I0222889

SANCTIONS AS WAR

Studies in Critical Social Sciences Book Series

Haymarket Books is proud to be working with Brill Academic Publishers (www.brill.nl) to republish the *Studies in Critical Social Sciences* book series in paperback editions. This peer-reviewed book series offers insights into our current reality by exploring the content and consequences of power relationships under capitalism, and by considering the spaces of opposition and resistance to these changes that have been defining our new age. Our full catalog of *SCSS* volumes can be viewed at https://www.haymarketbooks .org/series_collections/4-studies-in-critical-social-sciences.

Series Editor
David Fasenfest (Wayne State University)

Editorial Board
Eduardo Bonilla-Silva (Duke University)
Chris Chase-Dunn (University of California–Riverside)
William Carroll (University of Victoria)
Raewyn Connell (University of Sydney)
Kimberlé W. Crenshaw (University of California–LA and Columbia University)
Heidi Gottfried (Wayne State University)
Karin Gottschall (University of Bremen)
Alfredo Saad Filho (King's College London)
Chizuko Ueno (University of Tokyo)
Sylvia Walby (Lancaster University)
Raju Das (York University)

SANCTIONS AS WAR

Anti-Imperialist Perspectives on
American Geo-Economic Strategy

EDITED BY
STUART DAVIS
IMMANUEL NESS

Haymarket Books
Chicago, IL

First published in 2021 by Brill Academic Publishers, The Netherlands
© 2021 Koninklijke Brill NV, Leiden, The Netherlands

Published in paperback in 2023 by
Haymarket Books
P.O. Box 180165
Chicago, IL 60618
773-583-7884
www.haymarketbooks.org

ISBN: 978-1-64259-812-4

Distributed to the trade in the US through Consortium Book Sales and
Distribution (www.cbsd.com) and internationally through Ingram Publisher
Services International (www.ingramcontent.com).

This book was published with the generous support of Lannan Foundation and
Wallace Action Fund.

Special discounts are available for bulk purchases by organizations and
institutions. Please call 773-583-7884 or email info@haymarketbooks.org for more
information.

Cover design by Jamie Kerry and Ragina Johnson.

Printed in the United States.

10 9 8 7 6 5 4 3 2 1

Library of Congress Cataloging-in-Publication data is available.

Contents

PART 2
Profiles of Sanctioned Nation-States

PART 3
Resistance to Economic Sanctions and Economic Sanctions as Resistance

Acknowledgments

This collection grew out of a series of public educational events, protests, and workshops organized by the International Committee of the Professional Staff Congress (PSC-CUNY) around the increasing prevalence of unilateral sanctions as a vicious "standard practice' in US geopolitical strategy. We would like to thank the International Committee, particularly the members of the Sanctions Subcommittee: Renate Bridenthal, Jackie DiSalvo, Tony Gronowicz, Ángel Martinez, Tony O'Brien, and Hamideh Sedghi. We would also like to thank those who discussed sanctions policy at the International Committee monthly meetings or at the PSC-sponsored roundtable "Should an Anti-War Union Oppose U.S. Sanctions?" in May 2019: Ervind Abrahamian, Dario Azzelini, Reza Ghorashi, Jeremy Kuzmarov, Hamideh Sedghi, Gregory Wilpert, and Daniel Younessi.

Illustrations

Figures

Table

Notes on Contributors

Editors

Stuart Davis
(PhD, University of Texas) is Assistant Professor of Communication Studies at Baruch College, the City University of New York. Centered on Latin America (specifically Brazil), his research focuses on digital media advocacy, protest politics, and digital media and public health. Since finishing his PhD in 2015 He has published 16 articles in journals including *Communication Theory*, *Communication Monographs*, *Information, Communication, & Society*, and *Digital Journalism* as well as chapters in edited collections including most recently *Political Communication in the Time of* COVID.

Immanuel Ness
is Professor of Political Science at Brooklyn College, City University of New York and Visiting Professor of Sociology at University of Johannesburg. Ness is author of numerous books and articles on labor, workers' movements, migration, and political economy. He is editor of the peer-review periodical *Journal of Labor and Society*. His most recent publications are *Organizing Insurgency: Workers' Movements in the Global South* and *The Oxford Handbook of Economic Imperialism*.

Contributors

Shireen Al-Adeimi
is an assistant professor of language and literacy at Michigan State University's College of Education. She researches classroom discourse and holds a doctorate from Harvard University. Additionally, Dr. Al-Adeimi is an expert on the war and humanitarian crisis in her country of birth, Yemen. She writes for In These Times, speaks frequently on Yemen globally, and has been featured on NBC, NPR/PRI, *The New York Times*, Aljazeera, *The Nation, Current Affairs*, and others.

Tim Beal
is a retired New Zealand academic who has written extensively on Asia, particularly on Northeast Asia and US imperialism. Recent publications include 'US Imperialism, the Korean Peninsula and Trumpian Disruption' (*International*

Critical Thought), 'Korea and Imperialism' (*The Palgrave Encyclopedia of Imperialism and Anti-Imperialism*), 'Insidious Aggression: Sanctions as Covert Warfare' (*Covert Action Magazine*) and 'In Line of Fire: The Korean Peninsula in US-China Strategy' (*Monthly Review*).

Renate Bridenthal

is Emerita Professor of History, Brooklyn College, The City University of New York. She has authored or edited many works, including *Becoming Visible: Women in European History, When Biology Became Destiny: Women in Weimar and Nazi Germany, The Heimat Abroad: The Boundaries of Germanness, Interactions: Transregional Perspectives on World History* and *The Hidden History of Crime, Corruption and States*, among other works.

Jesse Bucher

is Associate Professor of History and Director of the Center for Studying Structures of Race at Roanoke College. He has a PhD in African History from the University of Minnesota-Twin Cities. In 2012, he was a Postdoctoral Fellow at the Centre for Humanities Research at the University of the Western Cape. His research utilizes postcolonial and critical theory to interpret the history of political violence, colonialism, and racial politics in South Africa.

Gregory Elich

is a Korea Policy Institute associate and a board member of the Jasenovac Research Institute. He is a member of the Solidarity Committee for Democracy and Peace in Korea and the Task Force to Stop THAAD in Korea and Militarism in Asia and the Pacific. In 1999, he joined a delegation visiting Yugoslavia to investigate NATO war crimes. His articles have appeared in publications across the globe. His website is https://gregoryelich.org.

Manu Karuka

is Assistant Professor of American Studies and affiliated faculty in Women's, Gender, and Sexuality Studies at Barnard College. He is author *of Empire's Tracks: Indigenous Nations, Chinese Workers, and the Transcontinental Railroad* (University of California Press, 2019).

Jeremy Kuzmarov

is Managing Editor of *CovertAction Magazine* and is author of four books on US foreign policy including *The Myth of the Addicted Army* (Massachusetts, 2009); *Modernizing Repression* (Massachusetts, 2012); *The Russians are Coming, Again*, with John Marciano (New York: Monthly Review Press,

2018) and *Obama's Unending Wars* (Atlanta: Clarity Press, 2019). He has also published articles in academic journals such as *Diplomatic History, Class, Race & Corporate Power, The International History Review, Socialism and Democracy,* and others.

Fangfei Lin

is an Associate Professor in the Department of Sociology, School of Politics and Public Administration, Xinjiang University, P.R. China. She also is an anthropologist focusing on China's agrarian change and feminist political economy. Her current research is an action research mainly exploring possibilities of collaboration between the improvement of pastoral livelihood and ecological sustainability in northern Xinjiang.

Washington Mazorodze

born in Masvingo, Zimbabwe, holds a PhD in Public Administration (Peace Studies) obtained at the Durban University of Technology in South Africa. He is a Lecturer at the University of Zimbabwe in the Department of Peace, Security and Society. His research focuses on domestic Zimbabwean, regional Southern African, and international politics, governance, human security, peace and conflict studies, peacebuilding, conflict resolution and transformation.

Tanner Mirrlees

is an Associate Professor in the Communication and Digital Media Studies program at Ontario Tech University. He is the author of *Hearts and Mines: The US Empire's Cultural Industry* (UBC Press, 2016), *Global Entertainment Media: Between Cultural Imperialism and Cultural Globalization* (Routledge, 2013), co-author of *EdTech Inc.: Selling, Automating and Globalizing Higher Education in the Digital Age* (Routledge, 2020), and co-editor of *Media Imperialism: Continuity and Change* (Rowman & Littlefield, 2019).

Corinna Mullin

is an anti-imperialist scholar based in New York. She currently teaches at John Jay and Brooklyn College, City University of New York (CUNY). She researches, writes and teaches about: the politics and political economy of West Asia and North Africa, genealogies of global south security/carceral states, the politics of development, US imperialism, racial capitalism, anti-/decolonial theory and struggles, knowledge production, and popular education. Corinna has been involved in BDS struggles in the US, Tunisia and New York.

Junki Nakahara

is a doctoral student in the School of Communication at American University, Washington, DC. Her research focuses on nationalism and xenophobia in East Asian contexts, critical and cultural studies, feminist media studies, and international relations. She has presented her research at annual conventions of the International Studies Association, International Communication Association, and the Association for Education in Journalism and Mass Communication.

Nima Nakhaei

is an adjunct faculty in the Department of Politics at York University. His research sits at the nexus of Marxist political economy, Poulantzasian state theory and Gramscian discourse analysis. Within this approach, he explores the ways in which the political economy, state formations and identity discourses in the Middle East have been structured by the interiorization of imperialist relations and their crises. He is particularly focused on how the 'crisis of the neoliberal world order' has opened up spaces for new projects of domination and emancipation in the region.

Sarah Raymundo

is the director and a member of the faculty of the University of the Philippines, Diliman, Center for International Studies. She is a key political organizer for the International League of Peoples' Struggle and Bagong Alyansang Makabayan (BAYAN/New Patriotic Alliance) and the Chair of the Philippines-Bolivarian Venezuela Friendship Association.

Muhammad Sahimi

a Professor at the University of Southern California (USC) in Los Angeles, analyses Iran's political development, its nuclear program, and its foreign policy. He received his PhD from the University of Minnesota in 1984 and has been a faculty member at USC ever since. His analyses have appeared in major political websites, including the Huffington Post, The National Interest, Antiwar. com, and many others, as well as in *the New York Times, the Los Angeles Times, and Harvard International Review*. From 2008 to 2012 he was the lead political analyst at PBS/Frontline/Tehran Bureau website.

Saif Shahin

is Assistant Professor of Communication Studies at American University, Washington, DC. His research interests include critical data studies, digital culture, and media and politics in global contexts. His work has been published in journals such as *New Media & Society, Information, Communication*

& Society, Social Science Computer Review, The International Journal of Press/ Politics, and *Communication Methods and Measures.* He also serves as Associate Editor of the *Journal of Information Technology & Politics.*

Greg Shupak

writes fiction and political analysis. He teaches English and Media Studies at the University of Guelph-Humber and is the author of the book, *The Wrong Story: Palestine, Israel, and the Media* (OR Books, 2018). His work regularly appears in publications such as *Canadian Dimension, Electronic Intifada, Fairness and Accuracy in Reporting, The Guardian, In These Times, Jacobin, The Nation,* and *Salon.*

Gregory Wilpert

is a German-American sociologist and journalist who has covered Venezuela extensively for a wide variety of publications. He holds a PhD in sociology (Brandeis University, 1994) and is author of the book, *Changing Venezuela by Taking Power: The History and Policies of the Chávez Government* (Verso Books, 2007). He is co-founder of the website Venezuelanalysis.com. Currently he works as deputy editor at the Institute for New Economic Thinking.

Zhun Xu

is Associate Professor of Economics at John Jay College, City University of New York. His main research interests include Political Economy, Economic Development, and the Chinese Economy. He is on the editorial boards of Science and Society and the Journal of Labor and Society. His recent book is *From Commune to Capitalism: How China's Peasants Lost Collective Farming and Gained Urban Poverty* (Monthly Review Press, 2018).

Helen Yaffe

is a lecturer in Economic and Social History at the University of Glasgow, specialising in Cuban and Latin American development, and a Visiting Fellow at the Latin America and Caribbean Centre at the London School of Economics. Since 1995 Dr. Yaffe has spent time living and researching in Cuba. She is the author of *We Are Cuba! How a Revolutionary People Have Survived in a Post-Soviet World* (Yale University Press, 2020) and *Che Guevara: The Economics of Revolution* (Palgrave Macmillan, 2009).

CHAPTER 1

Introduction: Why Are Economic Sanctions a Form of War?

Stuart Davis and Immanuel Ness

The United States has maintained unrivalled global economic, political, cultural, and military hegemony for 70 years since the end of the Second World War in 1945 and reinforced with the fall of the Soviet Union and for 25 years since the end of the Cold War in 1991. However, by the 2010s, American dominance in each of these four spheres has come under renewed contestation on a global basis. Most notable are China's rise as an engine of economic development and growth in East Asia and beyond and the resurgence of the Russian Federation as a formidable regional military competitor in Europe and the Middle East. The shape of the emergent rivalry in 2020 is distinctive, as the US retains dominance in all four spheres but the incipient threats to its absolute domination has given rise to a new repertoire to defend and advance its imperialist advantages. At the peak of US power, the two decades from 1990 to 2010, the US controlled the global stage through rewarding and punishing regional challenges to its supreme neoliberal economic order through a global military alliance to overwhelm countries that challenged its dominance in every sphere. Thus, the era was denoted by expanding American-dominated global defense pacts, conquering nations that did not conform to neoliberalism, and opening up new lands and spaces for the accumulation of capitalist profits. In each case, the US has exploited its economic, political, cultural and military dominance to guarantee its world hegemony.

While the current era is marked by a succession of regional wars, the US has depended increasingly on economic, political and cultural hegemony as partial substitutes for military power through the application of economic sanctions. These sanctions generally work to punish states that did not conform to its will or pose a potential competitive threat on a regional or global basis. Furthermore, these sanctions have often been levelled at states that challenged global neoliberalism, the world economic system imposed by the US and its Western European partners. Specifically, challenges to the global neoliberal order and American hegemony are national redistributive policies, tariffs on free trade, and currency controls. States daring to violate American neoliberal policies would be subject to severe penalties from US-dominated multilateral agencies that would destabilize national currencies and drive economies into economic depression. Financial tools applied by the US and leading capitalist powers have been instrumental in pushing "rogue" nations into submission to neoliberal rule.

In response to economic and resource struggles with perceived competitors, the US countered with economic sanctions. These sanctions have been implanted in the liberal rhetoric of human rights as they are intended to punish governments who violate liberal norms established by the West in the post-Cold War era. These human rights protections include the preservation of freedom of expression (especially press freedoms) and opposition to governments who persecute whistle-blowers and political opponents. In addition, economic sanctions are employed against governments which maintain and use weapons of mass destruction or persecute oppress populations living within their own borders.

While economic sanctions are intended to punish the individuals, organizations, and states responsible for violating human rights, they are increasingly extended to include entire populations of nations. In addition, the US has augmented sanctions by banning all third parties from engaging in economic activities with designated countries. As a result, economic sanctions in effect punish entire populations of nation states. Thus, the US and its allies have applied economic sanctions as a means to foment dissent in hopes of destabilizing leaders and governing parties (often referred to in the parlance as "regimes") and often to overthrow and oust them from power and political leaders who are supportive of US policies. Often the US and its allies support NGOs as well as form oppositional organizations and political fronts to confront governments it opposes. If countries are enduring major recessions and economic collapse, these groups are instrumental in selecting opposition leaders and parties. This is a reason why economic sanctions are a vital aspect of imperialism and inter-imperialist rivalries.

This book examines the cause and effects of sanctions. We explore the use of economic sanctions by the US as an integral part of the growing inter-imperialist rivalry, the NGOs and imperialist government organizations which sustain sanctions, the legitimation of sanctions through the media, and the devastating effects of economic sanctions. The editors consider sanctions as harming entire nations, not just those purportedly harboring weapons of mass destruction or violating human rights. Ordinary citizens, especially the working class and those most vulnerable to economic deprivation, inevitably bear the weight of the damage. Sanctions create scarcity of essential goods and services, like food, oil, medicine, and spare parts for power stations which provide electricity. By preventing trade, national currencies lose their value, leading to hyperinflation, which fuels speculation, hoarding, and protracted shortages of essential goods and services. The economic contraction produced by sanctions generates famine, disease, unemployment, poverty, and foment civil strife. In this way, as an aspect of war, they resemble medieval sieges that starved out cities to compel surrender.

As of January 1, 2020, the US Treasury Department's Office of Foreign Asset Control (OFAC) has unilaterally imposed sanctions on the following countries: Belarus, Burundi, Central African Republic, Cuba, Democratic Republic of the Congo, Iran, Iraq, Lebanon, Libya, Mali, Nicaragua, North Korea, Russia, Somalia, Serbia, Sudan, South Sudan, Syria, Venezuela, Yemen, and Zimbabwe. While not exhaustive, this list of countries includes the poorest countries of the world which are unable to sustain the loss of trade and essential food and medicines. In many cases, sanctions also hinder the possibility of economic resuscitation as the US imposes sanctions on third-party states which engage in trade with countries on the Treasury Department list. Concomitantly, the vast majority of countries which are targeted by the US and its allies by sanctions are endowed with petroleum and strategic minerals and natural resources for new technology and military uses.

All in all, economic sanctions are a weapon wielded by the most powerful, the US and its allies in Western Europe and beyond, against the poor and weak in the poorest countries of the Global South. This is the first book to genuinely examine the causes, geostrategic dynamics, infrastructure, and devastating effects of economic sanctions.

Along with deconstructing the political and economic logic governing the application of sanctions and documenting their tangible effects on subjected nations, this book also examines historical and contemporary sanctions efforts (which the US and its allies have generally not favored) for the purpose of bringing to an end extreme inequality and exploitation by settler colonial states: apartheid South Africa against the Black majority and to encourage contemporary Israel to recognize the self-determination of the Palestinian people through the Boycott, Divest, Sanction movement. The book chapters examine and inquire on the unique differences that punctuate how sanctions are imposed on oppressed countries, which comprise the vast majority and those that are directed against oppressor states like apartheid South Africa and the present Israeli state.

1   Demystifying the Role of Sanctions within International
         Governance: Moving beyond Orthodox International
         Relations Theory

In an April 1964 speech to congress later published in *The State Department Bulletin*, US Undersecretary of State George W. Ball laid out what would become a longstanding formula for implementing American economic sanctions against the Republic of Cuba. Broken into four interrelated points that combine specific tactics with larger geopolitical strategy, this speech presents in embryonic form the geopolitical function of sanctions for the United States. The first three are particularly illuminating, as he writes: "The first goal of economic sanctions is to reduce the will and ability of the present Cuban regime to export subversion and violence; Second, to make plain to the people of Cuba and to elements of the power structure of the regime that the present regime cannot serve their interests; Third, to demonstrate to the peoples of the American Republics that communism has no future in the Western Hemisphere" (quoted in Gibbs 2010, 17). This formula, contemporaneously described by *The New York Times* as the "definitive platform" for American geo-economic diplomacy (Morley 1988, 457, fn. 123), captures the major elements of sanctions as war: the application of *totalizing* blockade-style measures to weaken the ability of a target state to provide for the material welfare of a population; the notion that application of pressure would sufficiently deplete public health and social reproduction to the point of regime change; and finally that the application of sanctions in a specific targeted state is inextricable from a larger American project of empire-building and maintenance. While formulated at the height of the Cold War, this formula of combining the strategic inflection of morbidity and death in the service of geopolitical hegemony has changed very little.

Though couched in a more technical and less ideologically apparent manner, contemporary academic and practitioner scholarship on sanctions tends to view these measures as a foreign policy panacea. Viewed as both a more "humane" and "precise" strategy for coercing nation-states perceived as "rogue" into compliance than overt military engagement, economic sanctions as a practice has increasingly become a preferred tool among geopolitically dominant states. In particular, the United States has employed sanctions regimes[1] at

---

1 Within foreign policy circles, terminologically "sanctions" refers to individual bans or conditions deployed against certain actors or states while "sanctions regimes" refers to the overall strategy regarding an opponent (i.e. "sanctions on oil trade" vs. "Sanctions regime against Iran") (Nephew 2019, 4).

a rapid rate in recent decades, expanding to over 30 different national contexts (as will be discussed in this collection. Ranging from the directed targeting of the bank accounts of individual perpetrators to rare commodities including caviar and purebred horses, sanctions are increasingly viewed as a privileged weapon for coercing non-compliant or threatening states. As Juan Zarate, deputy security advisor under George W. Bush and author of *Treasury Wars* (2013) has recently argued, the increasingly common and wide-ranging application of economic sanctions speaks to the perception of this approach as a "best practice for international relations" (Harrell and Zarate 2018).

Despite their strategic popularity within policy circles, economic sanctions remain relatively undiscussed, particularly from a critical, anti-imperialist, or anti-war perspective. Addressing the dearth in critical scholarship, this collection offers three novel interventions in the woefully under-analyzed area of economic sanctions as a foreign policy tool. The first intervention is a theoretical call to move beyond the popular dyadic antagonism between those who conceptualize sanctions as a strategic negotiating tool in the game of geo-economic statecraft (what we call the "orthodox international relations" approach) and those who decry sanctions for their impacts on civilian populations (the "humanitarian" view). The first approach, generally embraced by both mainstream political scientists and defense and intelligence communities, is built around the conceptualization of sanctions through the framework of game theory. If the US is able to create conditions within a controlled engagement that will present sufficient pressure on a rival nation it will be able to achieve strategic wins. This approach is fundamentally focused on effectiveness. The second approach, popular within human rights advocacy circles, views the application of economic sanctions as an existential threat to the physical wellbeing of civilian populations within opponent nations. Our book intends to interrogate these two positions, arguing that neither present a sufficiently robust conceptualization of the complex ways that sanctions regimes serve to decimate victim populations in the service of larger imperial demands.

The second intervention of this collection is the push for a much more extensive empirical analysis of why sanctions regimes are launched against certain "rogue" states and how sanctions operate to destroy the fitness and social order within target societies. To address this, we offer a series of chapters cataloging national case studies from the 1990s to the present. These short case studies serve to situate individual interventions within larger geopolitical conflicts as well as document in detail the impact of sanctions on the population and civil society within targeted nations. Though American or US-led sanction regimes against some nation-states like Iraq, Iran, and Venezuela have been documented to a certain degree (Arnove 2000, 2003; Weisbrot and Sachs 2019), other nations (ranging from North Korea to Sudan) have been largely ignored even within activist and human rights scholarship. Our collection aims to provide the first comprehensive cataloging of sanctions regimes globally.

Our third intervention will be to address the possible of dislocating the tool of economic sanctioning away from the imperial designs of the US and allies to see if they can be employed to promote progressive social change or combat despotic political regimes. Specifically, we will be turning to both historical cases like the 1980s boycott against the apartheid regime in South Africa and ongoing advocacy projects like the Boycott, Divest, and Sanctions (BDS) movement to ask if there are possibilities for employing economic sanctions as a tool for practicing solidarity and empowering marginalized populations.

2   Conceptual Trend 1: Sanctions' Regimes as Geo-Economic Games within a Traditional International Relations Approach

Sanctions as War seeks to move beyond this dichotomous opposition between mainstream international relations theorists/diplomats/policymakers on side and humanitarian activists on the other. In order to accomplish this, we must briefly address lacunae in each approach, beginning with the IR approach. For orthodox political scientists, pundits, and most American policymakers, the conceptual debate over economic sanctions centers on effectiveness. The question raised again and again within orthodox literature on economic sanctions has focused on their political efficacy as a tool for advancing geopolitical interests. Developed in the 1980s, the effectiveness question is built upon notions adopted from game theory that one can treat interstate conflict as a stable interaction between two rational actors (Brams and Kilgore 1988). Applied to sanctions, this approach attempts to determine which factors can be tweaked to increase effectiveness. Perhaps the most influential text in favor of sanctions as an effective tool of strategic geopolitical influence is Hufbauer, Schutt, and Elliot's *Economic Sanctions Reconsidered* (1985). This text attempted to develop the first framework for evaluating the effectiveness of sanctions. Surveying a number of cases from postwar American foreign policy (with a focus on the Carter era), the authors found that when combined with traditional public diplomacy sanctions could offer "a form of economic warfare that lowered human costs through precise economic targeting" (1985, 6). The most important innovation in this text was not its assessment of different kinds of economic sanctions but that it drew upon game theory to develop its lexicon. Thus, previous concerns about human costs, collateral damage, etc. (e.g. Galtung 1967) became tangential. In his even more widely cited responses to this argument (including the highly influential essay "Why Economic Sanctions Don't Work" (1997)), Robert Pape solidified the centrality of effectiveness to theorizing sanctions by presenting a series of case studies where sanctions did not achieve their intended effect (Pape 1997, 1998). The debate engendered by Pape's interventions has not abated in ensuing years. The process of metaphorization from multi-targeted/uncontrollable violence against a target nation's population to a strategic move in a geopolitical game remains rampant in the academic literature on sanctions. Richard Nephew's recent *The Art of Sanctions* (2019) presents the most recent and abstracted version of this theory with his "artistic formula" (7). For Nephew, former Deputy Coordinator for Sanctions Policy in the Obama State Department and self-proclaimed "major architect" of the sanctions policy in Iran in the 2000s–2010s, presents a model for economic sanction regime that "finessing the balance between the application of pain and the will of the population" (Nephew 2019, 22). Specifically, he develops "pain" as an analytical category, arguing for the strategic application of harm through measures ranging from banning trade relationships to damage national industries to imposing restrictions on international exchange for universities to damage education industries (Barrows-Friedman 2015) to cutting off supply lines for materials considered critical for the national economy (including some foodstuffs) (Nephew 2019, 53–62 *passim*). Falling squarely in the game theory tradition, Nephew's text represents one of the most recent and perhaps the most fully developed version of sanctions as game.

Crucially, these theorizations of sanctions as game depend on an abstract and power-neutral vision of geopolitics. Undergirding this gamefication of sanctions is the belief that the international geopolitical systems is governed through a stable network of both state and non-state actors including multilateral institutions, international regulatory organizations, and non-governmental organizations (Slaughter 2017). These actors serve as network nodal points representing a variety of interests from human rights to environmentalism. This network of state and non-state actors interacting together provides the cohesive tissue that enables sanctions to effectively engage in the initiation and management of sanctions regimes (*ibid.*). In a manner operating on a level of abstraction similar to theorizations of sanctions, this idea of a highly rational and accountable network of international institutions (what Anne-Marie Slaughter labeled "the web under the chessboard of international security" (2017, 30)) supporting state-to-state interactions creates the fantasy of a Manichean world of "good guys" who will help sanctioning nations fight the non-pliant "bad guys". To return to Zarate: "Sanctions work through the combination of strategic suasion and the role of non-state, networked actors, working alongside classical state power, to influence the world for good" (Zarate 2013, 432).

What's wrong with this gaming approach? First, for the US sanctions games are never "fair". As Edward Herman has powerfully argued, these sanctions "games" are often designated as games only within the policy papers and official reports of the nation or multi-lateral configuration issuing the sanctions. As these actors are the ones designating sanctions policies as "games" and their side as protagonists, they set the rules: "One of the tricks of imperialism has been to set unrealistic demands, then pretend that a targeted enemy has been offered a negotiating option, quickly claim that the option has been rejected, and move to even harsher sanctions" (Herman, cited in Arnove 2003, 23). Many international relations theorists have argued that the "game" of sanctions cannot be delinked from the hegemonic assymetries in global geopolitics. Written immediately in the wake of the US invasion of Iraq in the first "gulf war crisis", Lisa Martin's *Coercive Cooperation: Explaining Multilateral Economic Sanctions* (1992) offers an illustrative case for why the deployment of sanctions is much more complex than strategic moves within a stable game. In her account, Martin argues that the American imposition of sanctions has always included attempts to coerce or, in many cases, bully other nations, multilateral organizations, and NGOs to support the deployment of sanctions. Furthermore, for proponents of sanctions, "winning" is often conceptualized so broadly (in terms of a variety of objectives ranging from "renegotiation" to "influencing global public opinion") that even using the terminology of winning and losing represents an extreme conceptual stretch (Martin 1992, 32). As a metaphor for the exercise of economic sanctions, gaming is both naïve towards international power differentials and inappropriately sophisticated to understand geopolitical dynamics. In short, mainstream IR theorizations of sanctions as games suffer from an extreme lack of empirical insight.

This lack of empirical consideration has significant human costs within sanctioned nations. What is wrong with this gaming approach for those cast as "opponents"? "Gaming" as metaphor relies on a metaphorical abstraction wherein "two actors are locked in strategic application of pain and resilience" (Nephew 2019, 24). This abstraction masks the empirical reality of the situation on the ground: military actions are not against abstract actors but affect areas often populated with non-combatants and rife with collateral damage and human cost. Outside of the lineage of mainstream international relations theory, this notion of the gamification of war stands as part of the development of what Paul Virilio and Sylvere Lotringer have called the civilianization of war (Virilio and Lotringer 1983). This shift, also referred to as full-spectrum domination, describes a situation wherein the observed line between combatant and civilian as well as between enemy and citizen is consistently blurred to the point that no space of civil society is deemed off limits. This shift is also deeply linked to the rise of "dirty wars" (Scahill 2013), conflicts that refuse to observe any of the traditional signposts of conventional warfare. Political theorist Brian Massumi recognizes the drastic results of this gamification of coercive violence: "When the civil is no longer demarcated from the military, nor offense from defense, it becomes impossible to say where the exercise of force begins and ends" (Massumi 2015, 68). From this perspective, sanctions regimes represent the erosion of any traditional conventions within inter-state warfare. Therefore and crucially, sanctions are not an alternative to traditional warfare but instead an expansion that has the potential to leach into all aspects of civil society within targeted nations and beyond.

3   Conceptual Trend 2: Opposition to Sanctions on Humanitarian
       Grounds and the Problem of Criticism without Structural Critique

Recognizing that sanctions clearly violate several basic human rights as defined by the United Nations and while not discounting the position of critics who question the utility of sanctions for either strategic objectives or geopolitical game, this book adamantly rejects the centrality of "effectiveness" as a lens for understanding the role of economic sanctions within the global world system. The systematic human suffering unleashed on the poorer and working classes of targeted nations cannot be encapsulated under a framework of "effective suffering" (or as Nephew puts it, the sanction regime's "pain calculus" (2019, 41)). However, we also eschew narratives built around simple or reductive explanations that focus exclusively on the human cost of economic sanctions within targeted nations. The lion's share of this sort of opposition to economic sanctions regimes has been raised by transnational activist networks (TANS), faith-based organizations, or NGOs and have focused on humanitarian crises arising with their implementation. Anti-sanctions activists argue that these measures operationally amount to a blunt weapon of non-military warfare as they wreak havoc on targeted areas. Crucially, those who oppose sanctions on humanitarian grounds share IR theorists' skepticism about the effectiveness of sanctions as a tool for producing calculated intended consequences within specifically singled out target areas. However, the skepticism of humanitarian activists comes from a much different place. For IR theorists, policymakers, and diplomats, sanctions regimes' ineffectiveness poses a problem with their coercive capabilities as a form of non-military pressure. For humanitarian activists, the problem with sanctions is that instead of having the intended effect of providing a non-lethal and more diplomatic alternative to military assault, their actual effect is to produce an immense degree of human suffering, albeit not in the form of bodily harm and dismemberment. To reiterate, for these critics sanctions are just as much of a deadly weapon as an AR15 or a lethal drone. They are just a different kind of weapon.

The central assertion of humanitarian-based critics is that even the most focused of economic sanctions regimes produce what Human Rights Watch (2019) and others have identified as "knock-on effects", ripples within the targeted nation that resonate widely. Sanctions aimed at individual actors, administrations, or industries inevitably produce cascading effects. A recent example from sanctioned Syria illustrates this cascade. Since 2011 the US government has initiated a number of sanctions against the administration of President Bashar al-Assad, including a sanction on US citizens receiving payment for work conducted in Syria by any financial institution with ties to the Syrian government (McDowall 2018; Ghisn 2020). These sanctions have created a host of problems for a variety of actors from aid organizations like the International Red Cross to non-American companies trying to contract with the Syrian government to reconstruct roads and other essential infrastructure. The result is that a wide variety of crucial industries from transportation to pharmaceuticals to food production/distribution are left fallow in the wake of sanctions. The Syrian case is not unique. From massive unemployment to widespread malnutrition, the consequences of sanctions are often just as lethal as military tactics—albeit within a somewhat longer time frame.

While criticisms of US sanctions on humanitarian grounds have been raised at different points in time and in relationship to distinct US campaigns (notably catalogued in Anthony Arnove's collection *Iraq Under Siege* (2003)), the basic argument is relatively unchanging: economic sanctions cause a form of existential human suffering that violates "the inherent dignity and the equal and inalienable rights of all members of the human family" (UN General Assembly 2011 [1948], p. 1), to quote the first line of the "Universal Declaration of Human Rights". Variations on this position exist. For example, the Cato Institute's Daniel Griswold offers a conservative Christian version of this humanitarian position, claiming that sanctions limit the possibilities of citizens within a country to experience political liberty and practice market freedom (Griswold 2000). Nonetheless, the fundamentally existential nature of this position shines through. The most recent version of this humanitarian criticism of sanctions is a series of calls from policy-making bodies, anti-war activist groups, and others for the Trump administration to suspend sanctions against targeted nations (namely Iran and Venezuela) in response to the global public health crisis caused by the 2019–2020 Novel Coronavirus pandemic. A geographically dispersed group including anti-war activists like CODEPINK: Women For Peace (Gold and Benjamin 2020), US congress members (Huffman 2020), and UN High Commissioner for Human Rights Michelle Bachelet have recently pushed the US government to suspend sanctions as a way of helping damper the impact of this pandemic among the populations of nations under sanctions regimes.

There is no question that sanctions regimes have produced a plethora of drastic impacts in sectors ranging from public health to media and communications infrastructure. However, hinging one's critique on the claim that the human suffering and the existential threat to human life posed by economic sanctions does not provide a sufficiently robust analytical framework for understanding and thus critiquing their connection to larger geopolitical/ economic power structures. Though sympathetic to humanitarian impulses, we argue an effective resistance to sanctions is not grounded solely in an existential commitment to preserving human life. Instead, the question becomes what kind of geopolitical and economic logic does this kind of project aim to extend or maintain? Sanctions represent a systematic *and totalizing* attempt to extinguish life (particularly of the most vulnerable). In their totalizing ambitions sanctions regimes represent what Achille Mbembe has identified as the founding dream of American global power: "the generaliz[ation] of forms of power and modes of sovereignty whose key characteristic is to produce death on a large scale" (2020, p. 3). The last step toward establishing a critique is to address possibilities why the US Empire desires to produce death on a planetary scale.

4   US Sanctions and American Imperialism: Overlapping Economic
       and Geopolitical Concerns in the Waning American Century

In this collection, we aim to understand how the employment of economic sanctions regimes fits within the larger framework of US economic and political hegemony at the global level. Shifting lexicons from international relations to Marxian political economy, we hope to address the place of sanctions within what David Harvey (2003) and others have labeled the "new imperialism". This "new imperialism" can be characterized by an intensifying friction between geo-economic and geopolitical interests around the American state, two often overlapping but not irreducible agendas. In

Empire of Capital (2005), Ellen Meiksins Wood offers a useful explication of this tension: "The political form of globalization is not a global state but a global system of multiple states, and the new imperialism takes its specific shape from the complex and contradictory relationship between capital's expansive economic power and the more limited reach of the extra-economic force that sustains it" (2005, 6). As Vivek Chibber argues in his critique of the book, it is incorrect to understand the relationship between economic and extra-economic as a "soft functionalism" where the political activity of an imperial state follows a logical set up of steps to support the economic (Chibber, quoted in Callinicos 2009, 79). Instead, the relationship between the economic and the political is much thornier and non-deductive. For some of these authors (particularly Harvey and Giovanni Arrighi) intensifying military engagement in Iraq and other contexts is borne out of burgeoning inter-state competition after the end of the cold war turned into inter-imperial struggle as the transnationalizing economic activities of first nation-states within Western Europe and later China threatened American primacy (Harvey 2003, 65–69 *passim*; Arrighi 2005, 2008). Though sanctions have been employed by other actors than the United States in a variety of ways, at this moment the vast majority of the most extensive economic sanction regimes are coercive tools in service of empire-maintenance as a form of "extra-economic force".

Though it advocates neither an anti-imperialist nor necessarily anti-sanctions position, Johan Gultang's influential essay "On the Effects of International Sanctions" (1967) begins to point to the kind of political rationality that pushes the US to increasingly and more cruelly apply economic sanctions regimes to those perceived as threatening or non-compliant to its economic and political adventures. The "punishment-orientation attitude" towards imposing sanctions is especially enlightening for our project: "This punishment-oriented attitude is fairly widespread, particularly as applied to the inter-national [*sic.*] system and serves to maintain negative sanctions. If compliance is not obtained, there is at least the gratification that derives from knowing (or believing) that the sinner gets his due, that the criminal has been punished" (Galtung 1967, 380). For an American Empire facing the challenge of rising financial competitors coupled with global economic decline coupled with a perhaps unprecedented legitimation crisis as a political actor under the Trump administration, understanding how sanctions work might hopefully begin to establish frameworks for theorizing their undoing as a tool of human destruction.

5   Organization of the Book

The book is divided into three discrete sections: "Part 1: Theorizing and Situating Economic Sanctions in International Political Economy", "Part 2: Profiles of Sanctioned Nation-States", and "Part 3: Resistance to Economic Sanctions and Economic Sanctions as Resistance".

5.1   *Part 1: Situating Economic Sanctions in International Political Economy*

Part 1 appraises the theoretical and conceptual basis for sanction regimes in the contemporary era and how governments deemed as bad actors by the imperium are assumed, incriminated, and convicted as guilty even if both the original charge is rooted in geostrategic politics and economic competition rather than certifiable evidence. Historically, little or no consideration has been given to the consequences of sanctions on the broad masses who are purportedly the victims of governments that do not comply with the dictates of the United States and its allies. Primary salience is placed on convincing the peoples living within Europe and North America of criminal activity and human rights violations perpetrated by geopolitical rivals, rather than applying universal norms and thorough investigation. The chapters in Part 1 examine the sources and validations of sanctions applied by the United States and its political allies through use of the apparatuses of ideological hegemony—communications and the media—and their application and consequences on countries that have been targeted. In this first chapter, we have attempted to apply a new explanation of sanctions within the system of international governance by developing and extending an analytical construct beyond the established international relations theories. We view sanctions as the application of a range of coercive measures that are a stage in the production of geostrategic competition and warfare.

Part 1 then turns to an examination of the instruments of coercive sanctions and how they are bound by the American imperium's resolve to staunch real and perceived loss of global power to perceived or authentic rivals to its military, economic, political, and cultural dominance. In Chapter 2, Tim Beal examines and applies a conceptual rubric of sanctions as an instrument of coercion, revealing the approaches and boundaries to sanctions as well as the outcomes and limitations to their application by states possessing a range of tools and capacities. As the United States retains the largest array of palpable sanctions, the focus is on its utilization of the array of coercive instruments to enforce and maintain its power through threats and intimidation. Calling attention to the perceptible decline in American hegemony, Beal provides evidence on how economic, political, military, and cultural sanctions are increasingly utilized as coercive mechanisms to enforce consent.

In Chapter 3, Manu Karuka provides a construct of the coercive utilization of sanctions and the range of responses of those forced to survive without the necessary means. The application of sanctions on subject populations are conceived as a form of siege warfare, where blameless populations of targeted states are left vulnerable through entrapment within a defined and "limited space", as the hegemonic power denies the targeted countries with the capacity of self-preservation, nourishment, medicine and supplies essential for customary survival. In turn, "besieged" countries do not have the capacity to counter the hegemonic powers in equal measure but are left in a chaotic environment to assume "defensive fortifications", to do all they can to conserve essential goods and basic necessities, most crucially their unity, to survive through the equivalent of a modern-day siege. If outlasted, besieged nations must comply with the demands of the hegemonic force, ostensibly seeking to improve the lot of civilians through denial of basic supplies, fomenting unrest, and the overthrow of state leaders and their replacement with opponents who will comply with the hegemonic powers. Aptly, Karuka asserts, through joining "the mechanisms of war and finance to attack the political and economic independence of poorer nations, sanctions comprise an exemplary form of contemporary imperialist siege warfare. This essay situates contemporary US sanctions within a longer history of imperialist siege warfare."

Building on the previous chapter's claim that sanctions serve as a form of contemporary siege warfare, in Chapter 4 Stuart Davis addresses the ways that economic sanctions regimes stifle the development of communication infrastructure within targeted states. Beginning by describing innovative attempts that Cuba, Venezuela, and other nations facing sanctions have utilized to develop their own public access film and television production programs and government-subsidized Internet, Davis tracks the ways that the exercise of sanctions has curtailed these initiatives. After discussing the debilitating impacts of sanctions on public programs for media access, Davis's chapter discusses the larger impacts that the employment of economic sanctions has caused on Internet access within sanctioned states, particularly during the COVID pandemic. The chapter concludes by arguing that the economic damage wrought by sanctions on the civilian population's access to media complicates contemporary work within media and communication studies on freedom of the press and communication rights which largely treat these questions in terms of a Manichean struggle between an authoritarian government and individual citizens.

In Chapter 5, Junki Nakahara and Saif Shahin turn to an examination of how modern news coverage of sanctions bolsters, sustains, and legitimizes the American presidential establishment, and by extension, US hegemony. Nakahara and Shahin's study of a decade of news coverage on Iran, North Korea, and Venezuela in the leading print media reveal that C. Wright Mills' conception of a power elite remains a compelling construct today in discerning the significance of the American government's capacity to apply a range of coercive sanctions on states. The writers validate the view *of a propaganda model*, advanced by Edward Herman and Noam Chomsky that a power elite manufactures consent through a convergence of class interests, including maintaining the US as the predominant global hegemonic power. Purveying accurate information and empirical evidence is inimical to preserving political and economic power, and thus the media eschew accuracy to maintain the prevailing status quo through filtering dissenting and contrary information and views in favor of the establishment narrative, which predictably reinforces the efficacy of sanctions on rival states and their allies.

In Chapter 6 Immanuel Ness analyses how human rights non-governmental organizations (NGOs) have grown as a force in expanding the American sanctions regime. Pretending to act in the interest of oppressed populations living under autocratic rule, in reality human rights NGOs are a major global force for the imposition of sanctions on poor countries by the United States and its allies. After more than two decades of sanctions, NGOs have sought to recast their sphere of activity to identifying specific government elites who are perpetrating violations of Western norms, thereby mitigating detrimental consequences on the population as a whole. Ness reveals that applying sanctions on opponents in targeted countries has not mitigated the deleterious consequences of sanctions, which inevitably redound upon the vast majority of people. Led by Human Rights Watch (HRW), the chapter shows that economic sanctions devastate entire economies. HRW's default to impose economic sanctions fails to account for the pattern of global sanctions, which rich countries impose on poor countries, asserting that NGOs serve as useful instruments of the US and its allies.

In the final chapter of Part 1 (Chapter 7), Tanner Mirrlees provides a detailed explanation for the rise in the trade war between China and the United States which has intensified into a widespread competition for dominance over new technology, and, in turn "geopolitical conflict." Indeed, Mirrlees provides abundant evidence that Big Tech are in support of the confrontational American stance toward China to maintain and advance dominance over the development of new technology. In this way, Mirrlees views the ostensible trade war as the new frontier of conflict in the 21st century, taking the form of "irregular warfare," playing itself out on the world stage through cyberwarfare, notably "network attacks on corporate and military infrastructure, digital hacking and espionage." The sphere of competition over control over digital technology has intensified conflict between Silicon Valley and China's Big Tech for control over a rapidly transforming industry, which has significant implications for dominance over lucrative international markets. Mirrlees scrutinizes the nature of the competition, and, as the US is not maintaining market dominance, the conflict is slipping into "economic war," and even intensifying conflict in the political and military arenas.

5.2   *Part 2: Case Studies of Sanctioned Nation-States*

Part 2 of this collection offers a series of 11 case studies of nation-states who have been subject to sanctions imposed either unilaterally by the US or multilaterally through collaboration between the US, other nation-states, regional associations (e.g. the European Union), or international organizations like the UN or World Trade Organization. Organized chronologically, the section begins with a discussion of the economic embargo launched against Cuba by the US shortly after the Cuban Revolution of 1958 and concludes with unilateral sanctions imposed by the US against China and Russia as recently as late 2020. Across these 11 cases a larger historical arc begins to come into view. The earliest cases come from the 1950s and focus on American-led unilateral economic embargos against individual states with affiliations to the Soviet Union, including North Korea, Cuba, and China (though the embargo against China was lifted in the early 1970s). In the wake of the Soviet Union's decline and eventual demise, sanctions regimes initiated or supported by the US took on a significantly more multilateral character. The 1990s, labelled the "sanctions decade" (Cortright and Lopez 2000, Hufbauer and Oegg 2003), was characterized by draconian sanctions regimes supported by the US in concert with the UN, the European Community, and other multilateral organizations against perceived rogue states like Zimbabwe, Iraq, and the former Yugoslavia. Cases from the 2000s–2010s (particularly the 2010s) show the return of unilateral sanctions regimes or individual sanctions launched by the US government against individual nation-states, particularly those perceived as geopolitical competitors like Venezuela, Russia, and China, or those that serve as sites for proxy struggles including Yemen and Syria (seen as extensions of a continued American conflict with Iran). This current phase of sanctions is linked less to concerns about acts perceived as violating international political or juridical norms (like the 1990s cases) and more to explicit rivalries with perceived economic or political rivalries, specifically Russia and China. This newest phase of economic sanctions, we argue, represents a shift back to Cold War logics of challengers to American imperial ambitions.

Addressing the longest ongoing sanctions regimes discussed in our collection, in Chapter 8 Helen Yaffe presents a comprehensive analysis of the history of American sanctions against Cuba, the link between sanctions and American politics, and the material impacts of sanctions on the Cuban people. Crucially, Yaffe makes a compelling case that American economic warfare against Cuba is best conceptualized as a unilateral blockade: unilateral in the sense that it is launched by the US without buy-in from potential partner nation-states; and a blockade due to its attempt to prevent any other nation-state or company from conducting business within Cuba. As a blockade, therefore, the US sanctions regime against Cuba in effect has created "an economic stranglehold on the island which not only prevents the United States intercourse but also effectively blocks commerce with other states, their citizens and companies" (quoted in Yaffe, this volume).

Chapter 9 provides an in-depth case study of the historical development and impacts of economic sanctions on the Democratic Public's Republic of Korea (DPRK), often colloquially known as North Korea. Framing his analysis in terms of the centuries long attempt of the US to exert economic and political control over East Asia, Tim Beal tracks the history of American and multilateral economic sanctions against North Korea. He specifically links the history of sanctions against North Korea to the history of American geopolitical conflict with China. Comparing the sanctions against China to sanctions against North Korea, Beal analyzes how sanctions against North Korea serve a paradoxical function of using them as part of a push for regime change while at the same time refusing to fully commit to regime change as it would sacrifice the US's strategic position in the region.

In Chapter 10, Muhammid Sahimi's analysis of economic sanctions against Iran situates contemporary sanctions—namely those associated with the Joint Comprehensive Plan of Action (JCPOA) in the 2010s—within the long durée of conflictual relations between the US and Iran that spans across a hundred years and multiple administrations in each country. Tracking this history, Sahimi constructs a narrative that illustrates the way that the exercise of sanctioning reflects geopolitical conflicts between the two nation-states. This historicizing strategy permits the deflation of claims by the US Department and others that sanctions are levied against Iran as a punitive response to rights abuses or geopolitical meddling. Instead, Sahimi presents a cogent position arguing that the employment of sanctions against Iran depends not on affronts to human rights or other violations of international order on the part of the

Iranian government but on American geopolitical aims in the region at the time of sanctioning.

With Chapter 11, we move into the "sanctions decade" of the 1990s with a discussion of the expansive sanctions launched against former Yugoslavia. Gregory Elich's discussion of the role of economic sanctions in the implosion of former Yugoslavia offers one of the three case studies in our collection of sanctions regimes that arouse during the UN's "sanctions decade". Working under this framework, Elich traces the interrelationship between the imposition of sanctions first by the European Community then the UN from 1992–1994 and the application of military force against Yugoslavia and its constituent states. Chronicling in detail the domestic, regional, and international political configuration that produced the sanctions regime against Yugoslavia, Elich's case history offers two crucial points for our study. Firstly, it vividly depicts the way that the sanctions against Yugoslavia served as a form of what Arnove (2003) and Karuka (this volume) label "siege politics": cutting off Yugoslavia from trade produced a form of hyper-inflation that made it impossible for citizens to receive sufficient nutrition. Secondly the case of Yugoslavia provides an example of the convergence between the geopolitical interests of the US and its proxies (e.g. NATO) with multilateral organizations like the UN. We will see the overlap between the US agenda and other stakeholders begin to diverge in later cases.

Chapter 12 offers another case study of a sanctions regime launched in the 1990s. Washington Mazorodze argues that the ambiguously defined and capriciously employed targeted sanctions against Zimbabwe have contributed to the steady worsening of health and safety conditions within the country and the continued justification for the ruling ZANU PF government's own abuses of power. Echoing chapters on Venezuela and other sanctioned states, Mazorodze argues that the rationale for the continued imposition of sanctions by the US and partners is defined in such a maximalist and ambiguous way that the current regime could never address them—thus pushing a regime change agenda. However, sanctions have not triggered regime change. Instead, as sanctions continue to damage the population, they simultaneously provide a rationale for governmental abuse of power. Adopting the concept of framing theory from media sociology, he argues that the ZANU PF government is able to blame a variety of political and economic problems within the nation on the sanctions regime. Instead of "supporting grassroots efforts at building democracy" as they claim (Mazorodze, this volume), sanctions serve the opposite function: providing a catch-all excuse to be used by the ZANU PF administration for any problem facing Zimbabwe.

Nima Nakhaei's discussion of the sanctions regime against Iraq in Chapter 13 argues that the employment of a series of economic sanctions regimes represents a brutal but informative case for understanding American imperialist strategy within the Middle East. Beginning in 1990 with an emergency resolution from the UN Security Council that authorized a supposedly "temporary" US-led blockade against Iraq in response to Iraq's invasion of Kuwait, the sanctions regime imposed on Iraq would continue and intensify in the 1990s through the "Oil-for-Food" program and eventually a military invasion in early 2003. The trajectory of the sanctions against Iraq illustrate how closely sanctions act as a tool of war and a handmaiden to military intervention. Within this case study two geopolitical tendencies arise that will be seen in other applications of sanctions: (1) the employment of sanctions as a regime-change instrument of a certain government; and (2) a break within the American approach to sanctions away from multi-stakeholder-based participation by international organizations to an approach built around "unilateral coercive measures" where the US imposes sanctions without consultation with the international community.

In Chapter 14 Gregory Shupak analyzes the links between economic sanctions launched against Syria in the 2010s–2020s and an American attempt to assert geopolitical control in the region in the wake of the Arab Spring. This chapter represents the first case in the collection of the third historical phase of American sanctions. In the chapter, Shupak builds on his experience as a journalist covering American foreign policy in the Middle East to offer a synthetic account that simultaneously documents the damages caused to the Syrian people by economic sanctions while framing these measures explicitly in the context US empire maintenance. His analysis foregrounds the American attempt to assert its geopolitical superiority against Iran and other competitors by employing sanctions to systematically weaken civil society within Syria, a state perceived as a direct threat to US influence in the region. Resultingly, the Caesar Act of 2020 and other sanctions directed against Syria represent unilateral coercive measures imposed without concert with other nation-states or multilateral organizations. After analyzing the political context behind these sanctions and their impact within Syria, Shupak concludes by addressing the complicity of American mainstream media in quelling public outrage about the destruction wrought by sanctions by under-reporting the human costs these policies for the Syrian population.

While many case studies in this collection describe the employment of sanctions as a form of specialized economic warfare with its own logic and metrics of effectiveness, Shireen Al-Adeimi's discussion of sanctions in the context of contemporary Yemen in Chapter 15 situates them as an economic component of a brutalizing military campaign launched by Saudi Arabia and the United Arab Emirates with US and British support against the Ansarrullah (or "Houthi") movement. A significant part of this campaign is a comprehensive blockade enforced by military support that cuts off access to the major trade and travel routes into Yemen. Purportedly designed to prevent the sale of military supplies to the Houthis, this draconian blockade has produced calamitous effects on all aspects of trade and daily life in Yemen including food supply and health infrastructure. Documenting how this blockade creates a veritable wall around Yemen, Al-Adeimi's chapter strips economic sanctions regimes of the technocratic specialized language in which they are often couched by academics and policymakers. As she argues, the blockade against Yemen is tantamount to a military siege.

Whereas the Yemen and Syria cases are inextricably linked to US geopolitical conflict in the Middle East, the final three national case studies represent attempts by the US to mobilize economic sanctions against national governments perceived as either stumbling blocks to the continued growth of a US-centered geopolitical imperialism (Venezuela) or potential competitors threatening American hegemony (Russia and China). In his case study of Venezuela in Chapter 16, Gregory Wilpert argues that the increasingly brutal sanctions regime is fueled by a combination of ideological commitment on the part of the US government and the economic interests it serves. On an ideological level, Wilpert argues that sanctions against Venezuela arise from the fear that the social transformations enacted by Hugo Chavez and the Bolivarian Process present a threat to US political and economic interest across Latin America. On the economic level these sanctions represent an attempt to ouster a series of Venezuelan governments who present roadblocks to the expansion of transnational capital. Drawing on the work of William Robinson, Leo Panitch and Sam Gindin, and others, Wilpert argues that the sanctions on Venezuela benefit transnational economic elites who stand to gain from the overthrow of an administration hostile to foreign investment, privatization of major industries, and other neoliberal concessions.

Jeremy Kuzmarov's analysis of the recent sanctions regime imposed by the US and allies against the Russian Federation in Chapter 17 (specifically the Magnitsky Act) illustrates the deep ties between the imposition of sanctions and American geopolitical rivalries as well as provides a counter-point to other cases by pinpointing the ability of the Russian government to engage in economic planning including import-substitution to mitigate the impact of sanctions on the civilian population. In this way the case along with the discussions of China and (to a lesser degree Iran) serves as a counterpoint to other cases this volume that document the ability of sanctions to derail civil society and wreck extensive damage to human life in targeted states. In tracing the imposition of sanctions against Russia, Kuzmarov's discussion details the geopolitical context that produces them. This context is constructed around a complex web linking the economic interests of US elites who have extensive business interests in Russia, heightened cultural Russophobia arising in the period following the 2016 US elections, and the bipartisan efforts by American congress to push forward a confrontation with Russian President Putin as part of a potential new Cold War. While the editors recognize Russia's position as a transactional state motivated by its own economic and political interests (as are many nation states), we recognize the importance of this chapter in pinpointing the shortcomings of US sanctions regime against Russia.

In Chapter 18 Zhun Xu and Fangfei Lin argue that sanctions against China are inextricably linked to the perceived threat it raises to American geopolitical hegemony. Since the success of the Chinese Revolution in the late 1940s, the position of China as a competitor to the US has been a central concern of US imperialism. While during the post-revolutionary period American sanctions aimed at regime change in similar manner to Cuba, subsequent sanctions of China have vacillated depending on the state of its economic rivalry with the US. Xu and Lin argue that the employment of sanctions against China is intimately linked to anxieties over threats to American geopolitical power, intensifying as American hegemony has waned in recent decades. Reading current economic sanctions through the lens of this rivalry, the authors conclude their case study by presenting extensive evidence to deflate the supposed human rights claims invoked by the US to legitimate its most recent round of unilateral sanctions.

5.3   *Part 3: Resistance to Sanctions and Sanctions as Resistance*

Part 3 serves a dual function. It first attempts to document the strategies utilized by national governments, companies, and activists within sanctioned states attempt to circumvent, fight back, or even attempt to survive under the boot of economic sanctions. From the formation of new economic relationships between sanctioned states to local attempts to provide food aid and medical support for hard-hit communities, this section documents ways that targeted states are resisting sanctions regimes. The second function of Part 3 is to provide examples where economic sanctions are mobilized by grassroots social movements in order to fight back against oppressive governments, specifically in the context of the anti-apartheid movement in South Africa and the ongoing Boycott, Divestment, and Sanctions (BDS) campaign in Palestine.

Chapter 19 presents examples of blowback facing the US as in response to the imposition of sanctions regimes. In the face of the ever-expanding list of states targeted by sanctions, Renate Bridenthal tracks the negative unintended consequences of imposing economic sanctions for US geopolitical aims. Analyzing the ways that third party actors facilitate the circumvention of sanctions regimes, Bridenthal provides numerous examples of where sanctions failed to achieve their strategic goals. In the process, she tracks new alliances and forms of geopolitical cooperation (e.g. between Iran and Venezuela), rapidly developing monetary alternatives to the US Dollar within global trade, and the development of transnational grey markets that bypass imposed restrictions within sanctioned states. Her analysis points to the key insight that the act of leveeing economic sanctions never happens in a geopolitical vacuum.

Chapter 20 discusses how activists working within sanctioned states work to build networks of solidarity and support. Focusing on Venezuela, Sarah Raymundo looks at grassroots responses to the damage wrought by sanctions. Framing the imposition of economic sanctions as a form of counterinsurgency, Raymundo discusses the ways that international solidarity between social movements provide powerful avenues for support within sanctioned states. Labeling sanctions as "counterinsurgency" due to the way they purposefully inflict damage indiscriminately against designated combatants and civilians alike, Raymundo tracks how Venezuelan civil society, in coalition with transnational activist networks, fight these sanctions. To understand this resistance, she draws upon ethnographic research conducted in Venezuela that examines how public programs aimed at helping the population, from agricultural communes to food stamps to health care, continue despite sanctions. She also draws upon her own work within a social movement organization in the Philippines aimed at building solidarity with Venezuela to look at how collaboration between movements offers further possibilities for fighting sanctions and other forms of geopolitical domination.

The remaining two chapters in Part 3 interrogate cases where the acts of calling for boycotts and attempting to impose sanctions are utilized as part of resistance movements on behalf of marginalized communities. In Chapter 21, Jesse Bucher and Stuart Davis present a historical case study of how boycotts and sanctions can be utilized by marginalized communities to successfully challenge politically oppressive governments. Drawing on a discussion of the anti-apartheid movement in South Africa undertaken by the African National Congress (ANC) in the 1940s–1980s, they begin by tracing how the act of boycotting shifted from being one tool among others utilized by the ANC for fomenting social revolution within South Africa to the central strategy for gaining international support against the apartheid regime. This shift ushered in a period of simultaneously encouraging transnational corporations to participate in the boycott and building support for national governments in the

Global North (particularly the US and the UK) to enact legislation enacting sanctions against the apartheid government. Bucher and Davis argue that while this shift was instrumental in ending the apartheid regime it simultaneously represented a withdrawal from the ANC's earlier aspirations for larger revolutionary transformations.

In Chapter 22, Corinna Mullin offers a powerful geopolitical analysis of the Boycott, Divestment, and Sanctions (BDS) movement launched in solidarity with civil society actors and activists in occupied Palestine in the early 2000s. Framing the discussion in terms of the larger questions of American eco-economic power that underpin the Israeli-Palestinian activists as well as the history of boycott campaigns launched by anticolonial or other movements representing oppressed peoples, she adeptly returns the conversation to questions of political and economic imperialist ambition that begin the collection

References

Arnove, Anthony. (2000). "Iraq Under Siege: Ten Years On." *Monthly Review* 52 (7): 14–25.

Arnove, Anthony. (2003). *Iraq Under Siege, Updated Edition*. Boston, MA: South End Press.

Arrighi, Giovanni. (2005). "Hegemony Unravelling." *New Left Review* 32: 23–40.

Arrighi, Giovanni. (2008). *Adam Smith in Beijing: Lineages of the 20th Century*. New York: Verso.

Barrows-Friedman, Nora. (2015). *In Our Power: US Students Organize for Justice in Palestine*. Washington, DC: Just World Books.

Brams, Steven, and Kilgore, D. Marc. (1988). *Game Theory and National Security*. London: Wiley.

Callinicos, Alex. (2009). *Imperialism and Global Political Economy*. London: Polity.

Galtung, Johan. (1967). "On the Effects of International Sanctions with Examples from the Case of Rhodesia." *World Politics* 19 (3): 378–416.

Ghisn, Ziad. (2020). "How Economic Sanctions Negatively Affect the Health Sector in Syria: A Case Study of the Pharmaceutical Industry." *London School of Economics Research Reports*, 16 April.

Gibbs, Jessica. (2010). *US Policy Towards Cuba Since the Cold War*. New York: Routledge.

Gold, Ariel, and Medea, Benjamin. (2020). "To Help Stem Coronavirus End Sanctions on Iran." CODEPINK, 13 March.

Griswold, Daniel. (2000). "Going Alone on Economic Sanctions Hurts the US More than Foes." The Cato Institute, 27 November.

Harrell, Peter, and Zarate, Juan. (2018). "How to Successfully Sanction North Korea." *Foreign Affairs* Blog, 30 January.

Harvey, David. (2003). *The New Imperialism*. New York: Oxford University Press.

Hufbauer, Gary, Schutt, Jeffrey, and Elliot, Kimberley (1985). *Economic Sanctions Reconsidered*. Cambridge, MA: MIT Press.

Hufbauer, Gary, and Oegg, Barbara. (2003). "The Impact of Economic Sanctions on US Trade: Andrew Rose's Gravity Model." Policy Briefs, Peterson Institute for International Economics. PB03–04.

Huffman, Jared. (2020). "House and Senate Members Call on President Trump to End Sanctions Against Iran During COVID-19." Press Release from the Office of Representative Jared Huffman. 31 March.

Human Rights Watch. (2019). "'Maximum Pressure': US Economic Sanctions Harm Iranian's Right to Health." *Human Rights Watch* Blog, 29 October.

Martin, Lisa. (1992). *Coercive Cooperation: Explaining Multilateral Economic Sanctions*. Princeton, NJ: Princeton University Press.

McDowall, Angus. (2018). "Long Reach of US Sanctions Hits Syria Reconstruction." Reuters, September 22, 2018.

Massumi, Brian. (2015). *Ontopower: War, Powers, and the State of Perception*. Durham, NC: Duke University Press.

Mbembe, Achille. (2020). *Necropolitics*. Durham, NC: Duke University Press.

Meiksins Wood, Ellen. (2005). *Empire of Capital*. New York, Verso.

Morley, Morri. (1988). *Imperial State and Revolution: The US and Cuba, 1952–1986*. London: Cambridge University Press.

Nephew, Richard. (2019). *The Art of Sanctions: A View from the Field*. New York: Columbia University Press.

Pape, Robert. (1997). "Why Economic Sanctions Do Not Work." *International Security* 22 (2): 90–136.

Pape, Robert. (1998). "Why Economic Sanctions Still Do Not Work." *International Security* 23 (1): 66–77.

Scahill, Jeremy. (2013). *Dirty Wars: The World as a Battlefield*. New York: Nation Books.

Slaughter, Anne-Marie. (2017). *The Chessboard and the Web: Strategies of Connection in a Networked World*. New Haven, CT: Yale University Press.

UN General Assembly. (2011) [1948]. *Universal Declaration of Human Rights*. New York: The United Nations.

Virilio, Paul, and Lotringer, Sylvere. (1983). *Pure War*. New York: Semiotext(e).

Weisbrot, Mark, and Sachs, Jeffrey. (2019). "Economic Sanctions as Collective Punishment: The Case of Venezuela." Report for the Center for Economic and Policy Research, 25 April.

Zarate, Juan. (2013). *Treasury Wars: The Unleashing of a New Era of Financial Warfare*. New York: Public Affairs Books.

PART 1

Theorizing and Situating Economic Sanctions in International Political Economy

..

Sanctions as Instrument of Coercion: Characteristics, Limitations, and Consequences

Tim Beal

States have a range of instruments of coercion at their disposal. Michael Beckley of the American Enterprise Institute (AEI) gives a short, and very incomplete list: '...the United States would deploy every tool in its coercive arsenal—tariffs, financial sanctions, visa restrictions, cyber-espionage, and drone strikes' (Beckley 2020). The efficacy will vary with the state and here the focus is on the United States since it has the full range and, in most cases, the most effective instruments, even though its power is in decline. Indeed, any analysis of contemporary sanctions must be centered on the United States. It uses sanctions most often and with greater economic consequences than any other country. Moreover, it is usually the instigator and enforcer of the application of sanctions by other countries either through bilateral dominance or through its ability to utilize the United Nations Security Council (UNSC). In 2019 the US had some 30 sanctions programs, the UNSC a further 14 and a number of other countries such as Australia, Canada, the European Union, Japan, South Korea had their own additional programs, but all of them it is safe to say were consistent with US foreign policy, and probably a result of American 'guidance' (Gordon 2019). American dominance is slipping, especially in relation to peer competitors but at the moment the global sanctions regime speaks with an American accent.

1 Taxonomy of Sanctions

Sanctions can be divided up in various ways.

1.1 *Form of Economic Activity*

Restraints on trade in goods has a long history. In times of war there have been attempts at blockading the enemy, preventing all trade. The Napoleonic war presented the first modern attempt at that. In times of peace the restraints have been less and usually related to trade disputes. The Cold War brought in another phase where US geopolitical strategies used restraints on goods, especially high tech and dual use goods, and financial services to impoverish and weaken the Soviet bloc. 'Dual use' is a very flexible phrase because there are few things that do not have military as well as civilian use.

As services have become increasingly important in the international economy so have sanctions on them. Examples include the sanctioning of North Korea over migrant labor (Kim and Denyer 2019) and the Trump administration's moves against Chinese apps WeChat and TikTok (Bradsher and Zhong 2020). China's ability to retaliate is adding a completely new dimension to sanctions which has tended, at least since 1945 to be a cost-free coercion instrument for the US.

Other kinds of sanctions are linked to finance and banking and affect the use of the US-dominated 'international financial and banking system'. They may be absolute—North Korea but also currently Iran and Venezuela—or partial. As with other forms of coercion a threat may be nearly as effective while avoiding the complications, and potential blowback, of implementation (Lew and Nephew 2018). They may be complemented by the seizure of assets; some estimates put the amount of 'frozen' Iranian assets at $155 billion (2016a). Because finance and banking are so information rich this gives the US amazingly precise power and foreign individuals can be targeted quite easily. Carrie Lam, the Chief Executive of Hong Kong has been placed on the Specially Designated Nationals and Blocked Persons List, or SDN List, maintained by US Treasury's Office of Foreign Assets Control (OFAC) with the result that she is not able to have a bank account and her government salary is paid to her in cash (Taylor 2020).

1.2   *Reach: Unilateral vs. Multilateral*

Many US sanctions are unilateral although Washington usually expects other countries to comply either through secondary sanctions or through its assumption of extraterritoriality, where US law applies throughout the world. The Trump administration, impatient with its client states, was particularly fond of unilateral sanctions

Multilateral sanctions have the advantage of enabling the US to utilize its imperial power to multiply the reach of sanctions. This becomes especially important with the growth of globalization and transnational supply chains. It is likely that the Biden administration will put more effort into dragooning subordinate states into serving US sanctions strategy, even when, as is often the case, it is against their interests (Kim and Kim 2020). To have sanctions endorsed by the UN Security Council is the gold standard because it both gives extensive reach, being mandatory for all UN member states and also gives a veneer of legitimacy. No doubt some sanctions are useful in reducing conflict and are relatively disinterested but the list of sanctioned countries, and crucially the countries not on that list, such as Israel and Saudi Arabia, suggests an alignment with US foreign policy goals (2020). US imposed secondary sanctions have increased greatly in recent years, because of globalized value chains, and the way they extend US sanctions power (Walsh 2020).

1.3   Focus and Effects

Sanctions vary in focus from general to targeted. They can cover trade with a whole country, even a group such as the Soviet bloc, and often in petty-fogging detail. Americans cannot conduct any trade with a number of countries unless they are given special permission. However sanctions can be narrowly focused on economic sectors and industries (coal, oil, and armaments), companies (such as Huawei), groups of people such as Iran's Islamic Revolutionary Guard Corps (Hagedorn 2020) and individuals. Sanctions often have various indirect effects which enlarge their impact. For instance, Americans are not allowed to buy anything from North Korea and that includes postage stamps. Dispensation may be granted but the procedure imposes barriers of cost and effort (Chace 2013). This is what happens with sanctions evasion; the goods may get through but at great cost in money, effort and sometimes lives (Go 2020).

2   Objectives and Functions of Sanctions

The key questions about sanctions are what their objectives are and how to set about achieving them. We soon encounter a problem because the real, underlying objectives are often hidden behind a hypocritical screen of obfuscation and mythologizing. This is not surprising because one of the big attractions of sanctions as against kinetic military action or other exercises in physical coercion is this chameleon-like ability to deceive.

Sanctions are often portrayed not merely as a 'humane alternative to war' but as good in their own right, driven by benevolence and good intentions. Are they linked to good relationships, security threat, concern for foreign citizens? It is dubious which of the three is the more implausible. And if some of the consequences are unfortunate it is claimed that is unintended (Schott 1998). In reality, sanctions and other forms of coercion are usually intended to benefit the coercer at the expense of the coerced. Otherwise, what need of coercion? Moreover, the level of obfuscation tends to rise with the goal and impact of the sanctions

2.1   *Sanctions as Warning*

Sanctions can, on occasion, be acts of retaliation intended to warn the other side against proceeding further and to persuade them to rethink and desist. There is a certain neutrality about sanctions of this sort in that deciding whether they are aggressive, or defensive is a matter of interpreting the context in which they take place. Many US sanctions can be seen as warnings but whether they can be considered as justified and peace-enhancing is another matter. For instance, David Asher's argument, in testimony to Congress, that Treasury's designation of foreign jurisdictions or financial institutions as a 'primary money laundering concern… served as a powerful warning shot to financial institutions around the world, deterring them from accepting similar business relationships with the likes of North Korea and Hezbollah' was literally correct (Asher 2013). However, this threat of sanctions is more properly seen as an act of extraterritorial arrogance, serving to extend American power.

2.2   *Trade Disputes and Declining Competitiveness*

Sanctions, or the threat of them, are often used in trade wars or similar conflicts of economic interests between states. The Trump administration was notable for its use of tariffs against 'friends and enemies alike' in trade disputes (Long 2020). Of course, tariffs have been used for these purposes for centuries, and the only disguise employed is that protectionism, for good or bad reasons, is hidden behind the accusation that the other side—one country or a number of them—is engaged in unfair trade practices, including a 'manipulated' exchange rate. A generation ago the main culprit for America's trade deficit was seen as Japan but the Plaza Accord, forced on Tokyo in 1985 brought to an end its high-speed economic growth, at that stage the greatest in history, and led to decades of stagnation. Trump was unlucky; China is not Japan. It is independent rather than a conquered foe, and US corporations are more dependent on it than they were on Japan (Roach 2019).

The US is also in decline and experiencing an unprecedented loss of competitiveness. The failing competitiveness is not quite so new—Japan was ahead in many fields in the 1980s—but the difference this time is that the challenge comes from outside the empire. This means that economic disputes overlap with, and are couched in term of geopolitics which pressures allies to cooperate where they would be reluctant to do so in a purely commercial dispute (Detsch 2020).

This chapter will naturally focus on the upper end where the impact of sanctions has the greatest impact, both on politics and on people and that is where the objective is the subjugation of a country rather than modifying its behavior.

2.3   Subjugation/Regime Change

'Destabilization' is a frequent objective given in the studies of US sanctions programs by the authoritative team led by Gary Hufbauer (Hufbauer *et al.* 2009). Amongst them is America's longest-running sanctions program, that against North Korea initiated in 1950 but there is an extensive list of targets. The range runs from other small and medium countries such as Iran, Syria, Yugoslavia, Libya, Chile, Cuba, Venezuela, etc., up to the peer competitors Russia/Soviet Union and China. Destabilization occurs when the people lose confidence in their government's ability to run the country and the way is open to consider alternatives. Sanctions are a potent tool to bring about this situation though they are not, in themselves, sufficient to bring about satisfactory regime change. There must be acceptable alternatives waiting in the wings, either largely home-grown or facilitated and funded by external actors, which in the contemporary world usually means the United States. Victoria Nuland boasted after the coup in 2013 that the US had 'invested' $5 billion to bring about a 'secure and prosperous and democratic Ukraine', by which she meant a pro-American government, the security and prosperity being yet to be delivered (Nuland 2013).

Whether destabilization is successful or not the key point is that the people, albeit unconsciously and unwillingly, are participants rather than mere onlookers, the 'innocent civilians' of propaganda. That means they must suffer not as some 'unintended consequence' of sanctions but as an essential part of it. If only the top elite were affected by sanctions but not the people, they would have no grounds for rebellion.

Moreover, as sanctions produce economic and social degradation governments tend to see themselves forced to take remedial action which are by their nature unwelcome and if there is no societal acceptance of their necessity the countermeasures become increasingly unpopular; we see that with lockdowns and other measures against COVID-19. If all goes according to plan the government becomes more repressive, fueling discontent.

People will flee the country, even at huge danger. This displacement of people, the creation of refugees/asylum seekers/defectors can be portrayed as further evidence of the wickedness of the target government, with unhappy citizens voting with their feet. The role of sanctions is seldom discussed; a Senate hearing on the 'plight of refugees' from North Korea does not mention the word (2002).

To gain admittance to countries of sanctuary refugees naturally say what they think will allow them entry. This then is seized upon by hawks to argue for the intensification of sanctions (Lee and Stanton 2016).

2.4 A Complement to Covert Kinetic War or Precursor to Military Action

Sometimes, as with Yugoslavia 20 years ago or Syria today, sanctions complement kinetic war. In the case of Syria, although there are US forces on the ground (and in the air) most of the fighting to unseat the Syrian government is done by proxy forces with sanctions providing in effect a second flank, in the hope that the shortage of food, medicines, etc., will weaken morale and be blamed on the government (Sly 2019).

In other cases, Iraq being the classic example, sanctions are used to degrade the economic and social infrastructure to sap the morale of the military. All going well the country is then ripe for military intervention although that is not the way things are presented—military intervention becomes imperative because sanctions have been 'ineffective' and it is necessary 'to forcibly compel foreign governments to change their policies' (Schott 1998) And if the foreign government does not change its policies, then the government must itself be changed.

3 Sanctions and Soft Power

The use of sanctions is an exercise in power; as such it must be situated within the context of the other forms of power that states, and here principally the US, deploy. Sanctions are, by their nature, usually a reflection of the imbalance of economic power between states but that works in conjunction with other forms of power. The US can have the UNSC impose sanctions on North Korea in violation of the UN Charter because it has the *diplomatic power* to do so. It can interdict and seize North Korean ships in international waters, in violation of the norms of international law because it has the *military power* to do so, and its action is legitimized by its previous use of diplomatic power. It can control the narrative of the events because it has the *soft power*. Sanctions thus do not occur in a vacuum but as part of an arsenal of coercion.

Soft power, and control over the media are of such importance that they are covered in separate chapters—'Sanctions and Soft Power' and 'Media Coverage on Sanctions'.

3.1 Economic

Since sanctions are primarily an economic instrument the relative economic strength of the contending parties is a crucial factor. As by far the world's largest economy it is not surprising that the US has used them enthusiastically and more extensively than any other country. The rise of China, which is transforming the situation. This is discussed further in chapter of this volume "The Western Frontier" (Shih 2020).

3.2   *Military*

The use of military power, or the threat of it serves as an import adjunct to the implementation of sanctions. Military superiority is employed when the US (or its proxies) interdict ships at sea, both in the action itself and preventing the victim resisting or retaliating. An example of this was the seizure of Iranian oil en route to Venezuela in August 2020. The US utilized either mercenaries or proxy forces, rather than its own military, so there was no danger of American causalities, and 'persuaded' the Greek owner of the oil to comply with US sanctions (Jakes and Schmitt 2020).

3.3   *Political/Diplomatic*

In the deployment of sanctions American power acts on governments and crucially, on global institutions through pressure on governments, on individuals and on individuals as citizens of subordinate states. This extraterritorial reach is both a force multiplier, enhancing the power of the US to inflict economic and other damage, but also increasingly necessary in the globalized economy; the US may have competitive advantage as the supplier or market for a particular product but if needs must countries can, in theory, turn elsewhere. It is important, therefore, to block off alternative avenues.

Since sanctions have traditionally been employed against small economies there has been little cost to other countries in joining in sanctions. Oil has long been a partial exception and now the rise of China presents real challenges to collaboration with the US. The case of Huawei is perhaps the best example, with some countries such as Australia complying with gusto (Needham 2020) and others, such as Germany (Sanger and McCabe 2020) proving more resilient. There are also variations in responses to US efforts to prevent Russia building new pipelines to customers in Europe. The sanctions have commercial aspects as well as geopolitical ones, Russian gas being much cheaper and the US is encountering resistance from countries as disparate as Germany and Serbia (Zakaria 2020, 2021).

The deployment of subordinate states greatly increases the economic power of American sanctions but the harnessing of international institutions, especially the United Nations and its agencies gives a patina of legitimacy to economic coercion. NGOs which are so often dependent on government grants and support from the foundations emanating from oligarchs—Gates,

Rockefeller, Ford, Bertelsmann, etc.—often play a supporting role in this legitimization process (Weisbrot 2016; Norton 2020).

The United States has been very successful in getting its preferred candidate chosen for leadership positions in the UN and international agencies by harnessing its allies, though this is now being challenged a bit by China (Lee 2020). If the US-backed candidate should subsequently go rogue and display too much independence, then steps are taken. There have been a number of high-profile cases including UN Secretary-General Boutros Boutros-Ghali (Meisler 1999) and José Bustani, Director General of the Organization for the Prohibition of Chemical Weapons (OPCW) (Simons 2002). Since people who occupy senior positions in the UN and agencies are often diplomats or officials seconded by their governments this chain of authority provides another means for the US to achieve compliance.

The United States has had many successes in its utilization of the United Nations and agencies to advance its geopolitical objectives. Of special note has been its ability to get the UNSC to condemn and sanction troublesome countries (2020). The jewel in the crown has been the devastating program of sanctions against North Korea, in blatant violation of the UN Charter (Davenport 2018; Beal 2016).

3.4   Science and Technology Dominance

For a century and a half, the United States has been a world leader in science and technology and the manifold benefits derived from that. Its dominance increased greatly after 1945, despite challenges in some fields from the Soviet Union and it is only recently that China's rise has threatened to unseat its primacy (Miles 2018).

For many years it has used a plethora of export controls to stop the flow of technologies to those considered adversaries. As well as its own control over US exports (2012) Washington has also employed the multilateral entities it has created such as the Cold War Coordinating Committee for Multilateral Export Controls (COCOM) and the post-Soviet collapse "Wassenaar Arrangement" (Lipson 1999).

In the contemporary economy where international supply chains are so important bilateral sanctions prohibiting technology transfer can be complemented by interdiction elsewhere in the supply chain. A case in point is the attempt to prevent Huawei using chips produced by American-made chip making machines wherever they might be (Shepardson, Freifeld, and Alper 2020).

4   Sanctions and US Imperialism: Rationales and Ethical Considerations

4.1   *Sanctions as War*

Firstly, to re-iterate the theme of this book, sanctions are not an alternative to war but a mode of waging it. Apologists for sanctions attempt to circumvent or obscure this essential point. War may be justified—see the discussion on *jus ad bellum* under ethics below—but to pretend that a form of war is not war is specious. It conceals the devastating and widespread impact of imperialism on the world, shackles analysis and impedes resolution of the issue. A particular case in point is the well-meaning, but counterproductive call by many people for a 'peace declaration' or even a 'peace treaty' in Korea without demanding an end to US-led sanctions as part of that (Chun 2020). You cannot have peace while one side is continuing to wage war. This fantasy is self-defeating because Pyongyang will recognize it for what it is, whilst Washington will continue to inflict economic devastation largely shielded from condemnation (Lederer 2019). And peace will be no nearer.

The United States is by far the biggest user of sanctions in the world (Gordon 2006). Sanctions are also one of the twin active instruments of US power; in the background is the huge military apparatus, the 700–1000 bases spread throughout the world, the military exercises, the freedom of navigation operations (FONOP) off the shores of adversaries (and sometimes in disputed waters) on the other side of the globe (Dutton and Kardon 2017; Valencia 2019) and the intricate network of 'alliances'. But in the foreground are assassination (Cockburn 2015) and sanctions.

If we see sanctions as essentially emanating from the US in pursuit of imperial objectives, rather than, as usually represented, measures that are taken in defensive response to foreign aggression, then interconnectedness becomes apparent. Sanctions against one country are related to those against others. Moreover, sanctions interlock with other instruments of power. Contextualization thus becomes an essential part of the analysis.

4.2   *Militarization and US Imperialism*

The United States spends a greater proportion of its GDP on the military than any of the other NATO countries and US allies, other than Israel (Baker 2017). Militarization permeates US society more than it does in any other country except those under immediate threat. The US government privileges military over non-military instruments—the Pentagon's budget vastly exceeds that of the State Department by some 24 times (Prashad 2017). Socially the military is the most trusted institution in America, which is intriguing given its fairly constant failure since 1945 (McCarthy 2018). However, there are countervailing forces and of special note is the Quincy Institute for Responsible Statecraft which defines its mission as promoting '... ideas that move U.S. foreign policy away from endless war and toward vigorous diplomacy in the pursuit of international peace' (2019). It was established in 2019 with declared funding of US$0.5m each from the Open Society Foundation of George Soros and Charles Koch's Koch Foundation. Other familiar names amongst funders are Rockefeller and Ford. The president is Andrew J. Bacevich, a former army officer who has frequently written articles critical of militarization (Bacevich 2020). The anti-militarization advocates are not benign, pacifist or anti-imperialist, it would be naïve to expect that (Porter 2020). They merely prefer a more intelligent and nuanced projection of power.

This struggle between militarization and its opponents is especially important in the context of any analysis of sanctions. This is because sanctions are a form of coercion that is acceptable to both camps. For the anti-militarization camp, they are a non-military enforcement of power. The Pentagon does not object—sanctions are complementing military power and by destabilizing and breaking the morale of target population make victory easier. Moreover, sanctions do not take funding from the military budget, so both the Pentagon and the military-industrial complex are happy.

4.3   *Ethics of Sanctions as a Form of Soft Warfare*

With the passage of time ethics, or at least lip-service to it, has become a major issue in geopolitics. A number of approaches are taken in respect of the ethics of sanctions.

One is to claim that sanctions are not war, so the strictures against war do not apply. Woodrow Wilson, who managed to combine drawing the US into World War I and racism with moral probity, or posturing as you prefer, declared that 'Apply this economic, peaceful, silent deadly remedy and there will be no need for force. The boycott is what is substituted for war' (Gordon 2006).

From the perspective of the sanctioner the advantage of sanctions not being considered war obviates the troublesome concepts of *Jus ad bellum* and *Jus in bello*:

> *Jus ad bellum* refers to the conditions under which States may resort to war or to the use of armed force in general. The prohibition against the use of force amongst States and the exceptions to it (self-defence and UN authorization for the use of force), set out in the United Nations Charter of 1945, are the core ingredients of jus ad bellum ...*Jus in bello* regulates the conduct of parties engaged in an armed conflict.
>
> 2015

Sanctions can be imposed with far less scrutiny than military action would attract. In the sanctioning country/ies this is primarily of course a matter of there being no danger of casualties but in terms of the literature of ethics in international affairs the legal aspects are important.

Ethicists do examine *Jus in bello* in respect of sanctions, mainly in terms of the effect on the general population, but they usually pay scant regard to *Jus ad bellum*, or the geopolitical framework in which sanctions sit, and this tends to vitiate their analysis. In fact, most uncritically accept the case for sanctions and the objectives they serve. It is like decrying the horrors of Auschwitz and then adding that the death camps did not get rid of the Jews. But surely the major ethical problem with Auschwitz was that it was part of a program to consolidate Aryan German supremacy? To take one instance, consider an article by well-known peace activists Medea Benjamin and Nicholas Davies—"U.S. Sanctions: Economic Sabotage That Is Deadly, Illegal, and Ineffective":

> There is one more critical reason for sparing the people of Iran, Venezuela and other targeted countries from the deadly and illegal impacts of U.S. economic sanctions: they don't work. Twenty years ago, as economic sanctions slashed Iraq's GDP by 48% over 5 years and serious studies documented their genocidal human cost, they still failed to remove the government of Saddam Hussein from power.... We firmly believe that no combination of these or any other rationale can ever justify the genocidal human cost of economic sanctions in Iraq, North Korea, Iran, Venezuela or anywhere else.
>
> BENJAMIN AND DAVIES 2019

They are, in effect, accepting the right of the United States to remove an unwelcome government from power and install a more compliant one; they are merely objecting to the human cost involved.

However, if we accept the UN Charter amongst other expressions of international law, neither the United States, nor any other country, has that right. This should be the starting point and foundation of a critique of 'regime change' sanctions. Even Hazel Smith, whose studies of ethics of sanctions of North Korea are a benchmark makes this mistake:

> If the legal foundation and political consensus underpinning United Nations resolutions suggests that North Korea's denuclearization can be understood as a just cause, were the means used by the United

> Nations also just? This essay draws on jus in bello analogies to analyze
> UN sanctions via standard ethical criteria of effectiveness, necessity and
> proportionality.
>
> SMITH 2020

The 'if' is the problem in this statement. Gavan McCormack, amongst others, has pointed out that means such as the indiscriminate sanctions, such as those banning coal export and oil imports, are a violation of international law, and the Charter (McCormack 2017). However, the issue goes deeper than that; the very basis of the discriminatory condemnations of North Korea is illegal and is basically a manifestation of US political and soft power.

Why is denuclearization of North Korea a just cause and not that of other nuclear powers?

The answer usually given is non-proliferation, which is applied notably now to North Korea and Iran but not to other countries such as Israel, which is a substantial, if undeclared nuclear power. When the possible nuclearization of countries such as Japan or South Korea is discussed, the verdict is usually of disapproval and regret, sometimes approval but very seldom the forceful con-demnation which is reserved for Iran or North Korea (Sanger, Choe, and Rich 2017; Daiss 2016; Bandow 2016). Many people regard non-proliferation as hugely important, sacrosanct, even existential, and so justifying rigorous methods. Although starvation of a population is usually considered a war crime (2016b) the Editorial Board of the *Wall Street Journal* explains that 'Withholding food aid to bring down a government would normally be unethical, but North Korea is an exceptional case'(Board 2017).

The issue of nuclear weapons is of immense consequence; a major nuclear war could destroy the planet. However, non-proliferation is not the same as the abolition of nuclear weapons and despite promises to the contrary given in the Nuclear Non-Proliferation Treaty (NPT) the Nuclear Weapons States (NWS) have not moved towards nuclear disarmament. This is particularly relevant in the case of the United States which has been the most vocal, and the most aggressive in demanding that the non-nuclear states keep to their side of the bargain (2014). In reality, non-proliferation serves to preserve the monopoly of nuclear weapons by the NWS, not least the United States (Erästö 2019). Non-proliferation is like inequality; it does not abolish wealth but merely concen-trates it in a few hands.

Intuitively it seems plausible that the proliferation of nuclear weapons increases the danger of nuclear war, and then this is segued into the assump-tion that the spread of nuclear weapons makes war more likely. This is a logical fallacy. The possession of nuclear weapons by small states to deter stronger predators in fact makes war less likely. This is what Kenneth Waltz argued in respect of Iran (Waltz 2012) which seeks to deter two nuclear powers—the US and Israel, which officially not a NWS is well known to possess nuclear weapons (Birch and Smith 2014). In such circumstances proliferation is peace-enhancing, and this is certainly the case with North Korea. The substantive ethical challenge is the possibility of kinetic war—which is all around us—not potential but unlikely nuclear war.

There are other fallacies prevalent in discussion of the ethics of sanctions, but two stand out. One is that there is a distinction to be made between the general populace and the government, one being 'innocent' and the other 'guilty'. However, in the context of aggression, here specifically that against North Korea, the distinction is invalid. There is nothing 'wrong' about defending one's country against aggression. Moreover, victims of crime are, in that context, innocent. Victims—of state aggression, individual rape or murder—may well have contributed to their plight but the moral culpability lies squarely with the criminal. To talk of innocent and guilty in respect of the victims of aggression serves to obscure the criminality of that aggression. One variant of this theme is the false distinction between civilians and soldiers, with the implication that the killing of the former is wrong but that of the latter is permissible. Again, the context of aggression invalidates that distinction. Another is genderization where the effect of sanctions on women is emphasized to the degree that it is implied that damage done to men does not count (Feron *et al.* 2019). We do not make this distinction when discussing murder, why bring it in when discussing murder on a larger scale? It may well be that in practice women are affected more than men, but ethically they are equal victims.

Ethical obfuscation is one of the major soft power instruments imperialism uses to disguise self-interested aggression under the mantle of disinterested benevolence, such as 'humanitarian intervention' (Chomsky 2008). To counter this the discussion of the ethics of sanctions requires a dispassionate, critical approach, free of double standards and hypocrisy.

5   Attractions, Pitfalls and Efficacy of Sanctions

Sanctions can be analyzed in terms of function- the objectives they seek to achieve—and type—the mode employed. A specific function may be addressed by a number of different types. The broader and more ambitious the objective the more types employed. Each combination of function/type will have its own advantages and disadvantages. However, there are general points that can be made, with the focus naturally on the US.

5.1   The United States and the Attraction of Sanctions

As noted above the US is the main user of sanctions, either directly or via its control or influence over other states and the UNSC, and sanctions are the main non-kinetic coercive tool in its arsenal. Sanctions offer the US some very strong benefits (though the rise of China is diminishing them):

1. They utilize its great superiority in economic, financial and political power over any other state;
2. They cause no American casualties and have limited economic costs;
3. There is the opportunity to slough off responsibility for the effects of sanctions, such as child malnutrition, and fix that on the government of the sanctioned country;
4. The standard of justification for sanctions is lower than that for military intervention and this has facilitated manipulation of the UNSC so that sanctions, notably against North Korea have been given its imprimatur and hence accorded legitimacy.

5.2   Unintended Consequences

Despite their perceived strategic function in forwarding US goals, sanctions produce numerous deleterious unintended consequences. Sanctions are like antibiotics in that excessive and indiscriminate use leads to degradation of efficacy and may, especially in the long term, exacerbate US problems.

5.2.1   Financial Sanctions

Financial sanctions are especially popular with the US because they utilize its immense control over the international financial system and banking, and the traditional use of the dollar as the unit for international trade, and as a reserve currency. However, there is increasing concern in the establishment that 'misuse' is having negative consequences, eroding US power. This is particularly pronounced in the Trump administration's sanctions against Iran in violation of the Joint Comprehensive Plan of Action (JCPOA) agreement signed by the Obama administration to which its main European allies (together with Russia and China) were party (Lew and Nephew 2018). Germany, France, and the United Kingdom set up the Instrument in Support of Trade Exchanges (INSTEX) to continue trade with Iran under JCPOA (Farrell and Newman 2019). Further out China is pushing for the Cross-Border Interbank Payment System (CIPS) to supplant the Brussels-based, but US dominated SWIFT payment system (Wen 2020) and Russia has been developing the System for Transfer of Financial Messages (SPFS). These developments are seen by many US commentators facilitating de-dollarization of international finance with the consequent serious erosion of US power (Zakaria 2020).

5.2.2   Goods and Services

Sanctions preventing or hampering trade in goods can have a devastating effect. Loss of export income means less can be imported. However, these effects may propel the government into self-reliance and diversification of trade away from US-dominated countries (Jung 2017). If the target country is small these may have little impact of the US, but when it comes to large countries, especially China the future consequences can spell real danger to US dominance. America's onslaught on Huawei, on the high-tech sector in general and semi-conductor chips in particular will cause problems for China in the short-term and the United States in the long-term (Koo 2020). Similarly, sanctions on Chinese service companies such as Tik-Tok, restraints on scientific cooperation with China, the curtailment of the flow of Chinese students into the US and the general hounding of scientists, and others of Chinese (and East Asian) ethnicity will rebound to America's detriment, and China's advantage (Krige 2020).

5.2.3   Secondary Sanctions

America's traditional financial dominance and the lure of its own huge domestic market have enabled it to impose secondary sanctions on allies and adversaries alike (Spetalnick *et al.* 2020). Secondary sanctions, with their assumption of extraterritoriality are unpopular with affected countries and them an incentive to move towards de-dollarization.

5.2.4   Collateral Repercussions

The US sanctions many countries and sometimes sanctions against one have negative consequences in respect of sanctions against another. The major instance of this now is the raft of US sanctions against China and Russia which impact on their willingness, always reluctant but increasingly so, to cooperate on US-led sanctions against North Korea. The US government and media is constantly complaining that they, and particularly China are not 'implementing' sanctions (Talley 2020).

5.2.5   Targeted Sanctions

Sanctions which target individuals tend to have little effect beyond irritation—consider Carrie Lam's closed bank account- but are probably counterproductive. CEO Lam has said that it is 'an honor to be "unjustifiably sanctioned" by the U.S. government' and sanctions against leading members of the National People's Congress, China's version of Congress, attracted derision. It is likely that such actions fortify the resolve of Chinese leaders to stand up against what they rightly perceive as US meddling in China's internal affairs (Ramzy and May 2020).

5.2.6   Efficacy and Destabilization for 'Regime Change'

The main issue in the literature on sanctions is their efficacy. Do they achieve what they are intended to? For light impact sanctions such as those in trade wars the results may be easily verifiable. When it comes to ongoing deep impact programs such as those against Iran, Venezuela, North Korea and China assessment is far more difficult.

Kinetic wars have battles and defeats or victories, and it is usually easy to decide who is winning. Sanctions operate in a cloudy environment so judging whether they work is not clear-cut. However, there is a more substantive problem and that is ascertaining what the objectives are, especially when it comes to 'regime change' programs. The real objectives, both final and intermediate are usually hidden under a blanket of hypocrisy and obfuscation. For instance, we are told that 'Sanctions Against Syria Will Help, Not Harm, Civilians' (Adesnik and Dershowitz 2020) and 'The Coronavirus Is Absolutely No Excuse to Lift Sanctions on Iran' because 'The Iranian people are suffering at the hands of their own leaders on top of a pandemic. They know all too well that their own government is the problem, not U.S. sanctions' (Dubowitz and Goldberg 2020). This last quotation is the standard perverse argument for 'regime change' sanctions.

However, short of an invasion as in Iraq in 2003, the regime change must be carried out by the people, or in reality a powerful section of the society. For that to happen they must necessarily suffer and blame their suffering on the regime that needs changing. The suffering part is easily arranged but getting people to blame their government rather than the foreign one waging economic war is rather more difficult, though not impossible. That is what destabilization attempts to achieve.

Commentators tend to be skeptical about the efficacy of sanctions to produce regime change *on their own* (Morello 2020). You still have to drop the bombs, fire the missiles and send in the troops before the natives have the good sense to produce a government of your choosing. And that presents a problem to the Biden administration because the preceding ones have picked all the low-hanging fruit. Military action against Iran or North Korea, let alone Russia or China, is a daunting prospect.

That this dilemma will effect a change in US sanctions policy is unfortunately unlikely.

6 Conclusion: Sanctions as an Instrument of Coercion

Sanctions are often portrayed, by those that utilize them, as a humane alternative to war, a well-intentioned, proportionate and restrained effort to preserve peace and good international relations. The targeted countries are described as belligerent states intent on wreaking destruction on the innocent and benevolent 'international community'. Their leaders are depicted as indifferent to the sufferings of their people, happy to starve them in pursuit of their evil designs.

This book and this chapter convey a different message. Sanctions are a mode of war and an instrument of coercion usually in pursuit of hegemonic objectives. Sanctions tend to be wrapped in shrouds of obfuscation and hypocrisy and their facility for being disguised in objective and consequence is a great source of attraction for their users. Like kinetic war they tend to be employed by the strong against the weak and so are nearly always aggressive.

However, like war in general, they can be dissected. Objectives can be revealed, dreadful consequences of economic and social devastation laid bare. Moral outrage against sanctions should be complemented by dispassionate analysis of their characteristics and their strengths and weaknesses. Too often well-intentioned people agonize over some aspects—the malnourished children, the blighted lives—but do not penetrate further than that accepting without critical scrutiny the self-serving narratives created by politicians and officials and disseminated by the media.

It is vital to demolish the carapace of propaganda to expose what lies beneath. The dreadful effects on countless people around the world but even more important the coercive objectives that drive sanctions and cause the devastation. Madeleine Albright's assertion that "the price is worth it' is seldom given the analysis it deserves. The price was half a million Iraqi children but outrage is insufficient. We need to ask what was the 'it' that was worth such a price. Imperialism cannot be defeated until its motives, nature, and instruments of coercion are understood.

References

Adesnik, David, and Dershowitz, Toby. (2020). "Sanctions Against Syria Will Help, Not Harm, Civilians." *Foreign Policy*, 17 June. https://foreignpolicy.com/2020/06/17/sanctions-against-syria-will-help-not-harm-civilians/.

Asher, David L. (2013). "Pressuring North Korea: The Need for a New Strategy." *Testimony before the House Foreign Affairs Committee*, 5 March. https://css.ethz.ch/en/servi ces/digital-library/publications/publication.html/162593.

Bacevich, Andrew. (2020). "The Endless Fantasy of American Power." *Foreign Affairs*, 18 September. https://www.foreignaffairs.com/articles/united-states/2020-09-18/endless-fantasy-american-power.

Baker, Peter. (2017). "Trump Says NATO Allies Don't Pay Their Share. Is That True?" *New York Times*, 26 May. https://www.nytimes.com/2017/05/26/world/europe/nato-trump-spending.html.

Bandow, Doug. (2016). "Let Them Make Nukes." *Foreign Affairs*, 26 July. https://www.foreignaffairs.com/articles/japan/2016-07-26/let-them-make-nukes?cid=nlc-twofa-20160728&sp_mid=51937637&sp_rid=dGltQHRpbWJlYWwubmVoL m56So&spMailingID=51937637&spUserID=MjEwNDg3NTA4OTQ3So&spJobID =964120253&spReportId=OTYoMTIwMjUzSo.

Beal, Tim. (2016). "Satellites, Missiles and the Geopolitics of East Asia." In *North Korea: Political, Economic and Social Issues*, edited by Marvin Harrison, 1–118. New York: Nova Publishers.

Beckley, Michael. (2020). "Rogue Superpower: Why This Could Be an Illiberal American Century." *Foreign Affairs*, November/December. https://www.foreignaffairs.com/articles/united-states/2020-10-06/illiberal-american-century-rogue-superpower.

Benjamin, Medea, and Nicolas J.S. Davies. (2019). "U.S. Sanctions: Economic Sabotage That Is Deadly, Illegal, and Ineffective." *Common Dreams*, 17 June. https://www.commondreams.org/views/2019/06/17/us-sanctions-economic-sabotage-deadly-illegal-and-ineffective.

Birch, Douglas, and R. Jeffrey Smith. (2014). "Israel's Worst-Kept Secret." *The Atlantic*, 16 September. http://www.theatlantic.com/international/archive/2014/09/israel-nuclear-weapons-secret-united-states/380237/3/.

Board, Editorial. (2017). "Options for Removing Kim Jong Un." *Wall Street Journal*, 4 September. https://www.wsj.com/articles/options-for-removing-kim-jong-un-1504556500.

Bradsher, Keith, and Raymond Zhong. (2020). "After Trump's TikTok Ban, China Readies Blacklist of Foreign Companies." *New York Times*, 19 September. https://www.nytimes.com/2020/09/19/technology/china-tiktok-wechat-blacklist.html.

Chace, Zoe. (2013). "Stamps, Jeans, Beer: What Americans Want From North Korea." *WRVO Public Media*, 26 July. https://www.wrvo.org/post/stamps-jeans-beer-what-americans-want-north-korea.

Chomsky, Noam. (2008). "Humanitarian Imperialism: The New Doctrine of Imperial Right." *Monthly Review* 60 (4): 22.

Chun, Simone. (2020). "Will Biden finally declare the Korean War over." *Responsible Statecraft* [*Quincy Institute*], 1 December. https://responsiblestatecraft.org/2020/12/01/will-biden-finally-declare-the-korean-war-over/.

Cockburn, Andrew. (2015). "The Kingpin Strategy: Assassination as Policy in Washington and How It Failed, 1990-2015." *The American Empire Project*, 28 April. http://aep.typepad.com/american_empire_project/2015/04/the-kingpin-strategy.html.

Daiss, Tim. (2016). "Japan Could Go Nuclear 'Virtually Overnight' Joe Biden Tells Chinese President." *Forbes*, 25 June. https://www.forbes.com/sites/timdaiss/2016/06/25/japan-could-go-nuclear-virtually-overnight-joe-biden-tells-chinese-presid ent/#4d817fd0161c.

Davenport, Kelsey. (2018). "UN Security Council Resolutions on North Korea." *Arms Control Association*, April. https://www.armscontrol.org/factsheets/UN-Security -Council-Resolutions-on-North-Korea.

Detsch, Jack. (2020). "U.S. Set to Finally Sanction Turkey for Buying Russian Arms." *Foreign Policy*, 10 December. https://foreignpolicy.com/2020/12/10/trump-sanction -turkey-s400-russia-f35/.

Dubowitz, Mark, and Goldberg, Richard. (2020). "The Coronavirus Is Absolutely No Excuse to Lift Sanctions on Iran." *Foreign Policy*, 31 March. https://foreignpolicy .com/2020/03/31/the-coronavirus-is-absolutely-no-excuse-to-lift-sanctions-on -iran/.

Dutton, Peter, and Kardon, I.B. (2017). "Forget the FONOPs — Just Fly, Sail and Operate Wherever International Law Allows." *Lawfare*, 10 June. https://www.lawfareblog .com/forget-fonops-%E2%80%94-just-fly-sail-and-operate-wherever-internatio nal-law-allows.

Erästö, Tytti. (2019). "The NPT and the TPNW: Compatible or conflicting nuclear weap- ons treaties?" *Stockholm International Peace Research Institute (SIPRI)*, 6 March. https://www.sipri.org/commentary/blog/2019/npt-and-tpnw-compatible-or-conf licting-nuclear-weapons-treaties.

Farrell, Henry, and Newman, Abraham. (2019). "By Punishing Iran, Trump Is Weakening America." *Foreign Policy*, 24 April. https://foreignpolicy.com/2019/04/24/by-punish ing-iran-trump-is-weakening-america/.

Feron, Henri, Eriksson Fortier, Ewa, Gray, Kevin, Kim, Suzy, O'Reilly, Marie, Park, Kee B., Yoon, Joy. (2019). "First Comprehensive Assessment of the Impact of Sanctions Against North Korea Shows Adverse Consequences for Civilians, Especially Women." *Korea Peace Now*, October. https://koreapeacenow.org/first-comprehens ive-assessment-of-the-impact-of-sanctions-against-north-korea-shows-adverse -consequences-for-civilians-especially-women/.

Go, Myong-Hyun. (2020). "Not Under Pressure- How Pressure Leaked Out of North Korea Sanctions." *ASAN Institute for Asian Studies*, 18 June. http://en.asaninst.org/ contents/not-under-pressure-how-pressure-fizzled-out-of-north-korea-sanctions/.

Gordon, Joy. (2006). "A Peaceful, Silent, Deadly Remedy: The Ethics of Economic Sanctions." *Ethics & International Affairs* 13 (1): 123–142. https://www.researchgate .net/publication/229658377_A_Peaceful_Silent_Deadly_Remedy_The_Ethics_of _Economic_Sanctions.

Gordon, Joy. (2019). "Introduction [to issue of Ethics and International Affairs]." *Ethics and International Affairs*, September. https://www.ethicsandinternationalaffairs .org/2019/introduction-3/.

Hagedorn, Elizabeth. (2020). "US issues fresh Iran sanctions targeting IRGC's 'web of front companies.'" *Al-Monitor*, 26 March. https://www.al-monitor.com/pulse/origin als/2020/03/us-iran-sanction-irgc-web-front-companies.html.

Hufbauer, Gary Clyde, Schott, Jeffrey J., Elliott, Kimberly Ann, and Oegg, Barbara. (2009). "Economic Sanctions Reconsidered, 3rd Edition." *Peterson Institute for International Economics*, June. https://piie.com/bookstore/economic-sanctions -reconsidered-3rd-edition-paper.

Jakes, Lara, and Schmitt, Eric. (2020). "In Diplomatic Doubleheader, U.S. Seizes Iranian Fuel From Ships Headed to Venezuela." *New York Times*, 14 August. https://www.nyti mes.com/2020/08/14/world/middleeast/trump-iran-venezuela-fuel-tankers.html.

Jung, In-hwan. (2017). "North Korea stresses "self-reliance" in response to new oil sup-ply reductions." *Hankyoreh*, 19 September. http://english.hani.co.kr/arti/english _edition/e_northkorea/811621.html.

Kim, Jin-myung, and Kim, Eun-joong. (2020). "Korea Could Face Fresh Pressure to Join U.S.' War on Huawei." *Chosun Ilbo*, 7 December. http://english.chosun.com/site/ data/html_dir/2020/12/07/2020120701614.html.

Kim, Min Joo, and Denyer, Simon. (2019). "A U.N. deadline is forcing North Korea's global workers to go home. Some never will." *Washington Post*, 22 December. https:// www.washingtonpost.com/world/asia_pacific/a-un-deadline-is-forcing-north-kor eas-global-workers-to-go-home-some-never-will/2019/12/20/cf59ac04-1c14-11ea -977a-15a6710ed6da_story.html.

Koo, George. (2020). "Trump's war on Huawei is self-defeating." *Asia Times*, 31 May. https://asiatimes.com/2020/05/trumps-war-on-huawei-self-defeating/.

Krige, John. (2020). "Scholars or Spies? U.S.-China Tension in Academic Collaboration." *China Research Center* [*Georgia universities*], 12 October. https://www.chinacenter .net/2020/china_currents/19-3/scholars-or-spies-u-s-china-tension-in-academic -collaboration/.

Lederer, Edith M. (2019). "UN investigator: 11 million North Koreans are undernour-ished." *Associated Press*, 23 October. https://apnews.com/e2499ddf9e594c848b615 7a4e64127dc.

Lee, Kristine. (2020). "The United States Can't Quit on the UN." *Foreign Affairs*, 24 September. https://www.foreignaffairs.com/articles/united-states/2020-09-24/uni ted-states-cant-quit-un.

Lee, Sung-Yoon, and Stanton, Joshua. (2016). "How to get serious with North Korea." *CNN*, 15 January. http://edition.cnn.com/2016/01/15/opinions/lee-stanton-north -korea-sanctions/index.html.

Lew, Jacob J., and Nephew, Richard. (2018). "The Use and Misuse of Economic Statecraft." *Foreign Affairs*, November/December. https://www.foreignaffairs.com/ articles/world/2018-10-15/use-and-misuse-economic-statecraft.

Lipson, Michael. (1999). "The reincarnation of COCOM: Explaining post-Cold War export controls." *The Nonproliferation Review* 6 (2): 33–51.

Long, Heather. (2020). "Trump threatens Europe with fresh tariffs in Davos, deepening a rift with longtime U.S. allies." *Washington Post*, 22 January. https://www.washingtonpost.com/business/2020/01/21/trump-threatens-europe-with-fresh-tariffs-davos-deepening-rift-with-long-time-us-allies/.

McCarthy, Niall. (2018). "The Institutions Americans Trust Most And Least In 2018." *Forbes*, 29 June. https://www.forbes.com/sites/niallmccarthy/2018/06/29/the-institutions-americans-trust-most-and-least-in-2018-infographic/#2b106ba92fc8.

McCormack, Gavan. (2017). "North Korea and a Rules-Based Order For the Indo-Pacific, East Asia, and the World." *Asia Pacific Journal—Japan Focus*, 15 November. http://apjjf.org/2017/22/McCormack.html.

Meisler, Stanley. (1999). "The Revenge of Boutros Boutros-Ghali." *Stanley.Meisler.com*, 21 July. http://www.stanleymeisler.com/news-commentary/revenge.html#.U4EWSumKDIU.

Miles, Tom. (2018). "China drives stunning growth in global trademark applications, U.N. says." *Reuters*, 4 December. https://www.reuters.com/article/us-global-economy-innovation/china-drives-stunning-growth-in-global-trademark-applications-u-n-says-idUSKBN1O21FV.

Morello, Carol. (2020). "Trump's turn to military against Iran shows limits of economic 'maximum pressure.'" *Washington Post*, 5 January. https://www.washingtonpost.com/world/national-security/trump-administrations-maximum-pressure-campaign-against-iran-enters-a-new-military-phase/2020/01/04/fe237c5a-2f32-11ea-be79-83e793dbcaef_story.html.

Needham, Kirsty. (2020). "Australia faces down China in high-stakes strategy." *Reuters*, 4 September. https://www.reuters.com/investigates/special-report/australia-china-relations/.

Norton, Ben. (2020). "Billionaire-backed Human Rights Watch lobbies for lethal US sanctions on leftist governments as Covid crisis rages." *GrayZone*, 8 April. https://thegrayzone.com/2020/04/08/billionaire-human-rights-watch-sanctions-nicaragua-venezuela/.

Nuland, Victoria. (2013). "Address by Assistant Secretary of State Victoria Nuland." *US-Ukraine Foundation*, 13 December. http://www.state.gov/p/eur/rls/rm/2013/dec/218804.htm.

Porter, Gareth. (2020). "Anti-Interventionist Think Tank's Debut is a Dud." *Consortium News*, 28 February. https://consortiumnews.com/2020/02/28/anti-interventionist-think-tanks-debut-is-a-dud/.

Prashad, Vijay. (2017). "The Demise of Diplomacy." *Counterpunch*, 12 May. http://www.counterpunch.org/2017/05/12/the-demise-of-diplomacy/.

Ramzy, Austin, and May, Tiffany. (2020). "U.S. Imposes Sanctions on Chinese Officials Over Hong Kong Crackdown." *New York Times*, 8 December. https://www.nytimes.com/2020/12/08/world/asia/hong-kong-china-us-sanctions.html.

Roach, Stephen. (2019). "Japan Then, China Now." *Project Syndicate*, 27 May. https://johnmenadue.com/stephen-s-roach-japan-then-china-now-project-syndicate-27-5-2019/.

Sanger, David E., Choe, Sang-hun, and Motoko, Rich. (2017). "North Korea Rouses Neighbors to Reconsider Nuclear Weapons." *New York Times*, 28 October. https://www.nytimes.com/2017/10/28/world/asia/north-korea-nuclear-weapons-japan-south-korea.html.

Sanger, David E., and McCabe, David. (2020). "Huawei Is Winning the Argument in Europe, as the U.S. Fumbles to Develop Alternatives." *New York Times*, 17 February. https://www.nytimes.com/2020/02/17/us/politics/us-huawei-5g.html.

Schott, Jeffrey J. (1998). "US Economic Sanctions: Good Intentions, Bad Execution." *Peterson Institute for International Economics*, 3 June. https://www.piie.com/commentary/speeches-papers/us-economic-sanctions-good-intentions-bad-execution.

Shepardson, David, Freifeld, Karen, and Alper, Alexandra. (2020). "U.S. moves to cut Huawei off from global chip suppliers as China eyes retaliation." *Reuters*, 15 May. https://www.reuters.com/article/us-usa-huawei-tech/u-s-moves-to-cut-huawei-off-from-global-chip-suppliers-idUSKBN22R1KC.

Shih, Gerry. (2020). "China threatens U.S. companies with sanctions following Trump's WeChat ban." *Washington Post*, 20 September. https://www.washingtonpost.com/world/china-threatens-us-companies-with-sanctions-following-trumps-wechat-ban/2020/09/19/08c4a0d8-fa55-11ea-89e3-4b9efa36dc64_story.html.

Simons, Marlise. (2002). "U.S. Forces Out Head of Chemical Arms Agency." *New York Times*, 23 April. https://www.nytimes.com/2002/04/23/world/us-forces-out-head-of-chemical-arms-agency.html#h.

Sly, Liz. (2019). "Assad loyalists are turning on Syria's government as living standards deteriorate." *Washington Post*, 25 March. https://www.washingtonpost.com/world/middle_east/assad-loyalists-are-turning-on-syrias-government-as-living-standards-deteriorate/2019/03/25/080b1562-44d7-11e9-94ab-d2dda3c0df52_story.html.

Smith, Hazel. (2020). "The ethics of United Nations sanctions on North Korea: effectiveness, necessity and proportionality." *Critical Asian Studies*, June. https://www.tandfonline.com/doi/abs/10.1080/14672715.2020.1757479?journalCode=rcra20.

Spetalnick, Matt, Psaledakis, Daphne, Pamuk, Humeyra, and Hunnicutt, Trevor. (2020). "Biden will keep using U.S. sanctions weapon but with sharper aim—sources." *Reuters*, 17 December. https://www.reuters.com/article/us-usa-sanctions-insight/biden-will-keep-using-u-s-sanctions-weapon-but-with-sharper-aim-sources-idUSKBN28Q1CV.

Talley, Ian. (2020). "U.S. Steps Up Pressure on China Over North Korean Coal Exports." *Wall Street Journal*, 8 December. https://www.wsj.com/articles/u-s-steps-up-press ure-on-china-over-north-korean-coal-exports-11607464646.

Taylor, Adam. (2020). "Hong Kong leader says she has 'piles of cash at home,' no bank account, due to U.S. sanctions." *Washington Post*, 29 November. https://www.was hingtonpost.com/world/2020/11/28/carrie-lam-cash-sanctions/.

Valencia, Mark J. (2019). "Who's bullying who in the South China Sea?" *East Asia Forum*, 2 November. https://www.eastasiaforum.org/2019/11/02/whos-bullying-who-in-the -south-china-sea/.

Walsh, Jack. (2020). "Secondary Sanctions: Broad Reach and Inconsistent Enforcement Present Compliance Challenges for Global Companies and Their Executives." *Association of Certified Sanctions Specialists*, 7 August. https://sanctionsassociation .org/secondary-sanctions-broad-reach-and-inconsistent-enforcement-present -compliance-challenges-for-global-companies-and-their-executives/.

Waltz, Kenneth N. (2012). "Why Iran Should Get the Bomb." *Foreign Affairs*.

Weisbrot, Mark. (2016). "Is Human Rights Watch Too Closely Aligned With U.S. Foreign Policy?" *Huffington Post*, 23 September. https://www.huffingtonpost.com/mark -weisbrot/is-human-rights-watch-too_b_12157040.html.

Wen, Wang. (2020). "China confident 'de-dollarization' is fast underway amid tense times." *Global Times*, 20 July. https://www.globaltimes.cn/content/1195115.shtml.

Zakaria, Fareed. (2020). "America's excessive reliance on sanctions will come back to haunt it." *Washington Post*, 28 August. https://www.washingtonpost.com/opini ons/global-opinions/americas-excessive-reliance-on-sanctions-will-come-back-to -haunt-it/2020/08/27/e73a9004-e89c-11ea-970a-64c73a1c2392_story.html.

Internet References

(2002). "Examining the Plight of Refugees: The Case of North Korea." *Subcommittee on Immigration of the Committee on the Judiciary, United States Senate*, 21 July. https://www.govinfo.gov/content/pkg/CHRG-107shrg86829/html/CHRG-107shrg86 829.htm.

(2012). "Overview of Export Laws and Regulations." *UC Davis*, 13 January. https:// research.ucdavis.edu/wp-content/uploads/Export-Control-Overview-of-Regulati ons.pdf.

(2014). "Adherence to and Compliance with Arms Control, Nonproliferation, and Disarmament Agreements and Commitments." *State Department*, July. https:// 2009-2017.state.gov/documents/organization/230108.pdf.

(2015). "What are jus ad bellum and jus in bello?" *International Committe of the Red Cross*, 22 January. https://www.icrc.org/en/document/what-are-jus-ad-bel lum-and-jus-bello-o.

(2016a). "Iran has seen only \$3 bn returned since nuke deal: Kerry." *AFP*, 19 April. https://www.yahoo.com/news/iran-seen-only-3-bn-returned-since-nuke-023958350.html.

(2016b). "Starvation 'as a weapon' is a war crime, UN chief warns parties to conflict in Syria." *UN News Centre*, 14 January. http://www.un.org/apps/news/story.asp?NewsID=53003.

(2019). "Quincy Institute for Responsible Statecraft." https://quincyinst.org/.

(2020). "Sanctions and Other Committees." https://www.un.org/securitycouncil/content/repertoire/sanctions-and-other-committees.

(2021). "Serbia Opens Pipeline for Russian Gas, Ignores US Opposition." *AP via US News & World Report*, 1 January. https://www.usnews.com/news/world/articles/2021-01-01/serbia-opens-pipeline-for-russian-gas-ignores-us-opposition.

CHAPTER 3

Hunger Politics: Sanctions as Siege Warfare

Manu Karuka

Sanctions are a form of siege warfare. A siege involves trapping a population within a limited space, preventing any movement of weapons, food, and other supplies into that space. Besieged forces rely on defensive fortifications, stores of supplies, and most crucially, their unity, to out-wait their attackers. Attacking forces in a siege rely on their ability to wait until the besieged have run out of food and other supplies, until their unity has splintered. Siege warfare is generally a very slow form of warfare. It fills the lives of civilians under its shadow with ruin and devastation, for as long as it lasts. In addition to more traditional elements of siege warfare, such as artillery and field fortifications, sanctions add control over currency and finance capital. By joining the mechanisms of war and finance to attack the political and economic independence of poorer nations, sanctions comprise an exemplary form of contemporary imperialist siege warfare. This essay situates contemporary US sanctions within a longer history of imperialist siege warfare. It discusses sieges in the development of the bourgeois state. It compares imperialist sanctions, following the collapse of the USSR, to anti-imperialist sanctions against apartheid. Finally, it considers the effects of imperialist siege warfare on imperial society, against the principle of the unity of the besieged.

Sieges have been associated with the medieval romances of feudal Europe, calling to mind Crusading knights capturing Levantine towns for Christendom, or dying heroic deaths in failed defenses. The romances, however, pay scant attention to peasants and townspeople, snagged in a feudal chain of obligations, caught between the rule of warlords. Stories of sieges serve to outline the borders between distinct identities, such as the Greeks and Trojans of the Iliad, or el Cid, whose leadership of a combined Muslim and Christian force in a siege on Valencia was poetically transformed into a story of Muslim expulsion. On January 2, 1492, Granada capitulated to an eight-month siege by the forces of Castile and Aragon. Nine months later, Columbus departed on what would be his first voyage to the Caribbean. A decade earlier, Portuguese traders had built the São Jorge da Mina, the first permanent European trading fortress in coastal West Africa. Within forty years of Columbus's voyage, a transatlantic trade in African captives would move through al Mina, as the slavers called it, under contract with the Spanish monarchy. Modern imperialism, revolving around the concentration of economic and political power, resulting in slavery, settler colonialism, and genocide, originated under siege conditions.

The seventeenth century saw major advances in siege warfare, under the leadership of the Dutch Baron van Coehoorn, and the French Marquis de Vauban. To break the resolve of forces defending against siege warfare, attacking armies had long employed basic forms of artillery, such as catapults. In the seventeenth century, experimenting with gunpowder, European military engineers transformed this use of artillery. Rather than a scattered approach, Vauban and Coehoorn focused artillery fire on specific areas to weaken and destroy defensive walls. Vauban is associated with the statement "more powder, less blood" (Cohen 1937, 169). Accordingly, the seventeenth-century Dutch and French armies employing these methods presented them as a more civilized form of warfare. The military officers who refined novel siege techniques during this period participated in the concentration and centralization of state power. Born into minor provincial nobility, Vauban rose through the ranks of the French military during the reign of Louis XIV, the self-proclaimed sun-king. Siege warfare marked but one element in the bourgeois overthrow of aristocratic power. Colonialism was the motor for this transformation. At the dawn of the eighteenth century, Vauban advocated full-scale colonization in North America, in order to stabilize and extend French territorial control against English competition (Farrell 1988, 38–39).

1   Siege Warfare and the Bourgeois State

Siege warfare, like colonialism, persisted across the transition from absolute monarchy to the bourgeois state. In an 1841 essay on Algeria, Alexis de Tocqueville, a descendant of Vauban, respectfully disagreed with fellow Frenchmen who "find it wrong that we burn harvests, that we empty silos... that we seize unarmed men, women, and children." In his rejoinder, Tocqueville argued that such tactics "are unfortunate necessities," forced on "any people that wants to wage war on the Arabs" (Tocqueville 2000, 70). Tocqueville insisted that such brutal tactics were justified in Algeria. In Europe, he explained, the French waged war against governments. In Africa, they waged war against peoples. French military victory in Algeria necessitated shattering Algerian political unity. To achieve this, Tocqueville continued, it would be necessary for the French to employ "all means of desolating these tribes," making life "intolerable" in order to splinter Algerians' alliance against French power. Noting that Arabs in Algeria relied on trade to sustain their communities, Tocqueville argued that the "interdiction of commerce" would be the most effective means to accomplish French aims. "They suffer a great deal," he concluded, "when we trap them between our bayonets and the desert" (ibid., 70–71). French military forces in Algeria were not involved in a purely military confrontation. Instead, they were deployed against the entire Algerian community. From this vantage point, Tocqueville observed in a later report on Algeria, "the true conditions of war in Africa appeared" (ibid., 135–136).

In 1849, French forces laid siege to Zaatcha, a fortified oasis in the Sahara. In the beginning of the summer, a tax revolt had sparked a broader uprising. Word of the revolt spread from Morocco to Mecca. After suffering a humiliating defeat that July, the French laid a siege in September. The besiegers breached Zaatcha's walls on November 26 and slew everyone inside. They then razed the town, leaving it, in the words of one observer, "a mass of ruins and corpses." The rebel leader's decapitated head was mashed onto a post in the middle of the French camp. Three years later, French forces laid another siege on a more populous town, Laghouat, in order to quell another rebellion. After breaking through the walls, French soldiers spent the day massacring several thousand people before sunset (Brower 2009, 81–89).

The French military in Algeria implemented lessons learned from US military tactics against Indigenous nations in North America. These French tactics, in turn, shaped the further development of US military engineering. In his 1865 *Elementary Course of Military Engineering*, Dennis Mahan, a faculty member at West Point, drew heavily on Vauban's theories, and on the experience of the US Civil War, to urge military measures that would result in "success, at the least expenditure of time and blood" (Mahan 1870, 226). Mahan outlined three distinct phases of siege warfare. In the first phase, attacking forces take all necessary measures to cut off access of the besieged area with the outside world. In the second phase, attacking forces raise fortifications which enable them to approach the area under siege, gaining the ground to stage an open assault. The final phase consists of all subsequent operations leading to the surrender of the besieged. Siege tactics, Mahan explained, center on a policy of avoiding hand-to-hand combat at all costs. Instead, besieging forces seek to achieve their goals through the use of artillery and through positional warfare, skillfully pushing their trenches forward to tighten the siege. Those subjected to siege conditions, Mahan noted, "are often constrained to a bolder course," exploiting any opportunities opened up by the besiegers' errors" (ibid., 284).

While the US Civil War, the context for Mahan's analysis, occurred primarily on land, it also saw the expansion and institutionalization of US naval power, in order to maintain a naval blockade against the Confederacy. In 1890, Dennis

Mahan's son Alfred Mahan published his classic text of naval warfare strategy, *Influence of Sea Power Upon History, 1660–1783*, which linked naval warfare with naval commerce. War on the seas defends or disrupts sea-borne commerce. The ability to raise and sustain sea-borne siege operations, to destroy the commerce of a targeted area, is at the core of Alfred Mahan's vision of naval strategy. Naval warfare centers around the power to control, and if necessary, to obstruct naval shipping and trade, suggesting a fluid line between piracy and officially sanctioned naval operations. Moreover, Mahan argued, sea-borne commerce necessitates the establishment and maintenance of colonies, to provide way stations for replenishing provisions and fuel. During a period when corporate trusts consolidated monopoly control over wide swathes of the US economy, Alfred Mahan urged the United States to develop its naval power, in order to erect "a shield of defensive power" (Mahan 1894, 49).

Sieges are core techniques of imperialism. The deliberate targeting of civilians under siege tells us something about the historical preconditions of imperialism. Siege warfare is a tactic uniquely suited to imperialist ends. In an 1894 manual *Attack of Fortified Places*, James Mercur, a professor of civil and military engineering at West Point, discussed the centrality of civilians to siege warfare. "A blockade," he wrote, "consists in so surrounding a place and closing its communications as to keep the garrison from receiving reinforcements, provisions, and supplies sufficient to enable it to continue the defence [*sic.*] and to avoid starvation." While seemingly focused on opposing armed forces, Mercur continued,

> Blockades are more effective in reducing cities and towns than in taking places occupied only by a military garrison, since the presence of a large number of non-combatants in a place rapidly exhausts its store of provisions, renders epidemics more likely to break out, and by the suffering and misery resulting demoralizes the garrison, unnerves the commander, and eventually causes its downfall. This justifies the apparent harshness of not allowing non-combatants to leave a beleaguered place.
>
> MERCUR 1903, 1–2

Drawing on the historical experience of wars against Indigenous nations (several of them, it should be noted, resulting in US military defeats), Mercur outlined techniques that US armed forces would employ within a few years in blockades of San Juan, Manila, and Santiago de Cuba. Siege warfare, Mercur makes clear, deliberately targets civilians for intense suffering through hunger and disease.

Woodrow Wilson would take up these ideas in 1919, while attempting to explain the principles of the League of Nations to the US public. Speaking in Indianapolis, Wilson argued that the economic isolation of Germany hastened the end of World War I. "A nation that is boycotted," Wilson insisted, "is a nation in sight of surrender." Wilson described this as a "peaceful, silent, deadly remedy" that makes force unnecessary, a "terrible remedy" that risks no lives outside of the boycotted nation (Wilson 1919, 108).

Germany, itself, would attempt to implement this "terrible remedy" twenty-two years later. The Nazi invasion of the Soviet Union was organized around a Hunger Plan, seeking to use food as a weapon to serve German strategic interests. The Hunger Plan intended to address the wartime shortage of food within Germany, making the isolation of Germany impossible. Targeting the industrialized areas of the Soviet Union for mass starvation would advance the destruction of communism. The guidelines drafted during the planning phase flatly concluded that "tens of millions of people will starve to death when we take what we need from the land" (Gerhard 2015, 86–90). As Field Marshall Erich von Manstein would testify at Nuremberg, the Hunger Plan was a core component of Nazi Germany's prosecution of a "special war" against the USSR, an ideological war aiming to achieve the "extermination of the Bolshevik system" (Nuremberg Trial Proceedings 1946, 12).

2   Sanctions as Hybrid Warfare

The politics of hunger would persist after the dissolution of the USSR, which sparked catastrophic drops in caloric intake, and millions of excess deaths over the following decade. The apparent Cold War victory of the capitalist bloc saw a widespread intensification of hunger across Eastern Europe and the formerly colonized countries. Internationally, the use of sanctions increased at such a rapid scale that the 1990's was memorialized as the "sanctions decade." The US has led this trend, imposing about two-thirds of sanctions since the 1990's. 75% of US sanctions have been imposed unilaterally (Gordon 1999, 387). As with siege warfare historically, sanctions have been presented as a gentler alternative to war. A policy of collective punishment, sanctions have been consistently justified as a means to trigger political pressure on governments. By enforcing economic isolation, sanctions have exacerbated the suffering of their primary victims: the poorest and most vulnerable people in targeted countries, producing widespread malnutrition, debilitating illness, and premature death (Arya 2008, 34–35). During a period of spectacular growth and concentration of international finance capital, the US and its allies have aggressively asserted political control by mobilizing the core institutions of international finance, and international currency flows. Human rights, defined in the narrowest terms of individual property rights, replaced anti-communism as the core justification for imperialist violence. Whereas anti-communism raised the specter of a communist threat to an "American way of life", human rights instead invokes US responsibilities as "the last best hope of man on earth." Human rights has provided the ideological cement for US unipolar power.

Sanctions are a core element of contemporary hybrid warfare, "a combination of unconventional and conventional means using a range of state and non-state actors that runs across the spectrum of social and political life" (Tricontinental 2019, 2). Hybrid war is rooted in older concepts of "low-intensity conflict" that targeted national liberation movements in the Third World (Galvin 1991, 12). The contemporary doctrine of hybrid warfare took shape in the aftermath of US military defeats in Afghanistan and Iraq, and Hezbollah's 2006 defeat of the Israeli Defense Forces. Twelve years before he became US Secretary of Defense, Lt. General James Mattis drew on his experience commanding the US siege of Fallujah to argue that in addition to fighting, distributing humanitarian supplies, and policing, US Marines should include "psychological or information operations aspects." Mattis presented this as a way to mitigate the violence of war. "Successful information ops," according to Mattis, "help the civilian population understand and accept the better future we seek to help build with them" (Mattis and Hoffman 2005). More powder, less blood.

The doctrine of hybrid war has developed out of a long tradition of US imperialist warfare, a tradition with historical origins in the capture and control of territory in North America itself. From its costly wars with the Seminole nation, to its decades-long failed occupation of the Philippines, to the popular warfare it faced in Korea and Vietnam, where again, the US was militarily defeated, to the pointless savagery unleashed on Afghanistan and Iraq, US military planners have long faced the truth that overwhelming firepower does not facilitate military victories for imperialism.

A combination of drones, long-range missiles, and satellites has enabled the US to dominate the air with minimal risk to US lives. In October 2011, US Vice President Joseph Biden remarked on NATO airstrikes on Libya: "In this case, America spent $2 billion total and didn't [sic.] lose a single life...This is more the prescription for how we deal with the world going forward than we have in the past" (quoted in Shanker and Schmitt 2012). Air war, however, does not facilitate regime change. For that, US military planners acknowledge, the long-term deployment of land forces is necessary. In land war, the US is vulnerable to military casualties. After decades of intensifying economic, political, and social crises roiling US society, there may be real limits to the long-term deployment of US land forces, largely drawn from the ranks of the US poor, mobilized through the ideology of the "volunteer army." The ghosts of the draft army sent to Vietnam, where soldiers began to turn their weapons on their officers, haunt US military doctrine.

Siege warfare responds to these limitations. Tomahawk missiles and drone strikes are the new siege artillery. No-fly zones join naval blockades to totally isolate those under siege. US cyber-warfare capabilities allow for country-wide disruptions of electrical and water infrastructure, with lethal impacts on the most vulnerable civilians. But perhaps the sharpest innovation of siege warfare has manifested through US control over the mechanisms of international trade, finance, and currency. US sanctions block the entire world from trading with targeted countries. The US backs this with three threats: denying access to the US market; denying access to the mechanisms of international exchange (which the US controls through its currency); US criminal court proceedings (as evidenced in Canada's December 2018 house arrest and extradition proceedings of Huawei's Chief Financial Officer, under the charge of skirting US sanctions on Iran). By forcing all countries and enterprises in the world to sustain its siege policies, US sanctions actually contradict core principles of capitalist competition. US sanctions seek to isolate entire countries from access to international trade and credit, from remittances that are crucial for survival at the household level, and even from basic retail banking services. The US can impose these measures because its currency is the international medium of exchange. Through sanctions, the US coordinates imperialist siege warfare between the Departments of Defense, State, and Treasury.

3   Anti-Imperialist Sanctions

Siege warfare has been uniquely suited to the centralization of political power, and to ideological forms of warfare. However, we should be clear that not all sieges serve imperialist functions. Recall Dien Bien Phu, where the Viet Minh held the French garrison under siege for two months, striking the decisive blow against French colonialism in their homeland. Vietnamese forces dismantled artillery and anti-aircraft batteries, carried them up the mountains surrounding the city, reassembled the artillery, and proceeded to shell the French and prevent aerial reinforcements.

As there are anti-imperialist sieges, there are anti-imperialist sanctions. The apartheid regime in South Africa served as a continental beachhead for imperialism. The international movement against apartheid supported a different future, not only for South Africa, but for the region as a whole. Multilateral sanctions against the apartheid regime, levied by international institutions, and by civil society, were important tools for this movement. As Winnie Mandela wrote, in her 1984 autobiography *Part of My Soul Went With Him*, "We are only interested in sanctions now. Every alternative has been examined by those men who have spent their lifetimes in prison. One doesn't dream for one minute that sanctions alone would bring the government down, or disinvestment alone. But it is part of a tool one can use. And in fact, tools of this nature which are instruments of liberation would lessen the bloodbath we are heading for..." (Mandela 1985, 125).

While the US has advocated and employed unilateral sanctions, it has also publicly stood against the use of multilateral sanctions. On June 16, 1964, only four days after the apartheid regime sentenced eight defendants, including Nelson Mandela, to life imprisonment at the conclusion of the infamous Rivonia trial, Adlai Stevenson addressed the UN in his capacity as US Ambassador. "My Government," Stevenson reported, "continues to believe that the situation in South Africa... does not today provide a basis under the [UN] charter for the application by the Security Council of coercive measures" (Stevenson 1964, 31). Stevenson highlighted a policy of US support for higher education in South Africa, a policy which subsequent US administrations would invoke to criticize the academic and cultural boycott of the apartheid regime.

In 1965, eight days after the white supremacist government of Rhodesia issued its Unilateral Declaration of Independence, the UN Security Council (with France abstaining) urged a diplomatic and economic boycott of the illegal Rhodesian regime (UN Security Council Res. 217). Prior to these sanctions, the US had obtained 40% of its chrome imports from what was then Southern Rhodesia. In 1971, the US Congress passed the so-called "Byrd Amendment," which forbade the US government from prohibiting or regulating imports of "strategic and critical" materials from non-"Communist-dominated countries or areas," in the absence of corresponding sanctions on the same materials from Communist countries (US Congress 1971). The US thereby resumed imports of chrome, nickel, and asbestos from Rhodesia through the end of the decade. Tellingly, while the US skirted multilateral sanctions on the Rhodesian regime, it later imposed unilateral sanctions in Zimbabwe in 2003, invoking human rights and political corruption. These sanctions persist almost two decades later. They have had devastating effects on the regional economy of Southern Africa.

In our own time, the Boycott, Divestment, and Sanctions Movement (BDS) targets Israel with a cultural and academic boycott, to pressure the Israeli government to comply with international human rights norms in its treatment of Palestinians. Unlike US sanctions, no one will be denied food or medicine because of BDS. Unlike US sanctions, BDS does not deliberately target the poorest and most vulnerable members of Israeli society. A core aim of BDS is to lift the blockade of Gaza, which has devastated health, medical systems, and life expectancy in Gaza since it was first imposed by Israel and Egypt in 2007, punctuated with semi-regular bombing campaigns and ground military assaults. On February 5, 2020, the US Senate passed the "Combating BDS Act." The bill had been introduced by Sen. Marco Rubio, who proudly announced that it "supports efforts by state governments and local communities to use the power of the purse to counter the BDS movement's economic warfare targeting Israel" (Rubio 2020).

4   Imperialist Fortifications, and the Unity of the Besieged

A basic building material for trench construction consists of brushwood collected into bundles, cut to an appropriate size for specific applications, called fascines. Ramparts built from fascines enable attackers to "repel a sortie of the besieged" (Mahan 1870, 182–184). From the Roman empire onwards, these building blocks of siege warfare have been represented as fasces, bundles of sticks that symbolize imperial power. Fasces recur frequently in US political imagery: on the seal of the US Senate, on the doorway to the Oval Office in the White House, and on the facade of the US Supreme Court building, among other places. Their recurrence suggests siege warfare as a core building block of the US political imaginary.

The dialectical counterpart of siege warfare is the construction of fortifications. Vauban, the French military engineer associated with major breakthroughs in siege warfare during the reign of Louis XIV, was also a celebrated architect of fortresses. By the end of his career, Vauban had overseen the construction of a large system of fortifications, built by tens of thousands of peasants and other poor people, mustered into uncompensated labor for the monarchy. Technical knowledge and experience gained in breaking fortifications during siege warfare enhanced the practical knowledge for building fortifications that could withstand enemy sieges. The fortifications designed by Vauban, incidentally, withstood attack until World War II, when they proved no match for the Wehrmacht's new tank divisions.

In an era of imperialist siege warfare, we should expect a corresponding renewal of imperialist fortifications. In the period after 9/11, US imperialist fortifications hardened under the rubric of "Homeland Security," in the largest restructuring of federal agencies since the National Security Act of 1947. First formed in November 2002, Homeland Security is the third largest department of the US executive branch, after Defense and Veterans Affairs, with a Fiscal-Year 2020 budget of $92.1 billion. The Department of Homeland Security (DHS) has funneled tens of billions of dollars to state and local law enforcement agencies under the ostensible guise of preventing terrorism. The high pitch of racism driving immigration policy within the US is a manifestation of imperialist fortifications. After the Transportation Security Administration was formed in November 2001, immigrants, who had made up much of the existing airport security workforce, lost their jobs due to new citizenship restrictions on their positions. Recall that the initial plan for DHS would have stripped 180,000 federal employees of their union membership. Homeland security, the fortification of North America on a continental scale, is a core site of class struggle. This is reflected in the title of fourth-generation warfare theorist H. John Poole's 2009 book, *Homeland Siege: Tactics for Police and Military*. Poole argued that China has infiltrated the US, subcontracting with MS-13 to distribute opioids throughout the "American heartland." To combat this, he recommended suffusing border policing throughout the US, the amplification of "drug war" operations in the Caribbean, and strict disruptions of international trade with China (Poole 2009).

Class struggle knows no borders. For example, specific aspects of the assault on the Venezuelan poor are mirrored in the assault on the poor within the US. The CLAP program, which provides food staples to over six million households across Venezuela, was placed under sanctions by the US Treasury Department, under the charge of corruption. US Treasury Secretary Steven Mnuchin charged that through the CLAP program, which provides rice, beans, cooking oil, and other staples, the Venezuelan government uses "food as a form of social control (US Department of Treasury 2019). In 1890, Alfred Mahan considered the possibility of a naval blockade of the United States, finding that an effective blockade of the entire US seacoast could not be effectively imposed. Nevertheless, he concluded, while "the People of the United States will certainly not starve... they may suffer grievously" (Mahan 1870, 86). Within the US, the Trump administration rolled out a series of measures to limit the Supplemental Nutrition Assistance Program (SNAP), formerly referred to as the Food Stamp Program. Imposing new work requirements, transforming the enrollment process to make millions ineligible for the program, removing hundreds of thousands of children from free school lunch programs, targeting immigrants for using the program, and penalizing recipients in northern states for accessing heating and fuel subsidies, these policies, to riff on Secretary Mnuchin, use *hunger* as a form of social control. The working class and the poor, of North America, and of Venezuela, have a concrete unity of interest, to fight hunger as a form of social control.

Communities subjected to siege warfare are faced with a fundamental question: maintain unity to withstand the siege, or surrender? Unity is necessary for a society to withstand intensified suffering under siege conditions, especially the withdrawal of food, water, medicine, fuel, and other key goods necessary to sustain people's lives. The unity constructed and sustained under siege involves a recognition that while siege warfare targets all of the people held under siege, whether military or civilian, regardless of their political orientation, siege warfare has its most immediate and deadly impacts on those who are physically, economically, and socially the most vulnerable. It is in this context that imperialist hybrid warfare techniques foster secessionist movements hoisting the umbrella of human rights, or fanning the flames of ethnic separatism, joining sanctions as part of an overarching strategy of imperialist aggression. After all, treason, spy-craft, and treachery are recognized as time-honored methods of breaching defensive walls (Watson 1993).

What bearing can those outside of the siege have on the debates over unity or surrender, debates taking place amidst the gnashing teeth of hunger? Those outside of the siege instead face the question of reinforcing or breaking the siege itself. This, in its way, is a question of unity or division among the besieging forces. Is the siege justifiable? Who benefits from it? Who will benefit from the ways society will transform, in the process of laying and sustaining a siege? Does the siege advance the emancipation of poor, working class, and oppressed people? Behind these questions lies a political imperative: the unity of the besieged—the international unity of the working class—in order to advance the unfulfilled project of decolonization.

References

Arya, Neil. (2008). "Economic Sanctions: the Kinder, Gentler Alternative?" *Medicine, Conflict and Survival* 24 (1): 25–41, 34–35.

Brower, Benjamin. (2009). *A Desert Named Peace: The Violence of France's Empire in theAlgerian Sahara, 1844–1902.* New York: Columbia University Press.

Cohen, Paul. (1937). "The Marquis de Vauban." *The Military Engineer* 29 (165) (May–June): 169–171.

Farrell, David R. (1988). "Reluctant Imperialism: Ponchartrain, Vauban, and the Expansion of New France, 1699–1702." *Proceedings of the Meeting of the French Colonial History Society,* vol. 12: 35–45.

Galvin, John R. (1991). "Uncomfortable Wars: Toward a New Paradigm," in Max Manwaring, ed., *Uncomfortable Wars: Toward a New Paradigm of Low Intensity Conflict.* Boulder: Westview Press.

Gesine Gerhard. (2015). *Nazi Hunger Politics: A History of Food in the Third Reich.* Lanham: Rowman and Littlefield.

Gordon, Joy. (1999). "Economic Sanctions, Just War Doctrine, and the 'Fearful Spectacle of the Civilian Dead'." *CrossCurrents* 49 (3) (Fall): 387–400.

Mahan, Alfred Thayer. (1984 [1894]). *The Influence of Sea Power Upon History, 1660–1783.* New York: Dover.

Mahan, Dennis Hart. (1870). *Elementary Course of Military Engineering*, vol. 1. New York: J. Wiley.

Mandela, Winnie. (1995). *Part of My Soul Went With Him.* New York: Norton.

Mattis, James N., and Hoffman, Frank. (2005). "Future Warfare: The Rise of Hybrid Wars," *Proceedings Magazine*, Nov. vol. 132/11/1, 233.

Mercur, James. (1903 [1894]). *Attack of Fortified Places: Including Siege-Works, Mining, and Demolitions.* New York: J. Wiley.

Nuremberg Trial Proceedings, Vol. 20, Morning session, 1946. 10 August. https://avalon .law.yale.edu/imt/08-10-46.asp.

Nuremberg Trial Proceedings, Vol. 21. Morning session, 1946. 12 August. https://avalon .law.yale.edu/imt/08-12-46.asp.

Poole, H. John. (2009). *Homeland Siege: Tactics for Police and Military.* Emerald Isle, NC: Posterity Press.

Rubio, Marco, The Office of. (2017). "Press Release: Rubio, Manchin Introduce Bill to Counter BDS Movement to Target Israel," 18 Jan.

Shanker, Thom, and Schmitt, Eric. (2011). "Seeing Limits to 'New' Kind of War in Libya." *New York Times*, 21 Oct. 21.

Stevenson, Adlai. (1964). "U.N. Security Council Condemns Apartheid in South Africa; Sets Up Committee to Study Sanctions." *Department of State Bulletin*, 6 July, 29–33, p. 31.

Tocqueville, Alexis de. (2000). *Writings on Empire and Slavery.* Baltimore: Johns Hopkins University Press.

Tricontinental Institute for Social Research. (2019). "Venezuela and Hybrid Wars in Latin America." Dossier No. 17, June.

UN Security Council Resolution 217. (1965). 20 Nov. https://undocs.org/S/RES/217(1965).

US Congress, Public Law 92–156. (1971). 17 Nov. https://www.govinfo.gov/content/pkg/ STATUTE-85/pdf/STATUTE-85-Pg423.pdf.

US Department of Treasury. (2019). "Press Release: Treasury Disrupts Corruption Network Stealing From Venezuela's Food Distribution Program, CLAP," 25 July. https://home.treasury.gov/news/press-releases/sm741.

Watson, Bruce Allen. (1993). *Sieges: A Comparative Study*, Westport: Praeger.

Woodrow Wilson, Indianapolis. (1919). Sept. 4. Reproduced in Saul K. Padover, ed. *Wilson's Ideals.* Washington, D.C.: American Council on Public Affairs, 1942.

CHAPTER 4

Economic Sanctions, Communication Infrastructures, and the Destruction of Communicative Sovereignty

Stuart Davis

This chapter offers two interrelated arguments regarding the place of communication within an anti-imperialist understanding of economic sanctions. The *first argument* is that economic sanctions cause significant damage to the communication infrastructures of nations targeted by the US and allies. "Communication infrastructure", an analytic category introduced by Sandra Ball-Rokeach and collaborators (Ball-Rokeach, Kim, and Matei 2001), refers to complex communication networks created within a national space as constituted through the interweaving of multiple kinds of media production and consumption. The communication infrastructure within a given area links different forms of media from film to Internet access into a larger communicative ecosystem. From this perspective, this chapter will draw on empirical examples from Iran, Cuba, Venezuela, and Syria to offer documentary evidence of how sanctions wreck financial damage on filmmaking, television production, and Internet access. The *second argument* leverages the empirical examination of economic sanctions' far-reaching deleterious impacts on national communication infrastructures within targeted states to make the claim that both academic and foreign policy-oriented discussions of communication rights and linked concepts (including freedom of the press) need to be expanded to attenuate the influence of sanctions. Most of these discussions are largely framed as existential struggles between heroic activists and authoritarian leaders attempting to stifle their speech and press rights—a position that Herring and Robinson (2003) and Wilpert (2007) have taken to task. Consequently, debates over communication rights largely ignore other factors creating or exacerbating problems with media and telecommunications industries in nations like Cuba, Iran, or Venezuela. Inserting the complicating impacts of economic sanctions into these conversations potentially adds geopolitical sophistication to foreign policy arguments that often view communication issues in sanctioned states as a Manichean "battle between regime and dissidents", as Piers Robinson (2007) describes it.

As economic sanction regimes' primary role as a coercive tool is to diminish the capacities of targeted nations through instigating hardships on the nation's population (Arnove 2002; Gordon 2010), the immeasurable damage they inflict upon the ability of both national governments and their civilian populations to engage in a wide variety of communicative processes is extensively felt not insufficiently analyzed. In order to assess the complexity of sanctions' impact, the goal of this chapter is *not* to speak authoritatively on the political or ideological struggles surrounding media production or the actions of individual national governments in various sanctioned states. Instead, the chapter limits itself to tracking the destruction wrought by sanctions in order to complicate positions regarding communicative sovereignty and communication rights.

1   Argument 1: Sanctions Damage Material and Logistical Support for
         Communication Infrastructures within Targeted Nations

The damage wrought by economic sanctions regimes on communication systems within target nations will be tracked through the central areas of communication infrastructure: filmmaking, community media production, and provision of Internet access. In all three of these areas logistical burdens have been caused through a combination of targeted sanctions on domestic governments and the perceived threat of violating sanctions edicts by non-domestic telecommunications firms and platforms like YouTube and Google; this anticipatory fear in turn creates barriers to access for local populations.

While one would never be able to tell from vilifying mainstream media perspectives on sanctioned nations like Iran, Venezuela, and Cuba (see MacCleod 2018; Nakahara and Shahin, this volume), these nations have been home to noteworthy public experiments in funding cinematic, television, and video production. Specifically, in many of these areas the government has *prioritized public spending* on media production, often to a comparable or in some cases greater degree than in the United States. While experiencing the weight of sanctions and other forms of economic distress, nations like Cuba and Iran have invested heavily in creating a subsidized national system for supporting media production and exhibition (including funding international film festivals); Venezuela under Hugo Chavez dedicated considerable financial resources to creating community television as part of building participatory democracy; and numerous sanctioned states have attempted to build infrastructure for Internet access.

Beginning with the assault on film production in Cuba followed by a consideration of the defunding of community production in Venezuela and finishing with a discussion of the multifaceted issues with Internet access in Venezuela, Iran, and Syria, the following three brief case studies will delineate some of the harms engendered by sanctions.

1.1   Film Production in Cuba

Of the over 40 nations subject to economic sanctions regimes instigated by the US or European Union (EU), Cuba has arguably the longest history of creating infrastructure for robust and internationally recognized cinematic production. The Cuban film industry was conceptualized as a constitutive element of the massive social transformations initiated during the revolutionary period in the wake of the 1959 revolution. Viewed as a component of the revolutionary process, film production was prioritized as a communicative strategy for both consolidating revolutionary culture within the national media-space and ushering in a period of concerted and substantial public investment in funding film production and exhibition. This material investment in mobilizing cinema for national consolidation led to the creation of El Instituto Cubano del Arte e Industria Cinematográficos (ICAIC), a publicly subsidized film institute designed to both train filmmakers and construct a nationwide film distribution network. In the institute's registration charter with the UN Education, Scientifical, and Cultural Organization (UNESCO), founding vice-director Dolores Calviño Valdés articulated the position that "filmmaking presents the most powerful and suggestive medium of artistic expression and the most direct vehicle of education for the Cuban people" (Valdes 1961). Embodying this philosophy, ICAIC's central task was defined as the provision of a cinematic language to raise consciousness levels of the Cuban population, many of whom had no experience with audiovisual media. As such, the institute sought to train cadres of filmmakers in how to depict the transforming ideolgical landscape within Cuba as well as provide exhibition avenues for films made by the institute. Through mass training and free nationwide exhibition networks the institute's goal was the reinvention of film as not an art form but a component of revolutionary praxis. As Julio Garcia Espinosa, documentary filmmaker and one of the institute's primary intellectual architect, famously stated in "For an Imperfect Cinema": "Film as not [arising from] the expressed determination of any particular artist, but because reality itself has begun to reveal symptoms (not at all utopian) which indicate that, to quote Karl Marx, "in the future there will no longer be painters, but rather men who, among other things, dedicate themselves to painting" (Garcia Espinosa 1979 [1971]). As Michael Chanan lays out in his history of the institute, the establishment of ICAIC and its experimental approach to film as collective labor provided a revolution-ary sense of experimentation for the Cuban industry: "Cuba had escaped the domination of its screens by the US majors and was liberated from the cultural imperialism of Hollywood. The overthrow of the old order unleashed tremen-dous creative energies and gave license to iconoclasm" (2018).

While its primary function was to mobilize filmmaking as a cultural tool for supporting the creation of a revolutionary national identity, ICAIC also acted as an intermediary between Cuba and international filmmaking cur-rents—including Hollywood. Though the embargo placed restrictions on film imports, ICAIC still imported and distributed some Hollywood films within Cuba—often using the films to discuss American culture in relationship to Cuba (Amaya 2003). Finally, in the 1990s, as part of the gradual loosening of the embargo with the US, the Ministry of Culture (of which ICAIC was incor-porated in the 1980s) allowed international co-productions, including with production teams from the United States (Oro and Perez 2016; Chanan 2018). As Venegas (2009, 2016) has documented, these co-productions provided an avenue of support for ICAIC as the Cuban economy contracted at the end of the Cold War. Furthermore, co-productions also provided a space for dip-lomatic engagement. For example, in 1998 the US State Department collab-orated with ICAIC to screen the film *Amistad* as part of an effort to build "cultural diplomacy" around shared histories of racial struggle (US Senate Committee on Ways and Means 1999). These outward-facing components of ICAIC's work provided a tool for negotiating the tenuous relationship between the need to produce and maintain an ideologically coherent Cuban national identity and the pressure of external forces (along with domestic economic woes).

In spite of the complex nature of Cuba's engagement with the US regarding film production and exhibition, the impact of sanctions on both state-funded and independent filmmaking has not proven as complex. In fact, the ongo-ing embargo has created *perpetual burdens* both for ICAIC's funding and the opportunities for Cuban filmmakers to engage in international co-productions and collaborations as well as present at international festivals. With the end of the Cold War and accompanying support from the Soviet bloc, the impacts of the US embargo created rippling effects on multiple parts of Cuban cultural patrimony including film production: ICAIC's film output in the 1990s–2000s decreased to roughly six films a year, less than 10% of its annual output at its highpoint in the1970s (Gonzalez-Machado 2013; Salazar Navarro 2020). Though the imprecise nature of sanctions along with lack of access to internal budget documents from ICAIC or the Cuban Ministry of Culture makes it impossible to exactly pinpoint the impact of these measures, it is clear that when Soviet support lessened the macro-level economic pressure from the embargo caused a significant contraction in the public film industry that has continued until the present.

A more tangible and perverse impact of American sanctions on Cuba is the enforcement of sanctions against any Cuban party be it filmmakers, producers, or anyone else involved in either a US co-production or an American film shot in Cuba. A *New York Times* exposé on the upsurge in Cuban filmmaking in the 2000s accompanying the rise in digital filmmaking captures this paradox, arguing that while new digital tools make film production cheaper, "what hasn't changed, however, are the financial and legal restrictions that make transferring money to Cuba illegal without a special license from the United States Treasury Department's Office of Foreign Assets Control" (Burnett 2014). Though the article situates the struggle of these filmmakers in a morally equivalent quagmire between socialist bureaucracy and American foreign policy, it nonetheless emphasizes in stark terms the impossible conditions for money transfer to Cuba due to the embargo. This paragraph from a recent US Treasury Department statement shows that not much has changed: "The terms of the embargo on Cuba authorizes, subject to conditions, only travel-related transactions and other transactions that are directly incidental to professional media or artistic productions of information or informational materials for exportation, importation, or transmission, including the filming or production of media programs (such as movies and television programs), the recording of music, and the creation of artworks in Cuba, provided that the traveler is regularly employed in or has demonstrated professional experience in a field relevant to such professional media or artistic productions (US Department of Treasury 2020).

1.2 *Counter-hegemonic Television Production in and beyond Venezuela*
The damage wrought by sanctions on communication infrastructure within targeted nations also affects national experiments in television production. In Venezuela, the intensification of economic sanctions during the Obama and Trump administrations put extreme financial pressure on innovative attempts to create community-based and purportedly counter-hegemonic news production. As part of the Bolivarian revolution initiated in the early 2000s, the Chavez government focused specifically on building infrastructure for both community-based television production (through the creation/subsidization of new community media projects and increased funding to existing projects) and for a regionally oriented pan-Latin American television network (TeleSUR).

Community-based television programs like the oft-discussed CatiaTV (Schiller 2018; Artz 2019) were enabled by the Chavez administration to provide avenues for Venezuela's most marginalized communities to document and broadcast their lived struggles. Funded through the National Ministry of Communication and through corporate social responsibility (CSR) money from PVDUSA (the Venezuelan state oil company), community television programs resonated with ICAIC's agenda in their attempt to bring television production to demographic sectors traditionally excluded from media production. In a somewhat complimentary fashion, TeleSUR aimed at promoting a new agenda for television news production within the region by providing a narrative to counter the hegemony of American and elite-centric news agendas. The most ambitious endeavor in this attempt to reprogram television news in South America and beyond was the launching of the VENESAT I satellite in 2009 in order to provide an extra-terrestrial channel for amplifying TeleSUR's programming to get around geo-blocking from the American company DirecTV that was interfering with the distribution of its signal (TeleSUR 2014; Fontes and Lessa 2019). In initial stages both of these endeavors were heavily subsidized by the Venezuelan state as ambitious attempts to create what the Chavez administration considered to be a comprehensive counter-hegemonic audiovisual landscape (Bisbal 2009; Schiller 2018).

The community media initiatives and TeleSUR have been widely debated—particularly the political tensions between representing the Chavista agenda and leaving room for deliberation and dissent within the larger mediascape in an attempt to preserve a pluralistic approach to reportage (see, for example, Schiller 2018, 2019). Bracketing these political struggles, we can see that their funding has been drastically cut—along with many other Venezuelan public programs—as a result of sanctions. Building on accounts by Wilpert (this volume), and others, it is important to note that sanctions on Venezuela have produced a panoply of detrimental downstream effects, throwing a wide array of public services into states of economic penury. This includes numerous public ministries, including the Ministry of Culture. As an integral part of the funding structure for both the community television initiatives and TeleSUR came through existing CSR streams within PVDSA, sanctions impacted funding in yet another manner: As PDVSA and its US branch CITGO continue to face sanctions within the US, the resources available for supporting media production are evaporating accordingly. One of the areas where the financial crunch experienced by TeleSUR is most tangibly felt has been the scaling back of its international coverage. Designed as part of the network's geopolitical strategy to counterbalance the hegemony of American and British English-language television news coverage on Latin America (TeleSUR English 2014), TeleSUR in English opened a space for anti-imperialist perspectives from a variety of English-speaking pundits. One high-profile example of the effects of the continued throttling of the Venezuelan economy as a result of sanctions on TeleSUR in English was the 2018 canceling of the "The Empire Files", a television program produced by US-based journalists Abby Martin and Mike Prysner. As Martin and Prysner described in an interview regarding the shuttering of the program in 2018: "Contract TeleSUR journalists, including at "The Empire Files", have had funding blocked by the US government for over six months. Even wire transfers not originating in Venezuela, but ally countries which also fund TeleSUR, have been severed" (*Liberation News* 2018). In unadorned language, this statement encapsulates how sanctions damage Venezuelan media production: the prohibition on financial transactions with any actor associated with the Venezuelan government wipes out the possibility of funding media production.

1.3   *Internet Service Providers and Telecommunication Infrastructure in Iran, Venezuela, Syria, and Cuba*

At a level closer to everyday life, the imposition of economic sanctions regimes has created problems for citizens when attempting to access the Internet or social media. This problem, in the words of technology researcher Neil Selwyn (2009), represents a case of the most basic or "first level" digital divide issues: the failure of access. This failure is experienced through two central effects: 1) It creates hurdles for individuals to access the Internet for a wide variety of everyday tasks by creating confusion around cooperation agreements and licensing within transnational telecommunications networks that impacts corporations and national governments far beyond the borders of targeted nation-states; and 2) it breaks down the communication networks for a variety of other key infrastructural sectors including education and public health. A brief discussion of impacts in Iran, Venezuela, and Cuba, will shed light on the quagmire created for Internet infrastructure within sanctioned nations.

Like many of the effects of economic sanctions regimes addressed in this volume, the bluntness and lack of clarity in implementation creates a situation that makes it hard for both domestic and international telecommunications firms or Internet service providers to create a robust nationwide coverage net. Economic sanctions detrimentally damage the ability for service providers to create and maintain robust access for individuals living within a country. Though many of the individual sanctions imposed on target states like Iran are purportedly aimed to punish national governments or individuals within these governments for specific freedom or speech of human rights curtailments, their cumulative effect is the creation of even greater barriers to access. As Mehta's legal analysis of the history of telecommunications sanctions against

Iran (2016) argues, there has been a steady increase of sanctions against both Iranian telecommunications companies and international telecommunications firms that contract with certain individuals or cohorts or individuals included in the OFAC list of sanctions. Furthermore, the chain of liability in many of these sanctions extends from the violating individual to their entire firm. Resultingly, a chilling effect is produced, impacting both Iranian and international companies. Mehta's conclusion is unambiguous: "The effect of the ICT sanctions regime has been to impede ICT companies from doing business in Iran due to the legal, reputational, and financial risks involved. Therefore, Iranian civilians do not have access to crucial ICT tools, and their freedoms have been restricted. As a result, the US government's intentions behind ICT sanctions have been undermined" (Mehta 2016, p. 778). A similar case of economic sanctions regimes bluntly impeding the ability of ISPs to provide Internet access occurred in Venezuela in November 2020. China National Electronics Import & Export Corporation, a Chinese electronic engineering company, was sanctioned by the US Treasury Department for providing infrastructural support to La Compañía Anónima Nacional de Teléfonos de Venezuela (CANTV), the central Venezuelan state-owned ISP (Psaledakis 2020). The argument, as stated in the words of the Treasury Department, was that supporting CANTV was part of a larger geopolitical strategy by China to undermine democratic opposition in countries that opposed US global order: "Nondemocratic governments use Chinese-exported technologies such as those CEIEC has provided to repress political dissent within their own borders. CEIEC has been supporting the Maduro regime's malicious cyber efforts since 2017" (US Treasury Department 2020). Similar to the case of Iran, the ultimate result was that a huge number of Venezuelan residents had their Internet cut as technical support subsided. Once again, the paradoxical effect of sanctions aimed against telecommunications infrastructure produced an impact that did not affect the regime in power but did create ripples of problems with connectivity for the larger population.

Paradoxically, the shambolic implementation of sanctions has also created the unintended consequence in some cases of damaging potential markets for US-headquartered telecommunications and television companies. In 2019 the US State Department reported on complaints received from American telecommunications firms that the sanctions made it hard for them to incorporate Cuba into their grid coverage: "U.S. companies informed the subcommittees they are often deterred from entering the market due to uncertainty caused by frequent changes to U.S. regulations concerning Cuba" (Reuters 2019). Similar stories from the legal and trade press (e.g. Nguyen and Mohsin 2021) point to a general and widespread sense of confusion from American firms when having to attempt to work in sanctioned markets.

To conclude this section, it is important to note that sanctions on telecommunications firms and national ISPs create downstream impacts in relationship to Internet access and national infrastructure in areas like education and scientific research (including epidemiological research). In the context of the COVID outbreak, the inability of sanctioned governments to utilize a stable Internet infrastructure has exacerbated crises experienced in these areas. In Iran and Syria, for example, the shift to online teaching accompanying social distancing measures created a substantial tax on the Internet infrastructure for subsidized education systems that already been significantly dismantled as a result of insufficient funding (Vishkaie 2020). This is compounded by the regulatory frameworks under which US-based companies like Zoom Video Communications (integral to distance education during COVID outbreak) cannot provide services to most states facing OFAC sanctions. As a company potentially at risk of violating one of the myriad OFAC sanctions, Zoom has avoided offering free or paid access to users in Cuba, Syria, Iran, and other sanctioned nations. The diffuse effects of these prohibitions to Zoom are not just felt in the area of public education. They also impact the ability of scientists, epidemiologists, and medical researchers to participate in sessions related to information-sharing with professionals from other nations; a potentially fatal omission given the transnational nature of both the COVID-19 virus and the scientific response. Though scientists from some sanctioned states are able on very rare occasion to circumvent sanction restrictions to participate in scientific meetings if sponsored by American organizations (specifically in one notable case, the National Iranian American Council), there are few exceptions (Ro 2020). With Zoom becoming the platform du jour of academic communication during COVID, limiting access due to concern for potential sanctions violation takes on a dire epidemiological importance.

In the cases of Cuban filmmaking, Venezuelan television production, and the Internet and telecommunications infrastructure within numerous targeted states, we see examples of how sanctions inhibit the development of communicative capacities for everyday citizens. Whether it is an aspiring filmmaker in Cuba or a student trying to attend classes via teleconference in Iran while social distancing during the COVID outbreak, sanctions are felt most tangibly by individual citizens. The infrastructural damage caused by sanctions within targeted nations creates hurdles for an array of communicative processes from the overtly political (in the case of TeleSUR) to the intimately interpersonal.

2   Argument 2: The Deployment of Economic Sanctions Regimes
         Complicates Debates over Press and Speech Rights within Targeted
         Nations

The destruction of communication infrastructure by sanctions points to a fundamental issue: the denigration of the ability of individuals within sanctioned
nations to communicate. The inability of citizens within sanctioned nations
to utilize the tools necessary to access avenues of media production (though
only a limited number access these tools) and the Internet (for the larger
population) threatens the communicative sovereignty (Reilly 2016) of these
states. Specifically, two elements of communicative sovereignty are under
attack. The first element, most clearly articulated in the Bolivarian Process in
Venezuela, is linked to the entitlements a state owes its citizens including "providing the opportunity for the majority to freely express themselves by way of
diverse and novel communications and social media" (cited in Reilly 2016, 99).
Undercutting the financial strength of governments through the application
of economic sanctions inevitably endangers these programs—as we saw in
the case of Venezuelan television. The second and more mundane destructive
impact of sanctions on communicative sovereignty is the denial of information, which violates "the right of everyone to be informed in a timely and sufficient manner" (Reilly 2016, 99). Taken simply, this refers to the fundamental
right of individuals to access information in their daily lives. As we have seen
in the previous section, collateral impacts of damage to the ICT infrastructure
leads to a host of problems. These two elements of communicative sovereignty,
the right to control the image of oneself and the right to access information,
are dealt serious blows by economic sanctions.

    To reiterate, this chapter does not intend to shift responsibility for viola-
tions of communicative sovereignty of citizens away from decisions made by
national governments in sanctioned states regarding censorship, denial of
access to certain websites, or other violations discussed ad nauseam by critics.
Furthermore, the ambiguous nature of sanctions as coercive tools has made
it often impossible for any actor to ascertain so-called "direct effects" of sanctions (Martin 1992). However, highlighting the role of economic sanctions in
damaging communicative infrastructures introduces a confounding factor in
most discussions of communicative sovereignty within academic and foreign
policy circles.

    In the context of media production, we see numerous highly abstract cri-
tiques that could benefit from this correction in course. Turning briefly to these
critiques we can see a singularity in focus on the behavior of governments
within sanctioned countries as the instigator of violations in communicative

sovereignty. Many critics—particularly those in the United States and Western Europe—have gone to lengths to raise freedom of the press claims by certain administrations like Chavez then Maduro in Venezuela and corruption within the state apparatus of various sanctioned nations. These attacks are myopic in their focus on decision-making at the centralized government levels. As Tanner Mirrlees (2020) recognizes, a hypocrisy is embedded in the way the concept of "freedom" is deployed the by the United States and its allies to attack the way geopolitical rivals like China abuse the free press but no consideration of its own attempts to stifle media actors perceived as "disobedient" (e.g. WikiLeaks).

Against this majority position, there are a few accounts that attempt to address the complexities of media production. As anthropologist Naomi Schiller argues based on her extensive ethnographic fieldwork with Catia TV, the discourse on press freedom as experienced in Venezuela is much more complex than a matter of dissidents being silenced by the government. Instead, she argues that these issues are also rooted in economic and social rights for marginalized populations, specifically poor people and Afro-Venezuelans. Until the Bolivarian process attempted to address these deeper issues, press freedom was a luxury of economic elites (Schiller 2019). Sujatha Fernandes draws on extensive fieldwork to make a similar form of commentary on Cuban cultural policy: "In contexts such as Cuba governance is not confined to the formal political apparatus and critical activity is often developed within or in collaboration with official institutions or actors" (2006, p. 6).

The conversation regarding Internet access in sanctioned nations like Cuba, Venezuela, Iran, and Syria within English-language academic and policy discourse is predominantly framed within a similar narrative as the one framing media production: *problems with Internet access in many sanctioned states is due to a unidirectional and Manichean struggle between individual citizens/consumers who want "free" Internet access and an authoritarian government who limits that access with a proverbial and/or literal flick of a switch* (e.g. Freedom House 2018). Without endorsing any national government, there again seems to be a thorough stripe of American exceptionalism in coverage of ICT blackouts in sanctioned states—for example, the copious media coverage of claims that the Venezuelan government blocked certain YouTube channels from its national ISP in spring 2019 (Herrera 2019). The critiques of sanctions from many US-based critics conceptualize the relationship between individual and state narrowly in terms of political speech invoking the individual activist whose access is "cut off" by the state. This depiction of online media usage misses key conceptual claims that the Internet is interwoven in a variety of social processes from education to public health.

3   Conclusion: Resource Denial and Communicative Sovereignty

The damages to communicative infrastructures wrought by sanctions are best seen as downstream consequences of the "resource denial" model within the mainstream literature on sanctions as a foreign policy instrument. The operant logic is that refusing targeted countries the financial resources necessary to maintain communicative infrastructures will keep them from controlling access to media production and Internet access. This process of resource denial is supported by a robust discourse from think-tanks and US-dominated multilateral organizations that serve to shift the onus of communicative damages felt within all media industries ranging from film to telecommunications on the authoritarian restrictiveness of individual sanctioned states. To put it simply, the argument follows that if you make it impossible for a sanctioned country to have a stable media production outlet and a stable ICT infrastructure through blocking its financial resources, that will push the nation to shift to a policy viewpoint more in line with the ambitions or values of the state or multilateral organization issuing the sanctions.

The larger argument of this chapter is that economic sanctions play a substantial if sometimes difficult to measure role in destroying the capacity of individuals within sanctioned nations to produce media, receive information, and participate in processes that are of vital importance. Sanctions also damage the ability of national governments, state-run corporations, and even American companies to work within the markets of target nations. In the process, sanctions also wipe out innovative experiments in communicative sovereignty ranging from revolutionary socialist filmmaking to an anti-imperialist satellite network along with basic informational infrastructures necessary to provide education and health services.

References

Amaya, Hector. (2003). "Viewing Political Selves in Film: A Comparative Reception Study of Cuban Films in Cuba and the United States." PhD Dissertation, Department of Radio-TV-Film, University of Texas.

Artz, Lee. (2019). "A political economy for social movements and revolution: Popular media access, power, and cultural hegemony." *Third World Quarterly* 41 (8).

Ball-Rokeach, Sandra, Kim, Yong-Chan, and Matei, S. (2001). "Storytelling Neighborhood: Paths to Belonging in Diverse Urban Environments." *Communication Research* 50 (3).

Bisbal, Martin. (2009). "TeleSUR: ¿Concreción de un Proyecto Comunicacional-Político Regional?" *Comunicación: Estudios venezolanos de comunicación* 146: 66–75.

Burnett, Victoria. (2014). "Struggling to Film in America's Chokehold." *The New York Times*, 8 April.

Chanan, Michael. (2018). "Iconoclasm & Experimentalism: From Revolutionary Roots to Today's Cuban Cinema." Walker Art Center. 12 Feb.

Garcia Espinosa, Julio. (1979). "For an Imperfect Cinema." Reprinted at *Jump Cut* https://www.ejumpcut.org/archive/onlinessays/JC2ofolder/ImperfectCinema .html.

Fernandes, Sujatha. (2006). *Cuba Represent! Cuban Arts, State Power, and the Making of New Revolutionary Cultures*. Durham, NC: Duke University Press.

Fontes, Pablo and Lessa, Monica. (2019). "Uma Política Cultural Inovadora no Panorama da Era Chávez." *Contexto Internacional* 41 (3): 11–30.

González Machado, Claudia. (2013). *El Riesgo De La Herejía: Cartografía De La Crítica Y El Discurso Fílmico En La Revista Cine Cubano (1960–2010)*. Havana: Ediciones ICAIC.

Gordon, Joy. (2010). *Invisible War: The United States and the Iraq Sanctions*. Cambridge, MA: Harvard University Press.

Herring, Eric, and Robinson, Peirs. (2003). "Too Polemical or Too Critical? Chomsky on the Study of the News Media and US Foreign Policy." *Review of International Studies* 29 (3): 560–562.

Liberation News. (2018). "US Sanctions Shut Down the Empire Files." *Liberation News* August 26. Available at: https://www.liberationnews.org/u-s-sanctions-shut-down -the-empire-files-with-abby-martin/.

MacCleod, Alan. (2018). *Bad News for Venezuela: Twenty Years of Fake News and Bad Reporting*. London: Routledge.

Martin, Lisa. (1992). *Coercive Cooperation: Explaining Multilateral Economic Sanctions*. Princeton, NJ: Princeton University Press.

Mehta, Pinky. (2016). "Sanctioning Freedoms: US Sanctions Against Iran Threatening Information and Communications Technology Companies." *The University of Pennsylvania Journal of International Law* 37: 763–811. Available at: https://scholars hip.law.upenn.edu/cgi/viewcontent.cgi?article=1915&context=jil.

Mirrlees, Tanner. (2020). "'Weaponizing' the Internet and World Wide Web for Empire." In Oliver Boyd-Barrett and Tanner Mirrlees (eds.), *Media Imperialism: Continuity and Change*. Lanham, MD: Rowman and Littlefield.

Nguyen, Lanah, and Mohsin, Saleha. (2021). "The New York Stock Exchange Weighs Reverting to Original Plan to Delist China Shares." *Bloomberg News*, Canadian Edition 5 January. Available at https://www.bnnbloomberg.ca/nyse-weighs-revert ing-to-original-plan-to-delist-china-shares-1.1544156.

Psaledakis, Demetri. (2020). "U.S. imposes sanctions on Chinese firm accused of under- mining democracy in Venezuela." *Reuters*, 30 November.

Reilly, Katherine. (2016). "Communicative sovereignty in Latin America: The case of Radio Mundo Real." *Journal of Alternative and Community Media* 1 (1): 97–113.

Reuters News Service. (2019). "U.S. Sanctions Put Telecom Firms Off Cuba, Internet Task Force Says." *Reuters*, 25 June.

Ro, Christine. (2020). "How Researchers Overturned US Sanctions on a Virtual Summer School." *Nature*, 7 August. Available at https://www.nature.com/articles/d41586-020-02347-9.

Robinson, Piers. (2007). *The CNN Effect*. London: Routledge.

Salazar Navarro, Salvador. (2020). *Cine, revolución y resistencia: La política cultural del Instituto Cubano del Arte e Industria Cinematográficos hacia América Latina*. London: Ubiquity Press.

Schiller, Naomi. (2018). *Channeling the State: Community Media and Popular Politics in Venezuela*. Durham, NC: Duke University Press.

Schiller, Naomi. (2019). "Crisis in Venezuela." *PoLAR: Political and Legal Anthropology Review*, 5 May.

Selwyn, Neil. (2009). "Reconsidering Political and Popular Understandings of the Digital Divide." *New Media & Society* 11 (3).

TeleSUR English. (2014). "TeleSUR English lands in the USA." Press Release, 14 July.

US Department of Treasury. (2020). "Treasury Sanctions CEIEC for Supporting the Maduro Regime's Efforts to Undermine Venezuelan Democracy." 30 November.

Valdes, Dolores. (1961). *Noticiero ICAIC Latinoamericano*. UNESCO Documents.

Venegas, Cristina. (2009). "Filmmaking with Foreigners." In Hernandez-Regaunt, A. (ed.), *Cuba in the Special Period: Culture and Ideology in the 1990s*. London: Palgrave-Macmilan.

Venegas, Cristina. (2016). "Cuban Filmmaking and the Post-Capitalist Transition." In Petro, P., and Ferguson, K. (eds.), *After Capitalism*. Rutgers University Press.

Vishkaie, Rojin. (2020). "The Pandemic, War, and Sanctions: Building Resilience for the Digital Divide in Education." *Interactions: Journal of the Association for Computing Machinery* 28 (4).

Wilpert, Gregory. (2007). "RCTV and Freedom of Speech in Venezuela." *Counterpunch*, 4 June.

CHAPTER 5

All the President's Media: How News Coverage of Sanctions Props up the Power Elite and Legitimizes US Hegemony

Junki Nakahara and Saif Shahin

1   Introduction

A substantial body of scholarship, emerging over decades, links US media coverage of international affairs to foreign policy objectives. This is disturbing because it not only brings into question the supposed independence of the media as an institution—a basic normative expectation in a democracy—but also because people depend primarily upon the media for learning and forming opinions about foreign affairs (Soroka 2003). In this study, we look at 10 years of news coverage of US-led economic sanctions against three adversaries—Iran, North Korea, and Venezuela—in major print and broadcast media. We contend that the coverage not only serves the interests of what Mills (2000/1956) called the *power elite*—the country's political, corporate, and military brass—but also reinforces the legitimacy of US hegemony in global politics.

Although scholars broadly agree that US policymakers influence media coverage of international news, they differ over the extent and nature of such influence. Three theoretical models are prominent. Three decades ago, Herman and Chomsky (2002/1988) proposed the *propaganda model*, a fairly instrumentalist view of how the elite make use of mass media to "manufacture consent" for their policies. Media companies, because of their "concentrated ownership" and "profit orientation," have to rely on governments and businesses not only for advertising revenue but also as their primary sources of information. They also want to avoid "flak"—attacks from organizations affiliated with centers of political and financial power. In addition, media personnel themselves tend to be committed to "anticommunism" as an ideology. These "filters" make it nearly impossible for voices critical of government policy, especially foreign policy, to make it into news.

To illustrate, Herman and Chomsky differentiate between the media coverage of "worthy" and "unworthy" victims. Individuals harmed by US foes—the worthy victims—are "featured prominently and dramatically" (p. 35), with an abundance of detail and contextualization serving to humanize them and

evoke sympathy from readers. This, in turn, serves as the justification for belligerent policymaking against the perpetrators. However, people who suffer at the
hands of US allies and client states—the unworthy victims—"merit only slight
detail, minimal humanization, and little context that will excite and enrage"
(p. 35). For instance, mainstream media reports about the murder of a Polish
priest by communists in 1984 were "generous with gory details and quoted
expressions of outrage and demands for justice" (p. 39). Meanwhile, coverage
of the killing of 100 religious victims in US client states in Latin America was
"low-keyed (and) designed to keep the lid on emotions" (p. 39)—even though
many of the victims were US citizens.

The propaganda model tends to assume homogeneity of opinion among the
policymaking elite. But that is not always the case. Bennett's *indexing* theory
posits that "news is 'indexed' implicitly to the range and dynamics of governmental debate" (1990, p. 103). In other words, if officials have a singular view
on a (foreign) policy issue, that is what the media would report: but if there are
differences of opinion, those too would enter the media coverage. Moreover,
the media could reach out to non-official sources "when those voices express
opinions already emerging in official circles" (1990, p. 106). But the indexing
theory views all political elite as potentially wielding the same degree of influence on news. In contrast, Entman's (2003) *cascading activation model* differ-
entiates between the influence exerted by different levels of elite power. In this
model, policy preferences of the administration—specifically, the President,
White House and state and defense departments—"cascade" down to members of Congress, other officials, and experts and further down to journalists
and news organizations, who then express it in the form of news "frames" that
are received by the public. Although there is potential for differences of opinion to creep into news framing at each level of the cascade, Entman argues that
"the ability to promote the spread of frames is also highly stratified"—with
lower levels requiring "extra energy" to push new ideas upward (p. 420).

These theories have found extensive empirical support (Aday 2017). A study
of media reporting on Venezuela found the propaganda model to shape not
just an "overwhelmingly negative" news coverage but also "a highly antagonistic newsroom culture that sees itself as the 'resistance' to the Venezuelan government and its purpose to defeat it" (MacLeod 2020, p. 273). Another study
concluded that, in line with the indexing hypothesis, leading US news organizations framed the Abu Ghraib prison abuse in Iraq as an "isolated case ... perpetrated by low-level soldiers" rather than a reflection of the administration's
"policy of torture"—despite "evidence and sources" available to support the
alternative framing (Bennett, Lawrence, and Livingston 2006, p. 467). Reese
and Lewis's (2009) interpretive analysis of the coverage of the so-called War on

Terror argued that journalists had "internalized" the administration's frame. As a result, the media "reify the policy as uncontested and naturalize it as a taken-for-granted common-sense notion" (p. 777).

2 Research Design

Empirical studies of US media coverage of international affairs and their effects on public opinion tend to focus on wars and conflicts (Aday 2017). There is little research on US media coverage of economic sanctions imposed by the United States on its adversaries—which may be viewed either as an alternative to war or, given their debilitating impact, as war by other means. In this study, we therefore turn our attention to how major US media organizations covered sanctions against three countries—Iran, North Korea, and Venezuela.

To sample data for our study, we searched the Factiva news archive for articles containing the word "sanction" (in any form) with the name of any of these three countries in their headlines or lead paragraphs. The search was limited to a 10-year period—January 1, 2011 to December 31, 2020—and focused on four major newspapers (*New York Times, USA Today, Wall Street Journal*, and *Washington Post*) and four major broadcast channels (CNN, Fox News, MSNBC, and NPR). It yielded a sample of 7,142 articles, including 5,023 for Iran, 1,621 for North Korea, and 498 for Venezuela. Duplicates were excluded from the sample. The analysis employed *topic modeling*, an algorithmic approach used "for discovering the main themes that pervade a large and otherwise unstructured collection of documents" (Blei 2012, p. 77). The algorithm parses the text of documents—in our case, news articles—to identify groups of keywords that have a high probability of occurring in proximity across one or more documents. Each group of keywords is assumed to represent a meaningful *topic*—although it is for the researcher to interpret the "meaning" of each topic based on semantic connections among the keywords it is comprised of. The method has come to be commonly used in the social sciences (Nelson 2020), especially for analyzing large volumes of news text (Jacobi *et al.* 2016; Shahin and Zheng 2020).

For our study, we defined the sample of US news coverage about each of the three sanctioned nations—Iran, North Korea, and Venezuela—as a document. The analysis was carried out in the R programming environment. Topic modeling was run concurrently on all three documents, revealing a common set of 10 topics across documents as well as the proportion of each topic in each document. To interpret the topics, we looked closely at the keywords comprising each topic (see Table 5.1) and their usage in news coverage. We found that

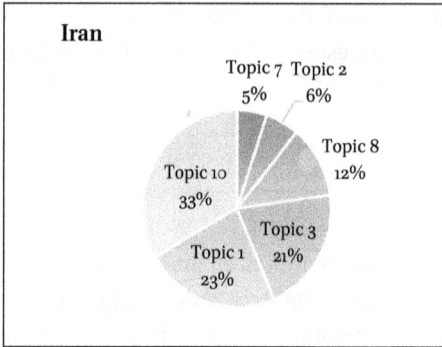

FIGURE 5.1   Topic proportions in news coverage of sanctions against Iran

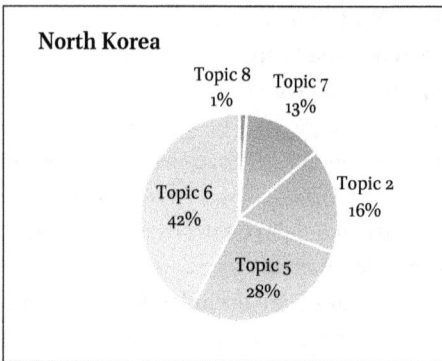

FIGURE 5.2   Topic proportions in news coverage of sanctions against North Korea

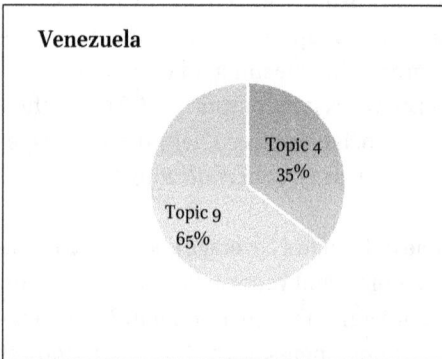

FIGURE 5.3   Topic proportions in news coverage of sanctions against Venezuela

despite topical differences in US media coverage of sanctions against each country (see Figures 5.1, 5.2, and 5.3), there were fundamental similarities in the composition of multiple topics. We now focus on three prominent themes that emerged from our analysis.

3   Yes, President

One set of common keywords across several topics was "president," "trump," "obama," "administration," "white," "house," and "secretary" (Table 5.1), suggesting that news coverage of sanctions, irrespective of topical focus, was oriented around the US administration and its senior officials. A closer look at the use of these keywords in the documents showed that President Donald Trump and his top administration executives, such as Secretary of State Mike Pompeo, Secretary of the Treasury Steven Mnuchin, and National Security Advisor John Bolton dominated the coverage. A frequently employed phrase was "U.S. officials say (or said)"—indicating that news reports relied heavily on statements and information obtained from interactions with US officials as their primary news sources. In contrast, non-official sources, including foreign policy experts, analysts, and scholars outside the government, NGOs/NPOs, and human rights activists, appeared to be sidelined.

As a result, the news coverage did not simply reflect an implicit alignment with "U.S. interests" (specifically, US interests as defined by administration officials) but blithely relied on US interests as the rationale for foreign policy decisions. For instance, CNN (2019) quoted Bolton speaking about the political crisis in Venezuela: "Now is the time to stand for prosperity and democracy in Venezuela ... We think stability and democracy in Venezuela are in the direct national security interests of the United States right now." And *Washington Post* (2017) reported, "President Trump is expected to announce next week that he will 'decertify' the international nuclear deal with Iran, saying it is not in the national interest of the United States."

Only one topic from each country included the names of Iranian President Hassan Rouhani (Topic 10), North Korean leader Kim Jong-un (Topic 6) and Venezuelan President Nicolás Maduro (Topic 9). Importantly, these topics simultaneously included references to US allies within these countries or in their respective regions, such as Saudi Arabia and Israel (Topic 10), South Korea (Topics 6 and 7), and Venezuela's "acting president" Juan Guaidó, an opponent of Maduro (Topic 9). These mentions were part of a related news frame—the delegitimization of the leadership of sanctioned countries on the grounds that it was not conducive to US interests or those of its allies. Simultaneously,

TABLE 5.1   Topic model of news coverage of sanctions against Iran, North Korea, and
             Venezuela

Topic number	Topic name	Terms
1	Iran nuclear deal under Obama/ Trump	administration, trump, president, deal, oil, obama, tehran, international, officials, program, military, washington, new, foreign, agreement, government, business, house, minister, point, policy, nuclear, financial, support, right, called, nations, security, treasury, end
2	Trump's nuclear deal with North Korea	president, trump, nuclear, deal, right, regime, security, first, officials, government, international, people, military, foreign, treasury, oil, live, million, bring, secretary, power, united, national, administration, house, good, white, big, chinese
3	US & EU sanctions against Iran	nuclear, people, president, trump, oil, international, tehran, government, washington, world, companies, security, program, white, house, officials, policy, european, obama, new, democrats, regime, statement, department, economic, administration, agreement, deal, weapons, donald
4	Trump policy on Venezuelan crisis	president, trump, government, administration, officials, power, new, washington, department, treasury, minister, america, market, foreign, regime, deal, international, people, house, security, leader, opposition, meeting, political, called, force, crisis, financial, companies, china
5	Trump's East Asia policy	trump, president, nuclear, people, security, russia, good, china, administration, foreign, officials, council, chinese, right, washington, world, use, first, program, pyongyang, talk, donald, investigation, end, coal, media, action, department, united, russian
6	East Asia nuclear crisis	kim, trump, china, new, south, un, pyongyang, house, nuclear, missile, president, people, military, right, weapons, jong, north, white, long, pressure, test, national, summit, chinese, international, commercial, thank, secretary, donald, bill

TABLE 5.1   Topic model of news coverage of sanctions against Iran, North Korea, and Venezuela (*cont.*)

Topic number	Topic name	Terms
7	Nuclear talks with North Korea	president, trump, new, china, nuclear, people, south, right, deal, world, international, russia, trade, administration, washington, report, war, economic un, chinese, talks, house, obama, security, case, business, meeting, john, nations, government
8	US pressuring of Tehran	trump, people, first, trade, new, deal, security, program, nuclear, prime, obama, officials, donald, economic, administration, russia, white, national, long, foreign, senate, move, congress, point, tehran, pressure, war, good, leader, united
9	Sanctions on PdVSA	maduro, oil, president, government, trump, people, new, administration, military, opposition, world, national, officials, russia, right, company, regime, economic, house, white, end, crude, guaido, million, russian, first, pdvsa, international, political, latin
10	Middle East nuclear crisis	nuclear, deal, president, new, trump, oil, world, agreement, foreign, israel, european, obama, administration, officials, house, department, right, congress, military, rouhani, companies, secretary, china, tehran, official, minister, saudi, middle, bank, talks

the coverage amplified the need for supporting pro-US opposition figures like Guaidó. For instance, *Wall Street Journal* (2019a) reported on Venezuela, "With much of the country deeming Mr. Maduro's leadership illegitimate, the US, the European Union and a host of countries across the Americas have urged him to cede power to the National Assembly." The delegitimization of leadership, in turn, served as an excuse to justify sanctions—such as Trump's sanctions against PdVSA, the Venezuelan state-owned energy company (Topic 9).

Within our sample, references to regional and global allies also allowed the media to portray US sanctions as an *international* enterprise. Indeed, "international" emerged as a common keyword across many topics, being used commonly across the coverage in phrases such as "international security problem," "international sanctions," "international agreement," "international community," "international partners," "international response," "international pressure," and so on. For instance, a CNN (2013) report claimed, "Pentagon spokesman George Little said North Korea 'will achieve nothing through threats of provocations, which will only further isolate North Korea and undermine international efforts to ensure peace and stability in Northeast Asia.'" This framing gave the impression that sanctions were collaboratively imposed and upheld by multiple nations, obscuring how the United States exploited its hegemonic power to coerce weaker countries.

News coverage of sanctions was thus in line with Entman's (2003) *cascading activation model,* with the President, the White House, and state and defense departments holding the most sway over the framing—just as they do in coverage of wars. However, the coverage was not always subservient. The media became increasingly critical of Trump's foreign policy over time and contrasted it with his predecessor, Obama. Several articles chastised Trump for his attitude toward all three countries. For example, a *USA Today* (2018) opinion piece, titled "Donald Trump is turning U.S. economic sanctions into an empty threat," criticized him for weakening the sanctions regime against Iran and North Korea (and Russia) because of his "go-it-alone" approach. The author of the article had served in the Obama administration. Thus, there was also some evidence of *indexing* (Bennett 1990), with differences among members of the policymaking elite making their way into news coverage.

4   New Cold War

Russia and China emerged as significant concerns in the US news coverage of sanctions against Iran, North Korea, and Venezuela. Russia featured in Topic 7 (Nuclear talks with North Korea), Topic 8 (US pressuring of Iran), Topic 9 (Sanctions on PdVSA), as well as the more general Topic 5 (Trump's East Asia policy). Meanwhile, China was included in Topics 5 and 7 as well as Topic 2 (Trump's nuclear deal with North Korea), Topic 4 (Trump policy on Venezuelan crisis), Topic 6 (East Asia nuclear crisis), and Topic 10 (Middle East nuclear crisis) (Table 5.1).

Two frames were evident in this coverage. First, the media portrayed both Russia and China as obstacles to the US-led "international" sanctions regime against the three countries. This was not only because of their veto power in the UN Security Council but also because of their respective bilateral relationships with Iran, North Korea, and Venezuela—specifically with the "illegitimate" leaderships of those countries. For instance, *New York Times* (2019) reported, "Mr. Maduro's friends in Cuba, China, Russia and Turkey have helped him cling on. The West has consistently underestimated his determination and lack of scruples." And Fox News (2018) claimed about nuclear talks with Iran, "They've already said they're not going to have anything to do with the renegotiation. They'll be backed up by Russia and China..."

Second, Russia and China's stance vis-à-vis the sanctions against these countries was framed as an example of the challenge they posed to American hegemony in global affairs. A *Wall Street Journal* (2017) article, titled "China's World: Trump Walks Dangerous Line with Beijing on Two Fronts," referred to North Korea as a key site of competition between the United States and China. Another article in the same newspaper, titled "Iran Courts Russia, China To Defy U.S.," discussed the competition between the United States, Russia, and China for sway over Iran (*Wall Street Journal* 2019b).

USA Today (2017) reported that after the UN Security Council approved US-sponsored sanctions against North Korea, China "pressed for a start of six-party talks involving North and South Korea, the United States, China, Russia and Japan"—but the proposal was rejected by the United States. The article quoted multiple US sources, including Jay Lefkowitz, a former US special envoy on human rights in North Korea; Susan Thornton, acting assistant secretary of state for the region, and Harry Kazianis, director of defense studies at the Center for the National Interest; to emphasize US skepticism toward China. Juxtaposed with the supposed effectiveness of US sanctions, China's proposal was portrayed as dubious, with Kazianis saying, "We have no reason to believe" in China.

Since the mid-1990s, scholars and pundits have spoken of a "new Cold War" between the United States on the one side and Russia or China, or even a Sino-Russian axis, on the other (Legvold 2014; Schoen and Kaylan 2014; Shambaugh 1995). Whether or not a new Cold War is ongoing, the talk of global competitors who, directly or through regional proxies, threaten American interests plays a key role in building domestic support for an ever-expanding military budget (Soroka 2003), much of which ends up in the coffers of the defense industry. Critical and feminist scholars have argued that the US military-industrial complex should in fact be called the "media-military-industrial" complex, drawing attention to the key role the American media plays in "manufacturing consent" for such expenditure (Herman and Chomsky 2002; Kumar 2006; Vavrus 2013). Media coverage of sanctions, as our analysis indicates, bolsters this narrative, framing the United States as locked in a competition with powerful rivals on a global scale that threaten its interests as well as its values—being authoritarian themselves and simultaneously propping up "illegitimate" totalitarian and anti-US regimes such as those in Iran, North Korea, and Venezuela.

5   Coal, Oil, and Power

Another set of keywords present across multiple topics included "military," "weapon," "business," "company," "financial," "commercial," "treasury," "economic," "oil," and "coal" (Table 5.1). This seemingly indicated coverage of the US military-industrial complex discussed above. But closer scrutiny of the usage of these keywords in the documents indicated the US media's focus, ironically, was the ties between military and industry in the sanctioned countries—specifically how the state-run oil industry in Iran and Venezuela and coal in North Korea enabled their respective leaders and militaries to remain in power.

Describing Maduro and his military's control over Venezuela's oil industry, the *Wall Street Journal* (2019a) said, "The military, which has helped Mr. Maduro thwart political challenges with violent repression, has increasingly become a major player in oil matters after Mr. Maduro last year ordered a purge of the technocrats that had long dominated PdVSA's upper echelon." This, in turn, helped justify the United States "blacklisting" PdVSA "in an effort to cripple a major revenue stream to the Nicolás Maduro government" (*Wall Street Journal* 2020). Several reports acknowledged that the sanctions made life difficult for ordinary Venezuelans, but the framing implied it was ultimately their government's fault.

Similarly, the coverage of North Korea suggested that coal and mineral industries funded the country's military and provided the foundation for nuclear weapons and ballistic missiles development. A 2018 *New York Times* report praised a UN Security Council ban on North Korea's export of coal and iron ore, among other materials, for "causing pain"—but also wondered if the sanctions were painful enough to break down the regime. It lamented: "Despite shortages, exchange rates and key consumer prices are stable, and there is no sign of an approaching famine" (*New York Times* 2018).

Reports also emphasized China and Russia's direct and indirect involvement—through their companies and other "entities"—in the military-industrial complex of the sanctioned countries. For instance, a CNN (2017) report, titled "U.S. targets Chinese, Russian entities funding North Korea's nukes," said imports from Beijing were a "lifeline" for Pyongyang and "prevent[ed] the U.S. from really putting the squeeze" on the country. It then quoted Anthony Ruggiero, a former deputy director of the U.S. Treasury, as saying, "In the end it's going to require going after Chinese banks and Chinese companies that are complicit in North Korea's sanction evasion." An NPR (2018) piece described US action against "27 companies and 28 shipping vessels" from different countries, including China, that were helping North Korea evade sanctions through "ship-to-ship transfers of fuel and other products." It quoted Treasury Secretary

Mnuchin as saying, "This action targets the deceptive shipping practices that have enabled the Kim [Jong-un] regime to fund its dangerous weapons programs."

Not all references to the military were in such contexts. Some news reports also compared the "military" option against Iran, strongly pushed by Israel in the early 2010s and also favored by the Republican party, with the Democratic Obama administration's decision to pursue economic sanctions instead. This was an especially common point of contention during the 2012 US presidential election between Obama and his Republican challenger, Mitt Romney. For instance, *Washington Post* (2012) reported Romney as saying, "If Barack Obama is reelected, Iran will have a nuclear weapon and the world will change if that's the case."

6   Conclusion

Our computational analysis demonstrates that major US print and broadcast media's coverage of economic sanctions is not all that different from their coverage of wars and conflicts. While manifest topics in news vary by country, the coverage is underpinned by a shared latent semantic structure. The same theories that have been used to explain the media's pliability in the coverage of conflicts also explain how they frame news about sanctions against different countries, from different parts of the world.

The coverage relies on statements, interviews, and on- or off-the-record interactions with the President, White House, and state and defense departments—as one would expect based on Entman's (2003) cascading activation model—by allowing them to define what constitutes US "interests" and "values" and drawing upon these definitions as touchstones for evaluating the sanctions regime. These definitions tend to serve the intertwined interests of the political, military, and corporate elite. Specifically, they present the United States as caught up in an unceasing war with hostile global rivals and their belligerent regional proxies, thus "manufacturing consent" for burgeoning "defense" budgets (Herman and Chomsky 2002)—tax dollars from everyday Americans repurposed as the fortunes of the military-industrial complex.

While these theories rightly emphasize the power of the US elite in shaping media coverage according to their interests, our analysis also suggests that the elite-media relationship ought to be viewed within the broader structure of international relations—and America's position within this structure. Media coverage doesn't simply toe the elite line: in doing so, it also reinforces the legitimacy of American hegemony as a *sine qua non* of global power politics.

Indeed, coverage remains pliant only to the extent that elite policies maintain this hegemony. The media become more unfriendly to the administration when its policies are deemed to be undermining American preeminence—as happened during the Trump years, especially vis-à-vis North Korea and Iran.

Both indexing theory (Bennett 1990) and cascading activation (Entman 2003) allow for the possibility that differences among policymakers can lead to the coverage becoming less pliant and more diverse. We argue that the media challenge the administration's line as a means of bringing policymaking itself "back on track." In other words, it is when the administration appears to be failing in its responsibility of upholding US dominance through ill-advised policymaking that the media take it upon themselves to prop up policy alternatives—although they still rely on sources from the policymaking world, such as opposition figures and foreign policy experts, to do so (see also, Shahin 2021).

If the coverage of sanctions appears to be of a piece with coverage of conflicts, it is because both sanctions and conflicts are part of this larger enterprise. Both serve their respective functions in preserving US hegemony—and so does their respective media coverage. That is why, while denouncing the leadership of US *adversaries* like Iran, North Korea, and Venezuela as authoritarian and therefore illegitimate, and supporting sanctions as well as threats of war against them, US media's coverage of autocratic *allies* like Saudi Arabia is quite the opposite. Few questions are raised when the administration provides military aid or sells weapons worth millions of dollars to such nations—weapons that are often used against their own populations (Kumar 2018).

This chapter began with the normative concern that elite influence over media coverage puts paid to the expectation of media's independence in a democracy. Our analysis, however, renders the question of media independence moot. The media emerge as not simply influenced by but instead as an integral part of Mills's (1956) *power elite*, with the same interests—and the same commitments—as the political, military, and corporate brass.

References

Aday, S. (2017). "The US media, foreign policy, and public support for war." In K. Kenski and K.H. Jamieson (eds.), *The Oxford handbook of political communication*, pp. 315–332. New York: Oxford University Press.

Bennett, W.L. (1990). "Toward a theory of press-state relations in the United States." *Journal of Communication* 40 (2): 103–127.

Bennett, W.L., Lawrence, R.G., and Livingston, S. (2006). "None dare call it torture: Indexing and the limits of press independence in the Abu Ghraib scandal." *Journal of Communication* 56 (3): 467–485.

Blei, D.M. (2012). "Probabilistic topic models." *Communications of the ACM* 55 (4): 77–84.

CNN. (2013). "North Korea vows end to nonaggression pacts after U.N. vote." 8 March. https://www.cnn.com/2013/03/08/world/asia/north-korea-sanctions/index.html.

CNN. (2017). "US targets Chinese, Russian entities funding North Korea's nukes." 22 August. https://www.cnn.com/2017/08/22/politics/us-treasury-sanctions-china-rus sia-north-korea/index.html.

CNN. (2019). "Trump approves sanctions on Venezuelan oil company." 28 January. https://www.cnn.com/2019/01/28/politics/us-sanctions-venezuelan-oil-company/ index.html.

Entman, R.M. (2003). "Cascading activation: Contesting the White House's frame after 9/11." *Political Communication* 20 (4): 415–432.

Fox News. (2018). "Trump administration keeps Iran nuclear deal with red line; Trump complicates efforts to reach bipartisan immigration Agreement; talk of removing Trump with 25th Amendment following Wolff Book." 14 January.

Herman, E.S., and Chomsky, N. (2002/1988). *Manufacturing consent: The political economy of the mass media.* New York: Random House.

Jacobi, C., Van Atteveldt, W., and Welbers, K. (2016). "Quantitative analysis of large amounts of journalistic texts using topic modelling." *Digital Journalism* 4 (1): 89–106.

Kumar, D. (2006). "Media, war, and propaganda: Strategies of information management during the 2003 Iraq war." *Communication and Critical/Cultural Studies* 3 (1): 48–69.

Kumar, D. (2018). "The right kind of "Islam": News media representations of US-Saudi relations during the Cold War." *Journalism Studies* 19 (8): 1079–1097.

Legvold, R. (2014). "Managing the new Cold War: what Moscow and Washington can learn from the last one." *Foreign Affairs* 93 (4): 74–84.

MacLeod, A. (2020). "Manufacturing consent in Venezuela: Media misreporting of a country, 1998–2014." *Critical Sociology* 46 (2): 273–290.

Mills, C. W. (2000/1956). *The power elite.* New York: Oxford University Press.

Nelson, L. K. (2020). "Computational grounded theory: A methodological framework." *Sociological Methods & Research* 49 (1): 3–42.

New York Times. (2018). "Sanctions Are Hurting North Korea. Can They Make Kim Give In?" 20 April.

New York Times. (2019). "What America doesn't get about dictatorships." 22 June. https://www.nytimes.com/2019/06/20/opinion/venezuelas-dictatorship-mad uro.html.

NPR. (2018). "Trump administration is trying to make it harder for North Korea to evade sanctions." 23 February. https://www.npr.org/2018/02/23/588374700/trump -administration-is-trying-to-make-it-harder-for-north-korea-to-evade-sancti.

Reese, S.D., and Lewis, S.C. (2009). "Framing the war on terror: The internalization of policy in the US press." *Journalism* 10 (6): 777–797.

Schoen, D.E., and Kaylan, M. (2014). *The Russia-China axis: The new Cold War and America's crisis of leadership.* Encounter Books.

Shambaugh, D. (1995). "The United States and China: A New Cold War?" *Current History* 94 (593): 241.

Shahin, S. (2021). "News and the neoliberal order: How transnational discourse structures national identities and asymmetries of power." Paper presented at the virtual annual convention of the International Studies Association.

Shahin, S., and Zheng, P. (2020). "Big data and the illusion of choice: Comparing the evolution of India's aadhaar and China's social credit system as technosocial discourses." *Social Science Computer Review* 38 (1): 25–41.

Soroka, S.N. (2003). "Media, public opinion, and foreign policy." *Harvard International Journal of Press/Politics* 8 (1): 27–48.

USA Today. (2017). "N. Korea tension brewing after new sanctions." 7 August.

USA Today. (2018). "Donald Trump is turning U.S. economic sanctions into an empty threat." 15 August. https://www.usatoday.com/story/opinion/2018/08/15/donald -trump-turning-american-sanctions-into-empty-threat-column/945745002/.

Vavrus, M.D. (2013). "Lifetime's Army Wives, or I Married the Media-Military-Industrial Complex." *Women's Studies in Communication* 36 (1): 92–112.

Wall Street Journal. (2017). "China's world: Trump walks dangerous line with Beijing on two fronts." 16 August.

Wall Street Journal. (2019a). "U.S. considers harshest Venezuela sanctions yet, on oil." 14 January. https://www.wsj.com/articles/u-s-considers-harshest-venezuela-sancti ons-yet-on-oil-11547510165.

Wall Street Journal. (2019b). "Iran courts Russia, China to defy U.S." 19 June.

Wall Street Journal. (2020). "U.S. Removes Sanctions on Nynas After Restructuring." 13 May.

Washington Post. (2012). "Mitt Romney says Iran 'will have a nuclear weapon' if Obama reelected." 4 March.

Washington Post. (2017). "Trump likely to declare that Iran nuclear deal is not in the national interest." 6 October.

CHAPTER 6

Transnational Allies of Sanctions: NGO Human Rights Organizations' Role in Reinforcing Economic Oppression

Immanuel Ness

Over the past 20 years, non-governmental organizations (NGOs) have been ubiquitous in demanding economic sanctions on nations and their leaders for alleged abuses of human rights activists. Though fully cognizant of the dele-terious effects of sanctions on the poor and frail, sanctions are viewed as the panacea for achieving compliance from rogue states, which are almost always at political odds with the United States (USA) and the West. To mitigate the detrimental consequences of sanctions on entire populations, human rights NGOs advocate that the USA, European Union (EU), and other rich countries should target sanctions against government officials and the elite. But in most instances, sanctions devastate entire economies, by systematically undermin-ing major industries controlled by political and economic power holders.

Human Rights Watch (HRW) is the most prominent NGO to repeatedly call on the USA and its affluent allies to apply sanctions on states they view as bad actors. Economic sanctions are almost always applied by rich states in the global North against the poorest countries that can least withstand restrictions on trade in a world which is ever more integrated through globalization. Since the formation and expansion of their influence in the 1970s, NGOs have trans-formed into agents of the USA and European allies, conducting an essential task that had previously been the preserve of the CIA, MI6, and government disinformation agencies. As conjectural independent entities, human rights NGOs wittingly or unwittingly serve as useful instruments of Western states. This chapter examines the formation of human rights NGOs and examines their actions in facilitating the sanctions regime.

1   Formation of Human Rights NGOs

Amnesty International (AI) was founded in 1961 in Britain by genuine human rights activists troubled by foreign states' imprisonment of political activists. Their goal was to monitor and publicize the jailing and ill treat-ment of governments' political opponents. In the formative years, it became apparent that AI had been infiltrated by British operatives as a means to target states that the government opposed. Peter Benenson, a founder and first General Secretary of AI, resigned five years later in 1961 in protest at the organization's refusal to condemn credible allegations about torture of political prisoners by the British government in Yemen. Benenson concluded that the human rights organization was infiltrated and incapable of fulfilling its founding goals (Clark 2010, 15). Nevertheless, Amnesty International persevered and maintained its status as a human rights watchdog. Along with HRW, AI has promoted its status as a leading human rights monitor of abuses worldwide, despite its continuous and reliable support for positions advanced by the USA, Britain, and Western states. In addition, whilst the two NGOs denounce human rights violations among opponents, they almost never criticize infringement of personal freedom at home. Since the 1980s, NGOs have become even more dependent on the US government to fund their democracy promotion operations. Thus, human rights and democracy promoting organizations lack independence and the credibility to be taken seriously by foreign states, even if they may convince the US media and sway public opinion. The National Endowment for Democracy (NED), founded in 1983, is a conduit for identifying and funding democracy promoting NGOs (Pee 2018, 693–711).

HRW was founded as Helsinki Watch in 1978 to monitor treatment of dissidents in the Soviet Union, 16 years after the formation of Amnesty International in 1961 in the UK. HRW's reputation as the leading human rights organization was enhanced in 1997 upon winning the Noble Peace Price with the International Campaign to Ban Landmines. HRW, deemed by academics and government officials to be the most respected human rights NGO in the world, along with AI, is a key linchpin in US sanctions policy. Habitually, HRW issues reports and press releases reproaching governments (routinely called "regimes") for violating human rights. Regimes are viewed as somehow maintaining power illegitimately, while governments adhere to Western norms of democracy. Yet, to various degrees, all countries violate what HRW would consider human rights, without recognition of how every nation has its own historic and cultural traditions that are at odds with Western norms. In addition, while the USA is a major perpetrator of human rights abuses at home and abroad, almost never have HRW and other human rights NGOs reprimanded the US regime, in power for nearly 250 years.

The infiltration by government intelligence agencies in the operations and policies of AI, HRW, and other leading human rights NGOs contributes to the general acceptance that they operate at the behest and with the support of

Western governments. In this way, AI and human rights NGOs are not viewed as independent arbitrators of abuses of personal freedoms, but appendages of Western intelligence organizations and state policies.

From the 1960s to the present, the CIA, MI6, and other Western intelligence agencies have increasingly shifted their modus operandi from direct operations against prospective political opponents to contracting out services to NGOs and other civil society organizations. These do their bidding and establish a case for taking action against ostensible targets. Rather than directly charging China and the Soviet Union, or politically and economically challenging opponents in the global South, intelligence agencies have outsourced operations to dependable civil society organizations to provide a patina of evidence (often without concern for factual or countervailing evidence) legitimizing economic, political, or armed action. Application of economic sanctions is among the most damaging actions imperial states can apply to weak states in need of essential goods for the survival of their most vulnerable citizens. HRW and AI have gained widespread public credibility from left to right through the extensive dissemination of counterintelligence and often spurious charges against US and Western nemeses (Stoner Saunders 2000).

Public perception of HRW as a human rights monitor means its reputation has surpassed even that of AI. Yet, in the past 30 years, the organization has come under harsh criticism from journalists and independent monitors for its obsequious support of US foreign policy; above all, the US State Department and foreign policy apparatus. HRW has painstakingly circumvented denunciation of human rights violations, violence, and abuses perpetrated by US allies, and has managed to maintain an imprimatur as an unbiased monitor of human rights even as it operates as an arm of the US State Department. When American allies have committed highly publicized violence and abuses against their own people, HRW has rarely issued critical reports and public statements. American allies such as Israel are rarely condemned for their suppression and massacre of Palestinian people, but in general, the NGO remained silent on the abuse of the Israeli state until a highly critical report on human rights abuses against Palestinians issued by HRW at the end of April 2021, in which the NGO equated Israeli policies with apartheid (Human Rights Watch 2021a). Although posturing as a civil society human rights NGO, HRW regularly engages in derogatory research and reporting on states that the USA and Western European foreign policy establishment oppose; almost always drawing conclusions corroborating Western policy positions.

2   Human Rights Watch Advocates Sanctions as Punishment

HRW openly considers sanctions as the antidote to virtually all state activities that it opposes. By its own admission:

> As a general matter, Human Rights Watch believes that sanctions and other measures taken against abusive individuals and governments are most effective and legitimate when they are imposed multilaterally by groups of states. In cases where multilateral action is not feasible or not the most effective option, Human Rights Watch supports unilateral targeted sanctions.
>
> Human Rights Watch 2021b

To justify sanctions, routinely erroneous and subjective evidence is gathered from NGO operatives based on the ground in states that the USA and Western establishment oppose. This is then disseminated to the media to demonstrate the necessity of sanctions, even on the basis of innuendo, ambiguity, or no evidence whatsoever. In many cases, the conclusions drawn by HRW are simply false or fabricated. However, HRW's accounts, disseminated to the media and the general public, serve as justification for the USA and other states to take severe actions, including military intervention and economic sanctions. Ironically, whistle-blowers with often valid opposing positions are discredited and belittled. While the purpose of this chapter is not to interrogate every single controversy involving NGOs and economic sanctions, the evidence is that in many instances HRW and AI base their conclusions on dubious and sometimes fraudulent claims. In July 2014, HRW, whose false claims had triggered US military intervention in Haiti (2004) and Libya (2011), was condemned and denounced by the World Summit of Nobel Peace Laureates for its close relationship to the US policy establishment:

> Human Rights Watch, a group that claims to "defend the rights of people worldwide" has come under fire from two Nobel Peace Laureates and a hundred other scholars and human rights activists. Among the criticisms against Human Rights Watch are its "revolving door" hiring policy from the US Government, its failure to denounce the practice of extrajudicial rendition, its endorsement of US military intervention in Libya and its silence during the 2004 coup d'état in Haiti.
>
> World Summit of Noble Peace Laureates n.d.

The hypocrisy advanced by the Noble laureates is that HRW had systematically concluded that economic sanctions or even foreign intervention by the USA and its allies are necessary and warranted to combat human rights violations. Yet HRW and other human rights NGOs based in the West almost always neglect to call attention to US foreign and domestic policies in response to human rights allegations that also frequently violate basic human rights and international law; such as severe, all-encompassing sanctions and military intervention to overthrow governments. In lockstep with US foreign policy, HRW stereotypically calls for sanctions on foreign governments it considers pariahs (Afghanistan, Burundi, Cuba, Democratic Republic of Congo, Iran, Korea, Myanmar, Sudan, Syria, Uganda, Venezuela), and others have been deposed internally or through foreign intervention. HRW particularly recommends sanctions against African states that are non-compliant with its norms: "Implementing targeted sanctions before a crisis fully emerges could make a notable difference in preventing further repression. Targeted sanctions are a useful tool to show the possibility of real, individual consequences for repressive acts, particularly when imposed in tandem with the European Union and/or the United Nations" (Human Rights Watch 2016).

3 Spotlighting Sanctions on Russia and China

The Russian Federation and China are repeatedly sanctioned economically for the alleged actions of client states or are directly subjected to calls by HRW and other human rights NGOs. The list of entreaties for sanctions by HRW, Avaaz, Freedom House, and other human rights NGOs, some funded directly by the US National Endowment for Democracy (NED), is endless. Reports by human rights NGOs rarely discuss the economic and political violence perpetrated by opposition forces, often funded, or formed by US organizations (Human Rights Watch 2020; Middle East Eye 2020; Reuters 2019; WorldECR 2019).

Sanctions are imposed by affluent states, typically the USA and EU, and less frequently by the United Nations (UN), on countries that are viewed as political, economic, military, and cultural opponents of the established imperialist order. State-imposed economic sanctions have grown dramatically from the 1990s to the present. State-sponsored sanctions are defined and exercised by states that claim to abide by democratic practices, especially the 'rule of law' and human rights. These principles have been advanced by the USA and Western Europe in the aftermath of the collapse of the Soviet Union in 1993. Scholars have noted that human rights have been used as an ideological tool to maintain and solidify hegemony over the world (Falkner 2005, 585–599; Köstem

2018, 726–752; Mallard 2019). In this way, as the leading economic power, sanctions were applied from the 1990s as a coercive measure to buttress US imperialist dominance on a global scale. Economic sanctions have been triggered by a range of assertions by the UN and intergovernmental organizations which have provided documented evidence of weapons of mass destruction in violation of treaties. Yet increasingly, Western governments have replaced the UN as the major force in determining that rogue states will be punished by economic sanctions. After all, the UN has limited power to enforce sanctions and penalize states for disregarding economic sanctions. Economic sanctions require rich countries to send sanctions that will one way or another lead dependent states to comply with their demands or cause internal oppositional forces to depose governments, usually referred to as "authoritarian regimes."

Although HRW and human rights NGOs have wide support among intellectuals, the media establishment, and the public, most international relations scholarship concludes that the application of economic sanctions almost never leads to regime compliance or the replacement of the governments of recipient states, and more often leads to entrenching state elites charged with abuses. In almost every case of general and targeted economic sanctions, the behaviour of alleged authoritarian governments is not changed, nor does a formidable political opposition congeal within civil society capable of overthrowing and replacing the existing leadership. In an empirical study of their effects from 1981 to 2000, international relations scholar Dursun Peksen finds that economic sanctions most often contribute to even greater damaging results through eroding "government respect for physical integrity rights, including freedom from disappearances, extra-judicial killings, torture, and political imprisonment." Peksen also finds that "extensive sanctions are more detrimental to human rights than partial/selective sanctions. Economic coercion remains a counterproductive policy tool, even when sanctions are specifically imposed with the goal of improving human rights" (Peksen 2009, 59).

From 2001 to the present, the Bush, Obama, Trump, and Biden Administrations have applied economic sanctions on the Russian Federation and China to challenge their human rights practices, with evidence marshalled by human rights NGOs. Yet the evidence shows that economic sanctions are applied for the purpose of gaining geopolitical and strategic hegemony. In most instances, these sanctions are supposedly intended to improve human rights in the target state; for example, the Magnitsky Rule of Law Accountability Act of 2012, against Russia, following a case in which an alleged whistle-blower was killed while in jail awaiting trial for participation in a fraudulent tax evasion scheme. The Magnitsky case is based on a distortion of facts, as the evidence reveals that the protagonist was not a whistle-blower, but an accomplice in a crime to defraud the Russian government (Nekrasov 2016).

Empirical justification and legitimation are decisive for sending states to apply economic coercion to non-compliant target governments to obtain submission using the threat of expulsion from multilateral international political and economic organizations. If the US government decides to "change behaviour" or replace a government in power, providing some form of proof and confirmation is often required to garner international support for sanctions as punishment. Before economic sanctions are applied, Western independent monitors with field operations within the target country are used to substantiate the violations justifying economic sanctions to either change the behaviour or depose the government in power. Human rights NGOs are principal agencies charged with conducting investigations and reports on target countries. Proponents suggest that human rights NGOs work together with the USA and Western allies to conduct unbiased independent investigations on human rights violations by target states. But NGOs most often provide limited substantiation of human rights abuses, particularly in the Russian Federation and China, where access is often difficult. Nonetheless, these NGO investigative reports are treated as sacrosanct. Given how human rights organizations situated in the West are viewed as independent and unbiased, they contribute to sending state decisions to apply sanctions on target countries. A fundamental justification for economic sanctions is that countries which 'violate' the 'rule of law' and engage in human rights abuses will be punished through economic isolation. A crucial facet to applying economic sanctions is the apparent belief that they will lead to the mitigation of human rights abuses by what are typically referred to as "authoritarian leaders," the improvement in human rights practices, or the overthrow of a government (regime). In addition, NGOs provide justification and legitimation to gain broad popular approval from sending countries' stakeholders and intellectuals, or at least a degree of support.

4 Colour Revolutions and the Limits of Regime Change

Since the dissolution of the Soviet Union, human rights NGOs have proliferated to support government opponents through monitoring potential abuses of power by states via government dissidents' reports or stationing personnel on the ground, often with the collusion of the NED, which provides financial and logistical support for civil society opponents of the leadership. Human rights NGOs often assist in developing and coordinating local civil society organizational infrastructure through cultivating existing opponents to the government in power, and by establishing local NGOs, supported by NED funding. Unequivocally, the effectiveness and capacity of foreign human rights NGOs to launch viable oppositional groups is dependent on the presence of extant oppositional structures and practices to establish organizational cohesion. HRW, AI, Avaaz, and other human rights NGOs seek to cultivate opposition to the government and assist in setting up operations in a range of states with the objective of regime change. This process began in states that emerged following the dissolution of the Soviet Union and former Yugoslavia, and extended to the Caucasus, Central Asia, and Africa.

Ironically, a targeted state with a democratic past, practices, and institutions, is far more vulnerable to these NGOs, which are permitted to freely send operatives to undermine the society. Perhaps the most notorious example of regime change is the development of opposition groups to depose Slobodan Milosevic, prime minister of the Federal Republic of Yugoslavia (now Serbia), in September 2000. Following a contested election, a crowd of no more than 2,000 supported the blocking of a major artery near parliament with a tractor commandeered by a far smaller number of protesters. Crucial was the presence of human rights NGOs, which helped form oppositional organizations with funding from the NED, among other groups. A relatively small group of about 1,000–2,000 opponents protested against the results of the election. The "success" of Milosevic's deposition in 2000 was replicated in a series of US-backed efforts to replace governments in Eastern Europe, the Caucasus, and Central Asia.

Reliance upon human rights NGOs and international monitoring organizations has been effective in subjecting the leadership of countries to international disparagement and vilification. But in this process, it is important to examine the political independence, stated objectives, and motivations of human rights NGOs. How independent are NGOs from the USA and its allies? Do NGOs have systemic and operational relations with the US foreign policy establishment? Is the goal of public criticism to improve human rights practices or to generate a public relations account that validates the US foreign policy establishment? Do the reports and statements advanced by human rights NGOs represent a means to advance the US foreign policy agenda or to tangibly improve conditions without social upheaval directed against the government in power? The record over the past 25 years demonstrates that most human rights NGOs have close relations with the USA and Western foreign policy establishment and share a common goal of expanding the systemic influence and power of the USA and its allies.

Human rights NGOs are devoted to providing counterintelligence disparaging the rulers, governing party, and political leadership of a country for the purpose of providing justification for the USA and its allies to implement sanctions. These sanctions are intended to contribute to popular economic insecurity, in the hope that such penalties will lead to reform or, preferably in most instances, to social and political upheaval strong enough to overthrow the leadership of the target country.

Human rights NGOs organize within a political framework which condemns and censures target states and leads to government crackdowns; these further corroborate claims of human rights abuses perpetrated by targeted state leaders. Through alleging human rights abuses, persecution, and repression of opponents, NGOs face an ethical and moral conundrum: while their raison d'être is to publicly expose and shame states in violation of societal norms established in the West, the entire population is punished for the policies and actions of targeted states' governments. In this way, NGOs direct their charges against countries which are infringing human rights yet, as they join forces with the USA and the West, the outcome of their reports and charges typically does not lead to mitigation of the violation, whether true or false. In most instances, the insertion of human rights NGOs inexorably leads to the immiseration of a far larger share of the population who are not engaged in claimed human rights abuses. In most nations, popular majorities are not the subject of government repression. More often, small organizations with a limited political base are the recipients of Western aid. Thus, human rights organizations are a tactical trigger to be activated in developing a set of charges against the target government for seeking to quash dissidents who would have no power were it not for US and Western aid. The NGO will seek to limit itself exclusively to counterintelligence to damage the reputation of the government and enable the USA and its allies to take tangible action to materially undermine the target.

The human rights NGO is caught in a moral and dialectical contradiction. By charging state leaders with human rights abuses, NGOs are often the source of economic sanctions, economic ruin, armed conflict, and even civil war. The NGO frequently serves as a willing conduit for the USA and Western states to provide legitimacy for condemning a government and then quickly disconnecting from the devastation that inevitably follows economic sanctions and sometimes war. In this way, the NGO, and the USA work together to undermine the targeted government in power. The NGO remains dependent on the US government and human rights foundations for the funds to conduct investigations and reports which are the basis for punitive action. The evidence is overwhelming that NGOs are wholly dependent on their imperialist paymasters to provide counterintelligence which provides the perceived evidence that a government is engaged in human rights violations.

While nation states engage in conflict, and may unilaterally impose sanctions on opposing countries, over the past 50 years, the application of sanctions through carrying out investigations, studies, and authoritative reports to validate the charges of human rights abuses has grown in significance. Why is it so important for the hegemonic US state to provide evidence of human rights violations? In every instance, states differ in political traditions and practices, yet the USA has sought to apply a neoliberal economy and 'rule of law;' a universal form for disparate states. Rather than recognizing different political traditions and differences in national conduct towards religious, ethnic, national, religious, and racial populations within states, US absolutist neoliberalism and 'rule of law' based on Western principles must be observed, or nations risk expulsion from the international system and possible sanction and military intervention. In the 1990s, NGOs expanded populations deemed under threat to include labour and workers, the environment, and particularly ethnic and religious minorities. However, rarely is class exploitation and oppression an issue for NGOs. The USA and its allies in the global North benefit economically from low-waged workers in the global South, who produce consumer goods at low cost. The USA may ask countries to comply with International Labour Organization conventions on workers' rights, but labour law violations are never used for the broad application of sanctions on a target country.

In no case has the USA applied economic sanctions and coercive punishment upon target countries which forced leaders into submission. Most often, if the USA is not successful in a colour revolution, the affluent and elite in small states are able to withstand economic penalties while workers and the poor are subjected to higher inflation and lack of access to food, medicine, and necessary commodities. Larger states, like the Russian Federation and China, are typically able to tolerate even sanctions that are applied broadly, by developing alternative economic partnerships or resorting to autarchic mechanisms to replace foreign products with locally produced goods.

5   Pushing Strong States into Sanctioning Weak Countries

In response to pervasive calls for action against China's meddling in the internal affairs of Hong Kong, Donald Trump signed the Hong Kong Human Rights and Democracy Act in November 2019, thereby sanctioning 11 Hong Kong officials. The next week, China announced that it would sanction key American NGOs and politicians in the USA. The Chinese government charged five NGOs and US political organizations with "interfering in China's internal affairs:" the NED (a funder of the Center of Democracy and Technology), HRW, Freedom House, the International Republican Institute, and the National Democratic Institute for International Affairs. China also announced sanctions for abetting and instigating the Hong Kong protests, and for those organizations' "egregious role" in instigating the protests which caused extensive economic disruption and property destruction for residents of the city. The US NGOS had all publicly supported the Hong Kong protests, which the Chinese government viewed as an attempt to foment a color revolution (Beach 2019). The NGOS, legislative officials, and media in the USA viewed the sanctions as unjust, and charged the Chinese government with "suppressing freedom and democracy (Morello 2020)." The article by *Washington Post* journalist Carl Morello made no references to the violence and destruction accompanying the civil unrest in Hong Kong, which certainly would have been de rigueur in a report on virtually any other country. In the aftermath of Beijing's sanctions against NGOS, HRW and Freedom House in January 2020 issued reports incredulously critical of the Chinese government, denying participation in the civil unrest and asserting that the sanctions suppressed press freedoms (Reuters 2020).

6   HRW Mantra: Sanction, Sanction, Sanction

Reading HRW reports and press releases, one theme seems to dominate: first sanction, then verify and mitigate. A smattering of HRW's recent press releases reveals these dominant themes that are intended to lead to regime change:

> Burma's military leaders are not communicating on the same wavelength as the rest of the international community. They are not prepared to appreciate or even hear its verbal denunciations and demands. So, the time has come to impose targeted sanctions and other measures that carry a real practical or financial cost on Burma's senior military command. It may be impossible to convince the military leadership to care about the Rohingya, but it might be possible to stop them from killing or displacing any more Rohingya—if the consequences of continuing such abuses create a burden that military leaders don't want to bear.
>
> SIFTON 2017

HRW consistently advocates that sanctions conform to US and Western efforts to isolate and undermine the political leadership of target states like Myanmar which are often supported by US rivals. Thus, sanctions against Myanmar can also be viewed as an extension of US efforts to weaken and discredit China. In an April 2021 report, HRW asserted that China may be blocking a UN Security Council vote to sanction Myanmar: "Could Beijing allow UN sanctions to pass with a mere abstention? The only way to identify China's limits is to circulate a draft resolution calling for targeted sanctions on junta leaders and an arms embargo; and start negotiating" (Ahmed 2021).

Testifying at the Senate Foreign Relations Committee in July 2015, HRW advocated a broad application of the Magnitsky Act. Indeed, on September 21, 2000, Luc Devigne, Managing Director of the European Union for External Action, noted that the EU Global Human Rights Sanctions Regime was engaged in discussions to reassesses the basis of the passage of the act. No such actions have been held by the US Congress. in the ensuing years, HRW actively lobbied the US Congress for the Global Magnitsky Act, which would authorize the US government to sanction countries violating human rights. The fact that the original law is based on ambiguous facts has not restrained HRW and other human rights NGOs from testifying for the passage of the law to punish authoritarian governments.

7   Conclusion

Human Rights NGOs have proliferated in the 21st century to monitor violations of personal freedoms and advancing Western concepts of the 'rule of law.' Focusing on HRW, this chapter has shown that NGOs operate as an integral part of the foreign intelligence and secret operations of the USA and its allies to destabilize governments through advocating sanctions, typically on dubious grounds. The chapter further shows that NGOs are wittingly or unwittingly engaged in discrediting states which oppose US and Western policies, leading to the imposition of damaging economic sanctions. NGOs have justified their position by encouraging targeted sanctions against state elites. Yet, in most instances, economic sanctions deleteriously affect strategic industries which are integral to foreign exchange earnings, thus contributing to economic deflation and the inability to purchase essential food, medicine, and integral supplies to meet human needs. In this way, HRW, AI, Avaaz, and other NGOs destabilize state economic capacities necessary for the development of human rights and legitimize public opprobrium within target states of foreign meddling, thereby bolstering the very governments they seek to overthrow.

References

Ahmed, Yasmine. (2021). "Why Britain Should Champion UN Action on Myanmar." *Human Rights Watch*, 16 April. https://www.hrw.org/news/2021/04/06/why-britain -should-champion-un-action-myanmar.

Beach, Sophie. (2019). "China Imposes Sanctions on US NGOs over Hong Kong Bill." *China Digital Times*, 2 December.

Clark, Ann Marie. (2010). *Diplomacy of Conscience: Amnesty International and Changing Human Rights Norms*. Princeton, NJ: Princeton University Press.

Falkner, Robert. (2005). "American Hegemony and the Global Environment." *International Studies Review* 7 (4): 585–599.

Freedom House. (2020). "Freedom House Urges Canada, U.K., to Join Global Magnitsky Sanctions Against Chinese Officials Violating the Rights of Uyghurs," 18 August. https://freedomhouse.org/article/freedom-house-urges-canada-uk-join-global -magnitsky-sanctions-against-chinese-officials.

Human Rights Watch. (2021a). "Abusive Israeli Policies Constitute Crimes of Apartheid, Persecution Crimes Against Humanity Should Trigger Action to End Repression of Palestinians," 27 April. https://www.hrw.org/news/2021/04/27/abusive-israeli-polic ies-constitute-crimes-apartheid-persecution.

Human Rights Watch. (2021b). "Myanmar, Sanctions, and Human Rights," 18 February. https://www.hrw.org/news/2021/02/18/myanmar-sanctions-and-human-rights# _What_is_Human.

Human Rights Watch. (2020). Press Release, "Human Rights First Urges Canada, UK, to Join Global Magnitsky Sanctions Against Chinese Officials Responsible for Violating the Rights of Uyghurs," 18 August. https://www.humanrightsfirst.org/press-release/ human-rights-first-urges-canada-uk-join-global-magnitsky-sanctions-against-chin ese-officials.

Human Rights Watch. (2016). "Human Rights Watch Testimony at Senate Foreign Relations Committee on US Policy in Central Africa: The Importance of Good Governance," 10 February. https://www.hrw.org/news/2016/02/10/human-rights -watch-testimony-senate-foreign-relations-committee-us-policy-central.

Human Rights Watch. (2015). "Human Rights Watch Testimony at Senate Foreign Relations Committee on Corruption, Global Magnitsky, and Modern Slavery," 16 July. https://www.hrw.org/news/2015/07/16/human-rights-watch-testimony-senate-fore ign-relations-committee-corruption-global.

Köstem, Seçkin. (2018). "Different Paths to Regional Hegemony: National Identity Contestation and Foreign Economic Strategy in Russia and Turkey." *Review of International Political Economy* 25 (5, October): 726–752.

Mallard, Grégoire. (2019). "Governing Proliferation Finance: Multilateralism, Transgovernmentalism and Hegemony in the Case of Sanctions against Iran." In Eric

Brousseau, Jean-Michel Glachant, and Jérôme Sgard (eds), *The Oxford Handbook of Institutions of International Economic Governance and Market Regulation*. New York: Oxford University Press.

Middle East Eye and Agencies. (2020). "Syrian and Russian Officials Should Face Sanctions over Idlib Strikes, States HRW." *Middle East Eye*, October. https://www .middleeasteye.net/news/syria-russia-idlib-strikes-hrw-sanctions.

Morello, Carl. (2020). *The Washington Post*, 10 August 2020.

Nekrasov, Andrei. (2016). *The Magnitsky Act: Behind the Scenes* (documentary film).

Pee, Robert. (2018). "Containing Revolution: Democracy Promotion, the Cold War and US National Security." *International Politics* 55: 693–711.

Peksen, Dursan. (2009). "Better or Worse? The Effect of Economic Sanctions on Human Rights." *Journal of Peace Research* 46: 1.

Reuters. (2020). "Human Rights Watch Report Blasts China as its Chief Barred from Hong Kong." *Reuters*, 14 January 2020.

Reuters. (2019). "Human Rights Watch Calls for Sanctions against New Afghan Defense Minister." *Reuters*, 13 January 2019.

Sifton, John. (2017). "Subcommission to the US Senate Foreign Relations Committee on the Rohingya Crisis in Burma," October 24. https://www.hrw.org/news/2017/10/24/ submission-us-senate-foreign-relations-committee-rohingya-crisis-burma.

Stoner Saunders, Frances. (2000). *Who Paid the Piper?: The CIA and the Cultural Cold War*. London: Granta Books.

WorldECR. (2019). "Human Rights Watch Calls for Sanctions against Nicaraguan Elite," 20 June. https://www.worldecr.com/news/human-rights-watch-calls-for-sanctions -against-nicaragua-elite/.

World Summit of Noble Peace Laureates. (n.d.). "Human Rights Watch is Roundly Criticized by Human Rights Activists," n.d. http://www.nobelpeacesummit.com/ human-rights-watch-is-roundly-criticized-by-human-rights-activists/.

CHAPTER 7

Sanctioning China's Tech Industry to 'Secure' Silicon Valley's Global Dominance

Tanner Mirrlees

1   Introduction: The US and China's Digital Divergence

From the world financial crisis of 2007–2009 to the global pandemic and new global slump of 2020, the US remained the world's dominant empire, but was one with much less clout and power than previously projected. For the past decade, international competition between US and Chinese corporations has been supported by each countries' security State, and as this intensified, so has geopolitical conflict. Nowadays, each country's business elites and political technocrats are restructuring their respective national societies to outmatch the other, regrouping to reshape the institutions, rules and relations of global order, and trying to push and pull other countries into their orbit. This epoch's new US-China "trade war" is accompanied by "irregular warfare", and "cyberwarfare"—network attacks on corporate and military infrastructure, digital hacking and espionage, and information operations—is the newest front in the 21st century's global battlespace (Johnson and Gramer 2020; Kahata 2020; Mirrlees 2019b; Perthes 2021). As global competition and conflict between the US and China mount, digital technology has emerged as a flashpoint in this fractious cross-border relationship (Inkster 2021; Kai-Fu 2018; Murdock 2019). Indeed, digital technology—its research and development, ownership and control, design, production and distribution, and usage—has become one of the most contentious sites in the US-China war to make the world's future.

This chapter probes the new international competition and conflict between the US and China over digital technology. The US is home to Silicon Valley, the biggest and most significant digital technology industry on the planet, but China's Big Tech industry is rising fast, and increasingly "going global." As digital technology corporations based in the US and China compete for international market dominance, the US and Chinese States are trying to "secure" their respective digital technology industries' interests, and frequently clashing in the process. The US State has long pursued a foreign policy of digital free trade with China in support of Silicon Valley, but with no success: the Chinese State opted to protect its nationally situated Big Tech industry from US-centred digital capitalists and promote that industry's international expansion. Having failed to tear down China's "Great Firewall" with digital free trade and facing China's digital expansion into the US territorial market and elsewhere, the US State is now sanctioning China's Big Tech industry to secure Silicon Valley. This chapter contends that the US State's sanctions on China's Big Tech industry are a tool of economic war that aims to defend Silicon Valley's global dominance and attack and proactively defeat the potential rivalry posed to this dominance by China's homegrown and globalizing digital capitalists.

To this end, the first section ("American Global Digital Dominance") demonstrates the US Empire's resilience vis-à-vis a rapidly rising China and highlights how digital technology is made and remade to serve the US Empire's means and ends of trans-national capitalist expansion, surveillance, public diplomacy and cyber-warfare. The second section ("China's Big Tech Boom") looks at the capitalist economics and nationalist politics of China's recent Big Tech boom. It highlights the Chinese State's strategy of protecting and promoting Chinese digital technology corporations as part of a broader sovereign strategy to become independent from Silicon Valley. The third section ("The US's Big Tech Ban") considers the US State's response to China's Big Tech boom, focusing on its imposition of sanctions on Chinese high-tech corporations, from chipmakers to smartphones to social media platforms. The US State's recent imposition of sanctions on China's Big Tech industry reflects a shift in US foreign policy away from trying to induce China into a US-centred global digital capitalism with peaceful digital free trade deals to directly attacking China's global technological ascendance and potentially rivalrous position with a blunt instrument of coercive power.

By interrogating the dynamics of this global technology competition and conflict between the US and China, the chapter contributes to current research on the geopolitical economy of communications and digital technology. Major developments in communications and media technology have always been shaped by or reconfigured to serve the world's Empires, and all of history's major Empires have strategized to exercise control and influence over new innovations (Schiller 1969, 1996; Schiller 2014; Mirrlees 2019a). The economic, military and cultural growth and maintenance of the US Empire have relied upon print, telegraphy, the motion picture, radio and TV broadcasting, and the Internet (Schiller 1996; Schiller 2014; Mirrlees 2019a). As this chapter shows, "digital technology"— personal computers, smartphones, wireless networks, software, websites, apps and data—is now of vital importance to the US Empire's ongoing expansion and solidity. That is why Silicon Valley's "Big Five"—Google, Amazon, Facebook, Apple and Microsoft—align with the US

State to fortify the US's position of global digital dominance against China, a rising challenger.

2   American Global Digital Dominance: The US Empire vs. China

Following the end of the US-Soviet Cold War and up until the US-led Global War on Terror hit the wall of the global economic slump of 2007–2008, the US was the planet's sole Empire. But during the presidencies of Barack Obama and Donald Trump, the US Empire was said to be declining due to the rise of China, a country that has grown rapidly and internationally over the past two decades and maintained its sovereignty in the face of the US State's use of a mix of persuasion and coercion to try to induce and pressure China to integrate into an American model of global capitalist order.

To plan and steer its own path of capitalist development, China's one-Party State incubated national corporate champions and protected their primacy within a massive national territorial market while promoting their international expansion through the "Belt and Road" initiative. The US and China are today the world's two largest capitalist economies, and they are connected by cross-border financial investments and debt holdings, commodity manufacture and supply chains, and trade (Inkster 2021; Johnson and Gramer 2020; Kahata 2020; Kai-Fu 2018; Perthes 2021; Prashad 2021; Watkins 2019). Yet, the political systems of these countries are very different: the former exhibits State support for capitalist industries under the auspice of neoliberal democracy, and the later entails significant State ownership of capitalist industries guided by authoritarian neoliberalism. The economic systems of the US and China are "capitalist", but their political superstructures (the State form and civil society) part ways. Nowadays, these countries are diverging, not because of a latent "clash of civilizations" or essential "cultural" differences, but as result of an intensifying US-China capitalist competition supported by each State's combative foreign policy. The US bourgeoisie and hawkish geo-strategists take China to be a troubling barrier to the global freedom of American corporations to access China's massive consumer market, and they also see China as a military threat to the security of the US and this Empire's many integrated neoliberal ally States.

In July of 2018, the Business Roundtable (2018), a lobby for corporate America run by the chief executive officers (CEOs) of US-based globalizing corporations such as Apple and Amazon, published "Recommendations for Reform to Address Chinese Trade and Investment Barriers." The report recognized China for offering "a large and growing market for U.S. businesses" but chastised its Communist Party for engaging "in harmful trade and investment practices that prevent U.S. companies from competing on a level playing field against Chinese domestic competitors." It called upon the US State to push "reforms for liberalizing the Chinese market and ensuring fair treatment of foreign [American] companies in China", and these included "new trade rules" bilaterally and "enhancing World Trade Organization rules" multilaterally. As it noted, "When U.S. companies can access global markets and compete fairly, the United States wins." Two months after the Business Roundtable published its advice, the US Department of Defense (DoD) released its "Summary of the National Defense Strategy of the United States" (2018) and declared its aim "To restore America's competitive edge by blocking global rivals [such as China] from challenging the U.S. and our allies" and "To keep those rivals from throwing the current international order out of balance." In that same year, the US National Security Council published a "US Strategic Framework for the Indo-Pacific" in which it declared the US's strategic goal in Asia was to "[m]aintain US primacy in the region" (USNI News 2021). Noting how China's "cutting-edge technologies" threaten American security interests, the doctrine declares that the US State would need to "[m]aintain American industry's innovation edge vis-à-vis China" with the support of key allies (USNI News 2021). With the above State and capitalist movements in mind, future US-China relations are unlikely to be characterized by peace and harmony (Prashad 2021).

As the US and China relationship unravels, the world is sometimes imagined to be becoming ever more "bi-polar," or, divided between the US and China, two "rival" Empires that possess an even match of power resources and which strive to integrate other countries into their spheres of influence. The US Empire has suffered a relative decline and China's economy and military are rising. As the cosmopolitan shine of the "Washington consensus" fades and the once polished American Dream rusts, some countries may be disinclined to follow the US's lead and resist its design for global order. Also, as global public opinion of America hits new all-time lows (Wike, Fetterolf, and Mordecai 2020) and American "soft power" campaigns miss their mark (Mathieson 2021), trans-national publics may be ever more willing to buy into China's authoritarian-capitalist societal model (Carminati 2020), and especially when on the receiving end of China's own successful "soft power" and emerging cultural imperialist campaigns (Sparks 2019). Nonetheless, the world is not yet truly bipolar because the US is indisputably still unmatched with regard to its grip on the lion's share of structural power resources (Mirrlees 2019c). While the US is certainly being challenged by China, for now, the US still outmatches China, economically and militarily, and especially with its digital technology industry.

Consider the following.

The US is the globe's largest economy with a nominal gross domestic product (GDP) of about $20.513 trillion, and China is now second largest, with a GDP of $14.86 trillion. According to the 2020 *Forbes Global 2000* list of The World's Largest Public Companies, the US is still home to most of the world's largest corporations, headquartering 588 while China is home to 324 (Tucker 2020a). A mere nine countries headquarter over three-fourths of the corporations on the list (the US, China, Japan, UK, Canada, France, Germany, South Korea, India), but just three of those (the US, China, and Japan) account for more than half. Of the top twenty largest global corporations, twelve are American and five are Chinese. The dollar, not the renminbi, is the world's reserve and most used currency. The US's capitalist strength is paralleled by its military might, which China does not match: the US's military expenditure of $778 billion in 2020 overpowered China's estimated $252 billion by more than three times (SIPRI 2021). From South Korea's Daegu Air Base to German's Spangdahlem Air Base, hundreds of US military installations and bases span many countries and also encompass to "contain" China. By comparison, China has only one foreign base in Djibouti, at a great distance from the US. Silicon Valley augments the US's Empire as the world's major centre of gravity for digital capitalism. Of the 161 digital technology corporations on *Forbes' Global 2000* list of The World's Largest Public Companies, almost half of these are headquartered in the US, and most of the biggest of these are American (e.g., Alphabet-Google, Apple, Facebook, Amazon, Microsoft, Intel, IBM, Cisco, Oracle). The US is also home to AT&T and Verizon, two of the largest global telecommunications corporations. China is also home to massive high-tech corporations, but these do not yet rival the US's globally (Tucker 2020b).

The Silicon Valley corporations that produce and sell digital hardware, software, sites services, and data are the vanguard of US capitalism, the leaders of the so-called "Fourth Industrial Revolution" (Mirrlees 2019b; Murdock 2019; Panitch and Albo 2020; van Dijck, Poell, and de Waal 2018; van Dijck 2019; Zuboff 2019). The US Bureau of Economic Analysis (2021) reported that in 2018, the US digital economy's goods and services accounted for about 9.0% of US gross domestic product (GDP), a whopping $1.8 trillion contribution to the US national economy. The corporations that rule this sector also serve global capitalism's general need for an advertising system. For example, Google, Facebook and Amazon currently control more than half of the American and transnational online advertising market, and together, they help other corporations create consumer demand for their commodity supply (Hagey and Vranica 2021). In 2020, Google used the data generated by the billions of users conducting billions of searches every day to generate $147 billion in ad revenue.

That same year, Facebook, one of the world's leading "platform imperialists" (Jin 2019), generated $84 billion in ad revenue, and each day, advertisers "bid" to buy what Facebook sells: the chance to expose target users to ads for their products. Amazon now ranks among the world's top digital ad sellers, and it annually rakes in billions by exposing billions of people to ads for the myriad products sold on its e-commerce platform. Silicon Valley plays a big role in expanding US capitalism and its advertising system around the world, and as these corporations cross borders, they search for labour exploit, consumers to sell to, investments to make, user data to mine and monetize, and adspend markets to control and profit from (Panitch and Albo 2020; van Dijck, Poell, and de Waal 2018; van Dijck 2019; Zuboff 2019).

Silicon Valley's power is not just a result of laissez-faire, though, as these corporations' growth and expansion at home and abroad is frequently boosted by different apparatuses of the US State (Schiller 2014; Block and Keller 2011; Mirrlees 2019a, 2019b). In 2009, 2011, and 2015, the presidency of Barack Obama launched US technological innovation strategies that allocated a portion of US GDP to the research and development of industries related to new and emerging digital technology and related ecosystems. Also, the US State supports the accumulation interests of American Big Tech corporations trans-nationally by pushing other States to open their borders to their operations (Mirrlees 2019b). In the post-war era, the US State rolled out the "free flow of information doctrine", conflating the freedom to impart and receive information across borders with a free-trade regime convivial to the profit margins of the US media and cultural industries (Schiller 1969, 1996). For the past twenty-five years, the US State has brokered digital free trade deals with other countries to lower borders to Silicon Valley's freedom to do business wherever it likes (Mirrlees 2019b). As the US Congressional Research Service's (2020) brief on Digital Trade explains, the US "has sought to combat barriers to digital trade through negotiation of rules and disciplines in free trade agreements (FTAs) and in multilateral fora", and it seeks "to remove barriers to trade in digital goods and services, ensure cross-border data flows, and eliminate and prevent localization measures." When some US-allied States propose to impose digital services taxes upon Big Tech's freedom to transact within their national jurisdictions, the US State Department and the Office of the US Trade Representative (USTR) retaliate with threats of tariffs on behalf of the likes of Google and Facebook.

In addition to boosting Silicon Valley's digital trade interests around the world, the US State frequently mobilizes new-fangled digital technology when conducting surveillance of the world's populations (Hills 2006; Zuboff 2019). The US National Security Agency (NSA) uses the Internet to conduct surveillance of people in almost every country on the planet (Levine 2018). As the "Big

Brother" of the NSA and the many "Little Brothers" of platform capitalism monitor, assemble, exchange, and use the data of billions for ends related to security and profit, the US State's surveillance of citizens is fusing with the corporate data-veillance of prosumers (Levine 2018). While the US Department of State's Office of Public Diplomacy (OPD) has longed pushed pro-American propaganda campaigns around the world through the Internet in support of American foreign policy goals, the OPD's propaganda now spreads digitally across all of the major social media platforms, from Facebook to YouTube to Twitter (Singer and Brooking 2018). Concomitantly, the DOD routinely declares the necessity of maintaining American global leadership in technology to ensure the US can fight and win future network-centric wars (Winseck 2008). To that end, it contracts Amazon, Google and Microsoft to undertake militarized R&D on the Internet of Things and artificial intelligence (A.I.), subsidizes and procures war-ready digital innovations, and "weaponizes" those for "cyberwarfare" against "enemy" States and non-state actors (Harris 2014). Touting his corporation's military service, Amazon CEO Jeff Bezos declared: "If big tech companies are going to turn their back on the U.S. Department of Defense, this country is going to be in trouble" (Mehta 2019). For the DoD, the digital technology of the global Internet is itself is a new "domain" of 21st century warfare (added to land, sea, air, and space), and Silicon Valley is all too eager to help the DoD exercise "command and control", so long as it can turn a profit when doing so (Dyer-Witheford and Matviyenko 2019; Levine 2018; Mirrlees 2019b; Singer and Brooking 2018).

Evidently, digital technology is integrated with the means and ends of the contemporary US Empire. While tensions between some Silicon Valley corporations and some US State agencies may flare up every so often, Big Tech and Big Government share a mostly amicable as opposed to antagonistic relationship to ensure that digital technology will be made and remade for their Empire's maintenance and extension. Silicon Valley corporations, backed by the US State, expand their products, sites and services, and profit margins to integrate other countries, communities, and populations into a US-centred global digital capitalism. The US State weaponizes the Internet to conduct surveillance, propaganda, and cyber-warfare within and across borders (Harris 2014; Levine 2018; Mirrlees 2019b; Singer and Brooking 2018). The US Empire's digital technology is formidable, but the doctrine of American technological exceptionalism—the idea that America is a uniquely great country because it possesses the greatest technology—encourages everyone from CEOs to politicians to publics to see American global digital dominance as benign, and to see those countries that wish to break free from reliance upon its wares, wires and services as outliers, even threats. Such is the way many view China.

3   China's Big Tech Boom: Capitalist Growth and National
        Independence

For nearly two decades, the Chinese State has pursued a national digital development strategy oriented to independence from the US by protecting and promoting the growth of China's own Big Tech industries (Kai-Fu 2018). Chinese
corporations such as Alibaba, Baidu, BOE Technology, Hikvision, China Mobil,
China Unicom, JD.com, Netease, Suning, Tencent Holdings (owner of WeChat
and Qzone), Xiaomi, ZTE and others appear on the *Forbes Global 2000* list,
and this demonstrates that Silicon Valley is not the only tech powerhouse in
the world, especially not in China. Also, China now has the world's largest
Internet population: nearly one billion users at the end of 2020 (Cheng 2021).
Furthermore, Chinese websites such as Tmall.com, Baidu.com, Qc.com, Sohu.
com, Taobao.com, 360.cn, JD.com regularly rank among the top ten sites in
the world, next to Google.com and YouTube.com (Alexa 2021), while Chinese
social media platforms proliferate and profit (Fuchs 2016). Moreover, many
Chinese technology corporations are traded on trans-national stock markets
and financialized (Jia and Winseck 2018). Evidently, China's Internet industry
is no "paper tiger", but a strong and globalizing capitalist force (Jia and Winseck
2018; Kai-Fu 2018; Murdock 2019).

The Chinese State has played a significant role in facilitating and legitimizing the growth of China's Big Tech industry through direct ownership of
key corporations, national development plans that have aimed to help China
achieve independence from largely US-based and other foreign technology
corporations, and a "Great Firewall" that blocks US Internet corporations, prohibits access to many of their sites and platforms, and filters the flow of digital
media content (Griffiths 2019; Hong 2017; Jiang 2012; Kai-Fu 2018; Roberts 2018;
Wu 2020; Zhao 2008).

The Chinese State controls some of the country's biggest corporations
through the State-Owned Assets Supervision and Administration Commission
of the State Council (SASAC) (Guluzade 2019; Jingrong Lin, Xiaoyan, Zhang,
and Zheng 2020; State-owned Assets Supervision and Administration
Commission of the State Council 2021). Responsible for managing ninety-
seven State Owned Enterprises (SOEs), SASAC is a boon to business of SOEs
both in China and around the globe. It doles out vast subsidies to them, privileges them with low-interest bank loans, appoints top CEOs to run them,
approves or rejects mergers and acquisitions and sales of key assets, and drafts
and approves the laws and regulations for governing their conduct in society.
The SASAC's five major communications and digital technology corporations
are the China Electronics Technology Group Corporation (CETC) (which also

owns Hikvision), China Telecom, China Unicom, China Mobile, and China Electronics Corporation (CEC).

From the turn of the millennium forward, China's Medium and Long-Term National Science and Technology Development Plan (2006–2020) helped these corporations to grow (Kai-Fu 2018; Wu 2020). Bemoaning China's dependence on Western corporations for core technologies and wanting to break free from digital dependency, this Plan advanced a strategy to achieve national independence in technological R&D and innovation (UNESCO 2016). To do so, the Chinese State protected Chinese national corporate champions from foreign competition while brokering partnerships with foreign investors. It subsidized and gave tax incentives to Chinese corporations to kickstart and reward innovation. It prioritized Chinese high-tech corporations for State R&D and procurement contracts. And it strengthened these corporations' intellectual property (IP) rights. This Medium and Long-Term Plan was interwoven with recurring Five-Year Plans that undergirded China's Big Tech boom (Kai-Fu 2018; Wu 2020). For example, the 10th Five-Year Plan (2001–2005) raised State R&D expenditure to more than 1.5% of GDP to enhance technological innovation. The 12th Plan (2011–2015) aimed to capture foreign direct investment (FDI) in the high-tech industries and transform coastal cities from the "world's factory" to hubs of R&D, technological innovation and consumer services (Kai-Fu 2018; Wu 2020).

The most significant State Plan for supporting China's Big Tech industry was the 13th (2016–2020). This Plan singled out "innovation" as key national priority and proclaimed to shift the country's mode of production from old manufacturing industries to new digital technology production and services sectors. The centrepiece of the 13th Plan was "Made in China 2025", a bold initiative to transform China from an offshore production facility for American and Western-owned companies looking to exploit low-cost labour into an independent technological dynamo that would lead the world in high-tech product and service production and circulation (Domínguez 2015; He 2020; Hopewell 2018; Kai-Fu 2018; Wu 2020). "Made in China 2025" declared the Chinese State's aim to strengthen ten high-tech sectors, empower Chinese corporations to rule the national market for these goods and services, and then, embolden them to expand internationally by making inroads into and capturing foreign markets (He 2020; Hopewell 2018; McBride and Chatzky 2019). In 2015, China's President Xi Jinping declared he would build China into a world leader in computers and smartphones, 5G networks and semiconductor chips. China's "Informatization of the National Economy Program" (2016) policy further emphasized China's ambition to not only become independent of foreign technology supply chains, but to one day lead to the globe in the "Fourth Industrial Revolution"

(Kai-Fu 2018). The 14th Plan (2020–2025) reiterated China's goal of technological independence (Kharpal 2021; Mark 2020). "Technological self-sufficiency
is a strategic pillar of the nation's development," explained China's Minister of
Science and Technology Wang Zhigang, "We must boost independent innovation and do our own job well...because key technologies can't be bought or
asked for [from others]" (cited in He 2020).

In addition to supporting the growth of its own Big Tech industry, the
Chinese State has constrained Silicon Valley's expansion into the national
territory and market over which it presides. With nationalist law and policy
oriented to bringing the global Internet under its national sovereignty, the
Chinese State has prohibited its population of over one billion Internet users
from accessing to non-Chinese websites, apps and services (Griffiths 2019;
Roberts 2018). For example, Apple, Amazon, Facebook, Google, Twitter, and
YouTube, are blocked in China, along with websites for US news sources such
as *The New York Times* and *The Economist* (Leskin 2019). This "Great Firewall"
of China is frequently explained with regard to the Chinese State's attempt to
secure the reigning "national culture" (however invented) from the threat of
American media or cultural imperialism and is often chastised for enabling a
one-Party State to exercise authoritarian control over national consciousness
by pre-emptively neutralizing any dissenting ideas that might put that State
in a negative light and foment revolutionary upheaval. But China's Internet
censorship regime is also an industrial policy that gave a massive, protected
territory and market to national digital technology corporations looking to
grow and prosper. By blocking Silicon Valley's websites and banning US-owned
digital media services, the Chinese State supports the prosperity of Chinese
Internet and digital technology corporations within the world's most populated country to ensure that they, not Google or Facebook, will be empowered
to sell to, and monitor and monetize, the data of nearly a billion Internet users.

Evidently, China has experienced a Big Tech boom over the past decade.
Like the US and other powerful countries, China increasingly takes digital
technology to be integral to its economic and military planning, and cultural
influence around the world. As the Chinese State partners with Chinese digital
technology corporations to protect and preside over the national market in
preparation to compete for the global one, the US Empire's bourgeoisie and
State administrators worry that China's rise might one day deplete if not defeat
American global digital dominance. Also, Silicon Valley is looking to invest in
and sell its wares, wires and services in China, but the Chinese State prevents
it from profit-maximizing on that national market turf. Given that the US is
home to the most expansive digital technology industry in the world and digitally delivered services amount to more than half of the US service trade, it is

no surprise that Silicon Valley and the State have constructed China's Big Tech boom and Great Firewall as a national security threat. Claims and statements about the "Made in China 2025" threat to the US amass, adding to an already massive elite and popular imperial discourse that represents China as America's enemy Other. The Council on Foreign Relations (2018) is a prominent US foreign policy think tank whose members include Google, Microsoft, AT&T, and Dell Technologies, and in 2018, one of its writers declared publicly that "Made in China 2025" threatens "US technological leadership" while others have echoed the Trump Administration's notion that this threatens global trade itself (McBride and Chatzky 2019).

For the past three years, US national security planners, Republican and Democratic politicians, think-tanks, Silicon Valley corporations, and news media outlets have lambasted the Chinese State for protecting China's digital technology giants and blocking digital services free trade with America. They've alleged that China is forcing US companies to transfer their technology IP to Chinese firms at America's expense. They've played upon Sinophobic fears that China's smartphones and social media platforms violate the privacy of American citizens by collecting their data and siphoning it back to China while saying little about how the GAFAM mine and extra the data of people around the world, transfer it back to the US for processing and profit. All in all, China's Big Tech boom has been framed as a major problem for American global digital dominance and for the US's prosperity, security and democracy (Barfield 2017; Business Roundtable 2021; Disis 2020, 2021; US Department of Defense 2018; US Congressional Research Service 2020; USNI News 2021; Thompson and Bremmer 2018). To "solve" this problem, the US State has moved to impose sanctions on Chinese digital capital.

4   The US's Big Tech Ban: Sanctioning Chinese Digital Capital to Secure Silicon Valley

The US is an empire, and the practice of US imperialism involves the US state's support of the trans-national interests of US-based corporations, legally, diplomatically, communicationally, and, frequently, with forms of coercion (Mirrlees 2019a). US imperialism has never been peaceful because far from relying exclusively on "soft power" or persuasion (e.g., propaganda campaigns, invitations and attractions, and trade incentives) to get other countries to do what it wants them to do, the US State has also consistently used "hard power" or brute force (wars, invasions and occupations, and sanctions) to punish and pummel countries that do not conduct themselves as US planners prefer. In world affairs, economic sanctions are a coercive power instrument that the US State uses with great regularity when pursuing its geo-strategic and national security interests vis-à-vis other States and whole countries (Masters 2019). While the Executive Branch or "imperial presidency" may unilaterally impose sanctions upon other countries without Congressional approval, the US Department of Treasury's Office of Foreign Assets Control (OFAC) carries them out. Also, the State Department's Office of Economic Sanctions Policy and Implementation (SPI) and the US Commerce Department's Bureau of Industry and Security (BIS) among other Federal agencies may also impose economic sanctions.

Economic sanctions can be conceptualized as a coercive tool of the US Empire's power in world affairs, and these encompass repressive as opposed to persuasive State tactics such as embargos, trade blocks and tariffs, as well as asset freezing and other financial restrictions. The US State uses sanctions pro-actively and reactively to prohibit and/or punish types of economic conduct and market activity by non-US States and corporations with the goal of achieving strategic ends, whether economic or geopolitical. Concretely, the US State uses sanctions to compel other States to change their conduct in a way that syncs with US national security interests, deter them from behaving in ways that may threaten those interests, and damage their reputation in the eyes of other States, corporations, and citizens around the globe.

From the Trump presidency to the Biden Presidency, The Office of the United States Trade representative (USTR), The Department of the Treasury (DoT), the Federal Communications Commission (FCC), the Department of Commerce (DoC) and the Department of Defense (DoD) have mobilized their personnel to impose massive sanctions upon China's Big Tech industry (Chen 2020; Kastrenakes 2018; McCabe 2020; Swanson 2020). The key moments in and targets of this campaign of sanctions are discussed in what follows.

Between 2015 and 2017, Chinese corporations were investing in major US corporations covering new and emerging technologies, as well as start-ups in A.I., virtual reality, and blockchain technology, but this raised concerns that China was using its investors' privilege for espionage and IP theft (Braw 2020; USTR 2018). Recognizing these, the DOT's Committee on Foreign Investment in the United States (CFIUS) launched the Foreign Investment Risk Review Modernization Act (FIRRMA) in September of 2018 (Blakey 2020). This Act gave the US State a mechanism for assessing the potential national security risks and costs of foreign investments in the US by other countries, especially China, and extended the CFIUS's jurisdiction over "certain non-controlling investments" into US corporations involved in "critical infrastructure", "critical technology" and "sensitive personal data" (Kalbfleisch and Pannu 2020). In addition to investing in the US, Chinese corporations were supplying US digital capital with high tech equipment and services for building the 5G wireless infrastructure. To arrest the flow, the USTR placed massive tariff on approximately $50 billion worth of Chinese imports originating from Chinese corporations that had supported or benefited from China's 2015 "Made in China 2025" plan (USTR 2018). As the USTR's head Robert Lighthizer declared: "Technology and innovation are America's greatest economic assets and...if we want our country to have a prosperous future, we must take a stand now to uphold fair trade and protect American competitiveness" (USTR 2018).

The US State also singled out ZTE and Huawei for sanction (Chen 2020; Kastrenakes 2018; McCabe 2020; Swanson 2020). These two Chinese telecommunications corporations were at the forefront of 5G wireless networking and smartphones, and they'd been making inroads into the US market, perhaps to the chagrin of AT&T and Verizon. In 2017, the DoC found ZTE to be in violation of a US sanction prohibiting it from selling its products and services to Iran and North Korea and issued a $1 billion fine. In 2018, the DoC imposed an export ban on ZTE that prohibited all US corporations from doing business with this company for seven years. By the end of that year, the Congressionally approved National Defense Authorization Act for Fiscal Year 2019 had banned the US Federal Government's use of technology produced and sold by both ZTE and Huawei, framing these corporations' goods and services as national security risks that might extend Chinese State surveillance into America and violate the citizenry's right to privacy. The Pentagon dutifully followed by blocking the sale of these corporations' digital devices in the retail outlets across its hundreds of bases in the US and worldwide after declaring they "may pose an unacceptable risk to the department's personnel, information and mission" (Liao 2018). Soon after, the FCC revoked ZTE and Huawei's authorization to sell their goods and services to corporations and consumers in the US market. By the summer of 2020, numerous Federal agencies were collectively barring *any* American corporation found to be using ZTE and Huawei products from receiving US State procurement contracts (Chen 2020; Kastrenakes 2018; McCabe 2020; Swanson 2020).

In August 2018, the DOC's Bureau of Industry and Security (BIS) dropped the hammer on China when expanding its sanctionable export licensing Entity List to include forty-four Chinese corporations. The DOC declared that these Chinese corporations were acting "contrary to the national security or foreign policy interests of the United States" due to being "involved in the illicit procurement of commodities and technologies for unauthorized military end-use in China" (Wu 2020). Between August 2020 and January 2021, the DoD fortified the DoC's position when publishing a blacklist of forty-four Chinese corporations that supposedly had links to China's People's Liberation Army and which had also been doing business in the US (Duffy 2021). Many of these Chinese corporations were at the forefront of digital technology. Then, in November of 2020, Donald Trump signed Executive Order 13959, "Addressing the Threat From Securities Investments That Finance Communist Chinese Military Companies," which was extended and expanded by Joe Biden in June 2021 (The White House 2021). This sanction prohibited all American citizens and corporations from investing in, buying or selling the shares of enterprises of what the DOD calls "Communist Chinese military companies." Some of the affected companies include the China Electronics Technology Group Corporation (CETC) and its subsidiary, Hikvision, as well as the Semiconductor Manufacturing International Corporation (SMIC). Also, in early 2021, the New York Stock Exchange (NYSE) had delisted China Telecom, China Mobile and China Unicom (Patridge 2021), and by March 2021, the US Securities and Exchange Commission (SEC) had adopted the Holding Foreign Companies Accountable Act, which instigated a stock value slump for some Chinese technology companies (Johnson and Murdoch 2021).

Hugely popular Chinese-owned social media platforms have barely endured the US State's new regime of blocking and banning Chinese Big Tech (Blitzer 2020; Glenn 2020; Jeong 2020). TikTok, a social media platform service that is used by millions of people to create and share short-form videos, was signalled out by the Republican and Democratic Parties for collecting user data, and potentially sending it back to China for processing by the State and/or Chinese surveillance capital. The Democratic National Committee warned its employees not to use TikTok on their smartphones because of the amount of user data it collected (Jeong 2020), and in a July 2020 interview with Fox News, US Secretary of State Mike Pompeo told American citizens that when they use TikTok, they put their "private information in the hands of the Chinese Communist Party" (Blitzer 2020; Glenn 2020). In August 2020, Trump released an "Executive Order on Addressing the Threat Posed by TikTok" to completely ban TikTok transactions in America unless its Chinese owner ByteDance sold it to an American firm, noting he had "credible evidence" that ByteDance might threaten US national security (The White House 2020).

Evidently, the US Empire's Federal agencies have unleashed a multi-faceted sanctions campaign that aims to punish China for pursuing technological independence at Silicon Valley's expense. These sanctions aim to put pressure on China to lower its Great Firewall so Silicon Valley can expand its digital goods and services trade in this vast market. They try to deter China from protecting its national tech titans while aiming to shield the US digital technology industry from a Chinese corporate takeover. They also aim to ensure that US corporations will prosper from new digital developments and be first in line to bid on and win lucrative government contracts for building the digital age. At the level of cultural politics, the US State's sanction campaign is a communicative act that works to generate fear of Chinese technology corporations, thereby depleting the currency of their brand images and diminishing their ability to prosper in the US and elsewhere. In all of these ways, US sanctions on China's Big Tech industry serve to weaken China and strengthen the US position in the current global battle over the future of digital technology.

5   Conclusion: The US-China Disintegration, Toward a New Imperial Rivalry?

This chapter probed the endurance of the US Empire vis-à-vis a rising China, and the US State's use of sanctions against China's Big Tech industry as a way to secure Silicon Valley, at home and abroad. The US State has long promoted the free flow of media and technology around the world, but its sanctions on China's Big Tech Industry represent a shift in the US's foreign policy away from engaging and trying to open China to Silicon Valley's bottom line, and toward more coercive measures to contain and constrain China's technological rise in order to secure Silicon Valley's digital dominance. In that regard, the US's commitment to global free-trade and the free flow of media and technology seems malleable: the US State advances a borderless world for Silicon Valley when it stands to benefit most but closes borders to non-US companies that may loosen Silicon Valley's global grip.

Today, competition and conflict between the US and China is a social fact of the global system, and digital technology is on the frontlines of these two countries' emerging rivalry to decide the digital future (Inkster 2021; Ku-Fai 2018). As the US and China move to decouple or potentially disintegrate their economic systems, partially or fully, each State will struggle to build and universalize their own specific "national" roads to the future (Johnson and Gramer 2020). Their strategic interests may run parallel to each other and when intersecting, may collide. Digital technology is now integral to the conduct of the US and Chinese States, and the ruling political and capitalist elites of both countries are working to try to prevail over the other. If this explodes into a full-blown rivalry, smaller countries around the world will be invited and cajoled to pick a side, and then find themselves enlisted into a junior officer or client role in the battle (Perthes 2021).

The global future is uncertain, but what is now clear is that the powers of Silicon Valley and the US State are aligning and more deeply integrating to protect and promote a global capitalist order wherein the US's digital model

presides, over which the US State makes and enforces the most important
rules, and in which America's nationalist ideology prevails over China's. In the
years to come, the US State will likely continue to try to secure American global
digital dominance and the economic, military and cultural power flowing from
it against the "threat" posed by China's rise. Opponents of this new cold war
will need to reboot and recharge an anti-imperialist politics that does not play
into or get played by a "nationalist-campist" outlook on the US-China rivalry,
and instead, works toward supporting internationalist working class struggles
and global-local forms of unity and solidarity, everywhere (Clarke 2021).

References

Alexa. (2021). *The top 500 sites on the web*. Available at: https://www.alexa.com/topsites.
Barfield, Claude. (2017). "Crafting an action-driven response to China's digital trade
    barriers." *American Enterprise Institute*, 25 January. Available at: https://www.aei
    .org/research-products/report/crafting-an-action-driven-response-to-chinas-digi
    tal-trade-barriers/.
Blakey, J. Russell. (2020). "The Foreign Investment Risk Review Modernization Act: The
    Double-Edged Sword of U.S. Foreign Investment Regulations." *Loyola of Los Angeles
    Law Review* 53 (4): 981–1014.
Blitzer, Ronn. (2020, August 2). "Pompeo warns TikTok users' personal info could be
    going 'directly to the Chinese Communist Party'." *Fox News*, 2 August.
Block, Fred, and Keller, Matthew. (2011). *State of Innovation: The US Government's Role
    in Technology Development*. Boulder: Paradigm Publishers.
Braw, Elisabeth. (2020). "How China Is Buying Up the West's High-Tech Sector." *Foreign
    Policy*, 3 December. https://foreignpolicy.com/2020/12/03/how-china-is-buying-up
    -the-wests-high-tech-sector/.
Business Roundtable. (2021). "Recommendations for Chinese Reforms to Address
    Trade and Investment Barriers." Available at: https://www.businessroundtable.org/
    recommendations-for-chinese-reforms-to-address-trade-and-investment-barriers.
Carminati, Daniele. (2020). "The State of China's Soft Power in 2020." *E-International
    Relations*. Available at: https://www.e-ir.info/2020/07/03/the-state-of-chinas-soft
    -power-in-2020/.
Chen, Shawna. (2020). "Trump bans Americans from investing in 31 companies with
    links to Chinese military." *Axios*, 12 November. https://www.axios.com/china-milit
    ary-trump-investments-ban-a0458e29-2245-4bde-920b-d1c6bc698370.html.
Cheng, Evelyn. (2021). "China says it now has nearly 1 billion internet users." *CNBC*,
    4 February. https://www.cnbc.com/2021/02/04/china-says-it-now-has-nearly-1-bill
    ion-internet-users.html.

Clarke, John. (2021). "The class struggle and geopolitics." *Canadian Dimension*, 19 March. Available at: https://canadiandimension.com/articles/view/the-class-struggle-and-geopolitics.

Council on Foreign Relations. (2018). "Why Does Everyone Hate Made in China 2025?" *Council on Foreign Relations*, 19 March.

Disis, Jill. (2021). "The China trade war is one thing Joe Biden won't be rushing to fix." *CNN*, 21 January. https://www.cnn.com/2021/01/21/economy/china-trade-tech-war-biden-intl-hnk/index.html.

Disis, Jill. (2020). "A New World War Over Technology." *CNN*, 10 July. https://www.cnn.com/2020/07/10/tech/us-china-global-tech-war-intl-hnk/index.html.

Domínguez, Gabriel. (2015). "Made in China 2025—The Next Stage of China's Economic Rise?" *Deutsche Welle*, 6 February. https://www.dw.com/en/made-in-china-2025-the-next-stage-of-chinas-economic-rise/a-18490377/.

Duffy, Kate. (2021). "The Trump administration blacklisted 9 more Chinese companies, including Xiaomi." *Business Insider*, 15 January. https://www.businessinsider.in/tech/news/the-trump-administration-blacklisted-9-more-chinese-companies-including-xiaomi-it-labeled-the-smartphone-giant-a-communist-chinese-military-company-/articleshow/80289356.cms.

Dyer-Witheford, Nick, and Matviyenko, Svitlana. (2019). *Cyberwar and Revolution: Digital Subterfuge in Global Capitalism*. Minneapolis: University of Minnesota Press.

Forbes. (2021). Global 2000: The World's Largest Public Companies List.

Fuchs, Christian. (2016). "Baidu, Weibo and Renren: The global political economy of social media in China." *Asian Journal of Communication* 26 (1): 14–41.

Glenn, Mike. (2020). "Pompeo: TikTok a national security threat." *AP*, 2 August. https://apnews.com/article/national-security-media-mike-pompeo-archive-united-states-ad6c62b894b9409e6d542f2bba2f821c.

Griffiths, James. (2019). *The Great Firewall of China: How to Build and Control an Alternative Version of the Internet*. London: Zed Books.

Guluzade, Amir. (2019). "The role of China's state-owned companies explained." *World Economic Forum*, 6 May. https://www.weforum.org/agenda/2019/05/why-chinas-state-owned-companies-still-have-a-key-role-to-play/.

Hagey, Keach, and Vranica, Suzanne. (2021). "How Covid-19 Supercharged the Advertising 'Triopoly' of Google, Facebook and Amazon." *The Wall Street Journal*, 19 March. https://www.wsj.com/articles/how-covid-19-supercharged-the-advertising-triopoly-of-google-facebook-and-amazon-11616163738.

Harris, Sean. (2014). *@War: The Rise of the Military-Internet Complex*. New York: Houghton Mifflin Harcourt.

He, Laura. (2020). "China wants to be less reliant on the United States. That's a tall order." *CNN*, 30 October. https://www.cnn.ph/business/2020/10/30/China-less-reliant-United-States-tall-order-.html.

Hills, Jill. (2006). "What's New? War, Censorship and Global Transmission." *International Communication Gazette* 68 (3): 195–216.

Hong, Yu. (2017). "Pivot to internet plus: Modeling China's digital economy for economic restructuring?" *International Journal of Communication* 11 (2): 1486–1506.

Hopewell, Kristen. (2018). "What is 'Made in China 2025' — and why is it a threat to Trump's trade goals?" *The Washington Post*, 3 May. https://www.washingtonpost.com/news/monkey-cage/wp/2018/05/03/what-is-made-in-china-2025-and-why-is-it-a-threat-to-trumps-trade-goals/.

Inkster, Nigel. (2021). *The Great Decoupling: China, America and the Struggle for Technological Supremacy.* New York: Oxford University Press.

Jeong, Sarah. (2020). "The US Declared War on TikTok Because it Can't Handle the Truth." *The Verge*, 7 August. https://www.theverge.com/21355465/tiktok-us-china-information-nationalism-online-propaganda.

Jia, Lianrui, and Winseck, Dwayne. (2018). "The Political Economy of Chinese Internet Companies: Financialization, concentration and capitalization." *The International Communication Gazette* 80 (1): 30–59.

Jiang, Min. (2012). "Internet Companies in China: Dancing between the Party Line and the Bottom Line." *Ifri Center for Asian Studies*, 29 January. https://www.ifri.org/en/publications/notes-de-lifri/asie-visions/internet-companies-china-dancing-between-party-line-and.

Jin, Dal Yong. (2019). "Facebook's Platform Imperialism: The Economics and Geopolitics of Social Media." In Boyd-Barrett, Oliver, and Mirrlees, Tanner (eds.), *Media Imperialism: Continuity and Change*, 187–198. New York: Rowman & Littlefield.

Jingrong Lin, Karen, Xiaoyan, Lu, Zhang, Junsheng, and Zheng, Ying. (2020). "State-owned enterprises in China: A review of 40 years of research and practice." *China Journal of Accounting Research* 13 (1): 31–55.

Johnson, Katanga, and Murdoch, Scott. (2021). "Chinese tech stocks slump as U.S. SEC begins rollout of law aimed at delisting." *Reuters*, 24 March. https://www.reuters.com/article/us-usa-sec-foreigncompanies-idUSKBN2BG2AI.

Johnson, Keith, and Gramer, Robbie. (2020). "The Great Decoupling." *Foreign Policy*, 14 May. https://foreignpolicy.com/2020/05/14/china-us-pandemic-economy-tensions-trump-coronavirus-covid-new-cold-war-economics-the-great-decoupling/.

Kahata, Akinori. (2020). "Managing U.S.-China Technology Competition and Decoupling." *Center for Strategic and International Studies*, 24 November.

Kalbfleisch, Adam, and Pannu, Alysha. (2020). "CFIUS' Jurisdiction to Review Foreign Investments Expands Effective February 13, 2020." *Bennet Jones*, 10 February. https://www.bennettjones.com/Blogs-Section/CFIUS-Jurisdiction-to-Review-Foreign-Investments-Expands-Effective-February-13-2020.

Kastrenakes, Jacob. (2018). "Trump signs bill banning government use of Huawei and ZTE tech." *The Verge*, 13 August. https://www.theverge.com/2018/8/13/17686310/huawei-zte-us-government-contractor-ban-trump.

Kharpal, Arjun. (2021). "In battle with U.S., China to focus on 7 'frontier' technologies from chips to brain-computer fusion." *CNBC* . https://www.cnbc.com/2021/03/05/china-to-focus-on-frontier-tech-from-chips-to-quantum-computing.html.

Lee, Kai-Fu. (2018). *AI Superpowers: China, Silicon Valley, and the New World Order*. New York: Houghton Mifflin Harcourt.

Leskin, Paige. (2019). "Here are all the major US tech companies blocked behind China's 'Great Firewall'." *Business Insider*, 10 October. https://www.businessinsider.com/major-us-tech-companies-blocked-from-operating-in-china-2019-5.

Levine, Yasha. (2018). *Surveillance Valley: The Secret Military History of the Internet*. New York: Public Affairs.

Liao, Shannon. (2018). "The Pentagon bans Huawei and ZTE phones from retail stores on military bases." *The Verge*, 2 May. https://www.theverge.com/2018/5/2/17310870/pentagon-ban-huawei-zte-phones-retail-stores-military-bases.

Mark, Jeremy. (2020). "China's fourteenth five-year plan: The technologies that shall not be named." *Atlantic Council*, 5 November. https://www.atlanticcouncil.org/blogs/new-atlanticist/chinas-fourteenth-five-year-plan-the-technologies-that-shall-not-be-named/.

Masters, Jonathan. (2019). "What are Economic Sanctions." *Council on Foreign Relations*, 12 August. https://www.cfr.org/backgrounder/what-are-economic-sanctions.

Mathieson, Rosalind. (2021). "Biden Faces Decline of American Soft Power." *Bloomberg*, 8 January. https://www.bloomberg.com/news/newsletters/2021-01-08/biden-faces-decline-of-american-soft-power.

McBride, James, and Chatzky, Andrew. (2019). "Is 'Made in China 2025' a Threat to Global Trade?" *Council on Foreign Relations*, 13 May. https://www.cfr.org/backgrounder/made-china-2025-threat-global-trade.

McCabe, David. (2020). "F.C.C. Designates Huawei and ZTE as National Security Threats." *The New York Times*, 30 June. https://www.nytimes.com/2020/06/30/technology/fcc-huawei-zte-national-security.html.

Mehta, Aaron. (2019). "Bezos: Country 'in trouble' if tech firms turn from DoD." *Defense News*, 8 December. https://www.defensenews.com/smr/reagan-defense-forum/2019/12/08/bezos-country-in-trouble-if-tech-firms-turn-from-dod/.

Mirrlees, Tanner. (2019a). "Mass Media and Imperialism." In Ness I., Cope Z. (eds.), *The Palgrave Encyclopedia of Imperialism and Anti-Imperialism*. New York: Palgrave Macmillan.

Mirrlees, Tanner. (2019b). "'Weaponizing' the Internet and World Wide Web for Empire: Platforming Capitalism, Data-Veillance, Public Diplomacy, and Cyberwarfare." In Boyd-Barrett, Oliver, and Mirrlees, Tanner (eds.), *Media Imperialism: Continuity and Change*, 213–231. New York: Rowman & Littlefield.

Mirrlees, Tanner. (2019c). "Not (Yet) the 'Chinese Century': The Endurance of the US Empire and Its Cultural Industries." In Boyd-Barrett, Oliver, and Mirrlees, Tanner (eds.), *Media Imperialism: Continuity and Change*, 305–320. New York: Rowman & Littlefield.

Mozur, Paul, and Myers, Steven Lee. (2021). "Xi's Gambit: China Plans for a World Without American Technology." *The New York Times*, 3 April. https://www.nytimes .com/2021/03/10/business/china-us-tech-rivalry.html.

Murdock, Graham. (2019). "The Empire's New Clothes: Political Priorities and Corporate Ambitions in China's Drive for Global Ascendency." In Boyd-Barrett, Oliver, and Mirrlees, Tanner (eds.), *Media Imperialism: Continuity and Change*, 291–304. New York: Rowman & Littlefield.

Panitch, Leo, and Albo, Greg. (2020). *Beyond Digital Capitalism-New Ways of Living: Socialist Register 2021*. London: Merlin Press.

Patridge, Joanna. (2021). "NYSE to delist three Chinese telecom firms, citing 'military links'." *The Guardian*, 1 January. https://www.theguardian.com/business/2021/jan/ 01/new-york-stock-exchange-nyse-to-delist-three-chinese-telecom-firms-alleged -military-links.

Perthes, Volker. (2021). "Dimensions of rivalry: China, the United States, and Europe." *China International Strategy Review*. https://link.springer.com/article/10.1007/s42 533-021-00065-z.

Petri, Peter A., and Dollar, David. (2020). "The US-China tech rivalry shapes the economic relationship." *Brookings Institute*, 8 June. https://www.brookings.edu/podc ast-episode/the-us-china-tech-rivalry-shapes-the-economic-relationship/.

Prashad, Vijay. (2021). "Biden Continues the US Conflict With China Through the Quad." *The Bullet,* 22 March. https://socialistproject.ca/2021/03/biden-continues -usa-conflict-with-china-through-quad/.

Roberts, Margaret. (2018). *Censored: Distraction and Diversion Inside China's Great Firewall*. Princeton University Press.

Schiller, Herbert. (1969). *Mass Communication and American Empire*. Boston: Beacon press.

Schiller, Herbert. (1996). *Information Inequality*. New York: Routledge.

Schiller, Dan. (2014). *Digital Depression: Information Technology and Economic Crisis*. Champaign, IL: University of Illinois Press.

Singer, P.W., and Brooking, Emerson T. (2018). *Like War: The Weaponization of Social Media*. New York: Houghton Mifflin Harcourt.

SIPRI (Stockholm International Peace Research Institute). (2021). "World military spending rises to almost $2 trillion in 2020." SIPRI, 14 June. https://www.sipri.org/ media/press-release/2021/world-military-spending-rises-almost-2-trillion-2020.

Sparks, Colin. (2019). "China: An Emerging Cultural Imperialist." In Boyd-Barrett, Oliver, and Mirrlees, Tanner (eds.), *Media Imperialism: Continuity and Change*, 275–290. New York: Rowman & Littlefield.

State-owned Assets Supervision and Administration Commission of the State Council. (2021). Directory. http://en.sasac.gov.cn/directory.html.

Swanson, Ana. (2020). "Trump Bars Investment in Chinese Firms With Military Ties." *The New York Times*, 12 November. https://www.nytimes.com/2020/11/12/business/economy/trump-china-investment-ban.html.

Thompson, Nicholas, and Bremmer, Ian. (2018). "The AI Cold War that Threatens Us All." *Wired*, 18 October. https://www.wired.com/story/ai-cold-war-china-could-doom-us-all/.

Tucker, Hank. (2020a). "Forbes Global 2000 Highlights: Inside the Numbers of the World's Largest Public Companies." *Forbes*, 13 May. https://www.forbes.com/sites/hanktucker/2020/05/13/global-2000-highlights-inside-the-numbers-of-the-worlds-largest-public-companies/?sh=384b4c596fec.

Tucker, Hank. (2020b). "World's Largest Technology Companies 2020: Apple Stays On Top, Zoom And Uber Debut." *Forbes*, 13 May. https://www.forbes.com/sites/hanktucker/2020/05/13/worlds-largest-technology-companies-2020-apple-stays-on-top-zoom-and-uber-debut/?sh=46a596983c03.

UNESCO (United Nations Educational, Scientific and Cultural Organization). (2016). "China: taking stock of progress towards becoming an innovation-driven nation." UNESCO, 2 December.

US Bureau of Economic Analysis. (2021). "Digital Economy." https://www.bea.gov/data/special-topics/digital-economy.

US Congressional Research Service. (2020). "Digital Trade." *US Congressional Research Service Brief*, 3 December. https://crsreports.congress.gov/product/pdf/IF/IF10770.

US Department of Defense. (2018). "Summary of the National Defense Strategy of the United States." https://www.jcs.mil/Portals/36/Documents/Publications/UNCLASS_2018_National_Military_Strategy_Description.pdf.

USTR (Office of the United States Trade Representative). (2018). "Update Concerning China's Acts, Policies, and Practices Related to Technology Transfer, Intellectual Property and Innovation." USTR, 20 November. https://ustr.gov/sites/default/files/enforcement/301Investigations/301%20Report%20Update.pdf.

USTR (Office of the United States Trade Representative). (2018). "USTR Issues Tariffs on Chinese Products in Response to Unfair Trade Practices." USTR, 15 June. https://ustr.gov/about-us/policy-offices/press-office/press-releases/2018/june/ustr-issues-tariffs-chinese-products.

USNI News. (2021). "US Strategic Framework for the Indo-Pacific." USNI *News*, 15 January. https://news.usni.org/2021/01/15/u-s-strategic-framework-for-the-indo-pacific.

van Dijck, Jose, Poell, Thomas, and de Waal, Martijn. (2018). *The Platform Society: Public Values in a Connective World*. New York: Oxford University Press.

van Dijck, José. (2019). "Guarding Public Values in a Connective World: Challenges for Europe." In Boyd-Barrett, Oliver, and Mirrlees, Tanner (eds.), *Media Imperialism: Continuity and Change*, 175–186. New York: Rowman & Littlefield.

Watkins, Susan. (2019). "America vs China." *New Left Review* 115 (Jan./Feb.): 5–14.

Wike, Richard, Fetterolf, Janell, and Mordecai, Mara. (2020). "US Image Plummets Internationally as Most Say Country Has Handled Coronavirus Badly." *Pew Research Center*, 15 September. https://www.pewresearch.org/global/2020/09/15/us-image -plummets-internationally-as-most-say-country-has-handled-coronavirus-badly/.

Winseck, Dwayne. (2008). "Information Operations Blowback: Communication, Propaganda and Surveillance in the Global War on Terrorism." *International Communication Gazette* 70 (6): 419–441.

Wu, Xiangning. (2020). "Technology, power, and uncontrolled great power strategic competition between China and the United States." *China International Strategy Review* 2 (1): 99–119.

The White House. (2020). "Executive Order on Addressing the Threat Posed by TikTok." *The White House*, 6 August. https://trumpwhitehouse.archives.gov/presidential-acti ons/executive-order-addressing-threat-posed-tiktok/.

The White House. (2021). "Executive Order on Addressing the Threat from Securities Investments that Finance Certain Companies of the People's Republic of China." *The White House*, 3, June. Available at: https://www.whitehouse.gov/briefing-room/ presidential-actions/2021/06/03/executive-order-on-addressing-the-threat-from -securities-investments-that-finance-certain-companies-of-the-peoples-republic -of-china/.

Zhao, Yuezhi. (2008). *Communication in China: Political Economy, Power, and Conflict*. Lanham, ML: Rowman & Littlefield.

Zuboff, Shoshana. (2019). *The Age of Surveillance Capitalism*. New York: Public Affairs.

PART 2

Profiles of Sanctioned Nation-States

∴

US Sanctions Cuba 'to Bring About Hunger, Desperation and the Overthrow of the Government'

Helen Yaffe

1   Introduction

The United States 'embargo' of Cuba, officially imposed since 1962, constitutes the longest and most extensive system of unliteral sanctions applied against any country in modern history. It is not merely a legal or a bilateral issue, as many of its proponents have claimed. It is a key instrument in the US toolkit to pursue regime change on the island. It is an act of war, a violation of human rights, designed to obstruct Cuban development, to undermine its example as a revolutionary alternative, and to intentionally cause suffering among the Cuban people. While the pretext for US actions against Cuba has changed over the last six decades, the objectives have not.

The driving motivations of the United States' post-1959 Cuba policy are established in the secret one-page memorandum written by Lester Mallory, US Deputy Assistant Secretary of State for Inter-American Affairs, on 6 April 1960. Under the subject title, 'The Decline and Fall of Castro', Mallory wrote:

> Salient considerations respecting the life of the present Government of Cuba are: 1. The majority of Cubans support Castro...2. There is no effective political opposition. 3. Fidel Castro and other members of the Cuban Government espouse or condone communist influence. 4. Communist influence is pervading the Government and the body politic at an amazingly fast rate. 5. Militant opposition to Castro from without Cuba would only serve his and the communist cause. 6. The only foreseeable means of alienating internal support is through disenchantment and disaffection based on economic dissatisfaction and hardship.
>
> MALLORY 1960

The CIA had already launched operations against Cuba's revolutionary government, in the second half of 1959, orchestrating acts of terrorism and sabotage and recruiting Cubans on the island as agents. But clearly, they were considered ineffective. How would the population be turned against the Cuban Revolution? Mallory proposed: 'that every possible means should be undertaken promptly to weaken the economic life of Cuba…denying money and supplies to Cuba, to decrease monetary and real wages, to bring about hunger, desperation and overthrow of government" (Mallory 1960). The human rights of the Cuban population were not on the radar. Furthermore, although Cuba's revolutionary government had already carried out the Agrarian Reform in 1959, confiscating unproductive plantations over 1,000 acres, and in January 1960, expropriated 70,000 acres from US sugar companies, Mallory does not frame sanctions as retaliation for nationalisation, or to pressure the government over the issue compensation; a claim subsequently made to justify the US 'embargo' in international law (White 2019). The concern expressed is over communist influence, not nationalisations.

One year later, on 16 April 1961, 'communist influence' was confirmed when, on the eve of the invasion at the Bay of Pigs/Playa Giron, Fidel Castro announced: "This is what they cannot forgive…that we have carried out a socialist revolution right under the nose of the United States!" (Castro 1961). The early measures of Cuba's new revolutionary state (693 new laws, resolutions and decrees in 1959, 229 more in 1960 and 93 in 1961, according to Valdés (2003, 2)) rapidly encroached on private interests, domestic and foreign, dismantling the economic and political institutions of the old Cuba, a US client state, building new institutions, power structures and social relations, adopting a centrally planned socialist economy and founding the organisations of the masses. Notably, while it was the threat of communism, in the context of broader geopolitical factors, that marked Cuba as a target for US sanctions, it was the adoption of socialism, and the shift to trade with the USSR and the socialist bloc countries, which enabled Cuba to survive the economic devastation wrecked on the island by the US blockade.

2   US Embargo? US Blockade?

This chapter refers to US sanctions against Cuba as a 'blockade', even while citing US legislation which states that it is an 'embargo'. The difference in terminology is political and has implications for whether US sanctions are regarded as legally justified and a bilateral issue, or whether they are regarded as an act of war. Formally, an embargo is when one nation establishes a policy not to trade with another nation and not to allow its own ports or territory to be used for commerce with that nation. It is usually a penalty in response to some action. Establishment of an embargo is the prerogative of any nation. A blockade is when a country uses a military threat or force to close the coast of another entity to international commerce; it prevents third parties from undertaking normal commercial activity. A blockade is an act of war rather than a country exercising its own prerogatives. However, as international law scholar Nigel White concludes: "While the US measures against Cuba do not amount to a blockade in a technical or formal sense, their cumulative effect is to put an economic stranglehold on the island, which not only prevents the United States intercourse but also effectively blocks commerce with other states, their citizens and companies" (White 2019, p. 163, fn. 1; Davalos Fernandez 2012). The United State imposes a blockade on Cuba.

3   A History of Incremental Sanctions

In July 1960, three months after Mallory's memorandum, President Eisenhower used the Export Control Act of 1949 to cut Cuban sugar exports to the United States purportedly in response to Cuba's nationalisations of US sugar interests in Cuba. Cuba responded with further nationalisations of US businesses whose owners were instructed by the US government to reject Cuban offers of compensation. To comprehend how devastating a measure this was intended to be it is necessary recall that Cuba had a monocrop economy dependent on sugar exports to the United States. Cuba was the world's largest producer and exporter of sugar in the 1950s. Sugar and its by-products accounted for 86% of exports, and 80% of Cuban sugar exports were shipped to the US. The USSR stepped in to purchase all sugar exports dropped from the United States. The successive tit-for-tat retaliations between the Cuban and US governments has been well-documented (Franklin 1997). It culminated in a full diplomatic and economic rupture between the countries on January 03, 1961.

Subsequent to those first sanctions, the US blockade of Cuba has been enforced through six main statutes: section 5(b) of the 1917 Trading with the Enemy Act; section 620(a) of the 1961 Foreign Assistance Act; the 1963 Cuban Assets Control Regulations; the 1992 Cuban Democracy Act, known as the Torricelli Act; the 1996 Cuban Liberty and Democratic Solidarity (Libertad) Act, known as the Helms-Burton Act; and the 2000 Trade Sanctions Reform and Export Enhancement Act (Amnesty International 2009, p. 7). The scope of these regulations is outlined below. These sanctions have been targeted at key economic and strategy areas of development in Cuba; sugar and nickel exports, tourism and, more recently, biotechnology, as Joy Gordon points out, adding, "and the projects that could significantly change Cuba's economic prospects, such as oil drilling and major infrastructural improvements" (Gordon 2016, 477).

In January 1961, President Eisenhower's administration considered sanctioning Cuba under the (1917) Trading with the Enemy Act (TWEA), which prohibits, limits or regulates trade and financial transactions, including those related to travel, transport or business, in times of war or when a national emergency has been declared.[1] This legislation was invoked in 1963 under President Kennedy. Today, Cuba remains the only country in the world subject to US sanctions under the TWEA, which is extended yearly by presidential signature. President Obama did this in 2015 and 2016, confirming Cuba's status as an official 'enemy', despite restoring diplomatic relations with Cuba and declaring his opposition to the US blockade.

In September 1961, the US Congress approved the Foreign Assistance Act, to restructure US overseas support, distinguishing between military and non-military 'aid', and setting up the United States Agency for International Development (USAID) to manage the latter.[2] Section 620 of the Act states: 'No assistance shall be furnished under this Act to the present government of Cuba. As an additional means of implementing and carrying into effect the policy of the preceding sentence, the President is authorized to establish and maintain a total embargo upon all trade between the United States and Cuba.' The pretext was the issue of "equitable compensation to citizens and entities for property taken... by the Government of Cuba" (Foreign Assistance Act of 1961, 219). The Act goes on to prohibit assistance "to any Communist country" and other countries assisting Cuba, thus already endowing US sanctions with

---

1 The Amnesty International report suggests that Eisenhower suspended trade with Cuba under the Trading with the Enemy Act in January 1961. *US Embargo Against Cuba*, 7. However, according to Benjamin A. Coates the Eisenhower administration discussed the idea but left the decision for the incoming administration of Kennedy, 'The Secret Life of Statutes: A Century of the Trading with the Enemy Act' in *Modern American History*, 1, 2018. Evidence for this version appears in a memorandum by US Secretary of State, Christian A. Herter, to President Eisenhower, 5 January 1961. Available here, https://history.state.gov/historicaldo cuments/frus1961-63v10/d12. Section 5(b) of the Trading with the Enemy Act was added by US Congress in 1933.

2 The backdrop to this was US President John F. Kennedy's 'Alliance for Progress' a ten-year plan launched in August 1961 in which the United States committed to invest $20 billion in Latin American development (and security), with a further $80 billion pledged by regional governments. This was motivated by Kennedy's fear that the Cuban Revolution would inspire neighbouring countries to address the continents' poor socio-economic conditions through revolutionary means. By alleviating the worst of those conditions, the Alliance would undermine the potential for revolution, and tie Latin American development to US institutions and interests.

an extraterritorial character. On 3 February 1962, eight months before Soviet missiles were deployed in Cuba, Kennedy issued Presidential Proclamation 3447, based on the Foreign Assistance Act, to suspend all trade with Cuba. This legislation remains in force.

By 1963 the Cuban Assets Controls Regulations (CACR) were issued under section 5(b) of the TWEA, with the expressed goal to "isolate the Cuban government economically and deprive it of U.S. dollars" (cited in Amnesty International, 2009, 8). Cuban assets in the United States were frozen, and all financial and commercial transactions were prohibited unless approved by a permit, as were the direct and indirect export of US products, services and technology to Cuba, while Cuban exports to the US were prohibited. Also banned were transactions in US dollars in Cuba by any citizen of the United States or any third country (Ministerio de Relaciones Exterior 2018). This was enforced by the US Treasury Department through penalties imposed for violations by its Office of Foreign Asset Controls. Penalties rose to a maximum ten years in prison, corporate fines of up to $1 million and individual fines of up to $250,000 with civil penalties up to $55,000 (Amnesty International 2009).

These sanctions might have brought the Cuban Revolution to its knees. Since the Platt Amendment of 1901, followed by the Trade Reciprocity Treaty of 1904, the Jones-Costigan Sugar Act of 1934 (later the Sugar Act of 1937), US legislation in the early 20th century had fostered Cuba's economic dependence on the United States, for trade, investment and loans. Meanwhile, the US dollar was established as the basis for international trade in 1944. The Soviet Union's decision to step in and assist the Cubans, after Deputy Premier Anastas Mikoyan visited the island in February 1960, threw a lifeline to the revolutionary government. Cuba's trade with the USSR and the socialist bloc, and its full integration from the mid-1970s into the Council for Mutual Economic Assistance, was not without problems from the technical, geographical, and economic perspective. However, there is no doubt that this was decisive for the survival of the Cuban revolution and cushioned the island from the impact of the United States blockade.

That came to an end, however, between 1989 and 1991, as the socialist bloc collapsed, generating a severe economic crisis as Cuba lost around 87% of its trade and investment. Cuba's GDP nosedived by one-third in three years. The story of how Cuba's socialist system survived this 'Special Period' of economic crisis is told elsewhere (Yaffe 2020). The Cuban economy was restructured for reintegration into a capitalist world market operating under neoliberalism and dominated by its nemesis, the United States. The Cubans demonstrated remarkable resilience and creativity, even while opponents in the United

States, government agencies and right-wing Cuban exiles, acted fast to hasten the Revolution's downfall.

In 1992, President George W. Bush signed the Cuban Democracy (Torricelli) Act. Its key sponsor, Democrat Congressman Robert Torricelli, boasted that the legislation would 'wreak havoc on that island' (Franklin 1994).[3] The legislation prohibits foreign-based subsidiaries of US companies in third countries from trading with Cuba or with Cuban nationals, banned foreign ships docking in Cuba from entering US ports for six months, barred travel to Cuba by US citizens, and limited family remittances to the island. Foreign countries providing assistance to Cuba would be ineligible for foreign assistance and debt reduction or relief. The Torricelli Act declares medical goods can be exported to Cuba 'if the President determines that the United States Government is able to verify, by onsite inspections and other appropriate means, that the exported item is to be used for the purposes for which it was intended and only for the use and benefit of the Cuban people.' (HR 5323, 1992) Donations of medicines for humanitarian purposes can be made to NGOs, but not Cuba's public healthcare system. Exports must be granted an export licence, but applications for most goods 'are subject to a policy of denial' (Bureau of Industry and Security, n.d.). Section 6006 states that 'Food, medicine, and medical supplies for humanitarian purposes' can only be made when Cuba has taken steps to introduce what the US President deems were free and fair elections for a new government.

For sanctions to be waived, the President must report to Congress that, among other conditions, Cuba has 'held free and fair elections', 'is moving toward establishing a free market economic system' and 'has committed itself to constitutional change' (HR 5323, 1992). In imposing these conditions, the Torricelli Act blatantly violates the declaration of the United Nations General Assembly of December 1960, which states that: 'All peoples have the right to self-determination; by virtue of that right they freely determine their political status and freely pursue their economic, social and cultural development.' (UN General Assembly 1960).

By 1996, Cuba had turned the corner in its economic crisis, returning to growth with new international partners investing in the tourism industry. This became a target for Cuba's opponents in the United States; government sanctions sought to block foreign investors and visitors, while militant Cuban

---

3   In 1988, Torricelli had visited and praised Cuba: 'Living standards are not high, but the homelessness, hunger and disease that is witnessed in much of Latin America does not appear evident'. After receiving generous campaign contributions from the Cuban American National Foundation, however, he sponsored the Cuban Democracy Act.

exiles sought to terrorise tourists through bombing campaigns. In March 1996, after Cuban military forces shot down exile flights invading Cuban airspace from the United States, President Bill Clinton signed the Cuban Liberty and Democratic Solidarity (Libertad) Act into law, known as the Helms-Burton Act for the names of the law's sponsors, Jesse Helms and Dan Burton (H.R.927, 1996). In addition to strengthening the extraterritorial character of the US blockade and planning the transition government in a post-Castro government, the Helms-Burton Act 'codified' the US blockade into law, so the capacity to lift the blockade now lies with Congress, not the US President.

The Helms-Burton Act has four titles: Title I: 'Strengthening international sanctions against the Castro government' reaffirms the CDA measures obstructing Cuba's trade with, or assistance from, third countries, with the threat of fines, and bars Cuba's membership of, or loans from, international financial institutions.[4] Title II of the Act: 'Assistance to a free and independent Cuba', establishes the steps for lifting or suspending the US blockade, including 'democratic elections' in Cuba and the return to US nationals of property nationalised by the Cuban government after 1 January 1959 and 'ensure coordination between the US Government and the private sector in responding to change and promoting market-based development in Cuba'. It describes the humanitarian and economic assistance the US will provide to a transition government, 'economic, food, medicine, medical supplies and equipment'; essentials denied to the population under US sanctions.

Title III, 'Protection of property rights of United States Nationals' authorises US nationals with claims to nationalised property in Cuba to file suit in US courts against persons 'trafficking' in that property. A legal abnormality of this law is that it provides the protection of US courts to individuals who were not US citizens when their properties were nationalised but became US citizens after the event (Roy 1997, 83). Title IV on 'Exclusion of certain aliens' allows foreigners and their families who are 'involved in the confiscation of property, or the trafficking in confiscated property...which is owned by a United States national' to be denied entry to the US.

---

4   Cuba is blocked from membership of the International Monetary Fund, the International Bank for Reconstruction and Development, the International Development Association, the International Finance Corporation, the Multilateral Investment Guarantee Agency and the Inter-American Development Bank. Any loan or assistance provided by any of these institutions to the government of Cuba will result in the withholding of the same amount by the US Secretary of Treasury from payment to that institution. Amnesty International, *US Embargo Against Cuba*, 11.

4   International Repudiation

From the outset every US President suspended Title III beginning with six months by Clinton and subsequently on a biannual basis until Trump in 2019. This was a concession made in response to protests at the extraterritorial character of these unilateral sanctions, particularly Title III, from Canada and the European Union (EU), who adopted blocking and 'claw-back' legislation and threatened legal action within the North American Free Trade Agreement and the World Trade Organisation respectively (Smis and van der Borgt 1999, 228). On paper, EU and UK citizens and businesses complying with the 1996 Helms-Burton Act can be fined. But in April 1997 the EU and the US made a deal: the US would limit the impact of certain provisions on European companies and citizens and in return the EU agreed to freeze legal action in the WTO. The US would continue suspending Title III every six months, 'so long as the EU and other allies continue their stepped up efforts to promote democracy in Cuba' (*ibid.*, 232). In 1996, the EU adopted the Common Position on Cuba, "to encourage a process of transition to a pluralist democracy and respect for human rights and fundamental freedoms".

Even with Title III suspended, the US Treasury's Office of Foreign Asset Controls (OFAC) has issued million- and billion-dollar fines on banks and companies in third countries for dealings with Cuba, while in the EU and UK anti-US blockade legislation is not enforced.[5] The United Nations advised member states to legislate against the US blockade's extraterritorial reach, but no legal action was taken so international trade with Cuba was severely restricted. Since 1994, when it was first delivered, Cuba has received overwhelming support for its resolution to the United Nations General Assembly on 'the need to put an end of the economic, commercial and financial blockade imposed by the United States against Cuba.' The only steadfast opponents have been the United States and Israel and in 2016 even they abstained, while the rest of the world voted in support of Cuba.

In 2000 the TSRA was approved by the US Congress, authorising the sale of agricultural goods and medicines to Cuba for 'humanitarian reasons'. In 2005, further US regulations stipulated that Cuba must pay for goods in full,

---

5   The only exception appears to be when in April 2016 a district court in Dortmund, Germany, issued an order against PayPal for applying US laws in the country. Details are included in *Cuba's Report, On Resolution 70/5 of the United Nations General Assembly entitled "Necessity of ending the economic, commercial and financial blockade imposed by the United States of America against Cuba"*, June 2016. http://misiones.minrex.gob.cu/en/articulo/cubas-report-resolution-705-united-nations-general-assembly-entitled-necessity-ending.

in cash, before shipment, with transactions made through banks in third countries. The Act also limited travel to Cuba by US citizens to 12 authorised categories requiring a licence. Amnesty notes that 'Although the TSRA contemplates the export of medicine, this legislation does not supersede the Cuban Democracy Act of 1992 and therefore the necessity of a presidential certificate through on-site verification remains in force.' (Amnesty International 2009, 11).

In addition to those six statutes other regulations have been applied (Ministerio de Relaciones Exterior 2018). Under the Export Administration Act of 1979, Cuba was included in a list of countries for which the US President could set special export controls on the basis of national security considerations. It established a general policy of refusal for exportation and re-exportation to Cuba up to the present (US Department of Commerce 2019). Section 211 of the Supplementary and Emergency Allocations Act for fiscal year 1999, prohibited recognition by US courts of the rights of Cuban companies on trademarks associated with nationalised properties.

The result is as complex web of overlapping legislation. 'Our legal consultants say nobody understands the embargo anymore, it's so many regulations accrued over so much time,' said Dr Kelvin Lee from Roswell Park Cancer Institute in New York state, outlining the challenges they faced in requesting authorisation to carry out clinical trials on Cuba's cancer immunotherapy CIMAVax-EGF during the second Obama administration. They had to meet with many federal authorities and state authorities to discuss whether collaboration was feasible, 'given the myriad laws bound up in the embargo' (Lee, Interview with author, 2017). And while they finally received authorisation for the trials, in general US citizens, and populations in other advanced capitalist countries, are denied access to the lifesaving and life-improving medicines produced by Cuba's world-leading biopharma sector (Yaffe 2020).

5   Republican? Democrat? Two Sides of the Same Coin

Given the comprehensive regime of sanctions already established, new laws have hardly been required since 2000, although 13 new Bills have been proposed by Cuban American politicians between 2013 and 2018 (Domínguez López and Barrera Rodríguez 2020). However, the implementation of sanctions, and associated fines by OFAC continued to increase post-2000. From January 2001–January 2020, US sanctions legislation was applied 121 times against Cuba, according to research by Cuban scholars Ernesto Domínguez López and Seida Barrera Rodríguez. Their analysis demonstrates how these were used as a political tool to mobilise, award or compensate key electoral sectors (that is, the Cuban exile community which has huge political leverage in Florida, a decisive State in the US presidential race); sanctions were applied more frequently in electoral and post-electoral years (Domínguez López and Barrera Rodríguez 2020, 184). Under President George W Bush's administration from 2001, 38 sanctions were imposed in eight years, a rate of 4.75 per year. This rose to 51 during Obama's eight years from 2009, with 6.38 per year, and 32 in Trump's first three years, from 2017 to 2019, soaring to 10.67% per year (*ibid.*, 186). Most of these sanctions were what Domínguez López and Seida Rodríguez define as 'continuing' (ongoing) sanctions, for which legislation is introduced to revive existing sanctions. For example, third parties are prohibited from selling to Cuba equipment in which there are a proportion of US components; this proportion has fluctuated between 10% and 25%. The cap on remittances permitted by Cuban Americans has also fluctuated. The authors also identify the measures introduced to increase the 'flexibility', or reduce the reach, of sanctions: 11 under Bush; 42 under Obama (most in 2015 and 2016 following 'rapprochement') and 5 in Trump's first three years (*ibid.*, 184).

Meanwhile, since the 2000s there has been a renewed political onslaught to reinforce the pressure for regime change articulated in the Torricelli and Helms-Burton Acts. Sophisticated and multifaceted 'regime change' programmes were developed, from Clinton's 'People to People' programmes, to Bush's Plan for a Free Cuba, and Obama's 'civil society engagement' (Kornbluh and LeoGrande 2015). President Bush established a Commission for Assistance to a Free Cuba, 'to explore ways we can help hasten and ease Cuba's democratic transition.' (Powell 2004). The Commission's first report was published in May 2004 with over 450 pages of demonizing propaganda, plans for destabilisation, regime change and a tightly US-controlled transition to a 'democratic' capitalist Cuba. This required dismantling the socialist state apparatus, reorganising the economy and education system, and introducing multiparty elections from which Cuban communists and officials would be excluded.[6] The report's flagrant violations of national sovereignty and international law sparked outrage, not least from within Cuba. The Commission's second report, published

---

6   The report recommended drawing on the experience of transitions to capitalism in Poland, Hungary and the Czech Republic, and targeting Cuban youth. 'The program could draw on youth organizations in Central and Eastern Europe, especially in Poland, the Czech Republic, Albania, Serbia, and others, to travel to Cuba to organize and conduct training, develop informational materials, and conduct other outreach. Many of these groups have been successfully involved in similar efforts in other countries and have expressed a commitment to doing the same in Cuba'. *Commission for Assistance*, 23.

in July 2006, recommended $80 million be channelled into US programmes over the next two years to boost Cuban 'civil society' and plan for a post-Castro transition to capitalism, then $20m to be spent annually 'until the dictatorship ceases to exist' (Commission for Assistance 2006).[7] The report contained a 'secret annexe' classified for security reasons. Former President of Cuba's National Assembly, Ricardo Alarcón asked reporters: 'What on earth could the secret part say when the public part violates all kinds of international law?' (cited in Goldenberg 2006).

Over several decades, Alarcón led the Cuban side in official and backchannel talks with the United States.[8] This history has been detailed by US scholars William LeoGrande and Peter Kornbluh, who note that progress was scant while both sides imposed conditions (Kornbluh and LeoGrande 2015). The Cubans asserted that the US blockade must be lifted for Cuba and the United States to negotiate as equals. The United States placed preconditions just to talk about broader relations. 'I don't remember them ever saying "if you do this, we will lift the embargo",' explained Alarcón (Interview with author, 2016). Only once both sides dropped preconditions could the restoration of diplomatic relations finally take place under President Barack Obama's second term. Even then, Obama made clear that the objective of US policy had not changed, only the means to achieve it (Obama 2014).

6   Obama's Rapprochement: A Castle Made of Sand

In December 2014, the Presidents of the United States and Cuba simultaneously announced that, following 18 months of secret talks, they had agreed to a rapprochement. Subsequently diplomatic relations were restored and embassies opened; the US removed Cuba from its list of states supporting terrorism; the Havana Club rum label was finally registered in the United States, resolving a 20-year-long ownership dispute instigated by the Bacardi Corporation; coastguard cooperation issues were resolved; postal services and regular flights were

---

7   That level of annual expenditure in regime change programmes, euphemistically called 'pro-democracy' programmes has been maintained since then. In 2016, US journalist Tracey Eaton revealed that US government institutions had spent around $1 billion on such programmes in the previous 20 years (Eaton 2016).
8   Ricardo Alarcón was Cuba's Permanent Representative to the United Nations in New York, Minister of Foreign Relations and President of the National Assembly.

restored with restrictions on US citizens' travel to Cuba eased, although visits still required a license. High profile prisoner releases took place. Obama eliminated the 'wet foot, dry foot' policy, which encouraged illegal and dangerous emigration from Cuba. However, commercial and economic progress was minimal and financial restrictions remained. Obama used his executive powers to grant licences to selected US companies to operate in Cuba: six telecoms, four cruises, one hotel, eight airlines and two small banks. While the Helms-Burton Act codified the US blockade in law, Cuban officials claim that Obama could have done more to dismantle sanctions through decisive use of executive powers. Obama continued extend the Trading With the Enemy Act against Cuba. And while he issued regulations authorising financial institutions to provide Cuba with finance and credit, as long as Cuba remains on the list of countries under US sanctions, US and international banks remained too terrified of fines being imposed to try this. And with good reason, given his record-breaking sanctions list. Effectively, Cuba still could not use the dollar in the international economy, nor make deposits in international banks. Cuban goods still could not be exported to the United States.[9]

7   Trump Tightens the US Blockade

From 2017, the new President Donald Trump's administration ratcheted up hostility towards Cuba, with rhetoric reminiscent of the Cold War and an injurious tightening of the US blockade, particularly from autumn 2018. In spring 2019, Trump threatened to impose a 'full embargo' on Cuba unless it withdrew support to the Maduro government in Venezuela. Asked about this threat by US TV network MSNBC, Carlos Fernández de Cossío, Cuba's General Director of US Affairs pointed out: 'There is already a practically total embargo of Cuba. We've had it for over 60 years and it's been rejected, condemned by the UN almost unanimously for many years. What else can he do?' He was soon to find out as the Trump administration extended US sanctions to unprecedented levels, including threatening to fine shipping companies transporting Venezuelan oil to Cuba. This effectively generated a new energy crisis that briefly halted public transport and devastated agricultural production, as there was little fuel for tractors, replicating the severe economic crisis of the 1990s (Belly of the Beast 2020). The cost of finding unplanned,

---

9   The one exception was a shipment of 40 tons of artisanal charcoal produced by Cuban cooperative farms and imported in January 2017 by Scott Gilbert, the attorney who represented US government contractor Alan Gross, released from prison in Cuba in 2014.

unbudgeted replacement sources put terrible strain on the already weakened Cuban economy. The scenario was repeated in most sectors. Director of Cuba's Neuroscience Centre, Mitchell Valdes Sosa explained the revenues from Cuban medical products abroad, which are needed for investments into the island's healthcare sector, are obstructed because 'we cannot use the normal bank channels which are continuously blocked to us as part of the US persecution, that is trying to starve us into submission' (Interview with author, September 23, 2020).

In April 2019, on the 58th anniversary of the Bay of Pigs invasion in 1961, the Trump administration announced that Title III of the Helms-Burton Act would be enacted after 23 years of suspension; that 'U-turn financial transactions' (which Cuba's uses to circumvent sanctions and access hard currency and the US banking system) would be blocked; that non-family travel to the island would be limited; that remittances would be severely capped; and that visa restrictions would be enforced on foreigners 'trafficking in confiscated properties'. US Treasury Secretary, Steven Mnuchin declared: 'Treasury is denying Cuba access to hard currency, and we are curbing the Cuban government's bad behavior while continuing to support the long-suffering people of Cuba.' (US Department of Treasury 2019) The Monroe Doctrine, which stakes the United States claim to exclusive domination over the Americas against rival European powers, was declared alive and well (Newman 2019). The Trump administration introduced 242 new actions, sanctions and measures against Cuba and, in act of vindictiveness, returned Cuba to the list of state sponsors of terrorism just days before it ended.

8   Sanctions in a Time of Pandemic

The food, fuel, and medicine shortages suffered by Cubans because of US sanctions have been compounded by the pandemic since March 2020, which forced Cuba to close its borders, leading to a 75% fall in tourism, contributing towards an 11% fall in GDP in 2020. As the United Nations and other international bodies called for an end to sanctions that reduced the capacity for nations to respond effectively to the global health crisis, the Trump administration imposed more than 50 measures, actions, and sanctions. Unlike most countries, Cuba has no lender of last resort and no emergency funding to help it through crises. Rising at dawn to join queues for basic goods has become part of the daily grind for Cubans. Whilst dealing with the scarcity of resources and the huge mobilisation behind its regionally outstanding effort to control

COVID-19 at home, within a year Cuba had sent 57 brigades of medical specialists in disease control and disaster response to treat 1.26 million COVID-19 patients in 40 countries around the world, including in Europe.[10] To US imperialism, Cuba continued to represent the threat of a good example in international solidarity.

The Cuban healthcare system and biopharma sectors are admired globally; but less well known are the obstacles they face from US sanctions. Valdes Sosa provides examples: Cuba bought Phillips CT scanners for their hospitals, but the manufacturers would not sell them spare parts because they had US components. Cuba's biotech system used a chromatographical system purchased from a Swedish company, LKB which 'overnight' was bought out by a US company that refused to sell Cuba inputs for the system. 'Immediately we had to change all the systems in the country', he explains. A similar situation occurred during the pandemic, this time with the ventilators, which were urgently needed, for intensive care units. Cuba's previous supplier, Swiss companies, IMTMedical and Acutronic were bought out by US company Vyaire Medical which immediately cut sales to Cuba, even of spare parts for their existing machines (Valdes Sosa, interview with the author, 2020).

US sanctions and high international prices meant Cuba struggled to import PCR tests and PPE. Even donations were obstructed. Chinese billionaire, Jack Ma, co-founder of Alibaba Group, donated medical materials to Latin America, including Cuba, but the US airline transporting it could not land in Cuba to unload the cargo. Despite these obstacles, by April 2021, Cuba had five COVID-19 vaccines under clinical trials with two being rolled out nationally—the only country in the Americas, outside the United States, in that position. Cuba has made clear that these vaccines will be made available to the global south, bringing hope to millions. And yet the island is struggling to access cheap, and globally available syringes and equipment required for mass vaccinations, as well as US-manufactured reagents for their drugs. Crowdfunding pages set up by Cubans and solidarity activists overseas to support Cuba's efforts have been immediately closed—again due to US sanctions (Cubanos en UK 2021).

---

10   This act of solidarity was consistent with Cuba's astonishing record of medical internationalism. Prior to 2020, 400,000 Cuban medical professionals had already served overseas in 164 countries since 1960, providing healthcare that is free at the point of delivery. See Yaffe, chapter 5 'Cuban Medical Internationalism: An Army of Whitecoats' in *We Are Cuba!*

9   The Financial Cost of the Blockade to Cuba

In 2019, 88% of international transactions involved US dollars. The Wall Street Journal noted, 'That gives the US extraordinary power over nearly anyone who imports or exports anything anywhere' (Wall Street Journal 2020). US sanctions prohibit Cuba from using the US dollar in international trade or transactions through the international financial system. The island is obliged to purchase goods from third parties, or from far away, significantly increasing costs. While the Socialist bloc provided an alternative source of trade and investment for Cuba, between 1960 and 1990, the blockade was estimated to have cost Cuba (USD) $30 billion, or $1 billion annually. This rose to $3 billion annually between 1990 and 1995 (equivalent to over 20% of GDP in 1993) and rising again after the Helms Burton Act came into force (Rodriguez 2013). By 2018, the National Association of Cuban Economists calculated the cost at $4.4 billion annually, equivalent to $12 million every day. In the 12 months from April 2019 to March 2020, as a consequence of the Trump sanctions, the cost soared to $5 billion. In 2020, Cuba's report to the United Nations put the total cost of the US blockade at $144 billion dollars over six decades. In mid-April 2021, in his final speech from a leadership position in Cuba, Raul Castro told the 8th Congress of the Cuban Communist Party that this 'financial persecution achieved the characteristics of a veritable witch hunt against Cuban transactions, damaging our capacity to pay for imported products and services' (Castro 2021).

10   The Human Cost of Sanctions

Reports by international bodies, particularly since the 1990s have documented the high cost in terms of human suffering, as do the Cuban government's annual reports to the United Nations.[11] These reports note that the United States' unilateral sanctions are a violation of international treaties and conventions because of both their effect on the population and their extraterritorial character. The blockade violates the Universal Declaration of Human Rights and

---

11   For example, American Association for World Health (AAWH), *Denial of Food and Medicine: The Impact of the US Embargo on Health and Nutrition in Cuba*, 1997; *Cuba: Social Policy at the Crossroads: Maintaining Priorities, Transforming Practice,* An Oxfam America Report, 2002; and Amnesty International, *US Embargo against Cuba.*

the UN's treaty on International Covenant on Economic, Social and Cultural Rights (ICESCR), which the United States has signed, but not ratified (Amnesty International 2009).

US/UK sanctions on Iraq in the 1990s were estimated to have killed 1.5 million civilians: an average of 150 children every day. Cuba has protected its population for this level of devastation. In 1997, the American Association for World Health (AAH) reported how, while the US blockade of Cuba contributed to malnutrition, poor water quality, lack of access to medicines and medical supplies, 'a humanitarian catastrophe has been averted only because the Cuban government has maintained a high level of budgetary support for a health care system designed to deliver primary and preventative medicine to all its citizens' (AAH 1997). In other words, the socialist state has mobilised scarce resources and directed production and distribution, which it controls through the centrally planned economy, to prioritise the welfare of the population. The situation is different in Venezuela, another of the 30 countries worldwide under US sanctions. Although Venezuela has an extensive state welfare system, much of the economy remains in private hands, which weakens the government's capacity to protect the population. Between 2014 and 2020, US sanctions on Venezuela were estimated to have caused the death of 100,000 people, as imports of key medicines and healthcare equipment were blocked and had cost the country $120 billion. 'Ecuador would not survive for five months with the blockade [of Cuba]', acknowledged then-President of Ecuador, Rafael Correa in 2009 (Interview with author, 2009). How Cuba has survived should be examined and respected.

11   Sanctions under Biden?

That US President Biden had been Vice President to Obama during rapprochement gave hope to many that he would alleviate sanctions. By late-April 2021, the Biden administration had done nothing about Cuba beyond announcing that doing so was not a priority. Following the violent protests which took place in Cuba on 11 July 2021, the first such protests in 27 years, headed new sanctions on Cuba and gave instructions for further measures to be taken. US Attorney Robert L. Muse, an expert on US laws relating to Cuba, claims that 'the US President has the constitutional power to unilaterally terminate the embargo on Cuba', based upon the constitutional primacy of the president's office in managing US foreign relations (Muse 2020). Doing so, however, will require loosening the stranglehold of the right-wing Cuban exile community over US Cuba policy. There is new political movement among

Cuban Americas, mobilising alongside solidarity activists, who call on Biden to alleviate the suffering of their Cuban families on the island by eliminating sanctions. While they wait, however, Cubans continue to suffer from those measures.

The Cuban government describes the US blockade as 'genocidal'. For that claim to hold, according to Nigel White, 'it would be necessary to prove that the US government, or its leaders, had the intent to destroy, in whole or in part, the Cuban people' (White 2019, p. 177). Mallory's memorandum clearly stated the aim of economic aggression as generating 'hunger, desperation and overthrow of government'. The legal mechanisms, the sanctions regime, set up to achieve that remain in place. They are one instrument in the US toolkit to achieve regime change on the island. There has been little evidence that the objective of US policy towards Cuba has changed since then.

References

American Association for World Health. (1997). *Denial of Food and Medicine. The Impact of the U.S. Embargo on Health and Nutrition in Cuba.*Washington: AAWH.

Amnesty International. (2009). *The US Embargo against Cuba: Its impact on economic and social Rights.* https://www.amnesty.org/download/Documents/44000/amr 250072009en.pdf.

Belly of the Beast Cuba. (2020). *The War on Cuba*, 3 episodes, October.

Bureau of Industry and Security, US Department of Commerce. (n.d.). *Cuba.* https:// bis.doc.gov/index.php/policy-guidance/country-guidance/sanctioned-destinati ons/cuba.

Castro, Fidel. (1961). "Discurso pronunciado en las honras fúnebres de las víctimas del bombardeo a distintos puntos de la república, efectuado en 23 y 12, frente al cementerio de Colón." 16 April.

Castro, Raúl. (2021). "Informe Central al 8vo. Congreso del Partido Comunista de Cuba." *Granma* online, 16 April. http://www.granma.cu/octavo-congreso-pcc/2021-04-17/info rme-central-al-8vo-congreso-del-partido-comunista-de-cuba-17-04-2021-05-04-12.

Cubanos en UK. (2021). *Bloquear ayuda humanitaria a Cuba es criminal y vergonzoso,* 16 February. https://cubanos.org.uk/noticias/481-bloquear-ayuda-humanitaria-a -cuba-es-criminal-y-vergonzoso.

Davalos Fernandez, Rodolfo. (2012). *¿Embargo o bloqueo? La instrumentación de un crimen contra Cuba.* La Habana: Editorial Capitán San Luis.

Domínguez López, Ernesto, and Barrera Rodríguez, Seida. (2020). "La Conformación de la política de Estados Unidos hacia Cuba." *Estudios del Desarrollo Social: Cuba y América Latina* 8.

Eaton, Tracey. (2016). "Democracy Spending Down, but Controversy Remains." *Along the Malecon,* 01 October. https://alongthemalecon.blogspot.co.uk/2016/10/democr acy-spending-down-but-controversy.html.

Foreign Assistance Act of 1961. (1961). 4 September, 219. https://www.foreign.senate .gov/imo/media/doc/Foreign%20Assistance%20Act%20Of%201961.pdf.

Franklin, Jane. (1994). "The Politics behind Clinton's Cuba policy." *The Baltimore Sun,* 30 August.

Franklin, Jane. (1997). *Cuba and the United States: A chronological History.* Ocean Press.

Goldenberg, Suzanne. (2006). "US has $80m plan for Cuba after Castro." *The Guardian,* 4 July.

Gordon, Joy. (2016). "Economic Sanctions as 'Negative Development': The Case of Cuba." *Journal of International Development* 28 (4): 473–484.

H.R.927—*Cuban Liberty and Democratic Solidarity (LIBERTAD) Act.* (1996). https:// www.congress.gov/104/plaws/publ14/PLAW-104publ14.pdf.

H.R.5323—*Cuban Democracy Act.* (1992). https://www.congress.gov/bill/102nd-congr ess/house-bill/5323/text.

Kornbluh Peter, and LeoGrande, William M. (2015). *Back Channel to Cuba: The Hidden History of Negotiations Between Washington and Havana.* University of North Carolina Press.

Mallory, Lestor. (1960). *Memorandum From the Deputy Assistant Secretary of State for Inter-American Affairs (Mallory) to the Assistant Secretary of State for Inter-American Affairs (Rubottom),* 6 April. https://history.state.gov/historicaldocuments/frus1958 -60v06/d499.

Ministerio de Relaciones Exterior. (2018). "Republica de Cuba." *Cuba Vs Bloqueo: Informe de Cuba.*

Muse, Robert L. (2020). "The US President has the constitutional power to unilaterally terminate the embargo on Cuba." *Global Americans,* 8 October.

Newman, Lucia. (2019). "Trump revives Monroe Doctrine as warning to China and Russia." *Al Jazeera,* 19 June.

Obama, Barack. (2014). *Statement by the President on Cuba Policy Changes.* The White House Office of the Press Secretary, 17 December.

Powell, Collin L. (2004). "Foreword." *Commission for Assistance to a Free Cuba, Report to the President,* May. https://pdf.usaid.gov/pdf_docs/Pcaab192.pdf.

Rice, Condaleeza. (2006). *Commission for Assistance, Report to the President.* July 2006.

Rodríguez, José Luis. (2013). "Fifty Years of Revolution in the Cuban Economy." In Campbell, A. (ed.), *Cuban Economists on the Cuban Economy.* University of Florida Press: Gainsville.

Roy, Joaquin. (1997). "The Helms-Burton Law: Development, Consequences, and Legacy for Inter-American and European-US Relations." *Journal of Interamerican Studies and World Affairs* 39 (3).

Smis, Stefan and Kim van der Borght. (1997). "The EU-US compromise on the Helms-Burton and D'Amato Acts." *The American Journal of International Law* 93 (1): 227–236.

United Nations. *Declaration on the Granting of Independence to Colonial Countries and Peoples*. General Assembly resolution 1514 (XV). (1960). 14 December. www.ohchr.org/EN/ProfessionalInterest/Pages/Independence.aspx.

US Department of the Treasury. (2019). "Treasury Issues Changes to Strengthen Cuba Sanctions Rules," 6 September. https://home.treasury.gov/news/press-releases/sm770.

Valdés, Orlando. (2003). *Historia de la Reforma Agraria en Cuba*. La Habana: Ciencias Sociales.

The Wall Street Journal. (2020). "How Global Trade Runs on US dollars." 22 January. https://www.youtube.com/watch?v=jsDwMGH5E8U.

White, Nigel. (2019). "Ending the US Embargo of Cuba: International Law in Dispute." *Journal of Latin American Studies*: 163–186.

Yaffe, Helen. (2020). *We are Cuba! How a Revolutionary People Have Survived in a Post-Soviet World*. Yale University Press.

CHAPTER 9

The Western Frontier: US Sanctions against North Korea and China

Tim Beal

Sanctions are a mode of waging war, and war has causes as well as consequences. To understand US sanctions against North Korea and China we must put them in a context which embraces current geopolitics, including other types of coercion, and which is cognizant of its historical roots. The starting point is a very brief overview of the history of America's journey to its present confrontation in East Asia. This survey is necessarily brief; a fuller version can be found at (Beal, this volume).

1 Manifest Destiny and the Three Phases of US Imperialism in East Asia

The Manifest Destiny of the United States has propelled its domain over the continent, and across the Pacific picking up acquisitions along the way and transforming the ocean into an American lake. However, on the western shores of the Pacific lie the great powers of Japan, China, and Russia. Japan was defeated in 1945 and turned into a state that is both a client and a deputy. Russia and China remain independent and a challenge to American power with China threatening to deprive it of its hegemony. In between is the Korean peninsula, one half under American domination, with an American general in charge of its military, while the northern half remains independent and although battered by 70 years of sanctions and hostility, resilient and defiant.

This is the Western Frontier of the American empire. The establishment and its maintenance for both protection and expansion can be divided into three phases.

1.1 The First Phase: Competing with Japan over China

As part of its western expansion, a 'territorial aggrandizement that has few parallels' (Mearsheimer 2014) in the 19th and first half of the 20th century the United States competed with other imperialist powers, but mainly with Japan for supremacy in East Asia with China being the main prize. Two events from this phase are particularly salient.

The first was the Open Door Policy towards China enunciated by Secretary of State John Hay in 1899 (Hay 1899).This opposed the old imperialist concept of 'spheres of influence' and called instead for equal treatment for all countries in the China market, and 'respect for China's administrative and territorial integrity'. The logic behind this was clear. The US would use 'America's most potent weapon, economic supremacy' to dominate the China market and its burgeoning policy power to secure that 'informal empire' (McCormick 1967). Hay was confident that America would not only penetrate the Chinese market but also fend off any foreign competitors. 120 years later the US struggles against competition from China itself and has been turning to the old imperialist tools, including sanctions, to counter it. The main challenge to the US during this period came from the other rising imperialist power, Japan. Initially they made a deal between themselves. Under the Taft-Katsura Memorandum of 1905 it was agreed that the United States would get the Philippines and Japan, Korea. This facilitated Japan's colonialist push into mainland Asia (it had already taken Taiwan from China in 1895), initially Korea, followed by Manchuria then, in 1937 an attempt on the rest of China. This was intolerable to the US and, with Britain it imposed an embargo 'that threatened to starve the Japanese war machine' and led to the attack on Pearl Harbor (Goldman 2012).

1.2   *The Second Phase: The Road to the Korean War*

With the surrender of Japan, the United States was clearly the paramount power in East Asia, but it faced two major interrelated challenges, one from the Soviet Union and the other from anti-colonialism. The US used two instruments against the Soviet Union. The atomic bombings were not so much to defeat Japan, which was on the verge of surrender, but to send a warning to Moscow (Alperovitz 1995). Then it divided Korea to create a buffer to protect Japan, an act which would have great unforeseen consequences. Anti-colonialism was a more intangible problem. The US had a history of supporting anti-colonialism and in a sense Hay's Open Door Policy could be seen as part of that. But anti-colonialism in East Asia was generally led by Communists or other leftists, so when a choice had to be made, the US chose colonialism.

This was also the case in Korea where the opposition to the Japanese was led by leftists of various persuasions who set up a Korean People's Republic— a polyglot assemblage of communists, anarchists, trade unionists, Christian socialists, and social democrats'—in Seoul in September 1945 (Chang 2020). The solution was to spurn Korean anti-colonialism and bring in Syngman Rhee from the US where he had mainly lived since 1913. Lacking both popular support and a political movement Rhee turned to the repressive state apparatus left behind by the Japanese. This dependence on the legacy of Japanese colonialism, and particularly the generals which led his army set the stage for the Korean War, whose outbreak sometime became virtually inevitable (Cumings 2010). There is much controversary over which side precipitated the actual fighting; the simple answer is both (Gupta 1972). The real answer is that the question is essentially irrelevant.

The Korean War devastated the peninsula, killing millions of people. It had huge economic and political consequences. It was the first war that the US had not won. It ended in an armistice—a suspension of fighting but not of the conflict itself. If kinetic war was no longer possible the US turned to other forms to pursue its objectives including, not least, sanctions.

1.3   *The Third Phase: Continuing with War with Sanctions*

Although the US initiated sanctions against China and North Korea at roughly the same time the two programs have followed very different trajectories. The main reason for this is their very differing size. China is big, important and cannot be ignored, although the US did that for nearly 25 years. North Korea is small and poses neither substantial danger nor opportunity. It can only retaliate *in extremis*—the nuclear deterrent—and it has no value as a pawn against others.

These huge differences between the two sanctions programs have usually led them to be treated separately. That is a mistake because they are, in fact, two theatres in the same war. Korea is important mainly because of its location, where the US meets Japan, Soviet Union/Russia and China (Beal 2019). The peninsula was divided because of its strategic location. China is both a major reason for sanctions against North Korea and the key to their implementation. China has long been the focus of US foreign policy in Asia and now it dominates the global horizon. The linkages between the two should not be overlooked; the overarching theme is US imperialism which is an international enterprise for whom actions in one country have ramifications in the rest.

2   Sanctions against China

Sanctions against China can be broken into three periods, The first, from the establishment of the People's Republic (PRC) in 1949 until the 1970s, with the 'China card'. Then there was a period of quietude until fears about the rise of China led to Obama's 'Pivot to Asia' in 2011. Since then, there has been heightened confrontation and an increasing recourse to sanctions. But now China can retaliate to an increasing extent, which adds a new dimension to US sanctions, which hitherto had usually been risk-free.

2.1   The Embargo, 1949–1970

The US responded to the establishment of the PRC in October 1949 by imposing selective trade controls and these were extended in March 1950 to be coextensive with those against the Soviet Union. On the outbreak of the Korean War on 25 June 1950 the controls were expanded and by December all exports required a license, all imports were banned and Chinese assets in the United States seized. The basic objective was to slow economic growth and hopefully precipitate an economic crisis which would lead to the downfall of the regime—destabilization for regime change (Hufbauer *et al.* 2007a).

Curiously, there seems to have been little or no resistance within the American business community to the embargo. As time passed there was some relaxation of the embargo but what really rang the death knell for it was the belated realization of two things—the PRC was not going to collapse and the Sino-Soviet split offered opportunity. This led to Kissinger playing the 'China card', doing a deal with Beijing that enabled Washington to utilize it against Moscow. However, flowering of the economic relationship depended on the establishment of diplomatic relations (Eckstein 1975), which involved the thorny question of Taiwan. The Carter administration took the plunge and relations were established on 15 December 1978 despite vociferous domestic opposition. In 1979 Deng Xiaoping visited the US to cement relations. His visit was 'extremely successful as he charismatically wooed Congress, the media, and the American people. Journalists depicted the Chinese leader as personable, famously photographing 'him at a rodeo wearing a ten-gallon hat' (State Department Historian 2016). Deng was feted and was given the message: 'Help us against the Soviet Union, continue along the capitalist road, play by our rules and you can join the club'. His successors were to find out that this promise of accepting China's 'peaceful rise' came with conditions. The embargo had exacerbated Sino-Soviet relations because it forced China into an unnaturally high level of trade with the Soviet Union (Zhang 2001). Some argue that It was 'completely ineffective' in curtailing China's economic growth (Chen 2006). This is unpersuasive given the immense growth in China's foreign trade in following decades, and the high economic growth rates that facilitated.

2.2   China Card Rapprochement, 1970–2011

The embargo was lifted and for the next 40 years general sanctions against China faded from sight. There were controls on exports deemed to have military or technological significance, and after events such as the Tiananmen

Incident of 1989 limited sanctions were imposed and soon lifted (Rogin 2020). Sporadic sanctions were imposed as a result of the vagaries of US domestic politics and lobbying but the overall tenor was trade promotion rather than hindrance. The conventional wisdom in Washington was that trade and access to the US-dominated world would transform China and make it obedient and malleable. Membership of the club would have a civilizing influence on the Chinese who would come to acknowledge the superiority of American ways and the necessity of American leadership. They would not, of course, be admitted to the executive committee of the club but they would realize that was for the best.

After the establishment of diplomatic relations bilateral trade and investment grew substantially and by 2017, the last year for which data is available, the US exported US\$130 billion (8.4% of total exports) to China and imported US\$506 billion (21.6%), giving a bilateral trade deficit of US\$375 billion (2021b). 'Offshoring'—the manufacturing of goods in China by US companies to some extent offset this but it caused unemployment and contributed to Trump's 2016 victory. The rapprochement carried within it the seeds of its own discontent; China was just too successful. The trade balance and unemployment were not the only issues but they were perhaps the most visible.

2.3   *Heightened Geopolitical and Economic Confrontation, 2011–*
The unstated conditions in the promise given to Deng Xiaoping became increasingly evident by the time of Obama's 'pivot to Asia'. A modest military capacity against the Soviet Union/Russia was welcome but full modernization to protect China's borders, as in the South China Sea, was not. China was to respect US global hegemony. It was to remain low in the international value chain, utilizing cheap labor to manufacture cheap goods for Walmart but not challenge America's position at the top end. The US was to remain the place where the knowledge for tomorrow was created. Where it could China tended to accept these rules. For instance. it supported US moves in the UNSC to condemn and sanction North Korea, though that was against its own strategic interests. However, in other areas there was a degree of automaticity. The South China Sea is a chokepoint for much of China's maritime trade and has to be defended. China's modernization is on autopilot and the government in Beijing cannot turn it off just to mollify Washington. Even if China does not exert its growing strength its very existence is a problem; US sanctions against third countries, for instance, are losing their effectiveness because China offers 'an alternative to U.S. financial and economic dominance' (Harrell and Rosenberg 2019)

The American response has varied but there are two constants. US hegemony must be protected; the idea of sharing power in a truly multipower world and to accept the equal sovereignty of all nations as specified in the UN Charter is intolerable. The deep-seated domestic reforms that might help it weather these storms are off the agenda, so that leaves sanctions and similar actions against China and other challengers.

So far this is a familiar story. Sanctions have become the key component of American foreign policy and it has used them with enthusiasm and impunity. But with the rise of China and its concomitant growth in confidence and assertiveness we are entering a new phase in history, a historical transformation of the global architecture of power. The familiar narrative is fracturing. The American practice of imposing sanctions is very formalistic and usually entails a legal document issued by Treasury reflecting an assumption of extraterritoriality (2021a). The Chinese way is much more fluid and circumspect. What are effectively sanctions are portrayed in other terms, such as taking action against the violation of WTO regulations (Cutler and Green 2020). In respect of the US it has, so far, tended to threaten sanctions rather than impose them. However, in countering Trump's trade war it has imposed retaliatory tariffs (Chandran 2018) and it has started targeted sanctions against American politicians particularly vociferous in what it sees as interfering in its internal affairs (Dou and Fifield 2020).

Interfering in China's internal affairs is seen as crossing a red line. It was non-interference that was at the heart of China's retaliatory sanctions against Australia in 2020. Interestingly China took strong action against Australia because it was seen as a proxy for the US. The sanctions were a warning to Canberra but ultimately to Washington. The Australian government called in April 2020 for an 'independent inquiry' into China's handling of the coronavirus pandemic (Worthington 2020). By 'independent' it meant independent of the World Health Organization, but guided by the US. It was clearly meant to buttress attempts by Trump to divert attention from his mishandling of the pandemic by blaming China. The Scott Morrison government was also extremely critical of Chinese policies in Hong Kong and Xinjiang. Why the Australian government embraced the role of 'attack dog' for the Trump administration is a mystery since there was little to be gained and so much to lose. The likeliest explanation is that it was a short-sighted domestic political ploy to divert attention from the government's failures, of which the bushfires were the most obvious example and also to tap into the deep historical fear of the 'Yellow Peril' amongst large swathes of the Australian electorate(Kevin 2020).

The Chinese economic response was calibrated to serve as a warning to Australia (and the US) about interference in Chinese internal affairs while allowing it to step back and avoid further damage. A report in September 2020 on Chinese 'economic coercion' found that the effect of Chinese sanctions had been minimal and 'The PRC could inflict far worse trade punishment on Australia than it has done to date' (Laurenceson, Pantle, and Zhou 2020). In November China imposed tariffs of up to 212% on Australian wines as part of an investigation in dumping in violation of WTO regulations (Toh 2020). The dumping charges were probably justified but it was also clear that this was part of the retaliatory sanctions program (Butler 2020). Some suggested that Australia and other countries which sacrificed themselves should be supported by the US government establishing 'a special purpose vehicle to buy and hold foreign commodities that lose sales thanks to aggressive Chinese trade action' (Jiang and Schneider 2020). What is clear is that the Chinese will increasingly use sanctions as retaliatory warnings against countries which either collaborate with the US in actions which endanger it, as with THAAD in South Korea, or gratuitously interfere in China's internal affairs, such as Australia. Whether it will eventually go beyond that and use sanctions as an aggressive instrument of coercion on the American model is uncertain.

3   Sanctions against North Korea

Sanctions against North Korea are a rather simpler matter. It does not have the size and importance of China so the sorts of deals that Washington made with Beijing, particularly the 'China card', are not necessary. Concessions are not necessary and so are not given. However, the situation is more complex than commonly realized. The US divided the Korean peninsula in 1945, as we have seen, to protect its new acquisition of Japan from the Soviet Union and to provide a forward military position on the Asian mainland. That overriding geopolitical objective remains the basis of US strategy in the region to this day, though China has long supplanted Russia. Korea then was of no interest in its own right; it was really a matter of location but over time Korea grew in importance. The Korean War was a catalyst for this transformation and Korea became key component of the Cold War. South Korea is now a major economy and a very formidable adjunct to US military power against China. Although North Korea was for decades more successful economically than the South the collapse of the Soviet Union and the continuation of US sanctions put paid to that. However North Korea has proved to be surprisingly resilient politically, economically and militarily and that has been a source of frustration. The US response to this situation has been to mythologize a North Korean threat bordering on the bizarre (Reich 2016). North Korea, we are frequently told, is the major threat facing the US, though at times it has to compete with Islamic fundamentalism, Russia or China. It is 'perhaps the most dangerous country in the world today' (Gelb 1991), 'North Korea could kill 90 percent of Americans' (Woolsey and Pry 2017), it is an 'existential threat' (Reich 2016) and it 'is world's most worrisome nuclear threat' (Landler 2016). Although by any conceivable military metric such claims are preposterous the continual assertion by authoritative figures not surprisingly has been accepted by the American public (Smeltz *et al.* 2018). It is reported that Defense Secretary Jim Mattis used to sleep in his gym clothes in 2017 in case Kim Jong Un launched a nuclear missile at the US. Why Kim would do something with no conceivable purpose but which would be suicidal for his nation and him personally no-one thought necessary to ask (Woodward and Kelly 2020). The myth has become so embedded in US consciousness, both at elite and popular level, that it has become an item of religious faith, beyond reason. North Korea's nuclear program only makes sense as a deterrent and has no possible function as an offensive capability (Beal 2017).

The imagined threat provides a rationale for sanctions, but it also inserts conflicting objectives into the strategy. This 'threat' also serves to justify the US military presence in South Korea and Japan. It helps underpin the forward military presence from Guam westwards, which forms the northern flank of the containment of China. However, if the sanctions 'work' in some way and remove the threat, then what happens to the justification for the forward presence? Dropping the pretense of North Korea and just focusing on China might be acceptable in Tokyo which has its own history of confronting China, but would be more troublesome in Seoul. These conflicting objectives—to remove the threat but also preserve it—are basically the reason why American presidential attempts to negotiate with North Korea always run into the sand. Despite the rhetoric the best situation for the Pentagon is a continuation of the status quo—a horror-movie illusion of danger fueling tension.

Despite the contradictory objectives, sanctions fulfil several functions. They punish North Korea and its people for defiance, a punishment which must cause satisfaction in some quarters. They provide a post-facto justification for US policy—why would the United States, known for its good intensions and concern for human rights impose sanctions unless there was a good reason? But most important of all it forces North Korea to respond, thus fueling tension. Sanctions are an act of war which cause economic and social distress and cannot be ignored. The American people might think they are not still at war in Korea but in fact they are. When American commentors claim condescendingly that North Korea is seeking attention they are quite right, though their interpretation and proposals are perverse (Kaplan 2012). The history of sanctions against North Korea can be roughly divided into three periods.

3.1   Bilateral Sanctions, 1950–1993

President Truman imposed a total trade embargo against North Korea on 30 June 1950, just five days after the outbreak of the Korean War and this prohibition was continued despite the Armistice in 1953 (Hufbauer *et al.* 2007b). It is difficult to ascertain the direct consequences of US sanctions in this period. The North Korean economy was sheltered by its relationship with the Soviet Union, and China. However, we can surmise that the loss of potential benefit, as with China's experience of sanctions, was considerable.

Even bilateral sanctions have a wide collateral effect. For instance, companies from third countries will be unwilling to investing in factories if the output cannot be exported to America.

3.2   Entry of the UNSC, 1993–2006

In the early 1990s, after the collapse of the Soviet Union, the United States was much more able to bend the United Nations to its will, from the destruction of Yugoslavia to discriminatory treatment of North Korea. The main issue then, as now, was the nuclear program. Such programs, by their nature, have a dual nature—generating electricity but also potentially nuclear weapons. Details are contested but it seems likely that with the disappearance of Soviet protection, to be replaced by antagonism under Yeltsin anxious to please Washington, North Korea set to extend its existing rudimentary nuclear energy program into weapons production. It did not lose sight of nuclear energy and the Agreed Framework, signed with the Clinton administration in 1994 specified that US was to supply two reactors suitable for energy but not weapons grade fuel. The agreement was torn up by George W. Bush and the reactors were never completed (Carlin 2021).

In developing nuclear weapons in the early 1990s North Korea was doing what South Korea had attempted 20 years before, and for the same reason. In the 1970s Park Chung-hee faced with America's imminent defeat in Vietnam and fearing that it would withdraw from Asia, leaving South Korea to its fate, embarked on a clandestine nuclear weapons program. The Americans found out about it and forced him to close it down (Hayes and Moon 2011; Sneider 2008). The US took a much stronger line with North Korea and working through the International Atomic Energy Agency (IAEA) was able to exert a lot of pressure. The scrapping of the Agreed Framework and continued US hostility led to North Korea leaving the NPT and eventually succeeding in exploding a nuclear device in October 2006. With this the US was able to bring the UNSC into play.

3.3   UN Sanctions, 2006–

By getting the UNSC to impose sanctions the United States greatly increased the force of its own program. UNSC sanctions are mandatory for all members of the UN, although implementation has varied. The US has been able to utilize the UN to a large degree since the Korean War but 2006 marked a new stage with the imposition of sanctions. Resolution 1695 (15 July) imposed limited sanctions relating to Weapons of Mass Destruction or WMD (2006a) but it was Resolution 1718 passed on 14 October following North Korea's first nuclear test of 9 October that fully harnessed the UNSC to US policy and provided the basis for the UNSC sanctions program (2006b). This resolution established a sanctions committee—*Security Council Committee established pursuant to resolution 1718 (2006)'*—which was to administer the program (2020b). The bureaucratic apparatus was subsequently expanded with a *Panel of Experts* who monitored the implementation of the sanctions, and the measures taken by North Korea to circumvent them (2009).

The problems inherent in the UNSC actions against North Korea are evident. The US has conducted over 1000 nuclear tests without censure. The UNSC condemned the acquisition of nuclear weapons by North Korea but not their continued possession by the US. This discrimination is a clear violation of the Charter of the United Nations which holds that all nations are equal— 'the principle of the sovereign equality of all its Members' (1945). There was another, less obvious problem with Resolution 1718 and the whole UNSC program. That is the assertion that proliferation 'constitutes a threat to international peace and security'. This, of course, is what the United States and other states possessing WMD want us to believe but on examination it becomes clear that it is likely that the opposite is true. As Waltz has pointed out in respect of Iran, the possession of nuclear weapons by small, threatened states does not threaten peace but enhances it (Waltz 2012).

3.4   Effect and Efficacy of Sanctions against North Korea

One of the advantages of sanctions for the United States is that responsibility for the devastation caused can often be hidden or shifted onto the victim. There are no reliable assessments in any detail on the effects of the sanctions against North Korea. A report in 2010 claimed that up to 2005 the country had suffered losses of US$13.7 trillion from US sanctions and US$16.7 trillion from 'property losses' (2010a). Estimates of deaths during the 1990s when famine stalked the country following the collapse of the Soviet relationship vary considerably, but 300,000 seems the most dependable (2010c, 2010b). How much of this can be attributed to the US is another matter (Woo-Cumings 2002). Sanctions themselves may have had only a minor role but what the

Koreans call the US 'hostility policy' offers a better perspective because it includes the military threat which imposes a huge defense burden and the use of political power to deprive North Korea access to international bodies, investment, and markets.

We know from UN agencies that malnutrition is a continuing problem in North Korea and US hostility is surely the prime cause (Lederer 2019). Kim Jong Un in his speeches to the 8th Congress of KWP admitted that all sectors had fallen a long way short of planned targets (Choe). He identified the 'barbarous sanctions and blockade by the US and other hostile forces' as the main 'objective factor' for that, followed by natural disasters and coronavirus pandemic (2021c). The effect of sanctions, and the US hostility policy in general has undoubtedly been dire, blighting the lives of generations of North Koreans but what of 'efficacy'? If by that we mean unilateral nuclear disarmament or collapse of the state—'regime change' as the euphemism has it—then clearly US policy has not worked.

Whatever politicians and officials may claim, experts tend to be skeptical about the efficacy of 'regime change' sanctions (Cohen and Weinberg 2019). The basic reason is that the consequences of surrender, for the leadership and the country as a whole, outweigh the costs of struggling on. Libya became the emblematic example of the issues involved and their consequences. Secretary of State Condoleezza Rice assured Libyan leader Muammar Gaddafi that if he abandoned his nuclear deterrence program the United States would not attack. Secretary of State Hillary Clinton reneged on that promise (Hirsh 2006). Gaddafi was brutally killed and Libya devastated. This was widely seen as a warning about the folly of disarming in exchange for American promises (McDonald 2011) and when John Bolton wanted to derail the negotiations between Donald Trump and Kim Jong Un in 2018 the word 'Libya' never left his lips (Brunnstrom 2018).

However, efficacy must be measured against objectives and it is clear that 'regime change' is not necessarily the main one. An attack on North Korea, or precipitating its collapse through the destabilizing effects of sanctions, risked crisis and perhaps war with China. War with China is one of the options being considered but if it is judged that the time is not right, or the risks too high, then continuing the present state of tension, and stoking it when necessary without precipitating war, becomes a sensible objective. The sanctions program serves that function very well in which case the objective is realized.

4   The Conflicted Role of China

China's role in this is confusing and conflicted. It is the ultimate target of US policy towards North Korea but has sought since the 1970s to maintain the rapprochement. In the UNSC it has, like Russia, attempted to water down US proposals and then having achieved as much as it thinks it could, ended up voting with the US (DeThomas 2017). Subsequently the sanctions have been implemented with varying degrees of vigor, sending messages to both Washington and Pyongyang (Silberstein 2019). Beijing has been anxious not to provide Washington with any reason or excuse to impede its 'peaceful rise' and compromise on the Korean question must have seemed sensible. However, there are problems with this strategy which may now be coming to the end of its usefulness. The United States is being driven inexorably to take stronger measures to counter the Chinese challenge to its hegemony, and the measures taken by the Obama and Trump administrations will, in all likelihood, be continued under Biden (Baer 2020). China wants peace and stability on the Korean peninsula, but the US needs tension there to sustain its forward presence in Asia (Spetalnick *et al.* 2020). Appeasement offers no solution to these problems but instead deepens them. If pressure towards China increases under Biden, we might expect a further stiffening of Chinese resistance in Korea as elsewhere.

Mao Zedong likened the relationship to North Korea to that between 'lips and teeth'(Nanto, Manyin, and Dumbaugh 2010). Although there has been much friction over the years the metaphor continues to be valid. A North Korea not controlled by the US is vital to China's security. The Chinese economy and its intervention in case of an American attack are essential for North Korea. The reasons the US divided Korea in 1945 still hold good; when Washington looks at Pyongyang it sees Beijing. The three countries are locked together in a relationship and US sanctions policy must be seen in that context.

References

Alperovitz, Gar. (1995). "Hiroshima: Historians Reassess." *Foreign Policy* 99: 15–34.

Baer, Daniel B. (2020). "America Under Biden Won't Go Soft on China." *Foreign Policy*, 6 November.

Beal, Tim. (2017). "Hegemony and Resistance, Compellence and Deterrence: Deconstructing the North Korean 'Threat' and Identifying America's Strategic Alternatives." *Journal of Political Criticism*, December, 57–113. http://www.timbeal.net.nz/geopolitics/Beal_JPC21_Compellence.pdf.

Beal, Tim. (2019). "The Road to the Korean War, and the Path to Peace." *Korean Quarterly*, Winter.

Beal, Tim. (2021). "Korea and Imperialism." In Ness, I., and Cope, Z. (eds.), *The Palgrave Encyclopedia of Imperialism and Anti-Imperialism, 2nd Edition*. Cham, US: Palgrave Macmillan.

Brunnstrom, David. (2018). "Trump should insist on Libya-style denuclearization for N.Korea-Bolton." *Reuters*, 24 March. https://af.reuters.com/article/africaTech/idAFL1N1R5245.

Butler, Ben. (2020). "There could be more to this wine war than just another trade stoush with China." *Guardian*, 18 August. https://www.theguardian.com/australia-news/2020/aug/18/there-could-be-more-to-this-wine-war-than-just-another-trade-stoush-with-china.

Carlin, Robert. (2021). "KEDO: Long Gone, and Nearly Forgotten." *38 North*, 7 January. https://www.38north.org/2021/01/kedo-long-gone-and-nearly-forgotten/.

Chandran, Nyshka. (2018). "China responds to Trump tariffs with proposed list of 128 US products to target." *CNBC*, 22 March. https://www.cnbc.com/2018/03/22/china-responds-to-trump-tariffs-with-proposed-list-of-us-products-to-target.html.

Chang, Kornel. (2020). "Independence without Liberation: Democratization as Decolonization Management in U.S.-Occupied Korea, 1945–1948." *Journal of American History* (June): 77–106. https://academic.oup.com/jah/article-abstract/107/1/77/5862199.

Chen, Xin-zhu J. (2006). "China and the US Trade Embargo, 1950–1972." *American Journal of Chinese Studies* (October). https://www.jstor.org/stable/44288827.

Choe, Sang-hun. (2021). "Kim Jong-un Opens Party Congress With Admission of Failures in North Korea." *New York Times*, 5 January. https://www.nytimes.com/2021/01/05/world/asia/north-korea-kim-jong-un-party-congress.html.

Clinton, Hillary Rodham. (2011). "America's Pacific Century." *Foreign Policy*, November.

Cohen, David S., and Weinberg, Zoe A.Y. (2019). "Sanctions Can't Spark Regime Change." *Foreign Affairs*, 29 April. https://www.foreignaffairs.com/articles/united-states/2019-04-29/sanctions-cant-spark-regime-change.

Cumings, Bruce. (2010). *The Korean War*. New York: Modern Library.

Cutler, Wendy, and Green, James. (2020). "Collectively Calling Out China on Trade Aggression." *The Straits Times*, 24 November. https://asiasociety.org/policy-institute/collectively-calling-out-china-trade-aggression?mc_cid=7cc4fb695b&mc_eid=a8c89f909a.

DeThomas, Joseph. (2017). "UNSCR 2375: What Just Happened Here?" *38 North*, 15 September. http://www.38north.org/2017/09/jdethomas091517/.

Dou, Eva, and Fifield, Anna. (2020). "China puts sanctions on U.S. lawmakers, NGO chiefs, in tit-for-tat retaliation." *Washington Post*, 10 August. https://www.washingtonpost.com/world/china-sanctions-cruz-rubio-retaliation-hong-kong/2020/08/10/f8e221a4-dae2-11ea-b4f1-25b762cdbbf4_story.html.

Eckstein, Alexander. (1975). "China's Trade Policy and Sino-American Relations." *Foreign Affairs*, October. https://www.foreignaffairs.com/articles/china/1975-10-01/chinas-trade-policy-and-sino-american-relations.

Gelb, Leslie H. (1991). "The Next Renegade State." *New York Times*, 10 April. https://www.nytimes.com/1991/04/10/opinion/foreign-affairs-the-next-renegade-state.html.

Goldman, Stuart D. (2012). "The Forgotten Soviet-Japanese War of 1939." *The Diplomat*, 28 August. https://thediplomat.com/2012/08/the-forgotten-soviet-japanese-war-of-1939/.

Gupta, Karunakar. (1972). "How Did the Korean War Begin?" *The China Quarterly* (52): 699–716.

Harrell, Peter, and Rosenberg, Elizabeth. (2019). "Economic Dominance, Financial Technology, and the Future of U.S. Economic Coercion." *Center for New American Security*, 29 April. https://www.cnas.org/publications/reports/economic-dominance-financial-technology-and-the-future-of-u-s-economic-coercion.

Hay, John. (1899). "The Open Door Note [Submitted by U.S. Secretary of State, John Hay, September 6, 1899]," 6 September. https://www.mtholyoke.edu/acad/intrel/opendoor.htm.

Hayes, Peter, and Moon, Chung-in. (2011). "Park Chung Hee, the CIA & the Bomb." *Global Asia* 6 (3): 46–58.

Hirsh, Michael. (2006). "The Real Libya Model." *Newsweek*, 16 May. https://www.newsweek.com/hirsh-real-lesson-libya-110245.

Hufbauer, Gary Clyde, Schott, Jeffrey J., Elliott, Kimberley Ann, and Oegg, Barbara. (2007a). "Case 49-1 US, ChinCom v. China (1949–70: Communist control of China; 1950–53: Korean War, impair military potential)." In Hufbauer, G.C., Schott, J.J., Elliott, K.A., and Oegg, B. (eds.), *Economic Sanctions Reconsidered*. Washington: Peterson Institute for International Economics.

Hufbauer, Gary Clyde, Schott, Jeffrey J., Elliott, Kimberley Ann, and Oegg, Barbara. (2007b). "Case 50-1 US, UN versus North Korea (1950:- Korean War)." In Hufbauer, G.C., Schott, J.J., Elliott, K.A., and Oegg, B. (eds.), *Economic Sanctions reconsidered*. Washington: Peterson Institute for International Economics.

Jiang, Yun, and Schneider, Jordan. (2020). "The United States Needs More Wine to Stand Up to Chinese Bullying." *Foreign Policy*, 10 December. https://foreignpolicy.com/2020/12/10/united-states-australian-wine-chinese-bullying-strategic-shiraz-reserve/.

Kaplan, Fred. (2012). "Let's Ignore North Korea." *Slate*, 19 April. http://www.newamerica.net/publications/articles/2012/let_s_ignore_north_korea_66647.

Kevin, Tony. (2020). "How Australia sabotaged its own interests in relations with China." *Pearls and Irritations*, 6 December. https://johnmenadue.com/how-australia-sabotaged-its-own-interests-in-relations-with-china/.

Landler, Mark. (2016). "North Korea Nuclear Threat Cited by James Clapper, Intelligence Chief." *New York Times*, 9 February. http://www.nytimes.com/2016/02/10/world/asia/north-korea-nuclear-effort-seen-as-a-top-threat-to-the-us.html?_r=2.

Laurenceson, James, Pantle, Thomas, and Zhou, Michael. (2020). "PRC Economic Coercion: The Recent Australian Experience." *The Australia-China Relations Institute, University of Technology Sydney*, 14 September. https://www.australiachinarelations.org/content/prc-economic-coercion-recent-australian-experience.

Lederer, Edith M. (2019). "UN investigator: 11 million North Koreans are undernourished." *Associated Press*, 23 October. https://apnews.com/e2499ddf9e594c848b6157a4e64127dc.

McCormick, Thomas J. (1967). *China Market: America's quest for Informal Empire 1893-1901*. Chicago: Quadrangle Books.

McDonald, Mark. (2011). "North Korea Suggests Libya Should Have Kept Nuclear Program." *New York Times*, 24 March. http://www.nytimes.com/2011/03/25/world/asia/25korea.html?_r=2&scp=2&sq=north%20korea&st=cse.

Mearsheimer, John J. (2014). "Can China Rise Peacefully?" *National Interest*, 25 October. https://nationalinterest.org/print/commentary/can-china-rise-peacefully-10204.

Menn, Joseph. (2020). "Spy agency ducks questions about 'back doors' in tech products." *Reuters*, 28 October. https://www.reuters.com/article/usa-security-congress-insight/spy-agency-ducks-questions-about-back-doors-in-tech-products-idUSKBN27D1B1.

Nanto, Dick K., Manyin, Mark E., and Dumbaugh, Kerry. (2010). "China-North Korea Relations." *Congressional Research Service*, 22 January. http://www.fas.org/sgp/crs/row/R41043.pdf.

Ramzy, Austin, and May, Tiffany. (2020). "U.S. Imposes Sanctions on Chinese Officials Over Hong Kong Crackdown." *New York Times*, 8 December. https://www.nytimes.com/2020/12/08/world/asia/hong-kong-china-us-sanctions.html.

Reich, Simon. (2016). "Should America be focusing on ISIS when North Korea poses an existential threat? ." *The Conversation*, 13 April. https://theconversation.com/should-america-be-focusing-on-isis-when-north-korea-poses-an-existential-threat-57610.

Rogin, Josh. (2020). "The world failed after Tiananmen Square. We must not fail Hong Kong now." *Washington Post*, 5 June. https://www.washingtonpost.com/opinions/global-opinions/the-world-failed-after-tiananmen-square-we-must-not-fail-hong-kong-now/2020/06/04/c67ed2f4-a688-11ea-b473-04905b1af82b_story.html.

Silberstein, Benjamin Katzeff. (2019). "China's Sanctions Enforcement and Fuel Prices in North Korea: What the Data Tells Us." *38 North*, 1 February. https://www.38north.org/2019/02/bkatzeffsilberstein020119/.

Singh, Ajit, and Blumenthal, Max. (2019). "China detaining millions of Uyghurs? Serious problems with claims by US-backed NGO and far-right researcher 'led by God' against Beijing." *GrayZone*, 21 December. https://thegrayzone.com/2019/12/21/china-detaining-millions-uyghurs-problems-claims-us-ngo-researcher/.

Smeltz, Dina, Daalder, Ivo, Friedhoff, Karl, Kafura, Craig, and Wojtowicz, Lily. (2018). "America Engaged: American Public Opinion and US Foreign Policy." *Chicago*

Council. https://www.thechicagocouncil.org/sites/default/files/2020-11/report_cc s18_america-engaged_181002.pdf.

Sneider, Daniel C. (2008). "Strategic Abandonment: Alliance Relations in Northeast Asia in the Post-Iraq Era." *Joint US Korea Academic Studies.* https://keia.org/publ ication/strategic-abandonment-alliance-relations-in-northeast-asia-in-the-post -iraq-era/.

Spetalnick, Matt, Psaledakis, Daphne, Pamuk, Humeyra, and Hunnicutt. Trevor. (2020). "Biden will keep using U.S. sanctions weapon but with sharper aim— sources." *Reuters,* 17 December. https://www.reuters.com/article/us-usa-sanctions- insight/biden-will-keep-using-u-s-sanctions-weapon-but-with-sharper-aim-sour ces-idUSKBN28Q1CV.

State Department Historian. (2016 [?]). China Policy *Office of the Historian, State Department.* Retrieved from https://history.state.gov/milestones/1977-1980/china -policy

Toh, Michelle. (2020). "China slaps tariffs of up to 212% on Australian wine imports." *CNN,* 27 November. https://edition.cnn.com/2020/11/27/business/china-australia -wine-dumping-intl-hnk/index.html.

Waltz, Kenneth N. (2012). "Why Iran Should Get the Bomb." *Foreign Affairs.*

Woo-Cumings, Meredith. (2002). "The political ecology of famine:the North Korean catastrophe and its lessons." *Asian Development Bank, ADB Institute Research Paper 31.*, January. http://www.adbi.org/files/2002.01.rp31.ecology.famine.northkorea.pdf.

Woodward, Bob, and Kelly, Mary Louise. (2020). "Interview With Bob Woodward, Part 1." *NPR,* 14 September. https://www.npr.org/2020/09/14/912791401/interview -with-bob-woodward-part-1.

Woolsey, R. James, and Pry, Vincent Pry. (2017). "How North Korea could kill 90 percent of Americans." *The Hill,* 29 March. http://thehill.com/blogs/pundits-blog/defense/ 326094-how-north-korea-could-kill-up-to-90-percent-of-americans-at-any.

Worthington, Brett. (2020). "Marise Payne calls for global inquiry into China's handling of the coronavirus outbreak." *Australian Broadcasting Commission,* 19 April. https:// www.abc.net.au/news/2020-04-19/payne-calls-for-inquiry-china-handling-of-coro navirus-covid-19/12162968.

Zhang, Shu Guang. (2001). *Economic Cold War: America's embargo against China and the Sino-Soviet alliance, 1949–1963.* Washington, DC; Stanford, CA: Woodrow Wilson Center Press; Stanford University Press.

Internet Sources

(1945). "Charter of the United Nations and Statute of the International Court of Justice." *United Nations.* Last modified 26 June. http://www.un.org/en/charter-united-nati ons/index.html.

(2006a). "Resolution 1695 (2006)." *United Nations Security Council,* 15 July. http://www .un.org/ga/search/view_doc.asp?symbol=S/RES/1695%282006%29.

(2006b). "Resolution 1718 (2006)." *United Nations Security Council*, 14 October. http://www.un.org/ga/search/view_doc.asp?symbol=S/RES/1718%282006%29.

(2009). "Panel of Experts." https://www.un.org/securitycouncil/sanctions/1718/panel_experts/work_mandate.

(2010a). "N Korea seeks $75 trillion in compensation." *AFP via ABC*, 24 June. http://www.abc.net.au/news/stories/2010/06/24/2936414.htm.

(2010b). "[North Korea Census 2008] N.K. Census says 340 thousand died during N.Korea's March of Tribulation." *Hankyoreh*, 17 March. http://english.hani.co.kr/arti/english_edition/e_northkorea/410577.html.

(2010c). "Over 600,000 N. Koreans starve from 1995–2005." *Hankyoreh*, 23 November. http://english.hani.co.kr/arti/english_edition/e_northkorea/450171.html.

(2020a). "China condemns new US Hong Kong sanctions, Taiwan arms sale." *Associated Press*, 9 December. https://apnews.com/article/joe-biden-legislature-beijing-hong-kong-china-1dd4ofic0b084b10cdaa563e129fcbf8.

(2020b). "Security Council Committee established pursuant to resolution 1718 (2006)." https://www.un.org/securitycouncil/sanctions/1718.

(2021a). "Chinese Military Companies Sanctions." https://home.treasury.gov/policy-issues/financial-sanctions/sanctions-programs-and-country-information/chinese-military-companies-sanctions.

(2021b). "Direction of Trade Statistics." https://data.imf.org/?sk=9d6028d4-f14a-464c-a2f2-59b2cd424b85&sId=1409151240976.

(2021c). "Great Programme for Struggle Leading Korean-style Socialist Construction to Fresh Victory: On Report Made by Supreme Leader Kim Jong Un at Eighth Congress of WPK." *Rodong Sinmun*, 10 January. http://www.rodong.rep.kp/en/index.php?strPageID=SF01_02_01&newsID=2021-01-10-0004.

CHAPTER 10

A Century of Economic Blackmail, Sanctions and War against Iran

Muhammad Sahimi

1 Introduction

Due to its strategic location at the crossroads between Asia, Europe and the Middle East, as well as its natural resources, Iran was a focus of attention of European powers for at least a century. Russian and British empires competed over Iran and exerted great influence on its internal affairs during the 19th and early 20th centuries, blackmailing it frequently. Since 1945 the American establishment has espoused the idea that the security and prosperity of the United States requires it to be the Middle East's hegemon. Successive administrations have advanced this belief through various means, including military invasion and occupation, regime-change campaigns, drone wars, supporting dictatorships, imposing economic sanctions, and coups. A prime victim of this policy has been Iran and its people. As a result, over the last century, Iran has experienced two Western-supported coups; has been invaded twice, and its two revolutions, one from 1905–1911 and a second one in 1978–1979, did not achieve many of their goals, for which one main factor has been a century of economic and political blackmail, sanctions, coups, and wars imposed on that nation.

The purpose of this chapter is to take a look at this history of imperialist interventions in Iran, the resulting sufferings of the Iranian people, and their consequences.

2 Great Powers Rivalry: Russian and British Intervention in Iran

Through two wars and the Treaty of Gulistan in July 1813 and the Treaty of Turkmenchay in February 1828 Russia succeeded in taking control of a significant part of Persia [Iran] in the Caucasus region, which currently includes Georgia, Armenia, and Republic of Azerbaijan, and Dagestan that is part of the current Russian territory. In addition, the Persian Cossack Brigade was established in 1879 whose commanding officers were entirely Russian. The Cossack forces supported the counter-revolutionaries during Iran's Constitutional

Revolution of 1905–1911. When Mohammad Ali Shah of the Qajar Dynasty tried to overthrow the government that had been elected after the initial success of the Revolution in 1906, the Cossack forces supported him by surrounding the *Majles* [Iranian parliament] and shelling it. With the support of the Cossack commander, Colonel Vladimir Platonovitch Liakhov, Mohammad Ali Shah succeeded temporarily and ruled as a dictator for a short time. But, although his regime was overthrown by the revolutionary forces in July 1909 and the constitutional monarchy was restored, the Cossack forces continued to exert great influence on Iran's internal affair by occupying a large portion of the Iranian territory in northern part of the country.

Worried by Germany's rise to a global position of power and its Triple Alliance with Italy and Austria-Hungary signed in May 1882, Britain decided to form an alliance with Russia to counter Germany. The Anglo-Russian Convention of 1907 in St. Petersburgh, Russia, ended the rivalry between the two nations. One important outcome of the Convention was the agreement over recognizing the spheres of Russian and British influence in Iran. Britain agreed to not meddle in northern Iran and recognized it as Russia's sphere of influence. In turn, Russia agreed that southern part of Iran, including the shores of the Persian Gulf and the Sea of Oman, was Britain's region of influence. The results was chaos for over 15 years.

3   Persian Famine of 1917–1919

The Anglo-Russian alliance and partitioning of Iran into quasi-colonies of Russia and Britain had catastrophic consequences for the Iranian people, as it contributed significantly to the Persian famine of 1917–1919. Although Iran had declared its neutrality during World War I, Russia and Britain ignored it, as their forces occupied Iran. The entire granary of the Sistan province in south-eastern Iran on the present border with Pakistan was sold to the British forces in 1915. All the roads to and from the Khorasan province in north-eastern Iran were blocked by Russian forces to prevent transfer of grains, except those intended for them. All means of transportation were dedicated to transporting fuel and everything else from Khuzestan, Iran's oil-rich province in the south-west, to the forces of the two nations. The result was a great disruption in Iran's network of roads and transportation, making distribution of food extremely difficult. This gave rise to a great famine, not well-known in the West, which contributed to the death of at least two million Iranians (Abrahamian 2013), although estimates as high as 8–10 million have also been claimed (Majd 2003, 72). Iran's population at that time was about 19–20 million, and even if we accept the low estimate of 2 million, it still represented about 10 percent of the population.

After the October 1917 Revolution in Russia, the new Soviet Union renounced all the treaties that the old Russian empire had imposed on it, except for the Treaties of Gulistan and Turkmenchay. This left Britain as the most influential power in Iran, which wished to dominate Iran in order to protect its colony in the Indian subcontinent and, with discovery of vast amounts of oil, have access to cheap fuel for its navy.

4   The Anglo-Persian Oil Company and the Seeds of the First Economic Sanctions

Mozaffar al-Din Shah of the Qajar Dynasty granted an oil concession to the British businessman William Knox D'Arcy in May 1901 for a period of 60 years. The concession covered three quarters of Iran, all but the northern part of the country on the border with Russia, and gave exclusive rights to D'Arcy to prospect, explore, exploit, transport and sell petroleum, natural gas, asphalt, and mineral waxes in Persia. In return, the Shah received £20,000 in cash, another £20,000 worth of shares of the operating company, and Iran would receive only 16 percent of the annual "net" profit. On May 26 1908 oil began flowing from a well in Masjed-e Solayman, a town in Khuzestan. The Anglo-Persian Oil Company (APOC) [the present British Petroleum] was formed in 1909, hence laying the foundation for the future economic sanctions that Britain would impose on Iran as a result of Iran nationalizing its oil industry in 1951, as well as the US intervention in the Iranian affairs and its forty years of economic sanctions since the Iranian Revolution of 1979.

5   Britain's Own Men: The 1921 Coup and the Emergence of Reza Shah

Britain tried to use Iran to topple the new political order in Russia after the 1917 Revolution, or at the very least to contain it. Russia responded by supporting establishment in June 1920 of Persian Socialist Soviet Republic (Atabaki 2009, 63), also known as the Republic of Gilan (Abrahamian 2008, 58–61), an Iranian province in the northern part of the country on the Caspian Sea shores. The Republic was led by Mirza Koochak Khan, who had played a leading role in the Constitutional Revolution. He led a progressive movement called *jonbesh-e jangal* [Jungle Movement, a reference to the thick forests in Gilan]. But this was not the only perceived threat by Britain. Mirza Koochak Khan's forces, in alliances with other revolutionary forces from other parts of Iran, wanted to take Tehran, the Capital.

To prevent a leftist takeover of Iran, Britain brought its own men to power. First, in January 1921, General William Edmond Ironside, commander of the British forces in Iran, called the North Persian Force, promoted Reza Khan, a little-known commissioned officer in the Persian Cossack Brigade with a military rank roughly equivalent to Brigadier General, to be the overall commander of the force. Next, in a coup supported by Britain (Ghani 2001, 147), Reza Khan and his forces took control of Tehran on 22 February 1921, toppled the government, and installed Sayyed Ziae'ddin Tabatabaei—"a friend of the British" (Milani 2008, 551)—as the Prime Minister, while keeping Ahmad Shah, the last king of the Qajar dynasty, on the throne. Reza Khan was Minister of War in the coup government, taking the title *Sardar Sepah*, meaning commander-in-chief of the armed forces.

The new government lasted only four months and was replaced by another one. Reza Khan was appointed Prime Minister by Ahmad Shah in 1923. Eventually, Reza Khan forced the Majles to depose Ahmad Shah [who was in Europe at that time]. He wanted to transform Iran to a republic, but senior clerics, as well as Britain, opposed the idea. Thus, the Majles declared him the new Shah on 12 December 1925, beginning the Pahlavi dynasty. Reza Shah was also granted dictatorial power. Despite some achievements for reconstructing the country and founding Iran's modern bureaucracy, Reza Shah's reign is considered one of the darkest political periods in contemporary Iran, marked by political suppression, censorship, and jailing, exiling and even murdering political dissidents, hence destroying all the achievements of the Constitutional Revolution.

6   Cancellation of the D'Arcy Concessions and the Rise of Iranian Nationalism

From the beginning it was clear to the Iranian intelligentsia that the D'Arcy oil concession was unfair. However, because the country was in turmoil and the central government was weak, Iran did not have any leverage to renegotiate the oil concessions. But by the mid-1920s the unfair nature of the concessions had become so glaring that even Reza Shah was not willing to continue business as usual. Renegotiating the concessions was not, however, easy. Winston Churchill, who was the First Lord of the Admiralty at that time, wanted a secure source of "oil supply for His Majesty's Navy" and, therefore, introduced on 17 June 1914 a bill in the House of Commons to propose that the government invest £2.2 million in the APOC for acquiring 51 percent of its stock, and place two directors on its board of directors with powers to veto decisions unfavorable to Admiralty fuel contracts. In addition, a secret and separate document provided the Admiralty with a twenty-year contract for fuel oil, and a rebate to the Royal Navy from the company's profits (Ferrier 1982; Yergin 1991). By 10 August 1914 the British government had become the major shareholder of the APOC.

One main point of contention between Iran and the APOC was that although Iran was to receive 16 percent of net profit of the company, there was sharp disagreement over what constituted "profit." The APOC was excluding its profits from its operations outside Iran, and was deducting the discount that it was giving to the British Royal Navy as "operating expenses." Thus, new negotiations began in 1928 and continued until 1933, at the time when there was a worldwide deep economic depression. So, just when a new agreement was in sight, the APOC declared that Iran's proceeds from its 1931 operations had declined over the previous year by 76 percent, whereas the company's own profits had declined by 36 percent. This angered Reza Shah, prompting him to reject the emerging new agreement (Bamberg 1982). The Iranian government declared on 27 November 1932 that the D'Arcy oil concessions had been nullified, and reported it to the League of Nations (League of Nations documents 1933).

Sir John Cadman, Chairman of the APOC, arrived in Tehran in April 1933. He held two face-to-face meetings with Reza Shah. The second meeting on 24 April 1933 resulted in a breakthrough, and by the end of May 1933 a new agreement was in place. Iran did receive better terms: The APOC relinquished about 80 percent of the area covered by the 1901 concession. It agreed to pay Iran £1 million to settle all past claims. Royalties were to be calculated based on physical volume of oil; small payments were to be made as local taxes, and Iran would receive 20 percent of the distribution of dividends that the APOC would pay to the ordinary stockholders or to the company's reserves above £671,250. The APOC also agreed to supply oil products to Iran with a discount of 25 percent for the government and 10 percent for the public. Several other minor concessions were made to Iran. But the concession's duration was extended to 1993 (from the original terminating year of 1961).

Despite better terms, considered the best of any oil concession in the world at that time (Yergin 1991), there were still many issues that Iranian nationalists were not happy about. One issue was extending duration of the concession to 1993. In addition, the royalty payments had been fixed at a fixed amount per ton of oil, regardless of the possible rise in oil prices. The payments as local taxes were not only very small and independent of the oil price and the AIOC's profits, but also independent of any changes in Iran's income tax laws. Although

Iran was to receive 20 percent share of the APOC worldwide profits, it would be calculated on the basis of distribution of dividends to the ordinary stockholders. But this was subject to the APOC decisions and its main shareholder, the British government, and large investment in other parts of the world.

But the issue most important to the Iranian nationalists was the question of control over the country's oil resources (Abrahamian 2013), which the 1933 agreement did not make any concession about it. As a result, the seeds of discontent planted by the 1901 concession produced rapidly growing shrubs by 1933, leading to a revolt against Britain and its looting of Iran's oil resources, nationalization of Iran's oil industry, and Britain's economic war against Iran and its people.

7   The Nationalization of Iran's Oil Industry

In 1935 Reza Shah changed the official name of the country from Persia to Iran [meaning land of Aryans]. Therefore, the APOC was also changed to Anglo-Iranian Oil Company (AIOC). Reza Shah also manifested sympathy for the Nazi regime in Germany. Thus, the Soviet Union and Britain invaded Iran on 25 August 1941 and occupied it. They deposed Reza Shah and exiled him to Johannesburg, South Africa, and put his 22 years old Crown Prince Mohammad Reza on the throne.

Between 1941 and 1953 Iran was a relatively democratic state. The young king had not consolidated his power, there were many political parties, many newspapers and weeklies had sprung to life, and there was fierce competition between the nationalists, leftists, Islamic forces, and other groups. At the same time, nationalism was on the rise due to occupation of Iran by the British and Russian forces as well as the pressure by American and British corporations to obtain exclusive rights for oil exploration and extraction in northern Iran. The most important nationalist figure of that era was Dr. Mohammad Mosaddegh, who had opposed the coronation of Reza Shah and had been jailed and exiled internally.

In the elections for the 14th session of the Majles in 1943, Dr. Mosaddegh, a candidate from Tehran, received the highest number of votes. In a fiery speech in the Majles, he spoke against the 1933 oil concession. In 1944 he proposed a new law, passed overwhelmingly on 2 December 1944, banning the government from granting any oil concession to any foreign corporation or government without the explicit approval of the Majles (Center for Majles Documents; Hurewitz 1979).

In the elections for the 15th session of the Majles in 1946 the intervention of the Imperial Court, the Army, and the then pro-Britain Premier Ahmad Ghavam, prevented Dr. Mosaddegh from getting elected. The nationalists and independents nominated Dr. Mosaddegh for the Premiership, but he fell short by one vote. They did succeed in approving a new law on 22 October 1947 that denied the Soviet Union any oil concession in the northern part of Iran that Ghavam had agreed to, and ordered the government to try to re-negotiate the 1933 agreement.

Sensing the rising Iranian nationalism, the AIOC begun negotiating with the Iran on 28 September 1948, led by Neville Gass, its managing director. Iran's negotiators pointed out, among other issues, that the royalties paid to Iran were much less than those received by Iraq, Kuwait, and Venezuela, and equal sharing of the profits had already been agreed to with Venezuela. But, the most contentious issue was again the question of use of Iranian engineers and experts by the AIOC, as well as Iranian control on its natural resources. Thus, the initial negotiations failed.

In 1949 Dr. Mosaddegh and his comrades founded the National Front, a coalition of various political forces and thinking. Abbas-Gholi Golshaeian, the Finance Minister, insisted that the October 1947 law would not allow acceptance by Iran of anything less equal sharing of the profits. The AIOC was forced to separate its Iran operations from the rest of the world, and then agreed to the principle of 50/50 profit sharing. An agreement, essentially a supplement to the 1933 oil concession, was reached and became known as the Gass-Golshaeian agreement. But the extension of the oil concession to 1993 remained in place. The pro-Britain deputies tried the get the new Majles to approve the Gass-Golshaeian agreement, but a large demonstration organized by the National front took place in Iran to protest the new agreement, enabling the nationalist deputies to prevent the approval of the agreement.

In the elections for the 16th session of the Majles in July 1949, the Imperial Court and its pro-Shah Prime Minister, Lieutenant General Haj-Ali Razmara, intervened and prevented election of Dr. Mosaddegh and his comrades. They protested the rigged elections, forcing the Shah to nullify the elections in Tehran and hold new elections in January 1950. Dr. Mosaddegh and seven of his comrades were elected. Together with several other pro-National Front and independent deputies, he led a minority but powerful faction of the Majles. The National Front put forward a proposal to nationalize the oil industry. On 15 March 1951, upon the recommendation of the Majles' special oil committee headed by Dr. Mosaddegh, nationalization of Iran's oil industry was approved by the Majles, on 20 March 1951 Iran's Senate approved the nationalization law.

The nationalization law had provisions for expropriation of the assets of the AIO, the settlement of claims and counter claims of the two parties, the establishment of the National Iranian Oil Company to operate Iran's oil industry, and uninterrupted sale of oil to the customers of the AIOC (Elm 1992, 91–93). Thus, Iran established its sovereignty, ownership, and control over its oil industry and resources. Another goal, eradicating British political and economic influence in Iran, was not achieved because of the CIA-MI6 coup of August 1953.

8   Britain's Economic Wars on Iran

Initially, the Truman administration supported Iran in its dispute with Britain, as it viewed Iranian nationalism as a bulwark against communism. There was fear in Washington that Iran might fall under communist rule, if Dr. Mosaddegh failed to achieve his objectives and fell from power. Dr. Mosaddegh visited the United States and was warmly received by President Truman. Britain embargoed Iran's oil, preventing Dr. Mosaddegh's government from exporting any oil. His government lost two-third of its foreign exchange earnings and 40 percent of the total revenue. Although the government took measures to boost non-oil exports, and decrease imports, which were highly successful, the oil embargo still caused great hardship for the Iranian people. According to a 1952 World Bank report on the nationalization of Iranian oil industry (World Bank Report 1952, 20), classified until 2003, Iran had only received just about one-fourth of its contractual share of the AIOC's income and was owed at least $1.2 billion. This was a dispute that never got to be resolved properly.

The AIOC also brought legal action against anyone who bought Iran's oil. Acting under the Defense Production Act of 1950 and with antitrust exemption, nineteen American oil companies formed a voluntary committee to coordinate and work closely with a similar British committee to move supplies around the world, so that the absence of Iran's oil would not be felt in the market. At the same time, Britain took steps to freeze Iran's assets outside the country. But the International Court of Justice declared that it had no jurisdiction over the Iran-Britain dispute, handing Dr. Mosaddegh a major victory. A joint Churchill-Truman proposal to Iran in August 1952 for settling the dispute was rejected by Dr. Mosaddegh in February 1953, because it still did not recognize Iran's sovereignty and control over its oil resources and industry.

9 The 1953 Coup

By then, the Eisenhower administration had come to power, and had concluded with Britain that Dr. Mosaddegh had to be removed from power. In fact, preparation for overthrowing Dr. Mosaddegh's government had already begun in November 1952, which was described in detail by Donald Wilber, the CIA agent who was the principal architect of the coup plot (Wilber 2000). The rest is a well-known history. Dr. Mosaddegh, the democratically-elected Prime Minister, was toppled in a joint CIA-MI6 coup on 19 August 1953, led by Major General Fazlollah Zahedi, "a worst grain-hoarder" (O'Sullivan 2015, 120–131) who had been imprisoned by British forces in 1941 (Maclean 1949, 263–274) for his pro-Nazi sympathies. Some of Dr. Mosaddegh's supporters, including some of the leading clerics, had also stopped supporting him, for which they have never been forgiven by the Iranian nation. Dr. Mosaddegh was imprisoned for four years, after which he was under virtual house arrest until he passed away on 5 March 1967.

10 The Coup Regime of 1953–1979

The Shah who had fled the country in August 1953, returned to Iran. With United States support, he transformed Iran from a relatively democratic state to one of absolute dictatorship. But while it is often said that the Shah was an ally of the United States, the fact is the United States never viewed the Shah and his regime as ally, but rather as a client state that should carry water for its interests in the Middle East. We will come back to this point at the end of this Chapter. As the Shah consolidated his power, corruption also increased dramatically. He also increased repression, to the point that in a speech in March 1975 he ordered all the political parties, which were docile and obedient to him anyway, to be dissolved and be replace by a single party, the *Rastakhiz* [resurrection] Party. In his speech he also said, "Anyone who disagrees with this, can obtain his passport and leave Iran." Such was his dictatorship, supported by the United States. Less than four years later he and his regime were toppled by the Iranian people.

11 The 1979 Revolution, the Hostage Crisis, and the Beginning of the United States Sanctions

Shah Mohammad Reza Pahlavi was toppled in February 1979 by "the last great revolution" of the 20th century (Wright 2000), led by Ayatollah Ruhollah

Khomeini. The Revolution had a strongly anti-American tone, simply because of the fact that a great majority of Iranians perceived the Shah's repressive and corrupt regime as lackey of the United States. The Shah and his family went into exile.

The revolutionaries, particularly the young university students, were worried that, similar to 1953 when the Shah had also fled the country, the United States would try orchestrating a counter-revolution. Their suspicion grew when on 22 October 1979 the Carter Administration allowed the Shah to enter the United States for medical treatment. He had cancer and needed treatment, but the revolutionaries viewed it as the first step toward another coup. The provisional revolutionary government was led by Mehdi Bazargan, a close aide of Dr. Mosaddegh and a relatively liberal figure in Iran's religious-nationalist movement (Sahimi 2011a). His foreign and defense ministers were, respectively, US-educated Ebrahim Yazdi and Mostafa Chamran. On 1 November 1979, the day in which huge demonstrations in Iran protested admission of the Shah by the US, Bazargan, Yazdi, and Chamran met in Algiers, Algeria, with Zbigniew Brzezinski, President Carter's national security advisor. As far as the revolutionary students were concerned, the Algiers meeting and the Shah being admitted into the US were the last straw. They decided to overrun the US Embassy in Tehran to force its closure, with the hope that Bazargan's government would fall. On 4 November 1979 the US embassy in Tehran was overrun by the students and its staff and diplomats were taken hostage (Sahimi 2009). Some of them, including women and African American staff, were released a few days later, but 52 of them were held, demanding that the Shah be extradited to Iran to be put on trial. The students had thought that the entire affair would end in one or two days. But they were wrong, as they and the hostages became pawns in a power struggle in Iran between the clerics and the more secular element of the revolution. Ayatollah Khomeini declared his support for the takeover, and Bazargan resigned. All the initial attempts for mediations between Iran and the US failed.

President Jimmy Carter's economic war on Iran began on 14 November 1979. Signing Executive Order 12170, Carter ordered the blocking of all assets owned by Iran's Central Bank of Iran within US jurisdiction, a move that largely helped Chase Bank and its chartered affiliates avoid encountering the possibility of a catastrophic bankruptcy. That explains why David Rockefeller and Henry Kissinger, a senior advisor of Chase Bank, used their immense influence and political prowess to make Carter resist his Secretary of State Cyrus Vance's strong opposition against allowing the shah to enter the US. On 7 April 1980 Carter severed all diplomatic ties with Iran, and issued Executive Order 12205, freezing Iran's assets in the United States, totaling about $12 billion, and imposing complete economic sanctions on Iran (Executive Order 12205, 1980). That began the US use of economic blackmail, sanctions and war against Iran, continuing what Britain had begun 80 years earlier. The goal of Carter's sanctions was ostensibly to force Iran to release the hostages. But, in fact, many, including the author, believe that the goal was to demonstrate the fundamental opposition of the United States to the Iranian Revolution.

After complete economic sanctions were imposed on Iran, President Carter resorted to military pressure. On 24 April 1980, he sent US Delta forces and Army Rangers into Iran to rescue the hostages, although many in Iran believed that the ultimate goal was toppling the government, since a secret CIA team had also been sent to Tehran (Hastedt and Guerrier 2011, 261). The plan, called Operation Eagle Claw (Bowden 2006), was fraught with difficulties. Eight helicopters flew to the staging area referred to as *Desert One*, in the desert in central Iran near the town of Tabas. But three of them developed problems, and since at least six operational helicopters were needed, the operation was aborted. But as the US forces prepared to withdraw from their staging area, one helicopter crashed into a transport aircraft that carried jet fuels with servicemen onboard, starting a fire that destroyed the aircraft and the helicopter, killing eight servicemen.

On 22 September 1980, Iraq invaded Iran. Although US officials have denied it, there is considerable evidence that the United States encouraged Saddam Hussein, at least indirectly, to invade Iran. For example, right after the hostage crisis began, the Carter administration approached Iraq to re-establish diplomatic relations, to which Saddam Hussein responded affirmatively. In fact, according to a New *York Times* piece from 1990, "Saddam later acknowledged that Iraq had accepted [David] Newsom's offer during the two months prior to the war between us and Iran," but "when the war started, and to avoid misinterpretation, we postponed the establishment of relations." Newsome was under-Secretary of State for political affairs. In addition, two exiled Iranian officials, Shapour Bakhtiar, the Shah's last Prime Minister, and General Gholam-Ali Oveisi were urging Iraq to invade Iran, and the CIA was in contact with both. Both were assassinated in Paris (Sahimi 2011b).

Joost Hiltermann, director of the Middle East and North Africa program for the International Crisis Group, was quoted by Blight *et al.* (2012) as stating that the US giving a "green light" to Saddam Hussein regime was also a belief among the Arabs. In fact, in August 1980, just before attacking Iran, Saddam Hussein travelled to Saudi Arabia during which King Khalid reportedly "gave his personal blessing to the invasion and promised Saudi backing" (Gibson 2010, 31–36). This was stated on page 2 of a top secret document prepared in April 1981 (National Security Archive 2012), which was a report on a trip to Saudi Arabia by Alexander Haig, President Ronald Reagan's Secretary of State, that, "It was also interesting to confirm that President Carter gave the Iraqis a green light to launch the war against Iran through [then Crown Prince] Fahd," meaning when Hussein had made his trip to Saudi Arabia in August 1980. Haig's interpretation of what he had been told by Fahd has, however, been disputed.

Serious negotiations for the release of the hostages began in September 1980, and were concluded with the Algiers Accords of 19 January 1981. The next day, 30 minutes after Ronald Reagan took the oath of office, the hostages were released. Point I, paragraph 1 of "the General Principles of the Declaration of the Government of the Democratic and Popular Republic of Algeria"— that is, the Algiers Accords—stated in the *The New York Times* in 1981: "Non-Intervention in Iranian Affairs—The United States pledges that it is and from now on will be the policy of the United States not to intervene, directly or indirectly, politically or militarily, in Iran's internal affairs." But the United States never delivered on its promise, and it is still intervening in Iran's internal affairs by supporting the exiled opposition, imposing economic sanctions, threatening military attacks, and various forms of blackmail.

12   Sanctions, Threats and Military Attacks in the Reagan Era

According to the Algiers Accords, the United States was obligated to lift its economic sanctions imposed on Iran, and President Reagan did deliver on it. Sanctions on the sale of military hardware to Iran remained in place, however. Given that between 1970 and 1978 the Shah had ordered the most modern US-made weapons worth $20 billion (Klare 1980), and had taken delivery of the most of them before he was toppled in February 1979, Iran badly needed spare parts for its weapons to defend itself against the Iraqi forces occupying a significant part of Iran.

In December 1983 Reagan dispatched Donald Rumsfeld to Baghdad as his special envoy. Rumsfeld met with Saddam Hussein (Battle 2003) and informed him that although US would remain officially neutral in the Iran-Iraq war, it was tilting toward Iraq. Thus, for the rest of the war, which ended in July 1988, the Reagan administration provided Iraq with several billion dollars' worth of economic aid, the sale of dual-use technology, non-US origin weaponry [mainly spare parts and ammunition for the Soviet weaponry that the Soviet Union had stopped supplying it to Iraq due to its opposition to the war], military intelligence, and special operations training. Italy and Britain played essential roles in helping the Reagan administrations to support Iraq (Friedman 1993). In 1984 Iraq attacked Iranian oil tankers and terminal at Kharg island in Persian Gulf.

Iran retaliated by attacking tankers that carried Iraqi oil transported to Kuwait and, later on, it expanded the attacks on oil tankers of any Arab nation of the Persian Gulf that was supporting Iraq. Hence, the so-called "tanker war" began. In 1987 Kuwait asked the US for help, and the US and its NATO allies offered their naval forces for support, flagging Kuwait's oil tankers with US flags, and escorting them through the Persian Gulf. In the same year, the Reagan administration imposed new sanctions on Iranian goods and services, "as a result of Iran's support for international terrorism and its aggressive actions against non-belligerent shipping in the Persian Gulf," which was in violation of the Algiers Accords.

On 14 April 1988 the frigate USS *Samuel B. Roberts* was badly damaged by an Iranian mine. The US retaliated 4 days later by destroying the Iranian warship *Sahand*, crippling another one, sinking 1 gunboat and 3 speedboats, and killing 55 sailors. In addition, the US Navy attacked two Iranian offshore oil platforms in the Persian Gulf and destroyed them. In November 2003 the International Court of Justice found (Bekker 2003) that the US attacks did not represent acts of self-defense, but the US never paid for the damage that it had inflicted on Iran. On 3 July 1988 the *USS Vincennes* shot down an Iranian passenger airliner over the Strait of Hurmoz, killing all 290 people onboard, including 63 children. The US attributed it to a mistake, claiming that the crew of Vincennes had incorrectly identified the Airbus as an attacking F-14 Tomcat jet fighter.

The war with Iraq finally ended in July 1988. As Akbar Hashemi Rafsanjani, the then Speaker of the Majles, put it, "we can fight with the Iraqis, but not with NATO."

13 The History of US Sanctions since the 1980s

13.1 *Sanctions Imposed by the George H.W. Bush Administration*
Although the George H.W. administration wished to improve the relations with Iran, President George H.W. Bush kept the sanctions imposed by the Reagan administration in place. In addition, due to the US-led coalition war with Iraq in 1991, Congress approved the Iran-Iraq Arms Non-Proliferation Act in June 1992 (House Resolution 5434, 1992), banning export of any materials to the two countries that could be used in the production of advanced weapons.

13.2 *Sanctions and Military Threats during the Clinton Administration*
From its inception in January 1993, the Clinton Administration was determined to pressure Iran, following its policy of "dual containment" (Gause 1994) of both Iran and Iraq, even though Iran sat out the war between the US and its

allies with Iraq in 1991 and did not support Saddam Hussein's regime. On the other hand, although the United States and its allies supported Iraq during its war with Iran, when Rafsanjani was elected Iran's president in 1989 [and for a second term in 1993], he was determined to improve US-Iran relations.

Thus, in 1994 Iran invested $350 million in an $8 billion oil consortium, which consisted mostly of Western oil companies, to explore and develop oil fields in the Republic of Azerbaijan. Under pressure by the Clinton Administration, Iran was forced to withdraw from the consortium. In January 1994 a bill was introduced by Alfonse D'Amato, the Republican Senator from New York that banned American companies from buying Iranian oil. Eventually, after also including Libya, the bill was approved in September 1996 (House Resolution 3107, 1996), and became known as the Iran-Libya Sanctions Act, which banned investing more $20 million in Iran's oil industry.

Despite such setbacks, the Rafsanjani administration granted on 6 March 1995 a large contract to the American oil company Conoco (the New York Times 1995) to develop two offshore oil fields in the Persian Gulf, even though Conoco's terms were less favorable to Iran than what it had received from European oil companies. In response, President Clinton signed Executive Order 12957 (Government Information 1995a) on 15 March 1995, prohibiting investing in Iran's oil industry, and buying Iran's oil and petroleum products, which prevented Conoco from moving forward with the project. Israel's lobby played a leading role in persuading Clinton to stop Conoco (Jewish Telegraphic Agency 1995). Executive Order 12959, signed on 6 May 1995 (Government Information 1995b), imposed complete economic sanctions on Iran.

In addition, during 1996–1997 Clinton contemplated attacking Iran in retaliation for the Khobar Towers bombing that destroyed a US Air Force barracks outside Dhahran, Saudi Arabia. The bombs killed 19 servicemen and wounded close to 400 others. The United States blamed Iran for the attack, even though Saudi Arabia intelligence believed that a Saudi terrorist group linked with al-Qaeda was the culprit, and Clinton's Defense Secretary William Perry acknowledged publicly much later that it had indeed been done by al-Qaeda-affiliated groups (United Press International 2007).

However, Clinton decided not to move forward with the military attacks because in May 1997 the reformist Mohammad Khatami won Iran's presidential elections in a landslide. He began a program of reforms, and improved Iran's relationships and trade with Western Europe. In the fall of 1998 Iranian reformists also swept nationwide elections for city councils, and then in March 2000 they scored huge victories for the Majles elections, taking control of the parliament. If the Clinton administration lifted at least the oil sanctions, it would have helped the cause of those in Iran who were advocating détente with the United States. But Clinton did not take any meaningful steps to lift the sanctions, and left them for the administration of George W. Bush. In March 2000 Secretary of State Madeleine Albright did acknowledge US role in the 1953 coup, and expressed regrets, but did not offer formal apology (Albright 2000).

13.3   Sanctions and Military Threats during the George W. Bush Administration

The George W. Bush administration kept the sanctions by its predecessor in place, but intensified its rhetoric against Iran, even though Iran cooperated with the United States when it invaded Afghanistan in the fall of 2001. Iran allowed the US to use its air space; provided crucial intelligence about the Taliban forces; and the forces that it had armed, trained and backed against the Taliban, namely, the Northern Alliance, were the first to enter Kabul, Afghanistan's Capital, on 13 November 2001 (Neville 2015, 43). In the conference in Bonn in December 2001 (United Nations 2001), Iran and its representative, Mohammad Javad Zarif (the current Foreign Minister) played a fundamental role in persuading the various Afghan factions to form a government of national unity.

Despite Iran's great help in Afghanistan, in his State-of-the-Union address on 29 January 2002, President Bush made Iran a charter member of the "axis of evil," with Iraq and North Korea as the other two members. Iran's initial response was stopping intelligence cooperation with the US for capturing senior leadership of al-Qaeda. The hostility intensified after it was revealed in summer of 2002, and officially admitted by Iran in February 2003, that since the 1990s Iran had had a secret nuclear program, trying to set up a uranium enrichment program, and carrying out a research program for understanding the process of producing nuclear weapons.

In August 2002 a British official had told the *Newsweek* (Krugman 2003), "Everyone wants to go to Baghdad. Real men want to go to Tehran." In February 2003, Israeli newspaper Ha'aretz reported that the then Under-Secretary of State John Bolton had told Israeli officials that, after defeating Iraq, the United States would "deal with" Iran, Syria and North Korea (Krugman 2003). After the US and Britain invaded Iraq in March 2003 and toppled the regime of Saddam Hussein with relative ease, US rhetoric against Iran intensified further. Then, General Wesley Clark, Supreme Commander of the Allied Powers in Europe from 1997–2000, revealed (Clark 2003, 130) that the Bush administration had plans to invade seven countries over a period of five years, namely, Iran, Iraq, Syria, Libya, Lebanon, Sudan, and Somalia. In response, in May 2003 President Khatami submitted a comprehensive proposal, a "Grand Bargain" (Kristof 2007), to the Bush administration to resolve all the issues between the two countries. In particular, Khatami proposed putting Iran's nuclear program under strict inspection by the International Atomic Energy Agency; help transform the Lebanese Hezbollah to a purely political organization, and recognize officially any agreement that the Palestinian people could reach with Israel. But the Bush administration rejected the proposal. The neo-conservatives, together with Israel and its lobby in the United States, were determined to prevent any détente with Iran, and invade it if possible.

Beginning in the fall of 2003 the Khatami administration froze Iran's nuclear program and began negotiating with three European powers, Britain, France and Germany. Iran agreed to limit the number of its centrifuges that were used in uranium enrichment to only 3,000, limiting the program to a research one, and grant unlimited access to the IAEA inspectors to monitor the program. But, according to Jack Straw, who was Britain's Foreign Secretary at that time, the negotiations failed (Oborne and Morrison 2013) because the Bush administration rejected it. The rejection of Khatami's proposal, as well as failure of the negotiations with the EU3, badly hurt Iran's moderates and reformist groups who were pushing for normalizing the relationships with the United States. They also contributed significantly to the rise to power of Mahmoud Ahmadinejad, who was elected Iran's President in June 2005. But, although unlike Khatami who proposed the concept of "dialogue of civilizations" as a way of starting dialogue between the two nations and peoples, Ahmadinejad was pursuing a confrontational foreign policy, he too sent an eighteen-page letter to Bush in 2006 (Radio Free Europe 2006), seeking to ease US-Iran tension. But that was also rejected by the Bush administration. Instead, in direct violation of the Algiers Accords of 1981 for not interfering in Iran's internal affairs, and with the support of the Bush administration, Congress approved in April 2006 (House Resolution 109–417, 2006) "Iran Freedom Support Act." Bush provided up to $400 million for Iran's exiled opposition (Harnden 2008).

The National Intelligence Estimate of November 2007 about Iran's nuclear program ended the Bush administration's effort for finding an excuse to attack Iran. The Estimate (Director of National Intelligence 2007) declared that Iran may have had a research program for nuclear weapons, but had stopped it in 2003. But this did not stop the Administration's push for referring Iran's nuclear dossier to the United Nations Security Council, even though no evidence had been found indicating that Iran had an active nuclear weapon program (Sahimi 2013). The result was five UNSC Resolutions against Iran, Resolutions 1696, 1737, 1747, 1803 and 1835, approved before Bush left office, approving limited sanctions against Iran's nuclear and missile programs, which the Obama administration used as the "legal" basis for imposing its harsh economic sanctions on Iran. Resolution 1929 was also approved in 2010.

13.4   Sanctions Imposed by the Obama Administration

Barack Obama campaigned for the US presidency as an antiwar candidate, and after he was elected in November 2008, he gave a speech in Cairo on 4 June 2009, entitled "a new beginning" (Obama 2009), offering peace to the Islamic world, and in particular Iran. He received the Nobel Peace Prize for that speech in the fall of 2009. Yet, he continued the policy of his predecessors against Iran. On 15 December 2009 the House of Representatives approved legislation, amending the aforementioned 1996 oil sanction law, to impose sanction on foreign companies that help supply gasoline to Iran. It was eventually signed by Obama on 30 June 2010 into law.

But Obama did not stop there. Beginning on 4 May 2011, he began signing a series of Executive Orders, E.O. 13574, 13590, 13622, and 13645, with the last one issued on 3 June 2013 (Federal Register 2013), imposing complete sanctions on all aspects of Iran's economy. Most importantly, the US, in complete cooperation by the European Union, succeeded in cutting Iran off from the Society for Worldwide Interbank Financial Telecommunications (SWIFT) system that allows international transfer of money. Thus, Iran's banks and financial institutions were completely removed from the international banking system, making it virtually impossible for Iran to export or import anything. In a speech on 4 March 2012, Obama boasted that "few thought that sanctions could have an immediate bite on the Iranian regime. They have, slowing the Iranian nuclear program and virtually grinding the Iranian economy to a halt in 2011" (White House 2012). However, Obama's boasting could not hide the hardship that his sanctions had imposed on the Iranian people. While Iran's rate of GDP growth in 2010, right before the new sanctions were imposed, was about 6 percent/ year, in 2012 it dropped to -7.5 percent, while in 2013 it was -0.2 percent (World Bank data; GDP growth). While the annual rate of inflation in 2010 was about 10 percent, by 2013 it had grown to about 37 percent (World Bank data; inflation).

After Hassan Rouhani was elected Iran's President in June 2013, negotiations between Iran and the 5+1 States—the five permanent members of the UN Security Council plus Germany—resumed in the fall of 2013. An agreement, known as the Joint Comprehensive Plan of Action (JCPOA)—was finally signed on 14 July 2015. Iran agreed to severely limit its nuclear program and put it under strict inspection by the IAEA. President Obama signed an Executive Order on 16 January 2016, lifting all the sanctions that he had imposed on Iran, but not those imposed by the Congress that require its approval.

13.5   *Sanctions Imposed by the Trump Administration*

Throughout his campaign for President in 2016 Donald Trump referred consistently to the JCPOA as "the worst deal ever." He also repeated the lie that the United States "had given Iran $150 billion." In reality, what Iran had received was about $55 billion of its own money that had been frozen in European and East Asian banks due to the sanctions that President Obama had imposed on Iran. During his campaign Trump also vowed that, if elected, he would take the United States out of the JCPOA and re-impose harsh sanctions on Iran.

That Trump would take such a position vis-à-vis JCPOA is not surprising. His most ardent supporter and financial backer was Sheldon Adelson, the Zionist billionaire that once suggested (Shwayder 2013) that the United States should attack Iran with nuclear bombs. Trump also received major financial backing from other Zionist billionaires (Clifton 2018), such as Bernard Marcus, founder of the Home Depot, and Paul Singer, founder and CEO of the hedge fund Elliott Management Corporation. In August 2017 Congress approved the Countering America's Adversaries Through Sanctions Act (CAATSA), which imposed sanctions against Iran's ballistic missile or weapons of mass destruction programs; the sale or transfer to Iran of military equipment or the provision of related technical or financial assistance, and Iran's Islamic Revolutionary Guard Corps (IRGC) and affiliated foreign persons. Note that Iran has no known program for producing weapons of mass destruction.

Trump delivered on his campaign promise and in May 2018 announced that the United States will withdraw from the JCPOA. His Secretary of State Mike Pompeo laid out a list of twelve demands that Iran had to satisfy *before* the United States would even agree to resume negotiations with Iran for replacing the JCPOA with a "better" agreement. The twelve demands were tantamount to capitulation by Iran, and were rejected immediately by Iran. In October 2018 the International Court of Justice ordered the United States to cancel all the sanctions against Iran. The unanimous decision was based on the 1955 US-Iran "Friendship Treaty" that the two sides had signed. In response, Pompeo withdrew the United States from the treaty. Full sanctions were imposed on Iran once again in November 2018. Pompeo and the Trump administration continued increasing the severity of the sanctions to absurd—some say sadistic—levels, to the point that even Mohammad Javad Zarif, Iran's moderate Foreign Minister, was sanctioned. The efforts failed to achieve its true goal, namely, the downfall of Tehran's regime, but failure did not change Pompeo (Sahimi 2020). Pompeo's mission in life seems to be bringing misery to the Iranian people. The Trump administration's exit from the JCPOA is completely illegal. Resolution 2231 of the UN Security Council, which approved and supported the JCPOA, was issued under Chapter VII of the UN Charter. Carrying out the provisions of such resolutions is mandatory for all the UN members. Re-imposing the sanctions on Iran, given that Iran had delivered on all its obligations, is both illegal and immoral.

The effect of the Trump's sanctions on Iran's economy has been catastrophic. Iran's economy that had grown by about 13.4 percent in 2016, contracted by about 6 percent in 2018 and another 6.7 percent in 2019. The rate of inflation that was 7.2 percent in 2016, jumped to 18 percent in 2018 and 40 percent in 2019.

Even at the height of the Coronavirus pandemic, the United States did not relax its sanctions, so that Iran could import critical medicine and medical equipment that it needed to confront the pandemic. Theoretically, exporting medicine to Iran is not sanctioned by the United States. But when Iran's banks and financial institutions are cut off from the SWIFT system and its European and East Asian bank accounts are frozen, how can Iran pay for the medicine?

14   Conclusion: The Effect of Economic War on the Social Fabric and National Development of Iran

The British-Russian interventions in Iran, the British economic war of 1951–1953, and the CIA-MI6 coup of 1953 halted Iran's progress toward a completely democratic state. Had Dr. Mosaddegh's government survived, Iran would have been a model of secular democracy in the Middle East. Instead, after Iranian people suffered the Shah's dictatorship for 25 years, they toppled his regime, but the political vacuum that he had created during his reign by jailing, executing, exiling, or forcing into silence his opponents, from the nationalists, to the leftist and moderate religious-nationalist groups, was a prime reason why the clerics succeeded in taking control of the Iranian revolution and setting up a theocracy, instead of a secular republic that most Iranians, including this author, had hoped for (Sahimi 2011a). It is not exaggeration to view the 1953 coup as the beginning of a process that not only led to the 1979 Revolution, but also to the 11 September 2001 terrorist attacks on the United States.

The hostility of the United States toward Iran over the past 42 years has deeply affected Iran's political and economic development. The eight-year Iran-Iraq war that Iraq began with at least indirect encouragement by the United States, inflicted terrible and heavy damage on Iran's infrastructure, economy, political development, and social fabric. At least 16,000 civilians lost their lives. Estimates of number of dead Iranian soldiers vary anywhere from 200,000 to 600,000 (Hiro 1991, 205), with another 320,000 to 500,000 injured (Mikaberidze 2011, 418). The economic loss is estimated to be at least $627 billion (Hiro 1991, 251), although estimates as high as $1 trillion have also been mentioned. The cost of caring for the veterans of the war, thousands of them injured by Iraq's chemical weapons is simply incalculable.

The war with Iraq also halted Iran's progress toward democracy. The ruling clerics used the war as an excuse to suppress the opposition. Thousands of political prisoners were executed in the 1980s. In particular, close to 4,000 political prisoners who had been given only jail sentences, were executed during summer of 1988, which was a grave crime (Sahimi 2011c).

The social fabric of the population was also deeply scarred. When a country losses close to one million young men, with another 1–2 million leaving the country to avoid being drafted into the army, the overall population suffers from imbalance. The war left deep scars on Iranian people's conscience and society that persist today.

Since the 1990s, not only has the United States imposed extensive sanctions on Iran, as described above, which has almost always been supported by its European allies, it has also imposed secondary sanctions on those countries or entities that would like to continue their trade with Iran. This is, of course, illegal, because no country has the right to approve sanctions by its parliament, but extend the boundaries of its applicability to overseas, which the secondary sanctions effectively do. The secondary sanctions have prevented large-scale foreign investments in Iran, and this is while Iran badly needs investments in its oil and natural gas sector. For example, after the Trump administration exited the JCPOA, the French oil firm Total withdrew from a $4.8 billion project that it had signed with the Rouhani administration for developing portions of South Pars, the giant gas field in the Persian Gulf. As a results, Iran's economic development has been badly hampered for over 30 years.

To better understand the effect of the US sanctions against Iran, consider a comprehensive study (Hufbauer *et al.* 2009, 155–178) that concluded that the US has imposed more political and economic sanctions against Iran than against the Soviet Union at the height of the Cold War. In other words, the United States political and security establishment has treated Iran even more harshly than its archrival during the Cold War. An important result of hampering Iran's economic development has been the brain drain that it has been suffering since the 1980s. Without foreign investments, the ability of the State for creating jobs for the population is severely limited. Thus, every year thousands of young and educated Iranians leave Iran. Part of this is undoubtedly due to the social and political limitation and repression in Iran. But, even the most democratic nation would not be able to create enough jobs and opportunity by itself and without foreign investments, particularly for a nation of 84 million people.

Three main excuses that the United States uses to impose sanctions on Iran are violations of human rights, Iran's civilian nuclear program, and its "meddling" in the Middle East through proxy groups. But, violations of human rights and lack of political freedom, free press, and freedom of expression were also rampant during the reign of the Shah, and despite being an un-democratic political system, the Islamic Republic is far more open than the Shah's regime ever was. Yet, the United States never seriously took issue with them and never imposed sanctions on the Shah's regime. In addition, Iran is a far more dynamic and open society than any of the US Arab allies in the Middle East, namely, Saudi Arabia, United Arab Emirates, Bahrain, and Egypt, which are far worse than Iran in violating the fundamental human rights of their own citizens. Israel's violation of the rights of the Palestinian people needs no explanation. As for the Islamic Republic's "meddling" in the Middle East, the Shah's interventions in the region on behalf of the United States was just as extensive, if not more so, than the Islamic Republic's. The Shah sided with Saudi Arabia in the Radfan Uprising, the South Yemen war of independence from North Yemen from 1963–1967. He supported the regime of Hafez al-Assad in Syria against his rival regime in Iraq. He armed and trained the Iraqi Kurds in the 1970s against the central government (Reisinezhad 2019). In the 1970s he also sent Iran's military to Oman to intervene in the Dhofar rebellion, a leftist insurgency (Allen and Rigsbee 2000, 72–73). When a leftist government came to power in Afghanistan through a coup in 1973, it was the Shah who first began training and arming the so-called Afghan Mujahedin (Cordovez and Harrison 1995, 15–16) and sending them into their country to fight with the central government. None of these raised any objections by Washington, simply because the Shah's Iran was a client state.

This is not to say that the Islamic Republic is without fault; far from it. Iran does share major responsibility for the state-of-affairs of its relations with the United States. But, much of what the Islamic Republic has done in the Middle East has been in reaction to what the United States and its allies have been doing against Iran and its interests, particularly, security interest, in the region. Constant threat of "all options are on the table" by the United States will rattle any nation, let alone Iran with its bitter history of its relationship with the US, not to mention its historical sense of insecurity, a result of being invaded by foreign powers.

Acknowledgment

The author would like to thank Dr. Amir Boozari for reading this chapter, and for his insightful comments and suggestions that helped improving it.

References

Abrahamian, Ervand. (2008). *A History of Modern Iran*. London: Cambridge University Press.

Abrahamian, Ervand. (2013). *The Coup: 1953, the CIA, and the Roots of Modern U.S.–Iranian Relations*. New York: New Press.

Albright, Madeleine. (2000). "Remarks before the American-Iranian Council, March 17, 2000." Washington, DC.

Allen, Calvin H., and Rigsbee, W. Lynn. (2000). *Oman Under Qaboos: From Coup to Constitution, 1970–1996*. New York: Routledge.

Atabaki, Touraj. (2009). *Iran in the 20th Century: Historiography and Political Culture*. New York: I.B. Tauris.

Bamberg, John H. (1982). *The History of the British Petroleum Company*, vol. II, *The Anglo-Iranian Years, 1928–1954*. London: Cambridge University Press.

Battle, Joyce (ed.). (2003). National Security Archive Electronic Briefing Book No. 82. *Shaking Hands with Saddam Hussein: The U.S. Tilts toward Iraq, 1980–1984*. https://nsarchive2.gwu.edu//NSAEBB/NSAEBB82/index.htm.

Bekker, Pieter H.F. (2003). "The world court finds that U.S. attacks on Iranian oil platforms in 1987–1988 were not justifiable as self-defense, but the United States did not violate the applicable treaty with Iran." *American Society of International Law* 8 (25).

Blight, James G., Lang, Janet M., Banai, Hussein, Byrne, Malcolm, Tirman, John, and Riedel, Bruce. (2012). *Becoming Enemies: U.S.-Iran Relations and the Iran-Iraq War, 1979–1988*. Plymouth: Rowman & Littlefield.

Bowden, Mark. (2006). "The Desert One Debacle." *The Atlantic*, May 2006.

Clark, Sr., Wesley K. (2003). *Winning Modern Wars: Iraq, Terrorism, and the American Empire*. New York: Public Affairs.

Clifton, Eli. (2018). "Follow the Money: Three Billionaires Paved Way For Trump's Iran Deal Withdrawal." *Lobelog*, 8 May. https://lobelog.com/three-billionaires-paved-way-for-trumps-iran-deal-withdrawal/.

Cordovez, Diego, and Selig, Harrison. (1995). *Out of Afghanistan: The Inside Story of the Soviet Withdrawal*. London: Cambridge University Press.

Director of National Intelligence. (2007). Iran: Nuclear Intentions and Capabilities. https://www.dni.gov/files/documents/Newsroom/Reports%20and%20Pubs/20071203_release.pdf.

Elm, Mostafa. (1992). *Oil, Power, and Principle: Iran's Oil Nationalization and Its Aftermath*. Syracuse: Syracuse University Press.

Executive Order 12170. (1979). "Blocking Iranian Government property," 14 November.

Executive Order 13645. (2013). "Authorizing the Implementation of Certain Sanctions Set Forth in the Iran Freedom and Counter-Proliferation Act of 2012 and Additional

Sanctions with Respect to Iran. 3 June. Federal Register." *Federal Register*, Volume 78, No. 108, 5 June.

Ferrier, Ronal W. (1982). *The History of the British Petroleum Company*, vol. i, *The Developing Years, 1901–1932*. London: Cambridge University Press.

Friedman, Alan. (1993). *Spider's Web: The Secret History of how the White House Illegally armed Iraq*. New York: Bantam Books.

Gause, Gegory. (1994). "The illogic of Dual Containment." *Foreign Affairs*, March/April.

Ghani, Cyrus. (2001). *Iran and the Rise of Reza Shah: From Qajar Collapse to Pahlavi Power*. New York: I.B. Tauris.

Gibson, Bryan R. (2010). *Covert Relationship: American Foreign Policy, Intelligence, and the Iran-Iraq War, 1980–1988*. Santa Barbara: ABC-CLIO, LLC.

Government Information. (1995a). Executive Order 12957—Prohibiting Certain Transactions with Respect to the Development of Iranian Petroleum Resources.

Government Information. (1995b). Executive Order 12959—Prohibiting Certain Transactions with Respect to Iran.

Harnden, Toby. (2008). "George W. Bush Raised $400 Million for Action Against Iran." *The Telegraph*, 30 June.

Hastedt, Glenn P., and Guerrier, Steven W. (eds.). (2011). *Spies, Wiretaps, and Secret Operations: An Encyclopedia of American Espionage* (in two volumes). Santa Barbara: ABC-CLIO.

Hiro, Dilip. (1991). *The Longest War: The Iran-Iraq Military Conflict*. New York, NY: Routledge.House Resolution 5434 (1992). The Iran-Iraq Arms Non-Proliferation Act of 1992.

House Resolution 3107. (1996). Iran and Libya Sanctions Act of 1996.

House of Representatives 109-417. (2006). Iran Freedom Support Act.

House Resolution 3364. (2017). Countering America's Adversaries Through Sanctions Act.

Hufbauer, Gary Clyde, Schott, Jeffrey J., Elliot, Kimberly Ann, and Oegg, Barbara. (2009). *Economic Sanctions Reconsidered*, 3rd ed. Peterson Institute for International Economics. New York: Columbia University Press.

Hurewitz, Jacob C. (1979). *Diplomacy in the Near and Middle East A Documentary Record, Volume II, 2nd ed*. New Haven: Yale University Press.

Jewish Telegraphic Agency. (1995). "Bronfman Leads Lobby Against Conoco Deal with Iran," 13 March.

Klare, Michael. (1980). "Military Madness." *New Internationalist*, 2 September. https://newint.org/features/1980/09/01/militarymadness.

Kristof, Nicholas D. (2007). "Iran's Proposal for a "Grand Bargain"." *The New York Times*, 28 April 2007.

Krugman, Paul. (2003). "Things to Come." *The New York Times*, 18 March 2003.

The League of Nations. (1933). "Dispute Between His Majesty's Government in United Kingdom and the Imperial Government of Iran," document C. 43. M.17. 1933.VII, 19 January.

Maclean, Fitzroy. (1949). *Eastern Approaches*. London: Jonathan Cape.

Majd, Mohammad Gholi. (2003). *The Great Famine and Genocide in Persia, 1917–1919*. Lanham: University Press of America.

Mikaberidze, Alexander. (2011). *Conflict and Conquest in the Islamic World: A Historical Encyclopedia*. Santa Barbara, CA: ABC-CLIO.

Milani, Abbas. (2008). *Eminent Persians: The Men and Women Who Made Modern Iran, 1941–1979*, volume 2. Syracuse: Syracuse University Press.

Neville, Leigh. (2008). *Special Forces in the War on Terror*. New York: Bloomsbury Publishing.

Obama, Barack H. (2009). "A new beginning," the speech in Cairo, Egypt, 4 June.

Oborne, Peter, and Morrison, David. (2013). "U.S. Scuppered deal with Iran in 2005 says then British Foreign Minister." *Open Democracy*, 23 September.

O'Sullivan, Adrian. (2015). *Espionage and Counterintelligence in Occupied Persia (Iran): The Success of the Allied Secret Services, 1941–45*. London: Palgrave Macmillan.

Radio Free Europe. (2006). "Iran: Text of Ahmadinejad's letter to Bush," 11 May.

Reisinezhad, Arash. (2019). *The Shah of Iran, the Iraqi Kurds, and the Lebanese Shia*. London: Palgrave Macmillan.

Sahimi, Muhammad. (2009). "The Hostage Crisis, 30 Years on." Tehran Bureau, PBS.

Sahimi, Muhammad. (2011a)."The Nationalist Religious Movmeent, Part 1." Tehran Bureau, PBS.

Sahimi, Muhammad. (2011b). "The Chain Murders: Killing Dissidents and Intellectuals, 1988–1998." Tehran Bureau, PBS.

Sahimi, Muhammad. (2011c). "The Bloody Red Summer of 1988. Grave Crimes Against Humanity." Tehran Bureau, PBS.

Sahimi, Muhammad. (2013). "Atoms for Peace." *The Cairo Review*. Summer.

Sahimi, Muhammad. (2020). "When it Comes to Iran, How Many Failures is Enough for Pompeo?". *Responsible Statecraft*, 14 September.

Shwayder, Maya. (2013). "Adelson: U.S. Should Drop Atomic Bombs on Iran." *The Jerusalem Post*, 24 October.

The National Security Archive. (2012). "Document 5: Talking Points." State Department, 12 October.

United Nations. (2001). Agreement on Provisional Arrangements in Afghanistan Pending the Re-establishment of Permanent Government Institutions (Bonn Agreement).

United Press International. (2007). "Perry: U.S. eyed Iran attack after bombing." 6 June White House Fact Sheet. 31 July 2012. Sanctions Related to Iran.

Wilber, Donald N. (2000). *Regime Change in Iran. Overthrow of Premier Mossadeq of Iran, November 1952—August 1953.* New York: Abm Komers.

World Bank Report. (1952). "Nationalization of the Iranian Oil Industry—An Outline of its Origin and Issues." http://pubdocs.worldbank.org/en/608151403270477052/wbg -archives-1806440.pdf.

World Bank. (2009). "GDP growth (annual%) Iran, Islamic Republic of, 2009." https:// data.worldbank.org/indicator/NY.GDP.MKTP.KD.ZG?end=2019&locations= IR&start=2009.

World Bank. (2010). "Inflation, consumer prices (annual%) Iran, Islamic Republic of, 2010." https://data.worldbank.org/indicator/FP.CPI.TOTL.ZG?end=2019&locations= IR&start=2010.

Wright, Robin. (2000). *The Last Great Revolution: Turmoil and Transformation in Iran.* New York: Random House.

Yergin, Daniel. (1991). *The Prize: The Epic Quest for Oil, Money, and Power.* New York: Free Press.

CHAPTER 11

Sanctions and Nation Breaking: Yugoslavia, 1990–2000

Gregory Elich

Like an iceberg, the bulk of US and Western European foreign policy is hidden from general view. Yugoslavia's breakup and descent into bloodshed illustrate many of the ways in which imperial powers can impose their will on other nations. American and European leaders deployed their entire arsenal of malign foreign policy tools to dismantle and reconfigure Yugoslavia. Economic sanctions were intertwined in the hybrid war against Yugoslavia and are properly understood in that context. Other components in the anti-Yugoslav project included diplomatic machinations, threats and intimidation, relentless media propaganda, support to opposition parties, subversion, covert operations, mobilization of violence, and kinetic warfare.

Aside from NATO's 1999 war, the West's role in the Balkans has largely faded into oblivion. Instead, we are presented with the manufactured image of a crisis that needed Western military intervention to put things right. Omitted is any suggestion that the West fomented mayhem in the first place. But then, it usually is only the targeted country that is fully aware that the United States and Western Europe conduct foreign policy as arsonists rather than firefighters. Political economist Amiya Kumar Bagchi has described imperialism as "the persistent tendency of mature capitalist state systems to generate violent conflicts" (cited in Karuka 2019). Although generally promoted as a "soft" option, sanctions are only another manifestation of violence in the harm that is done to people. However, in all of its forms, violence was what American and European leaders delivered to Yugoslavia's peoples.

Following the collapse of socialism in Eastern Europe and amid Mikhail Gorbachev's dismantling of socialism in the Soviet Union, Yugoslavia's independent socialist development model stood out as the last European challenge to neoliberal orthodoxy. Inevitably, that attracted Western attention. Sucked into the political vortex generated by events in Eastern Europe, Yugoslavia encountered internal divisions and a crisis of socialist confidence that the West capitalized on to disarticulate the nation and create small dependent states. Debt accumulated during Yugoslavia's growing reliance on international loans during the 1980s inevitably exposed the nation to vulnerabilities that the West tried to exploit. Market reforms were demanded. According to a CIA analysis, "Under pressure from the IMF and Western creditors, Belgrade in May 1988 launched its most ambitious economic reform effort to date," calling for "broader introduction of market measures and dismantling of much of the subsidies and benefits provided by the country's traditional system of 'workers' self-management socialism.' " However, those measures encountered stiff resistance, leading the CIA to complain, "Implementation of reform measures thus far has been slow" and the population "is in no mood for further belt-tightening" (CIA 1989).

Ante Marković became prime minister of Yugoslavia in March 1989, at a time of intense ideological struggle between those who sought capitalist restoration and those who remained committed to the socialist path. Marković's plan to accelerate the privatization process could only make slow headway. Appealing to the IMF for additional loans, Marković was rebuffed and told that no new loans would be forthcoming until neoliberal plans were carried out (Sinai 1989). Because Marković sought to destroy socially-owned property in a manner that would have allowed Western corporations to swoop in and grab the best assets at bargain-basement prices, the Yugoslav Assembly planned to hold a no-confidence vote. Panicked at the prospect of losing their man, US and Western European officials threatened to block all of Yugoslavia's financial accounts held abroad unless the Assembly cancelled its scheduled vote. In the international arena, the mere threat of sanctions can frequently be enough to compel obedience. So it proved on this occasion, and Marković stayed in office until resigning near the end of 1991.

According to Borisav Jović, who was Yugoslavia's president then, "They knew that the National Bank of Yugoslavia at the time had around 3.5 billion US dollars in foreign banks and that the blocking of accounts would finish off our already exhausted economy" (Jović 1992). The Socialist Federal Republic of Yugoslavia (SFRY) comprised six republics: Bosnia-Herzegovina, Croatia, Macedonia, Montenegro, Serbia, and Slovenia. Elements within the League of Communists began to favor separatist and anti-socialist policies. A walkout by the Slovenian delegation in January 1990 brought the 14th party congress to a quick close, and that hastened the party's dissolution. Moving quickly, Croatia and Slovenia held multi-party elections in April, in which anti-communist parties assumed power.

The United States expected Yugoslavia's four remaining republics to follow that example. In June 1990, a bill was introduced in the House of Representatives, which instructed American officials in international financial institutions to oppose "any assistance" to Yugoslavia unless multi-party elections were held in all six republics. That bill was signed into law on November 5

(US Congress 1990). By the end of the year, multi-party elections took place in the four remaining republics, in which capitalist-oriented parties were victorious in Bosnia and Macedonia. In contrast, socialist parties that were the League of Communists' offspring retained power in Serbia and Montenegro. The latter two republics' electoral outcome was the antithesis of US hopes and determined who would be marked for regime change.

Borisav Jović wrote in his diary that a reliable source had informed him that a US diplomat met with the leaders of Croatian anti-communist parties in Zagreb and that through them, the United States had chosen to destroy communism in Yugoslavia at the cost of shattering the country. Jović also learned that Austrian officials met in Ljubljana with secessionist-minded leaders from Croatia, Macedonia, and Slovenia. "Everything is clear," he concluded. "This is treason and the breakup of the country with international assistance" (Jović 1995).

Yugoslavia was led by a collective presidency that included one member from each republic and autonomous province. As first Slovenia, and then Croatia, waged a secessionist war against the Yugoslav People's Army (Jugoslovenska Narodna Armija—JNA), the nation was plunged into a crisis that called for an emergency response. However, the presidency was split, and no agreement was possible between members who wanted to save the country and those who hoped to destroy it. In March 1991, the JNA's General Staff met with the presidency. It proposed that a state of emergency be declared, authorizing the army to halt the nation's disintegration and prevent a civil war. It was not too late to defend the SFRY, but immediate action was needed. Under terms of the constitution, a state of emergency required a majority vote by the members. Unfortunately, the division in the presidency meant that the proposal failed to win approval (Jović 2020a). On June 25, 1991, Croatia and Slovenia declared independence, and their territorial troops attacked units of the JNA stationed in the two republics. The Krajina region of Croatia had a majority ethnic Serb population, which had no desire to be dragged away from Yugoslavia. Armed ethnic Serb militias battled Croatian territorial and paramilitary forces.

The position of president of the collective presidency rotated among members on an annual basis. On May 15, 1991, it was time for Croatia's representative, Stipe Mesić, to be named president, but the collective voted him down according to Article 327 of the Yugoslav constitution. Mesić's repeated vows to be the last president of Yugoslavia and his role in arranging illegal arms imports into Croatia made it clear that he would be a disastrous choice to lead the nation (Yugoslav Survey 1992). Those same qualities appealed to Western leaders, who saw in Mesić an effective means of achieving their objectives. Who better to lead Yugoslavia than a man who sought its destruction? It would be necessary to force Mesić on the nation against its will. Claiming to act in the interests of democracy, US Ambassador to Yugoslavia Warren Zimmerman warned that failure to appoint Mesić would prompt the United States to oppose Yugoslav access to international financial institutions (Tanjug 1991a). Since credit is essential in international trade, blockage would have dealt a severe blow to Yugoslavia's economy.

The European Community (EC) added threats of its own to those of Zimmerman. Together, they succeeded in strong-arming the Yugoslav presidency into reversing its vote on Mesić and naming him president. As Jović related, "Democracy was to be affirmed by accepting and appointing to the leading position a dynamiter who would plant explosives in Yugoslavia's foundation" (Jović 1992). In exchange for that vote, Croatia and Slovenia agreed to EC mediators' request to suspend independence plans for three months, a meaningless formulation in that it changed nothing. Certainly, Slovenia emphasized to EC diplomats that the delay did not mean it would drop its independence (Tanjug 1991b). Yugoslavia was spiraling ever deeper into crisis. Mesić obstructed the presidency's work by refusing to convene sessions in Belgrade and ignoring the presidency's repeated requests to schedule meetings. As the United States and European Community intended, the Yugoslav government was paralyzed when action was most needed (Tanjug 1991c). As armed conflict escalated, the EC dispatched three of its foreign ministers to Brioni, Yugoslavia. On July 8, they brokered an agreement between the parties, calling on the JNA to withdraw to its barracks. Croatia and Slovenia were obligated to deactivate territorial military units and stop blockading JNA facilities, terms they never honored.

The Brioni Declaration specified that "control of border crossings will be in the hands of Slovenian police," a crucial point in that it opened the floodgates for arms shipments to secessionist forces (UN 1991). Germany and Austria increased the supply of arms and military gear they were sending to Croatia and Slovenia. To list two examples among many, a truck convoy on October 4 delivered anti-tank weapons and 40,000 uniforms to Croatia, and another one eight days later brought 18,000 Kalashnikov assault rifles (Yugoslav Survey 1992; Vujičić 2014).

By October, the Yugoslav presidency could no longer remain idle. In the continued absence of Mesić and the Slovenian representative, the six remaining members voted unanimously per Article 328 of the constitution to govern, relying on those who chose to attend its sessions (Tanjug 1991d). The West's reaction was immediate, denouncing the Yugoslav presidency as anti-democratic and characterizing its decision to resume functioning as a "coup." There was still a split in the presidency. The only option the members could agree on was to accept the EC's offer to organize a Conference on Yugoslavia to arrive at a negotiated settlement among the parties. It would soon become apparent that the EC intended to use the conference as a battering ram to smash the SFRY. The EC wasted little time in guiding events towards its desired goal. In an early plenary session, Lord Peter Carrington, chairman of the conference, stopped Yugoslav Vice President Branko Kostić in the middle of his presentation, saying that he would not allow Kostić to represent the Yugoslav presidency (Kostić 1991).

On October 17, attendees at the Conference on Yugoslavia received copies of the EC's "Arrangements for an Overall Solution," which called for "sovereign and independent republics with an international personality for those wishing it." Furthermore, it continued, "the republics themselves will decide on their own armed forces" (Yugoslav Survey 1992). The document was the basis for talks, but what was there to negotiate when it already defined the outcome? At the end of October, the EC warned that "uncooperative republics" would face economic sanctions, and it delivered an ultimatum to the Republic of Serbia that it would be sanctioned if it did not accede to the EC's "basic principles" by November 5 (Tanjug 1991e).

By now, secessionist violence was out of control, and the moment to save Yugoslavia as a federation of six republics had passed. Months of paralysis due to Stipe Mesić blockading the presidency, coupled with the flood of Western arms shipments, ensured that Croatia and Slovenia were lost to the SFRY. Serbia's view was that the two republics could go, but that process should be arranged through peaceful negotiation rather than violence. Furthermore, separation ought to be based on the choice of peoples rather than internal administrative borders.

The EC's position was that any republic could secede, and Yugoslavia's internal administrative borders are sacrosanct while its international borders are erased. Serbia argued that the EC's principles should not be applied selectively only to those who wish to leave Yugoslavia, but must also include those who want to remain. It added that the conference had no right to start with the premise that Yugoslavia no longer exists (Tanjug 1991f; Tanjug 1991g).

In a speech delivered at the conference, Serbian President Slobodan Milošević rebuked the EC for its ultimatum to accept its principles as "an act of pressure and violence," adding that "we have never and also cannot now agree to Yugoslavia being written off with the stroke of a pen" (Milošević 1991). Retribution was swift in coming. On November 8, the European Community announced a package of sanctions on Yugoslavia, including termination of its trade and cooperation agreement and a reduction in exports of textile products (EC 1991a). Four days later, Mesić sent a letter to the Federal Reserve Bank in New York, demanding that it "refuse to comply with and reject any attempt by the Yugoslav National Bank to withdraw funds" (Radio Croatia 1991). Not long after, the EC voted to exempt the four secession-minded republics from sanctions, targeting only Serbia and Montenegro (Tanjug 1991h). Dissenting voices were not wanted at the Conference on Yugoslavia and needed to be stifled as much as possible. The EC organizers barred Yugoslav federal officials from speaking, and later did not even allow them to attend. Every request sent by federal officials to join the conference was ignored. The extraordinary situation is that decisions were made by Western powers and mostly secessionists, while Yugoslavia itself had no say in its fate (Yugoslav Survey 1992).

It came as no surprise when the EC announced on December 16 that it would recognize the independence of those Yugoslav republics that "wish to be recognized as independent states" (EC 1991b). Stipe Mesić, having already seen the writing on the wall, had by then announced in a speech before the Croatian Parliament, "I have accomplished my task. Yugoslavia is no more" (Yugoslav Survey 1992). The EC promptly recognized the independence of Croatia, Slovenia, and Macedonia. The latter republic was the only one to peacefully separate from the Yugoslav federation. The conference was reminiscent of the colonial era, in which European nations were in the practice of drawing other people's borders. Not long into 1992, Bosnia-Herzegovina announced its intention to secede, and the EC assigned José Cutileiro to chair talks between representatives of the republic's Croat, Muslim, and Serb peoples. On March 18, the parties agreed to a statement of principles as the basis for negotiations. American officials were not pleased. As Cutileiro recalled, some of them tended to "try to frame it in some kind of fight between good and evil," urging Bosnian Muslim leader Alija Izetbegović against negotiating (Cutileiro 2015). As revealed by an unnamed high-ranking State Department official: "The policy was to encourage Izetbegović to break with the partition plan" (cited in Binder 1993). In that endeavor, the Americans proved successful, and Izetbegović renounced the statement of principles that he had just signed. In the absence of cooperation, the talks limped along until June, when the Muslim side issued a formal rejection of the plan (Cutileiro 2015).

The Americans had another approach in mind. According to US diplomat Richard Johnson, "We pressed the Europeans to move forward on recognition" (Binder 1993). The Americans got their way, and on April 7, 1992, the EC recognized Bosnian independence, as did the United States. In the absence of agreement among Bosnia's peoples as to what that state should look like, immediate international recognition was a recipe for a three-way civil war, which was not long in coming. Muslim territorial units launched attacks on the JNA everywhere it was stationed, and internecine conflict erupted among

Bosnia's three peoples. Only Serbia and Montenegro remained in the SFRY, so in April, the two republics were reconstituted as the Federal Republic of Yugoslavia (FRY).

In the Western mindset, the abrupt recognition of Bosnia's independence instantly transformed JNA troops stationed there into interlopers, and the United States and European Community demanded the immediate withdrawal of the army to the FRY. UN Security Council Resolution 752 commanded the JNA in Bosnia to either withdraw or be disbanded. As punishment, the EC imposed an oil embargo on Yugoslavia (Tanjug 1992a). For the JNA, withdrawal was easier said than done, in that Muslim and Croatian territorial military units blockaded its barracks. Eventually, JNA units reached an agreement with the Muslim side on peaceful withdrawal from Sarajevo and Tuzla, only to be ambushed after exiting their barracks.

On May 30, 1992, the UN Security Council passed Resolution 757 to penalize the Federal Republic of Yugoslavia. By this time, JNA units in Bosnia had withdrawn to the FRY, except for individual soldiers with homes in Bosnia, who either entered civilian life or joined the three warring factions. Among other measures, the UN resolution banned trade with the FRY except for food and medicine and prohibited international financial transactions involving Yugoslavia (UN 1992a). That same day, US President George H.W. Bush issued an executive order blocking all Yugoslav property in the United States, including in US overseas financial branches (Bush 1992).

Western officials did not hide what prompted their animus. At a meeting of the Conference on Security and Cooperation in Europe (CSCE), Yugoslav delegate Vladimir Pavićević found himself engaged in difficult discussions with other members. "Some have told me openly that this is now an occasion, through acceptance of the criticisms of the CSCE, to really help Yugoslavia to experience further democratization and fit into the new order in the true sense of the word," he related. "Others say that this is a way in which additional pressure must be exerted to achieve the goal, regardless of consequences." The United States was applying "pressure for us to fit into the new European order. The United States wants Yugoslavia within the framework of the new international order, not outside it, and certainly not opposed to it. It has been saying this both publicly and in conversation" (Stošić 1992).

Yugoslavia's sin was in swimming against the neoliberal tide of the times. Socialized capital still accounted for over 93 percent of the FRY economy, and nearly all the rest was in individually-owned businesses (Dumezić 1992).

1   The Imposition of Sanctions

UN sanctions had an immediate impact on Yugoslavia. Crowds swarmed into stores, sweeping up goods that would soon be in short supply. Shelves that were fully stocked at the start of the day had been emptied by closing time (Čičić 1992).

The Bush administration closed Yugoslav consulates and announced that it would no longer recognize the nation's ambassador. The United States was also pressuring various international organizations to banish Yugoslavia (AFP 1992). That effort soon bore fruit, and on July 8, the CSCE suspended Yugoslavia's membership (Tanjug 1992b). Days later, the Organization for Economic Cooperation and Development followed suit (Tanjug 1992c). US Secretary of State James Baker was determined to punish the FRY by ousting it from the United Nations. The American delegation introduced the resolution to expel Yugoslavia from the General Assembly based on the contrived fiction that Yugoslavia no longer existed. That measure passed by majority vote, and Yugoslavia was gone from the organization (Kempster 1992; Lewis 1992). The professed justification was nonsensical but convenient. In logical terms, it was the same as arguing that the United States had ceased to exist in 1861 because its southern states had seceded. To this day, Yugoslavia remains the only country ever to be thrown out of the United Nations.

The vindictive nature of UN sanctions spared no one. Nearly 60,000 Yugoslav retirees had earned foreign pensions while working abroad, but sanctions immediately halted their monthly annuity payments, leaving them destitute. Many also lost foreign health insurance coverage in the process. Yugoslavia appealed to the UN sanctions monitoring committee for an exemption for retirees, only to be turned down (Tanjug 1992d). When it came to matters that the United States cared about, the UN sanctions monitoring committee acted with alacrity in issuing exemptions. The US government's request to import more than a quarter of a million dollars of equipment to the pro-opposition Studio B broadcaster won immediate acceptance, timed to arrive one month before elections (Binder 1992).

By the third month under the sanctions regime, Yugoslavia's industrial sector was already reeling, plummeting forty percent compared to the same period the year before (Ikonić 1992). Industry found it nearly impossible to obtain raw materials, supplies, and spare parts for machinery. The experience of the Trepča mining conglomerate in the province of Kosovo was typical. Shortages directly caused most of its facilities to grind to a near halt, forcing a ninety percent reduction in the workforce (Laketić 1992). At Novkabel, the largest factory in Novi Sad, General Director Djordje Širadović described his firm's predicament. "Our trouble is that we have not only lost important foreign trading partners, but we have stopped all investments... even if a few trucks get through, it is like feeding berries to a hungry lion" (Uzelac 1992).

US and Western European leaders were anxious about the impact sanctions were having on Yugoslavia's people. Their abiding concern was that sanctions were not causing enough pain. To rectify that problem, they employed a naval blockade in the Adriatic against Yugoslavia, and ships were issued stop-and-search orders to enforce the trade embargo (Wielaard 1992). A naval blockade is an act of war, but international law is not meant to apply to imperial powers. Western leaders were still not satisfied, and to tighten the noose, the UN Security Council passed a resolution to blockade traffic on the Danube River too (UN 1992b). With ruthless efficiency, economic sanctions drove down the Yugoslav economy. By the time 1992 came to a close, GDP had declined by nearly 32 percent, and the annual inflation rate stood at almost nine thousand percent (Bogetić, Petrović, and Vujošević 1999).

It had been a hard year, but far worse was to come. Early in 1993, the CIA analyzed the impact of sanctions. It deplored the fact that "the downward spiral of Serbia's economy" had "yet to impose sufficient hardships on local consumers needed to spark a groundswell of anti-regime sentiment." Something had to be done to deliver more pain to the Yugoslav people. "Only a prolonged determination by the West to impose even tighter sanctions...would offer any prospect of forcing Belgrade to make significant political concessions," the CIA helpfully suggested (CIA 1993).

The CIA did not have long to wait to see more pain delivered, and in April, the United Nations passed yet another set of sanctions on the FRY. UN member nations were directed to seize funds belonging to Yugoslav entities. The blockade on the Danube River was tightened. No commodity was allowed to be transported by land into or out of the FRY. The same restriction was applied to the Montenegrin port of Bar. UN member nations were instructed to impound Yugoslav vessels, vehicles, rolling stock, and aircraft in their territories and charge the expense of impoundment to Yugoslav owners (UN 1993).

The new sanctions forbade Montenegro's merchant fleet from sailing in international waters, and wherever its ships were anchored abroad, they were promptly seized. Not allowed to depart from foreign ports, the ships were nevertheless charged mooring fees where they were trapped. Because sanctions did not allow Yugoslavia to process international transactions, there was no way for Montenegrin maritime firms to pay the costs that mounted to astronomical levels. The only means of meeting the imposed debt obligations was for shipping companies to sell several seized vessels, with the proceeds going directly to creditors (Gregović 1995).

Unable to work and draw a paycheck, most of Montenegro's seamen sought employment on foreign ships (Ramović 1995). Montenegrin vessels rapidly decayed due to disuse and lack of maintenance (Vulić 1994). A ship impounded at Liverpool was representative. Trapped aboard, the crew had to rely on food handouts to survive. Bill Swanson of the Apostleship of the Sea characterized the policy of seizing ships as "slow strangulation, a gangster tactic." The ship in Liverpool, he sadly noted, "is falling apart through lack of use. It was a good ship in the past, but now it needs help" (Litherland 1994).

Although UN sanctions ostensibly exempted medical supplies and humanitarian aid on a case-by-case basis, the provision was mainly for show, meant to maintain a façade of compassion. In actual practice, reviews proceeded with a preordained negative outcome. By late 1994, the UN Sanctions Committee had rejected 550 requests by various nations and organizations to deliver humanitarian aid to Yugoslavia. In most cases, it was an objection raised by the United States that stood in the way (Tanjug 1994a).

Yugoslavia could neither import medicines nor obtain the necessary raw materials for pharmaceutical plants to manufacture drugs. "The drugs are scarce," explained Branko Radović, director of the Belgrade Pharmacy Institution, "because everything has been disrupted since back in November, when imports of the raw materials were banned because of the blockade." According to Miodrag Babić, general director of a pharmaceutical firm, there "are practically no legal ways of obtaining" import permits. "You can just imagine what will happen when this factory stops making infusion solutions and dialysis kits" (O. Popović 1993a).

Stock dwindled to nearly nothing, as pharmacy manager Dragana Slović reported. "Our pharmacies are completely empty. We still have a few antibiotics," and small quantities of other medicines but "the drug manufacturers want advance payment from the Pharmacy Institution, but we do not have money" (O. Popović 1993b). Radomir Stojićević, president of the Association of the Yugoslav Pharmaceutical Industry, complained that "there are no raw materials, although they are not covered by the sanctions. We are not covered by the sanctions, but actually we are subject to horrible sanctions" (B. Popović 1993). Hospitals were compelled to operate without all of the necessary surgical materials. Many facilities were no longer able to perform medical procedures requiring equipment that had become inoperable due to lack of spare parts. Tens of thousands of operations had to be postponed, putting many patients at risk (Lj. M. 1993; Ekonomska Politika 1993).

The health sector needed help. Instead, what it got was a kick in the teeth, as the World Health Organization (WHO) expelled Yugoslavia. The decision dismayed Dr. Viktorija Cucić, a consultant with the WHO: "We believed deeply that the World Health Organization is above and outside politics. However, we see this decision not only as betrayal, but also as misuse of an organization concerned with human health. We are very hard hit by the closed doors, the isolation, the vilification, and the condemnation, so that we have no drugs and must choose whom to treat and whom to let die" (O. Popović 1993c). British physician Mary Black was appalled at the conditions she found when visiting hospitals in Belgrade. Compared to the year before, she saw a "clear deterioration," as "surgical services are now in a catastrophic state, with supplies for only two to three days at a time and often the donated supplies are near their expiry date. Most elective surgery and nearly all plastic and reconstructive surgery has been cancelled. A shortage of artificial valves has denied surgery to some children with congenital cardiac defects" (Black 1993). Dr. Živorad Djordjević, director of an emergency surgical center in Belgrade, described his facility's calamitous situation. "We are rationed to fifty liters of intravenous fluid per day; previously, we used up to two thousand. Only one anesthetic machine is still working, and the wheelchairs are broken. Today the only antibiotic I have is penicillin. Soon all we will have left to work with is our hands" (Black 1993).

Requests to the United Nations to provide humanitarian aid were habitually denied. In one case, three tons of assistance from Nestle intended for orphans were rerouted to Peru when the UN refused to allow delivery to the FRY. Similarly, Austria turned back at its border an Italian donation of children's food meant for a Belgrade orphanage. "The UN Committee ferrets out procedural loopholes even for medicine, whose import is not embargoed," bitterly remarked Borislav Vuković of the Yugoslav sanctions monitoring committee (cited in Tanjug 1993a).

Yugoslav Prime Minister Radoje Kontić's repeated appeals for sanctions relief to meet the health crisis failed to yield results. "I have been writing requests for several months," he said, "asking for the import of medicines, raw materials for their production, and for additional energy supplies to be allowed, in order to save our newborn babies from dying and children in schools from freezing. In no case did they give approval... We have been pleading, begging, saying that we shall pay all the costs. No humanitarian organization has accepted (Logar 1993). Miodrag Babić, director of a pharmaceutical factory, met the UN sanctions monitoring committee, where he learned "that decisions are not made in the committee for sanctions" but by certain Western governments. Velimir Branković, director of the Galenika Factory, confirmed that impression. "It was a horrible discovery when we realized that, despite the fact that raw materials for medicines were not on the list of banned items, they were placed on it by an additional activity by the U.S. administration" (RTB 1993).

Yugoslavia signed a deal with Russia on the provision of natural gas to heat schools and hospitals over the winter of 1993–94. That contract remained stalled, as American and British members on the UN sanctions monitoring committee refused to issue a permit for delivery (Tanjug 1993b). It was not until 1995 that the UN committee approved a limited amount of gas to be delivered, but this apparent concession came with a poison pill. The United Nations would allow no shipment of natural gas unless the FRY paid the lodging and per diem expenses of the 120 international observers that the UN insisted must monitor consumption. Not only was payment required to be in foreign exchange, which Yugoslavia sorely lacked, but the observers' total expenses would exceed the amount needed to pay for the natural gas (Cebalović and Simić 1995). Western members of the committee had hit upon the perfect formula for blocking delivery without entailing the political embarrassment for having done so.

The oil embargo was a key factor in bringing Yugoslavia's economy to its knees. According to Branko Pavličić, Jugopetrol director in Kotor, "Montenegro's entire industry is shutting down—except for food production, and even they will not get petroleum products unless the approval comes from the United Nations for us to import fuel for humanitarian purposes. There is just enough fuel to keep industrial plants 'warm,' so there will not be a breakdown, and all available quantities have been allocated to hospitals, children's institutions, and food production" (J.P. 1993). By October, three-fourths of industrial facilities were idle due to the lack of fuel, raw materials, and spare parts (Tanjug 1993c).

Although gasoline ration coupons were issued to the population, the commodity could often only be obtained from smugglers offering it for sale in canisters along the streets. Long lines of vehicles waited for hours to cross the border into Macedonia in search of gasoline. One smuggler described his routine: "If you cannot put it in cans, then put it in bottles. Every day I bring some forty, but you could have even more. Just do a very good job of putting in the corks, so you don't blow up." Soon, the West pressed Macedonia to apply brakes to the trade to shut off the supply. As one Macedonian station owner explained to a Serb who had asked for fuel, "I do not dare give it to you. Do not get mad. It is a new law. If they catch me pumping into a Serbian car, that is the end! A huge fine" (Andjelković 1993).

Purchasing gasoline in Romania presented another set of challenges, and one had to be ready to pay hefty bribes at various points to transport the commodity out of the country. It often happened that the liquid that unscrupulous sellers billed as gasoline was water they had altered to fake its smell and appearance. It was also essential to elude Romanian police, who were on the lookout to catch smugglers. Despite such obstacles, the gains could outweigh the risks, as this trade provided the only means of survival for many people (Grubić 1993).

Some boat owners were able to make a living by engaging in smuggling operations on the Danube River. It was possible to purchase fuel from foreign boats at a high price, but the process became both more arduous and less lucrative over time. "When the embargo was just beginning, it was fine," stated one smuggler. "A hundred drums per vessel. Not any longer. As the ring is tightened, there is less and less petroleum. We here are the first to feel it. Sometimes we squat here ten days at a time, sleep, eat in this shed. It ruins your nerves and everything, and we do not get a single drumful." The trade was not without its dangers, the smuggler explained: "Try to go out on the Danube in the pitch dark and hook onto a vessel, and he speeds up and suddenly maneuvers to capsize you. This winter, there were icebergs floating here that could destroy you like anything. People tipped over with full boats; they drowned; full drums were floating down the Danube." Regardless, the trade had to continue, as it provided over seventy percent of farmers in the Srem District in the northern province of Vojvodina with the fuel they needed to plant crops. "I have a wife and children and a little bit of land," the smuggler continued. "There are quite a few people from villages who come and wait for a vessel, take a drum of petroleum, and go off to their field to plow and plant. What this is here, friend, is a struggle for life" (Šaponjić 1993).

Under severe pressure from the sanctions, the government tried to direct enough money to cover regional deficits and fund struggling socially-owned firms. As intended, sanctions had saddled the nation with towering needs that could not be adequately met. Hyperinflation hurtled along at an ever-increasing rate with each passing month, like an out-of-control locomotive. For 1993, inflation registered a staggering 116 trillion percent, one of the highest in world history (Bogetić, Petrović, and Vujošević 1999).

Rampaging prices catapulted the entire society into economic chaos. People waited for hours in line at banks to access cash, and despite repeated rounds of devaluation, presses at the Belgrade mint ran nearly round-the-clock, to the point of overheating. Shopkeepers updated prices multiple times a day. "Look at the prices," one shopper grumbled. "I cannot count all the zeroes anymore" (Lekić 1993). Monthly pensions had to be paid in installments, as their value vanished almost instantaneously. By July, the cost of a single tube of toothpaste was more than half the average pension. From the largest firms down to the individual, everyone sought foreign exchange, but sanctions sharply limited the supply (Tanjug 1993d). A flourishing black market quickly arose, and moneychangers became the go-to source for foreign exchange.

Price controls were established on essential goods to ensure availability for the impoverished population. However, speculators emptied the shelves at shops as soon as they were stocked, reselling price-controlled items on the black market at inflated prices. By October, stock at many food warehouses had been depleted. Producers no longer delivered goods, as the prices failed to cover their basic costs (Ivanović and Volf 1993). "There are no goods, and the list of articles that producers are ceasing to supply is getting longer," Milovoje Stanojlović, general director of Gorica market, reported. "Consumers are buying whatever they find in the store, and they almost never ask about the price; availability is the only important thing." Even when goods were obtainable, grocers generally lacked the cash to meet producers' demands for payment in advance (Trbojević 1993).

Regardless of how often salaries and pensions were adjusted, it was impossible to keep pace with inflation's celerity. Retiree Danica Jokić bemoaned the fact that her pension lost half its value the moment she received it. She could not even cover the cost of her family's medication. "We have worked all our lives, and now we have to wait to be given alms, from which we cannot even buy bread" (Rabrenović 1993). Life had become unmanageable, another pensioner explained. "I forgot what fruit, meat, and even milk taste like. I don't eat breakfast. I don't eat dinner. I don't drink coffee anymore... I don't have powder to wash clothes. I'm saving soap. I have no one to help me, and the last pension was 8 billion dinars, just as much as a roll of toilet paper" (Nišavić 2018a). By the end of the year, even the highest pension barely covered the cost of a single bar of soap (Nišavic 2018b).

People coped as best they could. Those having relatives in the countryside had more access to food, while city dwellers with small plots grew a few vegetables. Others were not so fortunate, as in the case of a physician named Milena. "It was so confusing to see empty shelves everywhere. For my whole monthly salary, that of a specialist clinical doctor, all I could buy was three eggs." A landscape architect later recalled, "We had a 50-kilo sack of flour in the pantry, and I baked three times a day, as there was hardly anything else to eat: bread for breakfast, pies for lunch, and buns for dinner, day after day, month after month. In the first six months after hyperinflation, I refused to turn on the oven—I was so fed up with baking" (cited in Bajić-Hajduković 2014). Foraging could be an option for those living in the countryside near a forested area, as was the case with a woman named Gordana. "I regularly made soups from nettle or wild mushrooms, both of which I collected in the forest near my village... This relationship with the land, both cultivated and wild—that was our lifeline during hyperinflation; this is what saved people from starvation" (*ibid.*).The nation hovered on the verge of plunging into the abyss of mass starvation. As long as sanctions remained in place, there would never be enough foreign exchange for Yugoslavia to cover even minimal needs.

A different monetary approach was needed to avert disaster. In January 1994, economist Dragoslav Avramović was appointed to develop an inflation-fighting program. Avramović, who would soon be named governor of the National Bank, introduced the so-called "super dinar." He sharply devalued the national currency and reduced the number of new dinars in circulation to only those backed by gold and hard currency. It took only two months for the new monetary program to achieve the remarkable feat of driving inflation down to near zero. The policy was not pain-free, though. Deep cuts were made to the budget, and austerity brought its form of hardship on people's lives. Because the National Bank no longer printed money to cover government deficits, the extent of assistance offered to people and socially-owned firms was reduced when it was most needed. No measure the government could implement, though, could alter the inexorable impact of sanctions. Catastrophic runaway inflation had been tamed, but economic chaos still reigned, and nearly half the population remained without work (Winter 1994).

Inflation continued to remain exceptionally low until late in 1994 when it began to creep back up, although it never again attained hyperinflationary levels. Avramović listed the pressures the economy still faced. "With our exports blocked because of the embargo, the demand for currency has increased, and because of the blockade as well, we cannot appeal for foreign capital. At the same time, people have grown accustomed to making a rush on the German mark, which acts as security as soon as inflation threatens." Moreover, "[W]e have not solved the problem of Yugoslav assets frozen abroad" (Calle 1995).

As Bosnia's war continued into 1995, the United States was concerned that the advent of peace would end UN sanctions, so it was planning how to maintain pressure on Yugoslavia. A CIA intelligence report complained, "Belgrade has made little progress toward free-market reforms." However, leverage could be applied due to the FRY being "in default on all its international obligations as a result of the freezing of its foreign financial holdings." Economic recovery from sanctions-induced damage would require financial borrowing, the CIA argued, and that presented an opportunity. The IMF and World Bank would be "likely to insist on...substantial progress on economic reforms, particularly privatization and banking reform" (CIA 1995a).

A "release of frozen assets" after the lifting of sanctions would pose a risk to the CIA's goal. If not handled "properly," Milošević "could get a massive infusion of cash that he can use to rectify his economy's most pressing problems." To forestall such a disastrous outcome, the CIA suggested ways to block or delay the release of Yugoslavia's funds so that the US could continue to punish the population (CIA 1995b). The day after a Bosnian peace agreement was agreed to in Dayton, Ohio, the UN Security Council voted to suspend sanctions. However, the UN made the suspension conditional on completing the Bosnian elections, so sanctions on the long-suffering nation remained in place for another year. Even peace brought no relief to the Yugoslav people (UPI 1996).

Western powers justified sanctions by blaming the FRY for the war in Bosnia, whereas Yugoslavia believed it had met all of the conditions for sanctions to be lifted. Yugoslavia was not a participant in the war, and it had consistently pressed Bosnian Serb officials to agree to each peace proposal. Yugoslav President Zoran Lilić sharply objected to Western sanctions. "Placing an entire nation and state under total isolation and such international pressure for something which is happening outside the borders of that state is unprecedented in modern political history. We are not in a position to resolve the Bosnian problem all by ourselves. Yugoslavia did what it could. It has invested maximum efforts for a speedier political settlement" (Tanjug 1993e).

The Bosnian Serbs' nitpicking and reluctance in agreeing to peace terms prompted the FRY to impose an economic blockade along the border to press them to reconsider and agree to peace terms no matter how imperfect (Brajović and Milosavljević 1994; De Luce 1994). Lilić emphasized to the Bosnian Serb leadership "that the war must end, that our peace policy has no alternative, and that we cannot allow any more killings in vain" (Tanjug 1994b). The irony is that no sanctions were directed at outside parties that actively intervened in the war. Throughout the war, tens of thousands of troops from Croatia fought in Bosnia to support their brethren. The United States, having first sabotaged a peace plan in 1992 that would have prevented war, proceeded to do the same with the Vance-Owen proposal in 1993 (Matthews 1993; Gibbs 2015; Komad 1993).

After the United States scuttled the once-promising Vance-Owen plan, negotiations continued on various proposals. Each party—Croat, Muslim, and Serb—leaned toward favoring proffered drafts on some occasions. At other times, each was more resistant. Simultaneous agreement among them all, however, proved elusive.

The war was unwinnable for anyone, but the US promise to provide military aid only increased intransigence on the Muslim side, encouraging it to believe it could win through conflict what it could not via negotiated settlement. Total military victory was the Clinton administration's goal, as well, and it fueled the war by arranging for Iran to provide the Muslims with regular arms shipments (Risen 1996). For its part, the United States also directly supplied arms (Krushelnycky and Mather 1994; Clare 1995; E. Popović 1995; Reuters 1995). Moreover, NATO, acting as an extension of US imperialism, was a belligerent in the war, carrying out multiple bombing attacks. In other words, sanctions were applied to the only party with an interest that was *not* intervening in the war. As Yugoslav Foreign Minister Vladislav Jovanović wryly observed in speaking of the United States, "You cannot speak of peace and prepare for war at the same time. The country that does this should explain it to the world" (Jovanović 1994).

On August 26, 1995, European Union (EU) envoy Carl Bildt, acting on behalf of the five-nation Contact Group, met with Bosnian Serb officials. He presented a more even-handed peace proposal than was customarily the case. Three days later, the Bosnian Serb People's Assembly adopted a statement in which it welcomed the plan and announced that it would join peace negotiations (SRNA 1995). The next day, NATO launched Operation Deliberate Force, a three-week-long bombing attack on the Bosnian Serbs. Official US mythology informs us that the bombing campaign brought the Bosnian Serbs to the negotiating table. Never mind the inconvenient fact that acceptance predated military strikes. The United States was caught off guard by the Bosnian Serbs' speedy acceptance of the Contact Group's plan and feared that the "wrong" lesson could be drawn from that. A different conclusion was necessary, one which offered the opportunity to define a new role for NATO in the post-Cold War era, shifting its mission to out-of-area offensive operations. In the years since the war, NATO's last-minute airstrikes have been praised as proof of the necessity for military violence and the need for US leadership. The mainstream narrative conveniently neglects to mention the US role in causing and prolonging the war. War-making had to be presented as a model for future interventions. The image of the United States as peacemaker through bombing was built in Bosnia upon a mountain of corpses, vast destruction, and mass displacement and emigration. A small price to pay to promote US militarism.

The war in Bosnia officially ended in late 1995, and while UN sanctions persisted through most of 1996, US officials continued planning for the years ahead. Sanctions had already caused $200 billion damage to the Yugoslav economy (Bilski 1996). The concern in Washington was how to add to that. As US State Department spokesman Nicholas Burns confirmed at the beginning of 1997, "The so-called 'outer wall' of sanctions means that Serbia can't be a member of the IMF and the World Bank... We're trying to tighten the pressure on Mr. Milošević." Access to the credit needed for rebuilding had to be blocked. Yugoslavia, Burns said, did not have economic contacts with the West "because the United States is using its effective veto in those organizations to make sure those organizations do not lend money to Belgrade" (Burns 1997).

Although the United States was capable of crippling the Yugoslav economy without end, something more forceful would be required to make further progress. Opportunity came knocking when a small ethnic Albanian group named the Kosovo Liberation Army (KLA) initiated a violent campaign aimed at secession. The KLA would need to be built into a more formidable force to lay the foundation for US intervention. Advanced weaponry soon found its way into the KLA arsenal through the black market, to which the West turned a blind eye (Carpenter 1998).

Western nations were doing their best to enhance the KLA's capabilities directly. According to Albanian Secret Service Director Fatos Klosi, CIA specialists "intensified" their activity in his country's northern region, an area under the KLA's control (AFP 1998). US Green Berets and the CIA ran training programs for the KLA in the north of Albania (Causholi 1998; Vujačić 1998; AFP 1999a) German commandos and military intelligence also conducted training, and Germany sent communication equipment, military uniforms, and weaponry inherited from the German Democratic Republic (Faligot 1999).

The West did much to fan the flames into a full-scale insurgency in the province of Kosovo. American officials intended to capitalize on the conflict as their path to military action. In a 1998 meeting with NATO allies, US Secretary of State Madeleine Albright outlined her goals in attacking Yugoslavia. War plans were developed that summer, and the decision to bomb was made (Večernje Novosti 2020). All that was needed was a pretext. Early in 1999, the United States organized what was portrayed as a peace conference between Yugoslavia and secessionist ethnic Albanians. To eliminate any possible threat of peace, US officials designed the process to fail. In that effort, the Americans were successful, and they abruptly cancelled the talks once their sabotage was complete. US officials dismissed Yugoslav appeals to resume negotiations and gave the go-ahead for NATO to start bombing (Elich 2019).

If economic sanctions, acting as a siege, can be regarded as a form of war, then the reverse can also be true. NATO demonstrated limited interest in striking military targets, destroying only 13 Yugoslav tanks, many of which were obsolete models deliberately left in the open as decoys. NATO instead focused most of its attention on destroying economic and civilian targets. Typical of the targets NATO selected was DIN, a tobacco factory which was one of the largest employers in the city of Niš. It was bombed on four occasions, causing an estimated $35 million in damage (Apostolović 1999). Cigarette production served no discernible military utility; the only purpose in striking DIN was to deprive many workers of their livelihood.

War acted as a multiplier effect on sanctions, accelerating the effect. In a mere 78 days, NATO inflicted $100 billion in economic damage on Yugoslavia, half the amount it had taken sanctions years to achieve (Dobbs 1999). The widespread destruction of worksites also had the desired punitive effect on ordinary people, resulting in 600,000 lost jobs (AFP 1999b).

The United States never lost sight of the purpose behind its aggression. At the height of the NATO bombing, US Balkan envoy Richard Holbrooke sent a memorandum to top American officials, advising that "the bombing must intensify—and continue until the Serbs change their position, preferably by changing their leader." Such advice hardly needed mentioning, as the entire Clinton administration was of like mind. Nevertheless, Holbrooke emphasized, "Our real goal, whether stated or not, must be a change in the leadership of Yugoslavia" (Holbrooke 1999). The presumption was that the United States had the inalienable right to dictate to other nations what government they could have and to rain death, destruction, and economic ruin on any country that chose to go its own way.

As NATO poured bombs and missiles into Yugoslavia, the nation was hit by more sanctions. The European Union imposed a ban on the export of petroleum and petroleum products to Yugoslavia (EU 1999). The United States quickly followed suit, placing a "total trade embargo" on Yugoslavia. The goal was clear, as a US National Security Council spokesman indicated. "The United States will continue to tighten the screws until our objectives are met" (CNN 1999). Before the war even started, the United States and the European Union had already banned foreign investment in Yugoslavia and frozen its foreign assets (Cornwell 1998). Under the outer wall sanctions regime, Yugoslav firms' representatives had to carry bags of money outside the country to purchase raw materials and spare parts, an onerous enough restriction. But with the reimposition by the US and EU of inner sanctions, that option was practically eliminated (Ranković 1998).

NATO attacks destroyed or damaged many power facilities that were already struggling due to sanctions. As a result, the FRY was forced to implement power cuts to get through the winter of 1999–2000. Citizens were urged to resort to alternative heating resources, as the nation's power supply system was said to be "on the verge of falling apart" (Reuters 1999). The trade and financial embargo took a heavy toll. The supply of goods dwindled at shops, and the value of the Yugoslav dinar plummeted. One pensioner complained, "For two days now I have been standing in the lines for milk. And this is the most basic foodstuff" (Gall 1999). News of this nature was always welcome in Washington. "The sanctions are having an impact," gloated a US State Department official. "Hard currency is very tight right now—so tight that they are clearly drawing down from funds they had stashed away" (DPA 1999).

2   Cashing In on Sanctions

National elections in the FRY were scheduled for September 24, 2000. For the United States and European Union, the time had come to cash in on sanctions. The United States ordered the fractious opposition parties to unite behind Vojislav Koštunica, the candidate it had handpicked in the race for president of Yugoslavia. The US and EU pumped tens of millions of dollars into the opposition's coffers and provided electoral training. Essentially, it was the West that directed the opposition campaign. Counting on a population weary from onerous sanctions, the European Union issued a "Message to the Serbian people," announcing that sanctions would never be lifted unless the people voted the opposition into power (EU 2000). Sanctions would remain "even if Milošević were returned by democratic vote," vowed one EU official (Meade 2000). The Western message to the Yugoslav people could not be missed: surrender and put our man in power, or we will crush you.

Neither Milošević nor Koštunica made it over the fifty percent threshold, which necessitated a runoff election that the West was determined not to allow. A long-planned CIA-backed operation to topple the government went into action and achieved its objective on October 5 (Elich 2013). Yugoslavia's newly installed comprador leaders wasted little time in privatizing socially-owned enterprises, offering advantageous terms to US and Western European corporations, and converting the workforce into a source of cheap labor. Once the economy was set on a neoliberal course, the West's next step was to eliminate Yugoslavia as a nation. EU official Javier Solana, who had been secretary-general of NATO during the bombing of Yugoslavia, devised a plan to rename the country to Serbia and Montenegro and put the two republics on a clear path to separation. In 2003, Yugoslav officials caved in under intense pressure from the European Union and accepted the plan, and three years later, the two republics divorced (BBC 2003; Simpson 2003).

The West not only destroyed Yugoslavia but also the very concept of a federation of South Slav peoples. Intervention by the West had taken a nation that had earned a prominent place in the non-aligned movement and fragmented it into several small, weak, and easily controlled states where neoliberal economic policies could prevail. Centuries under rule by the Ottoman and Austro-Hungarian empires taught the South Slav peoples of the need to unite to maintain independence. And it was the experience of an independent and self-reliant Yugoslavia that convinced the West of the necessity of demolishing that model to impose its domination.

There is a streak of paternalism, as well as an inability to see the other, underlying the Western belief in its right to meddle in the affairs of other nations and mete out punishment. There is also a manifest haughtiness and self-assumed superiority in the expectation that servility is the only acceptable role for foreign leaders. In the Washington establishment, sanctions against Yugoslavia are celebrated for demonstrating the efficacy of collective punishment in achieving foreign policy objectives. But sanctions alone did not ensure Western domination. It took all of the elements of the hybrid war to accomplish that primary goal.

Nevertheless, a few secondary demands remain to be met, as the United States tries to bully Serbia into distancing itself from friendly diplomatic and trade relations with China and Russia and instead cozy up to its Western tormentors. The United States is especially keen on forcing Serbia to recognize Kosovo's independence as a vindication of NATO violence. Western leaders are also determined to rip up the Dayton Accord that brought peace to Bosnia because it is based on the equality of the republic's two entities and Serb, Croat, and Muslim peoples. The US and EU are unyielding in demanding a new constitution to abolish Republika Srpska, the Bosnian Serb entity, and impose a one-sided arrangement. Compromise is not a word in the Western lexicon. But then, when has imperialism ever abandoned its presumption that politically-useful peoples have rights and others do not?

Madeleine Albright believed that Europe's division into capitalist and socialist camps "was the disaster of the 20th century," and that "we should try and finish the job in the Balkans." She added that there "are certain parts of the world...where the presence of the United States, in some form, makes a huge difference" (Albright 2000). The hybrid war against Yugoslavia helped define the template for future foreign policy adventures in pursuit of imperial objectives. Sanctions have become the weapon of first choice in the drive for global hegemony, and in the last ten years alone, the number of US financial sanctions has more than doubled (Imperiale 2020). The continuing reliance on UN sanctions, together with American sanctions, cause enormous economic damage and human suffering. When sanctions fall short, US leaders can borrow from the example of the hybrid war against Yugoslavia and choose from a menu of malevolent options as a supplement. Albright was correct in her assessment. The United States did indeed make a "huge difference" in the Balkans, as it continues to do today around the globe.

References

Due to space constraints it was not possible to include all of the references in the text. A complete list of references is available at the Sanctions as War site.

AFP. (1998). "CIA Helping Albania Upgrade its Own Secret Services." *Agence France-Presse*, 13 August.

AFP. (1999a). "KLA Guerrillas Training in Albania—OSCE." *Agence France-Presse*, 8 January.

AFP. (1999b). "NATO Raids Drive Up Unemployment in Yugoslavia." *Agence France-Presse*, 7 June.

Albright, Madeleine. (2000). Interview. PBS *Frontline*, 22 February.

Andjelković, Branka. (1993). "Sanctioned Max." *Nin* (Belgrade), 14 May.

Apostolović, Milivoje. (1999). Meeting in Niš between DIN Deputy Managing Director Milivoje Apostolović and author and other delegation members. 12 August.

Bajić-Hajduković, Ivana. (2014). "Remembering the 'Embargo Cake': The Legacy of Hyperinflation and the UN Sanctions in Serbia." *Contemporary Southeastern Europe* 1 (2).

Bilski, Ryszard. (1996). "Domagamy Się Jednakowego Traktowania Stron Konfliktu." *Rzeczpospolita* (Warsaw), 16 April.

Binder, David. (1993). "Rejected by U.S., Division of Yugoslavia Might Have Averted War." *The New York Times*, 29 August.

Black, Mary E. (1993). "Collapsing Health Care in Serbia and Montenegro." *BMJ*, 30 October.

Bogetić, Željko, Petrović, Pavle, and Vujošević, Zorica. (1999). "The Yugoslav Hyperinflation of 1992–1994: Causes, Dynamics, and Money Supply Process." *Journal of Comparative Economics* 27.

Brajović, Rade, and Milosavljević, Rade. (1994). "It Was a Forced Decision." *Večernje Novosti* (Belgrade), 14 August.

Calle, Marie-France. (1995). "Dragoslav Avramovic: 'We Will Need International Aid.' " *Le Figaro*, 24 August.

Carpenter, Dave. (1998). "Kosovo Rebel Group Grows and Rearms." *Associated Press*, 19 December.

Causholi, Arlinda. (1998). "Albanian Official Reportedly Admits CIA Operating in the Country, Even in the North Near Kosovo." *Associated Press*, 13 August.

Cebalović, M., and Simić, Z. (1995). "Oil Collection Center Opened." *Politika* (Belgrade), 15 April.

CIA. (1989). "Yugoslavia: Status and Outlook," 21 July.

CIA. (1993). "Serbia: Coping with Sanctions." *DCI Interagency Balkan Task Force*, 2 February.

CIA. (1995a). "Serbia: Rough Road After Sanctions." *CIA DCI Intelligence Report*, 7 February.

CIA. (1995b). "Controlling Release of FRY Frozen Assets under Plan B." *CIA*, 20 February.

Čičić, Dragan. (1992). "The Sanctions: A State in Prison." *Nin* (Belgrade), 12 June.

Clare, Sian. (1995). "U.S. Weapons, Advice 'Passed' to Bosnians." Press Association (London), 20 January.

Dumezić, Tomislav. (1992). "The Economy After the War." *Ekonomska Politika* (Belgrade), 23 November.

Ekonomska Politika. (1993). "Health Care: Epidemic of Distress." *Ekonomska Politika* (Belgrade), 2 July.

Elich, Gregory. (2013). "The Fall of Yugoslavia: the West's First 'Color Revolution'." *gregoryelich.org*, 20 October. https://gregoryelich.org/2013/10/20/the-fall-of-yugoslavia-the-wests-first-color-revolution/.

Elich, Gregory. (2019). "How Madeleine Albright Got the War the U.S. Wanted." *gregoryelich.org*, 13 May. https://gregoryelich.org/2019/05/13/how-madeleine-albright-got-the-war-the-u-s-wanted/.

Faligot, Roger. (1999). "How Germany Backed KLA." *The European*, 21–27 September.

Gregović, Savo. (1995). "Leasing Means Servicing Our Ships." *Večernje Novosti* (Belgrade), 12 January.

Grubić, Ljubomir. (1993). "Anus Mundi." *Nin* (Belgrade), 13 August.

Holbrooke, Richard. (1999). "Memorandum for: The Secretary of State, The National Security Advisor, The Secretary of Defense." 20 April.

Ikonić, Slobodan. (1992). "Prices – Spiral of Suicide: Before the Abyss." *Nin* (Belgrade), 27 November.

Imperiale, Johnpatrick. (2020). "Sanctions by the Numbers: U.S. Sanctions Designations and Delistings, 2009–2019." *Center for a New American Security*, 27 February.

Ivanović, D., and Volf, G. (1993). "Price Controls Have Emptied the Stores." *Politika* (Belgrade), 18 September.

Jovanović, Vladislav. (1994). "Jovanović: Sanctions Are the Greatest Obstacle to Peace." *Mladá fronta Dnes*, 3 September.

Jović, Borisav. (1995). *Последњи дани СФРЈ*. Belgrade: Politika.

Jović, Borisav. (1992). *Комадање Југославије*. Belgrade: Politika.

Jović, Borisav. (2020a). "Пуч и Конфузија у Армијском Врху." *Večernje Novosti*, 19 November.

Jović, Borisav. (2020b). "Немачка Мења Политичку Карту Европе." *Večernje Novosti*, 17 November.

J.P. (1993). "Montenegro: Petroleum Products for Just 20 Days. " *Borba* (Belgrade), 13 January.

Karuka, Manu. (2019). *Empire's Tracks: Indigenous Nations, Chinese Workers, and the Transcontinental Railroad*. Page 205, note 9. Oakland: University of California Press.

Kempster, Norman. (1992). "Baker Seeks Yugoslavia's Expulsion From U.N." *The Los Angeles Times*, 24 June.

Komad, Borislav. (1993). "The Permanent Guilty Party." *Večernje Novosti* (Belgrade), 4 September.

Kostić, Branko. (1991). Broadcast interview. *Radio Belgrade*, 18 October.

Krushelnycky, Askold, and Mather, Ian. (1994). "America 'Has Joined War' in Bosnia." *The European*, 18–24 November.

Laketić, M. (1992). "Production Almost Shutdown at Trepča." *Politika* (Belgrade), 6 October.

Lekić, Slobodan. (1993). "Inflation at 286,125,293,792 – and Climbing." *Associated Press*, 1 December.

Lewis, Paul. (1992). "U.N. Assembly Expels Belgrade Over Its Role in Bosnia Fighting." *The New York Times*, 23 September.

Lj. M. (1993). "The Alarming Consequences of Sanctions." *Politika* (Belgrade), 22 July.

Litherland, Susan. (1994). "Labor Rights: Seafarers Stranded Without Pay in Foreign Ports." *Inter Press Service*, 22 July.

Logar, Zvonko. (1993). "The World Has Us on its Conscience." *Dnevnik* (Novi Sad), 25 April.

Matthews, Mark. (1993). "Envoys' Bosnia Plan Criticized by Clinton." *The Baltimore Sun*, 6 February.

Milošević, Slobodan. (1991). Broadcast reading of speech. *Radio Belgrade*, 5 November.

Nišavić, Danijela. (2018a). "Kako Je Ovaj 'Super Deka' 1994: Uveo Novi Dinar i Razbio Dve Zablude o Srpskoj Ekonomiji." *Blic* (Belgrade), 30 January.

Nišavić, Danijela. (2018b). "Gorko Sećanje Na Januar 1994: Kako Smo Živeli Kada Je Od Cele Plate Mogla Da Se Kupi Samo Jedna Olovka." *Blic* (Belgrade), 5 January.

Popović, Bojana. (1993). "Interview with Radomir Stojićević." *Borba* (Belgrade), 22 April.

Popović, Eduard. (1995). "On 18 February, a Large Transport Plane Landed on the Runway in Zivinci Village Near Tuzla." *Globus* (Zagreb), 24 February.

Popović, Olivera. (1993a). "Pharmacies Empty Because of Imported Raw Materials." *Politika* (Belgrade), 5 March.

Popović, Olivera. (1993b). "Pharmacies Almost Empty." *Politika* (Belgrade), 28, July.

Popović, Olivera. (1993c). "After Decision to Exclude Yugoslavia from World Health Organization: Betrayal of Human Right to Health." *Politika* (Belgrade), 5 May.

Rabrenović, Ljiljana. (1993). "Art of Survival: On the Brink of Starvation." *Politika* (Belgrade), 22 July.

Ramović, Dino. (1995). "The Anchor is Being Weighed." *Monitor* (Podgorica), 24 November.

Ranković, Jovan. (1998). "The Threats are Expanding." *Večernje Novosti* (Belgrade), 14 June.

Reuters. (1995). "U.S. Supplied Bosnian Govt with Arms." *Reuters*, 17 November.

Risen, James. (1996). "Closer U.S. Role Seen on Bosnia-Iran Arms Pipeline." *The Los Angeles Times*, 23 December.

Šaponjić, Zoran. (1993). "'Wells' Beneath Multicolored Flags." *Borba* (Belgrade), 12 April.

SRNA. (1995). Srpska Republika News Agency (Pale), August 29.

Stošić, Branko. (1992). "Changes in the Country are the Purpose of All the Pressures." *Borba* (Belgrade), 16–17 May.

Tanjug. (1994a). "550 Requests Blocked in U.N. Sanctions Committee for Yugoslavia." *Tanjug*, 20 October.

Tanjug. (1994b). "Yugoslav President Says Yugoslavia Pursues Policy of Peace." *Tanjug*, 5 August.

Trbojević, Bogdan. (1993). "Fear for Tomorrow is Emptying the Shelves." *Politika* (Belgrade), 20 July 1993.

Uzelac, Milan. (1992). "The Firms Are Eating Themselves Up." Dnevnik (Novi Sad), 8 November.

Večernje, Novosti. (2020). "НАТО Још 1998. Осмислио Агресију На СРЈ, Опција Била и Рат Са Русијом." *Večernje Novosti* (Belgrade), 12 December.

Vujačić, Dragan. (1998). "Terrorists Under NATO Helmet." *Večernje Novosti* (Belgrade), 5 July 1998.

Vujičić, D. (2014). "Умро хрватски генерал Мартин Шпегељ." *Večernje Novosti*, 11 May.

Vulić, Novak. (1994). "From Loser to Accomplice." *Monitor* (Podgorica), 13 May.

Winter, Marko. (1994). "Serbien erhofft Stabilisierung trotz Sanktionen." *Neues Deutschland* (Berlin), 17 May.

Yugoslav Survey (1992). "Memorandum of the Government of Yugoslavia on the Yugoslav Crisis." *Yugoslav Survey* 1.

CHAPTER 12

Targeted Sanctions and the Failure of the Regime Change Agenda in Zimbabwe

Washington Mazorodze

1   Introduction

This book chapter traces the imposition of 'targeted' sanctions against
Zimbabwe by the Western countries—namely the United States—beginning
with the passing of the Zimbabwe Democracy and Economic Recovery Act
(ZIDERA) in 2001 (Grebe 2010) and the European Union in 2003 on allegations of mismanaging the economy, human and property rights violations
following the invasion of white owned commercial farms instigated by the
ruling party, Zimbabwe African National Union Patriotic Front (ZANU PF)
(Chingono 2010). There was, however, no consensus with regards to the objectives of these sanctions. The US and EU argued that sanctions were imposed
to promote democratic principles, institutionalize democracy, enhance political freedoms of Zimbabweans, and uphold human rights and rule of law in
Zimbabwe (Ogbonna 2015). Chogugudza further asserted that the EU and US
justified the imposition and renewal of sanctions against Zimbabwe on the
following factors: alleged election fraud, human rights violations, farm invasions and harassment of opposition activists (Chogugudza 2009). On the other
hand, ZANU PF leadership argued that these were not 'targeted' sanctions but
comprehensive economic sanctions that were imposed to punish the country
for embarking on land reform to empower its indigenous and historically marginalized people, making life unbearable for the majority of the people so that
they could revolt against ZANU PF government (Ogbonna 2017). Moreover,
Guvamatanga noted that ZANU PF always argued that the imposition of sanctions on Zimbabwe by the West was a result of the latter's anger over the land
reform that Mugabe initiated in 2000 (Golden 2009). This was also supported
by Ndakaripa who argued that ZANU PF perceived that those sanctions were
used by the West as a tool to influence Zimbabwean politics and to effect
regime change (Ndakaripa 2013). It is key to note that these accusations and
counter accusations have not been exhausted and continue to scuttle relations
between Zimbabwe and the West. This book chapter turns to the theoretical
framework which guides the discussion and then addresses difficulties with

removing ZANU PF from power, one of the principle objectives of 'targeted' sanctions.

2   Theoretical Framework: Agenda Setting and Framing

ZANU PF used state print and electronic mass media effectively to set the agenda and frame the sanctions narrative to its advantage. Page and Shapiro note that the role of mass media in policy formation, both foreign and domestic, has long interested scholars: repeated investigations point to the critical role played by mass communication in linking public opinion to government policy (Page and Shapiro 1992). Moeller further asserted that, "what we know about the world is circumscribed by what the media are able to tell us – and choose to tell us – about the world" (Moeller 1999). State-controlled print and electronic media is one area where ZANU PF dominated since independence and used it to its advantage to advance the sanctions narrative against its own policy failures. ZANU PF managed to maintain its grip on both print and electronic media in remote areas where the bulk of the news projected favorable government policies while denigrating the Western 'targeted' sanctions and the main opposition party Movement For Democratic Change (MDC), blaming them for all the economic challenges that the country experienced. Academics were also deployed to weigh in with their support for the ZANU PF sanctions narrative. These included university lecturers and analysts who fiercely defended ZANU PF government narrative about the impact of sanctions on the economy and were allocated editorial space in government owned daily and weekly newspapers, *The Herald* and *Sunday Mail* respectively. Based on this idea there is no doubt that the ZANU PF benefitted from its control of public media in telling people that sanctions were responsible for the poorly performing economy and lack of service delivery. These two theories that have emerged from the political role of mass media—agenda setting and framing—are therefore relevant in this case and were used by ZANU PF to retain power at all costs against regime change in Zimbabwe.

Agenda setting focuses on the ability of mass media to establish the importance of events and problems in the minds of the mass public through extensive and persistent coverage. In its agenda setting role the media brings visibility to issues and this has been referred to as the alerting function of mass media, a key component to what has become to be referred to as the "CNN Effect" (Shiras 1996). Sanctions were criticized by the Zimbabwean leadership as both illegal and imposed by the colonizers who wanted to recolonize the country with the help of the opposition MDC (Ogbonna 2017). Mugabe would usually tell his supporters that since the imposition of the so called 'targeted' sanctions which he considered to be a punishment for embarking on land reform, Zimbabwe was denied loans by the International Monetary Fund (IMF), World Bank and other international financial institutions who had been influenced by the US and EU against advancing any loans to the Zimbabwean government, indicating that the sanctions were a calculated move to subvert the Zimbabwean government

> ZANU PF election manifestos since the imposition of sanctions centered on fighting against Western sponsored opposition and 'illegal' sanctions (ZANU PF Manifesto, 2013). In the ZANU PF narrative, no mention was made of human rights violations and murders against opposition sup-porters as well as white commercial farmers who resisted eviction, corruption and mismanagement of resources which were the main reasons for the imposition of 'targeted' sanctions according to US and EU. Moreover, the term 'targeted' was never used by ZANU PF. People were told that Zimbabwe was under economic sanctions by the West for redistributing land from white commercial farmers to indigenous Zimbabweans. All this was covered in state-sponsored print and electronic media-the relied media source for most of the rural populace. This message became instru-mental in setting the ZANU PF agenda among rural voters. Potential vot-ers were further told that voting for the opposition meant that the land they occupied would be returned to the whites. Masunungure quoted one of the security chiefs threatening villagers against voting for the MDC: If you vote for MDC, you have seen the bullets, we have enough for each of one of you, so beware.
>
> MASUNUNGURE 2011

Sanctions and the intimidation of voters became ZANU PF's campaigning tools and they successfully helped the party to remain in power. State media put sanctions as the enemy number one and rural voters as well as some sections of the urban public did so too because of the suffering they endured allegedly due to 'targeted' sanctions imposed on the country by the West which to them had been invited by the opposition MDC. They were promised that as soon as the sanctions which were invited by the opposition MDC were removed the economy would be back to normal. It became the final nail in opposition coffin and ensured ZANU PF political survival.

ZANU PF also managed to use the media to transform the sanctions narra-tive to its advantage using framing. Framing refers to the way in which particu-lar events or problems are presented in mass media reporting and is significant for the way in which these are interpreted by mass public. Hall Jamieson and

Waldman argue that, "Frames tell us what is important, what the acceptable range of debate on a topic is and when the issue is resolved" (2004); Entman adds that, "the public actual opinions arise from framed information, from selected highlights of events, issues and problems rather than from direct contact with the realities of foreign affairs" (2003). In the 1990's the term "CNN Effect" was frequently used to capture the impact media were alleged to have on foreign policy decision making. The argument was that mass media had the power to force political elite to adopt policies such as intervention in humanitarian crises against their better judgement. Likewise, the media was used here in Zimbabwe through media control making sure that the government maintains tight control of the public media where they could provide propaganda on sanctions which ensured the survival of the government.

In rural areas commercial or privately-owned print media was banned by ruling party supporters. Furthermore, efforts to liberalize television services have been resisted by the government. This leaves the state broadcaster, ZBC TV as the sole television station in the country more than three decades after independence. ZANU PF made sure that its rural strongholds were not exposed to private media which focused reporting on corrupt activities and mismanagement.. Evidence from voting patterns and the support that ZANU PF gets in rural areas suggests that ZANU PF managed to manipulate the public media to its advantage regarding sanctions and the general view held by most Zimbabweans is that the sanctions are illegal and have ruined the economy more than corruption and economic mismanagement. Corruption by government officials and mismanagement of the economy were cited as secondary factors for the poor state of the economy, while sanctions which were deemed illegal were cited as the major cause of economic challenges that the country faced.

Public media controlled by the ruling party played agenda setting and framing roles with perfection choosing what to report and how to portray the sanctions debate for the benefit of the ruling party. Agenda setting and Framing theory was therefore used in this book chapter to show that ZANU PF set the agenda and framed the sanctions narrative in the state media to influence voters so as to prevent regime change which sanctions sought to achieve.

3   Literature Review: The Effectiveness of Sanctions

Much of the debate on economic sanctions as coercive tools of foreign policy has centered on their effectiveness. Sanctions can be defined as penalties threatened or imposed as a declared consequence of the target's failure to observe international standards or international obligations (Doxey 1986). Sanctions have also been defined as a broad range of reactions adopted unilaterally or collectively by states against the perpetrator of an internationally unlawful act in order to ensure the respect for and performance of a right or obligation (Decaux 2008). Sanctions have been referred to by the United Nations as a tool for all seasons (Ogbonna 2016). They are regarded as an alternative to military action and offer hope to solve conflicts without mass suffering and other negative consequences associated with war (Smith 2004). Sanctions are believed to be a soft approach that can be used to compel states to behave in line with the doctrine of the international community. There are different forms of sanctions which range from economic, social and political. Sanctions have been imposed against several countries for different reasons with notable examples including Iraq for invading Kuwait in 1992, Yugoslavia in 1999 for causing war in Bosnia and Kosovo, Libya in 1992 for supporting international terrorism, among others (Cortright and Lopez 2002).

Over the years there has been a gradual shift in the imposition of sanctions from general or comprehensive sanctions which targeted the whole economy to a more specific target to reduce the impact of sanctions on the general population after their devastating impact on Iraq in the 1990s (Thomas, Cortright, and Lopez 1997). 'Targeted' or 'smart' sanctions are designed to target specific persons, groups and entities responsible for the objectionable policies or behavior (Rudolf 2007). Such sanctions seek to freeze all funds and economic resources of the targeted persons and a prohibition on making funds or economic resources available directly or indirectly for the benefit of these persons and entities (Rudolf 2007). They can also be in form of travel ban on specific entity, group or persons. Gordon supported the use of targeted sanctions over comprehensive sanctions when she noted that sanctions against individuals and other non-state actors that were identified as a more direct threat to international peace and security than entire populations of a state were the effective course. She further noted that states imposing sanctions have a moral responsibility to protect civilians in the targeted state (Gordon 1999). By imposing targeted sanctions, it sends a clear message to those who have been subjected to them that their behavior is considered in violation of international norms and worthy of being sanctioned.

The concept of targeted sanctions aimed at the guilty individuals and elites evolved as an escape route to the ethical dilemma inherent in the implementation of broad sanctions (Kreutz 2005). Some studies on sanctions have shown that sanctions when strategically applied can achieve the desired political changes in the targeted state. A study of 115 cases between 1914 and 1990 showed a third of cases sanctions were effective when measured relative to

the direct goals of their imposition (Hufbauer *et al.* 1990). However, this analysis also showed that sanctions rarely forced a state into fundamental revision
of its policies. It has been found out that in autocratic government's general
sanctions have strengthened the regime as well as those groups supporting and
underpinning it. The question of the effectiveness of targeted sanctions has
been discussed by Brooks and Grebe. Grebe concluded that targeted sanctions
are ineffective (Grebe 2010), while Brooks argued that targeted sanctions are
effective against authoritarian regimes (Brooks 2002). Grebe went further and
concluded that US and EU targeted sanctions against Zimbabwe have failed to
achieve their intended political objectives.

This book chapter advances Grebe's argument that sanctions against
Zimbabwean political elite failed to achieve their political objectives. It then
goes further to call for the removal of the targeted sanctions as a way of exposing the failure of the government in Zimbabwe to transform the social and
economic conditions of Zimbabweans (Grebe 2010). While Grebe's research
might have been carried out under the Mugabe government, this research is
being carried out under a new regime which many have argued is old wine
in new bottles. This chapter analyzed the specific case study of Zimbabwe
and targeted sanctions against the Mugabe regime and the subsequent new
dispensation led by Mugabe's successor Emmerson Mnangagwa. This chapter
seeks to make it categorically clear that the main objective of Mugabe's regime
was to remain in power at any cost and his successor is no exception.

4   Effectiveness of Sanctions against Zimbabwe

The effectiveness of sanctions on the Zimbabwean government has been subject to international debate for some time. There are two contexts in which the
effectiveness of sanctions has been discussed. These are the effects of the sanctions on those sanctioned and the success of the intended objectives of those
who imposed sanctions (Grebe 2010). It is a mammoth task to measure the
effectiveness of sanctions; furthermore, the measurement of sanctions' effectiveness has tended to be limited to one primary objective while neglecting the
potential secondary objectives. In this chapter the effectiveness of sanctions
is measured against political objectives within which targeted sanctions were
imposed against individuals and institutions in Zimbabwe. These objectives
pertain to human rights observance, democratization, and ultimately regime
change. Examining whether or not these objectives have been achieved by the
imposition of targeted sanctions is the main aim of this section. When one
looks at the current situation in Zimbabwe, one cannot conclude that there

is any change in terms of the political objectives of the 'targeted' sanctions. The human rights record of the Zimbabwean government did not improve. If anything it has worsened even under the new government, which has witnessed journalists and political activists incarcerated without trial. The level of democratization has remained low, with elections characterized by threats on the electorate by the ruling party. Regime change remains a pipe dream for Zimbabweans. Peaceful demonstrations continue to be criminalized and outlawed. There was so much belief among opposition supporters that with the use of 'targeted' sanctions they could wrestle power from ZANU PF. But almost two decades of 'targeted' sanctions failed to produce regime change. Some might argue that the ouster of Mugabe in 2017, was a milestone development caused by 'targeted' sanctions, but this was an internal matter which was triggered by internal ZANU PF power struggles which had nothing to do with 'targeted' sanctions.

'Targeted' sanctions might have caused economic challenges in Zimbabwe, such as inflation, company closures, retrenchments, among others, but the government remained intact. Mugabe might have been toppled by his second in command but the system of Mugabeism which sought to keep power within ZANU PF remained unaltered for the foreseeable future. Ndlovu-Gatsheni contends that the term Mugabeism represents different things to different people. In the Pan African context, it represents an ideology that is opposed to all forms of imperialism and colonialism and dedicated to a radical redistributive project seeking to redress colonial imbalances. In a neo-liberal context which it has been popularized, Mugabeism is a form of racial chauvinism and authoritarianism marked by antipathy towards norms of liberal governance and disdain for human rights and democracy (Ndlovu-Gatsheni 2009). Though there are internal factions in the ruling party, members unite when faced with the common enemy such as 'targeted' sanctions, therefore minimizing the chances of losing power to the opposition which remained a pipe dream for the EU and US without success. It is therefore sufficient to argue in this chapter that 'targeted' sanctions against both individual ZANU PF members and the ZANU PF system have been ineffective based on the level one analysis which measures the effectiveness of sanctions on the basis of political objectives. The chapter goes further to argue that 'targeted' sanctions in Zimbabwe have outlived their usefulness and need to be removed. The following section explains how 'targeted' sanctions affected ordinary Zimbabweans as opposed to the alleged targeted elite who have been accused of human rights violations. The section also examines how ZANU PF created a "rally-around the flag effect" using targeted sanctions to prevent regime change in Zimbabwe.

5   How ZANU PF Created the Rally-Around Effect' against 'Targeted'
       Sanctions

There are a number of reasons which have led to the ineffectiveness of targeted
sanctions to effect regime change in Zimbabwe. These include the ruthlessness
of the government's security forces against political opponents instilling fear
in the minds of the general population, ZANU PF's hold over rural constituency and monopoly over resources, use of food aid in rural constituency, ZANU
PF monopoly over state media (television, radio), lack of unity in the opposition, and ZANU PF using poverty created partly by 'targeted' sanctions to its
advantage.

The government's security forces have been brutal in their response to
demonstrations against both the Mugabe regime and the new government.
There are several instances where opposition activists have been brutalized
by government forces acting on the instructions of the elite. At one moment
Mugabe boasted that his party has degrees in violence and the opposition
cannot match it. In another incident Mugabe mocked the late opposition
MDC leader Tsvangirai when he said that 'takachishagada', meaning we
'bashed him' and that he deserved to be beaten (*The Guardian* 2007). This
was after the opposition tried to hold a 'peaceful' demonstration against
the government for failing to run the economy; a demonstration which was
interpreted by ZANU PF government as a signal of a regime change agenda.
Many political activists have been abducted, beaten up, incarcerated, and
even disappeared. This state-sponsored violence against opposition activists prevented people from carrying out a revolution against the government
despite suffering from the effects of 'targeted' sanctions. This was more pronounced during Mugabe and has also been implemented by the current
government with success. This intimidation was more visible in the 2008
presidential election rerun when Mugabe deployed security forces in rural
areas to intimidate people to vote for ZANU PF. Masunungure illustrates how
the rural people were intimidated into voting for ZANU PF when he noted
that the security forces embarked on intense violent operation code named
"Operation Makavhotera papi?" meaning "Operation who did you vote for?"
(Masunungure 2011, 56). Masunungure further quoted one army chief threatening voters when he said that: This country came through the bullet not
through pencil. Therefore, it will not go by your X (voting mark) of the pencil.
We fought for this country and a lot of blood was shed. We are not going to
give up our country because of a mere X. How can a ballpoint fight with a
gun? (Masunungure 2011, 56).

This culture of violence against citizens continued into the so-called
new dispensation as witnessed by the killing of demonstrators who were

demonstrating against the delays in the announcement of presidential election results on 1 August 2018, alleging that the Zimbabwe Electoral Commission
was rigging in favor of Mnangagwa. This action resulted in the death of six people according to official government sources, although the government denied
being responsible for the deaths (Burke 2018). As if this was not enough, on 14
January 2019, in another demonstration against the rising cost of living, the
security forces responded heavy handedly resulting in the death of 14 people
countrywide (Zimbabwe Human Rights NGO Forum 2019). With such a show
of force by security forces and the resulting fear in the minds of would-be protesters, there is no room for a revolution or armed regime change in Zimbabwe,
which the crafters of the 'targeted' sanctions envisaged, despite so much suffering that the people of Zimbabwe have been subjected to, hence the need to
remove the sanctions as they have failed and will continue to fail to achieve
regime change in Zimbabwe. One interviewee noted that,

> US foreign policy is just good for no one. Saddam dug in, Maduro is dig-
> ging in, surviving coups and everything. Every dictator just digs in when
> US starts ramping up pressure. Now Zimbabwe is going the same way.
> 2023 will be tough. Gloves are off and we are fucked. And there is ain't
> [sic.] anything we can do about it.
> Interview with resident 2020

The majority of voters in Zimbabwe are rural based and ZANU PF has a strong
hold over rural voters which it has created and institutionalized over the
years since the time of the liberation war. During this war, ZANU PF adopted
a Maoist guerilla ideology that said the forces are the fish and the masses are
the sea, therefore the forces cannot survive without the sea. As a result, the
rural masses played a vital role in the liberation of the country where they
supported the liberation forces in a variety of ways. This bond continued after
independence and ZANU PF guarded jealously against any intrusion into this
stronghold by any opposition. Through the use of traditional leaders ZANU PF
has managed to maintain a rural constituency. This constituency is prone to
periodic droughts and ZANU PF has monopolized this constituency which it
declared a "no go area" for opposition. The ZANU PF government distributed
food aid through the traditional leaders which have been coopted into the
ZANU PF system of patronage. The aid is attributed to the ruling party not the
government and the poor rural voters vote for the ruling party with the threats
that failure to do so will result in them losing food aid.

Grebe argues that ZANU PF used these rural-oriented strategies to win both
presidential elections in 2002 and parliamentary elections in 2005, guarantee-
ing its stay in power (Grebe 2010b). These strategies included intimidation,

violence, abductions against opposition members, and the use of food as a political tool. No matter how biting the sanctions might be, the rural constituency was cushioned by food aid which was distributed through relief organizations such as the World Food Programme through ZANU PF politicians for their political benefit. Based on these facts one is tempted to argue that targeted sanctions have had minimum impact on Zimbabwe's rural constituency which resulted in ZANU PF recording successes in elections against opposition ever since targeted sanctions were imposed. This was despite the fact that the IMF and World Bank argued that the reasons for suspending loans to Zimbabwe had nothing to do with the sanctions but the non- repayment of loans by the Zimbabwean government to these institutions. Although ZANU PF government acknowledged that it owed the IMF and WB, it shifted the blame on Smith government arguing that the ZANU PF government inherited $700 million debt incurred by the Smith regime and the burden was transferred to them (ZANU PF Manifesto 2013). The debt had since ballooned to over $10 billion by 2013. All rallies and election campaigns organized by ZANU PF leadership criticized sanctions and the opposition MDC for inviting sanctions.

The effectiveness of sanctions to produce regime change has also been dampened by the monopoly over media by ZANU PF. Efforts by the opposition to lobby for media reforms were thwarted or frustrated by ZANU PF and piecemeal reforms have been implemented only with regards to radio services and print media. The only television station in the country has been used by ZANU PF to demonize the opposition and its "Western handlers" for the economic crisis brought by sanctions. The opposition is alleged to have invited the sanctions from the Western countries as punishment for carrying out land reform. The message is repeated over several times and people have as a result have loathed the opposition for their suffering. Through its monopoly on television services and newspapers, ZANU PF has dismissed the 'targeted' sanctions narrative, instead informing the nation that the country was suffering economically because of comprehensive sanctions instigated by the opposition.

Although some critics blamed ZANU PF's ruinous economic policies for the economic crisis that the country faced, their criticisms never reached the public domain due to ZANU PF control over media, which won sympathy not only in the rural areas but also in the urban areas where sanctions have been more severe. Moreover, during elections, the MDC and other political parties which posed a threat to ZANU PF were denied access to the media to campaign and spread their messages. Masunungure highlighted that in the 2008 elections, the biggest opposition in the country was denied access to state media which instead churned out savage attacks on the opposition as a Western-sponsored party that was created to remove ZANU PF from power (Masunungure

2011). This narrative subsequently won ZANU PF not only domestic but regional and some international support.

ZANU PF held on to power despite losing elections in 2008. The presidential run-off election in 2008 was one of the most violent elections in Zimbabwe, as ZANU PF government clung to power in the face of fierce opposition from MDC (Masunungure 2011). ZANU PF refused to concede defeat. It was the first time that the opposition defeated the ruling ZANU PF in both parliamentary and presidential elections. However, the opposition candidate for president failed to achieve an outright majority vote (50 plus one), though there were allegations that he had won the majority vote, but results were tampered with to make sure that the opposition did not assume power (Masunungure 2011). It took more than four weeks for results to be released which raised controversy over the authenticity of the released results which showed that there was no outright winner prompting a runoff which later turned violent.

Moreover, Mangwende (2009) asserted that the imposition of sanctions by the West gave ZANU PF an excuse for its failure and enhanced its chances of pillaging of the economy. Targeted sanctions affected the ordinary people more than they had affected the intended targets; hence their continued use was of no relevance (Brian 2009). In as much as ZANU PF has created mechanisms that ensure its retention of power, the opposition squabbles have also made it easy for ZANU PF to avoid regime change. There have been several main opposition MDC splits which began in 2005 with the split into two groups, where the other was led by late Morgan Tsvangirai and another was under the leadership of Arthur Mutambara and later Welshman Ncube. In 2013, another split occurred where founding members of the Movement for Democratic Change such as Tendai Biti, Elton Mangoma, Jacob Sikhala broke ranks with the Morgan Tsvangirai led MDC to form their own parties. In 2018, following the death of Tsvangirai there was another split where Nelson Chamisa was accused by Thokozani Khupe and some members of having assumed power illegally. Khupe remained with MDC-T and Chamisa formed MDC Alliance. At the elections in July 2018 there was splitting of votes which resulted in ZANU PF garnering two thirds majority in parliament. Had there been no such splits it is probable that sanctions could have achieved their intended objective of regime change in Zimbabwe, but unfortunately failed.

Despite sanctions generally believed to have failed in their primary objectives in Zimbabwe, their economic impact has been felt across the political and economic divide. It is not a coincidence that since the imposition of 'targeted' sanctions against Zimbabwe by the US and EU in 2001 and 2003 respectively, the economy has and continues to decline. Lack of foreign currency continues to cripple domestic businesses. Inflation reached its peak in 2008 and continues to soar under the new leadership with fuel shortages becoming a daily phenomenon, public hospitals ground to a halt with no basic medication and medical staff inadequately remunerated. Zimbabwe's inflation was officially estimated to be 231 percent in 2008, the second worst recorded in history. Steve Hanke of The Cato Institute estimated inflation at 89.7 sextillion percent in November 2008 (Hanke 2020). Partly due to the sanctions, the country was not able to access credit from international institutions such as the IMF and was unable to attract foreign direct investment. Sanctions brought suffering, unemployment and poverty to the majority of Zimbabweans as companies closed. Basic social services are in distress. Hospitals are now deathtraps; health personnel are on strike. The education system has nearly collapsed with teachers and lecturers always on strike for better salaries which have been eroded by inflation. The economy has struggled since the imposition of 'targeted' sanctions, but the victims of this economic crisis are the majority of the population who cannot access the country's natural resources. The 'targeted' sanctions did not stop the land reform, nor did it punish elites, but contributed to economic collapse and difficulties for ordinary people. Murisa and Bloemen highlighted that Zimbabwe's ability to manage its own economy as severely hampered by the US and EU sanctions and no country in the globalized world can both balance its budget and stabilize its economy without support from financial institutions (Murisa and Bloemen 2018). Zimbabwe survived in a globalized world without this support for more than two decades and Zimbabweans have paid a heavy price. They further argued that Zimbabweans have been unfairly treated by the EU and US as there are more countries who are committing human rights violations but are not sanctioned by the same Western countries. The targeted elite managed to shift blame on sanctions for their policy failures and maintained grip on power beyond the imagination of the sanctions imposers.

Magaisa, a human rights lawyer, noted that the problem is that it is the weak members of the society that are hit by the effects of the sanctions and democracy cannot flourish in poverty. It needs stable economic foundations (Magaisa 2005). This was supported by Hove who argued that it is the poor who have been most affected by sanctions either directly or indirectly (Hove 2012). Hove further advanced the argument that this chapter advocates the removal of sanctions need to be removed so that Zimbabwe can access credit lines to resuscitate its economy as sanctions have prevented Zimbabwe from accessing loans from international financial institutions. While the rationale for sanctions is to provide an alternative for war by avoiding mass suffering and negative consequences associated with war, the reality is that sanctions in Zimbabwe are not alternative to war but are actually a declaration of war on Zimbabweans judging by their humanitarian impact. Their impact on civilians is similar to the effects of warfare. The elite which are allegedly targeted by sanctions have not suffered from the effects of sanctions. The elite targeted by sanctions are looting the country's resources at the expense of the ordinary Zimbabweans. Recently, a close relative of the presidency was caught attempting to smuggle six kilograms of gold at Zimbabwe's largest airport, which points to the fact that the elite have been siphoning state resources while the general population is living in deep poverty yet the US and EU continue to argue that sanctions are targeting the elite. There is therefore no justification for the continued imposition of the sanctions. Despite sanctions having been deemed to be unsuccessful, they have been credited with some measure of success in changing the behavior of opponents. However, such kind of behavior has not been seen in Zimbabwe as human rights continue to be violated as highlighted by the continued abduction of political activists opposed to the government and all calls by the international community to respect the rights of political opponents have been ignored. Therefore, the primary purpose of 'targeted' sanctions has not been achieved. Hence the call for their removal.

6   Conclusion and Policy Recommendations

There is overwhelming evidence that the 'targeted' sanctions on Zimbabwe's political leadership failed to achieve their intended objective. The real aim of 'targeted' sanctions was to collapse the economy and thus mobilize people into the streets to overthrow or vote the government out of power. It looked possible for some time with violent demonstrations in the years 2005, 2007, 2016 but they all failed to remove ZANU PF from power as intended by the authors of the sanctions. There have been elections since the sanctions were imposed two decades ago but, in all instances, the ruling party managed to subdue the opposition through agenda setting and framing by state-owned media. The ruling party put in place measures meant to protect its power and prevent regime change. These measures included using the state security apparatus to suppress dissent, resisting all types of reforms such as media, security, political and electoral that could end its political hegemony, maintaining a monopoly over its rural constituency and infiltrating the opposition thereby causing divisions. The intended isolation and incapacitation of targeted leadership did not bear fruit. Based on these facts, there is no doubt that 'targeted' sanctions failed to bring about the much desired regime change in Zimbabwe and will not result in regime change in the foreseeable future, despite them affecting the generality of the population who are suffering in silence. 'Targeted' sanctions have in turn created a 'rally around flag' effect. The heavy-handed response of the security forces against protestors did not make it easy for regime change and its sympathizers riding on fighting against sanctions philosophy. Instead, sanctions must be removed and expose ZANU PF's failure to deliver and transform the economic and social lives of its citizens. As long as sanctions remain in place, ZANU PF will continue to use sanctions narrative propaganda to deny its responsibility for failure and suppress Zimbabweans to remain in power much to the detriment of the general populace. It is probable that without sanctions, ZANU PF would have accepted electoral defeats in 2002, 2005, 2008, 20013 and 2018 as the opposition claimed to have won all those elections but ZANU PF allegedly rigged to remain in office fearing reprisals and retributive justice from the joint collaboration of the opposition MDC and their alleged Western handlers who spearheaded regime change agenda through the imposition of targeted sanctions.

This chapter recommends that the Western countries must remove whatever form of sanctions against Zimbabwe as they hurt the ordinary people instead of intended elite targets. The ruling elite must implement political and economic reforms to promote good governance so that they get international support to remove sanctions. The country's leadership must fight against corruption as it has been entrenched in Zimbabwe' society and is negatively affecting the poor as well as eroding the moral fabric of society. The international community should encourage the US and EU to remove sanctions against Zimbabwe as they have caused untold suffering among the poor in Zimbabwe. Regional and continental leaders should encourage their counterparts in Zimbabwe to uphold people's human rights so that they can lobby the US and EU to remove sanctions.

References

Brooks, Risa. (2002). "Sanctions and Regime Type: What Works, and When?" *Security Studies* 11 (4).

Burke, Jason. (2018). "Zimbabwe's hopes for a new start after Mugabe dashed." *The Guardian*, 2 August.

Chingono, Heather. (2010). "Zimbabwe sanctions: An analysis of the "Lingo" guiding the perceptions of the sanctioners and the sanctionees." *African Journal of Political Science and International Relations* 4 (2): 66.

Chogugudza, Crisford. (2009). "Open Forum: The Long Story of Zim sanctions." *The Financial Gazette*, 16 September.

Cortright, David, and Lopez, George. (2002). *Smart Sanctions: Targeting Economic Statecraft*. New York: Rowman and Littlefield.

Decaux, Emmanuel. (2008). "The Definition of Traditional Sanctions: Their Scope and Characteristics." *International Review of the Red Cross* 90: 870.

Doxey, Margaret P. (1986). *International Sanctions in Contemporary Perspective.* New York: St. Martin's Press.

Entman, M. Robert. (2004). *Projections of power: Framing news, Public Opinion and US Foreign Policy.* Chicago, IL: University of Chicago Press.

Gordon, Joy. (1999). "Economic Sanctions, Just War Doctrine and the "Fearful Spectacle of the Civilians Dead"." *CrossCurrents* 49 (3): 387–400.

Grebe, Jan. (2010). "And They Are Still Targeting: Assessing the Effectiveness of Targeted Sanctions against Zimbabwe/Und sie sanktionieren weiter: Zur Wirksamkeit zielgerichteter Sanktionen gegen Simbabwe." *Africa Spectrum* 45 (3): 1–10.

The Guardian. (2007). "Opposition deserved to get bashed, says Mugabe." *The Guardian,* 30 March.

Guvamatanga, Golden. (2009). "Origins of Zim Sanctions." *The Herald,* 13 October.

Hall Jamieson, Kathleen, and Paul Waldman. (2004). *The Press Effect: Politicians, Journalists and Stories that Shape the Political News.* New York: Oxford University Press.

Hanke, Steven. (2008). "New Hyperinflation index puts (HHIZ) Puts Zimbabwe Inflation at 87.9 Sextillion Percent." The Cato Institute Working Papers.

Hove, Mediel. (2012). "The Debates and Impact of Sanctions: The Zimbabwean Experience." *International Journal of Business and Social Science* 3 (5): 77–80.

Hufbauer, Gary Clyde, Kimberley Elliott, and Barbara Oegg. (1990). *Economic Sanctions Reconsidered: History and Current Policy, 2nd Edition.* Washington: Institute for International Economics.

Kreutz, Joakim. (2005). "Hard Measures by Soft Power? Sanctions Policy of the European Union 1981–2004." Bonn: *Bonn International Center for Conversion* (online).

Magaisa, Alex. (2005). "Smart sanctions: who really do they hurt?" *The Independent,* 11 November.

Mangwende, Brian. (2009). "Further US sanctions detrimental to inclusive Government." *The Financial Gazette,* 18 March.

Masunungure, Eldred V. (2011). "Zimbabwe's Militarized, Electoral Authoritarianism." *Journal of International Affairs* 65 (11): 55–82.

Moeller, Susan. (1999). *Compassion Fatigue: How Media Sell Disease, Famine, War and Death.* New York: Routledge.

Murisa, Tendai, and Bloemen, Shantha. (2018). "Hey America, It is Time to End Zimbabwe's Economic Punishment." *African Arguments,* 8 November.

Ndakaripa, Musiwaro. (2013). "The Debate Over the Nature and Impact of the United States and European Union 'Sanctions' on Zimbabwe, 2001 to 2012." *OSSREA Bulletin* 10 (2).

Ndlovu-Gatsheni, Sabelo. (2009). "Making Sense of Mugabeism in Local and Global Politics: 'So Blair, Keep Your England and Let Me Keep My Zimbabwe'." *Third World Quarterly* 30 (6): 1139–1158.

Ogbonna, Chidiebere. (2015). *Politics of sanctions: Impact of US and EU Sanctions on the rights and wellbeing of Zimbabweans.* Munch: GRIN Verlag.

Ogbonna, Chidiebere. (2017). "Targeted or Restrictive: Impact of U.S. and EU Sanctions on Education and Healthcare of Zimbabweans." *African Research Review, An International Multi-Disciplinary Journal* 11 (3): 34–47.

Page, Benjamin I., and Robert Shapiro. (1992). *The Rational Public: Fifty Years of Trends in America's Policy Preferences.* Chicago IL: University of Chicago Press.

Rudolf, Peter. (2007). "Sanctions in International Relations. On the current state of research." SWP Research Paper: *German Institute for International and Security Affairs*: 14.

Shiras, Peter. (1996). "Big Problems, Small Print: Guide to the Complexity of Humanitarian Emergencies." In Robert Rotberg and Thomas Weiss (eds.), *From Massacre to Genocide: The Media, Public Policy and Humanitarian Intervention*, 93–114. Washington, DC: The Brooking Institution.

Thrall, Trevor A.. (2000). *War in the Media Age.* Cresskill, NJ: Hampton Press.

Weiss, Thomas, David Cortright, George Lopez, and Larry Minear. (1997). *Political Gain and Civilian Pain.* Oxford: Rowman & Littlefield Publishers.

ZANU PF Election Team. (2013). Team ZANU PF 2013: Presidential Address.

Zimbabwe Human Rights NGO Forum. (2019). "The New Deception. What has Changed? A Baseline Study on the Record of the Zimbabwe's New Dispensation in Upholding Human Rights." Harare, Zimbabwe, August 2019.

CHAPTER 13

Iraq: Understanding the 'Sanctions Warfare Regime'

Nima Nakhaei

It is perhaps a truism to say that since its foundation as a modern nation-state, Iraq has been repeatedly subject to the violent condensation of colonial and imperialist relations; condensations which were key in eliminating, ruptur- ing or delaying popular histories not just in Iraq, but also in the Middle East. Among the most prominent of such instances, one can refer to the suppression of the Revolt of 1920 through the "blanket bombing of villages" (Ismael and Ismael 2005, 611) and the use of chemical weapons by the British, the Gulf War, and the 2003 occupation. Such recurrent unleashing of genocidal violence is neither the 'unintended consequences' of other strategies ('smart' bombs!) nor exceptions. Rather, brute force has been a 'consciously chosen method' to contain and control the most geostrategic space in the Middle East (Alnasseri 2009, 77). This is not just in terms of Iraq's geographical location or vast hydro- carbon reserves, but also popular struggles which have consistently posed exis- tential threats to various colonial and imperialist projects in the region (the Revolt of 1920, the 14 July Revolution).

Within the above historical context, the imposition of the "most comprehen- sive sanctions regime the world has ever known" (D.J. Halliday 1999, 30) points to "the continuities rather than discontinuities of the imperialist project in relation to the modern history of Iraq" (Hammoudi 2019, 1). This is especially the case, if one considers how the imposition of the sanctions regime cor- related with the Gulf War, developed in conjunction with numerous bombing campaigns and in turn prepared the ground for the 2003 invasion. Nonetheless, taking such *longue duree* perspective risks overlooking the specificity of the sanctions regime. This is not just because of the unprecedented severity of the sanctions, but more importantly the extremely exceptional international and regional circumstances that made them possible; the crisis of the Eastern Bloc and the dissolution of the Soviet Union on the one hand and the unparalleled militarization of the Middle East region on the other hand. What is needed, then, is a 'conjunctural analysis' which approaches the sanctions regime as the concrete materialization of an imperialist strategy which was both made pos- sible and necessary in such a unique constellation. To do this, I will begin with a schematic periodization of the economic sanctions that were imposed on Iraq and then proceed to make two arguments. First, by pointing to a situation of 'war in permanence' in Iraq, I will argue that these economic sanctions were parts and parcels of what I term the 'sanctions warfare regime'. Second, after a brief discussion of the colossal changes in the international and regional relations of force, I will argue that the 'sanctions warfare regime' materialized through the relatively successful implementation of a three-layered American imperialist strategy; the 'war on rogue states', 'internationalization qua cantonization' (Alnasseri 2004) and asymmetrical containment.

1   The Economic Blockade

Immediately after Iraq's invasion of Kuwait on August 2, 1990, the United Nations Security Council passed resolution 660, which in condemning the invasion, placed Iraq under Chapter VII of the UN charter. Between August 6th and November 28th, as the American troops were being deployed to the Middle East, the Security Council passed 10 more resolutions. Collectively, these resolutions banned all trade with Iraq, froze government assets abroad, prohibited financial transactions, imposed a naval and aerial blockade and established a 'sanctions committee' to oversee the implementation of these measures (Ismael and Ismael 2004, 91). This economic blockade was seemingly a temporary measure "*determined* to bring the invasion and occupation of Kuwait by Iraq to end" (Resolution 661, 1990) in a non-violent manner (Hammoudi 2019, 10). Nonetheless, in the conjuncture between Iraq's withdrawal from Kuwait on February 27, 1991, and the 2003 invasion, the initial blockade proved to be only the first stage and the backbone for the most comprehensive economic sanctions that a country has ever faced.

After Iraq's withdrawal from Kuwait, the possibility of the removal of the economic sanctions were directly tied to Iraq's terms of surrender, which were laid out in Resolution 667. These terms included Iraq's commitment to repay its foreign debt, agree to a UN mediated boundary settlement with Kuwait, provide financial compensation for damages which Kuwait incurred during the invasion through a UN administered fund created by Iraq's oil revenues, destroy all of its weapons of mass destruction and unconditionally comply with the nuclear ban under international supervision. These measures, particularly the ones related to Iraq's current and future military capacity were far-reaching to an extent where they were "virtually unquantifiable" (Ismael and Ismael 2004, 97). In this sense, the terms of surrender not only allowed for the continuation of economic sanctions *ad infinium*, but also facilitated the creation of an institutional labyrinth on top of the committees that were established during the economic blockade. I will later return to the ways in which these institutions severely limited Iraq's sovereignty. For the time being, it is necessary to consider how these measures maintained the economic blockade that had been in effect since August 4, 1990.

Resolution 668 technically allowed Iraq to import foodstuffs and medicine and foresaw the approval of isolated exemptions to the oil embargo to ensure that essential civilian needs are met. In effect however, up until the institutionalization of the Oil-for-Food Program (OFFP) on May 1996, the blockade continued since the oil embargo remained in effect while all government assets outside Iraq were frozen (Alnasrawi 2001, 210).

2   The Oil-for-Food Program

The Security Council had proposed an Oil-for Food Program as early as August and September 1991 (Resolutions 706 and 712) and a modified version in April 1995 (Resolution 986). The Iraqi government however rejected both proposals because of their limited scope and violation of Iraq's sovereignty. After all, under these measures, Iraq was only allowed to export $1.6 billion worth of oil every six months ($2 billion under the Resolution 986) while the Sanctions Committee would be in charge of approving the oil contracts, administering the funds and supervising the import and distribution of humanitarian supplies. With the collapse of the Iraqi dinar since January 1995, high inflation and the inability of the government's food rationing system to meet the needs of the population, Iraq accepted the Oil-for-Food Program on May 20th, 1996, by signing a Memorandum of Understanding. In its initial stage, which began on December 10, 1996, the OFFP would allow Iraq to export $2 billion of oil every six months. Through an elaborate organizational structure, the United Nations would transfer 25% of the acquired revenue to the UN Compensation Commission (UNCC) to pay for Iraq's war reparations, 3% towards UN's administrative costs, 59% for humanitarian aid in areas under the control of the central government and 13% to the three Kurdish provinces. In the second stage of the OFFP, the ceiling on oil exports was increased to $5.2 billion on February 1998 and in the final stage, which began after the passing of Resolution 1284 on December 17, 1999 the ceiling was entirely removed (Katzman and Blanchard 2007). The crucial point here is that despite slightly easing the economic blockade, the OFFP institutionalized Iraq's loss of sovereignty over major aspects of its economy and provision basic civilian needs.

3   'War in Permanence'

Noting the catastrophic economic, social and ecological consequences of these economic sanctions, many critical observers have insisted that these sanctions were not an 'alternative to war' but rather a 'different kind of war' (Sponeck 2006). It is however more accurate to argue that the sanctions, whether in the blockade phase or after the institutionalization of the OFFP, were parts and parcel of what may be termed the 'sanctions warfare regime'. That is, a constellation when, the imposition of economic sanctions, their continuity and effectiveness are overdetermined by a situation of 'war in permanence'. From this perspective, Operation Desert Storm not only marked "a scale of destruction that has no parallels in the history of warfare" (Simons 1996, 4), but also the beginning of a protracted cycle where a mutually reinforcing relationship between 'economic sanctions' and 'warfare' was established.

Let me begin with Operation Desert Storm, the six-week American-led campaign in which 88,000 tons of bombs, "equivalent to seven Hiroshima-size atomic bombs", were dropped on Iraq (Simons 1996, 4). For the time being, my concern is neither the illegal nature of this military campaign and its conduct, nor how it eliminated all diplomatic efforts to resolve the invasion of Kuwait peacefully (Hammoudi 2019). The essential issue here is how the campaign was based on a strategy of accentuating Iraq's economic dependencies through a deliberate and massive destruction of the country's civilian infrastructure (oil facilities, electric power stations, water treatment and swage sanitation facilities, communication and transport infrastructure, industrial and agricultural plants, health and education facilities). Among other issues, this is manifested in how the American-led coalition tried to "create post-war leverage over Iraq" by destroying and damaging infrastructure which could only be revitalized through foreign assistance (Simons 1996, 11; Gellman 1991). The devastating magnitude of this strategy, which was indisputably unrelated to the 'liberation' of Kuwait, becomes all the more significant, when one considers the long-lasting ecological and health effects of the use of uranium-depleted weapons as well as the chemical and electromagnetic pollution (Bennis and Halliday 2000).

All in all, during the six-week military operation, Iraq's economy and civilian infrastructure was literally bombed back to the colonial era. For instance, "nearly four months after the war the national power generation was only 20%–25% of its prewar total, or about the level it was at in 1920" (Alnasrawi 2001, 210; Gellman 1991). At the same time, Iraq's health care system was "put back by at least 50 years" due to destruction of the health infrastructure, the exodus of health workers and lack of financial resources (World Health Organization, Division of Emergency and Humanitarian Action 1996, 17; Abdullah 2006, 75).

The Gulf War however did not end with the conclusion of Operation Desert Storm, but rather entered a new phase of 'sustained warfare'. Immediately after Iraq's surrender, popular uprisings swept much of Iraq's south and later the Kurdish-inhabited north while the government lost control over most of the provinces. Only after the coalition forces allowed the regime to suppress the uprisings, the United States (later joined by France and UK) began enforcing a No-Fly-Zone over the north of the 36th parallel (from June 1991) and later south of the 32nd parallel (from August 1992) and 33rd parallel (from 1996). The No-Fly-Zone which consistently expanded both in space and scope, was seemingly justified by Resolution 688 which had "condemned the repression of Iraqi civilian population" and demanded that Iraq "immediately end this repression" (Resolution 688, 1991). For the time being, the major point is not so much that "the longest sustained US air operation since the Vietnam War" (Richter 1999) was not authorized by the Security Council (Gray 2002). Rather, the crucial issue is how the enforcement of the No-Fly-Zone weakened Iraq's defensive capacities through intelligence gathering and bombing military installations. This gains all the more significance, when one considers how these dynamics worked in conjunction with the weapons inspections programme and the arms embargo (see Bennis and Halliday 2000, 37). What is more, the No-Fly-Zone not only facilitated the creation of a semi-autonomous region in Iraq's Kurdish provinces, it also accentuated the effects of the economic sanctions by targeting economic installations throughout Iraq (Aruri 2000; Abdullah 2006, 72).

4   The 'Sanctions Warfare Regime'

Now, the persistence of the war after the conclusion of Operation Desert Storm came against the background of an estimated $200 billion cost for restoring Iraq's damaged and destroyed civilian infrastructure (Simons 1996, 12). This is in a context marked by Iraq's near total reliance on the import of medicine and food in the pre-war years (70% of Iraq's food requirements were imported in the pre-war years) and oil exports as the main source of foreign exchange earnings. The conjunction of 'war in permanence' and an enduring 'economic blockade' not only made the restoration of Iraq's infrastructure impossible, but also created a situation where most Iraqis were living on 'semi-starvation diet', despite a 'disciplined government-run rationing system'. What is more, food insecurity, the health effects of illegal weapons used throughout the war, the debilitating of health care system and the basic infrastructure (particularly water sanitation plants) had a direct effect on rising illness and high mortality rates. This is reflected in epidemic outbreaks (malaria, typhoid, chloral), doubling of under-five child mortality in the 1994–1999 period and death of over half a million children as a direct result of sanctions (World Health Organization. Division of Emergency and Humanitarian Action 1996; Abdullah 2006, 74). As Alnasrawi notes, this situation remained the same under the various stages of the OFFP "since the revenue generated under this programme [was] too small to meet the basic needs of the population" (Alnasrawi 2001, 213).

Based on the above observations, we may then argue that the mutually reinforcing relationship between 'economic sanctions' and 'war in permanence' peripheralized Iraq in and through economic, territorial and political 'de-sovereignization' (Alnasseri 2004). That is, a) de-industrializing Iraq and peripheralizing its economy to the extent that the basic needs of the population could not be sufficiently met b) severely limiting Iraq's national autonomy by transferring central aspects of its economic sovereignty to the United Nations, creation of semi-autonomous regions in the north and weakening the country's defensive capacities.

5   Exceptional Circumstances

The 'sanctions warfare regime' emerged in large part due to the relatively successful implementation of a three-layered American imperialist strategy, which was both made possible and necessary by epochal shifts in the international and regional relations. Let me begin by a few words on the abrupt and tectonic consequences of the demise of the bi-polar world order from the perspective of the Middle East.

The 'sanctions warfare regime' emerged in the interregnum between the 'terminal crisis' of the Eastern Bloc and the collapse of the Soviet Union. For our purposes, what stands out with regards to this context is a three-fold process. First and foremost, the dissolution of the bi-polar world order put the United States in an extremely privileged position to push for a radical neo-liberlization of the (semi-)peripheries through 'enhancing the pressure' to enforce structural adjustment policies (Jessop 2010, 26). This was all the more accentuated in the Middle East since the crisis and dissolution of the Soviet Union came at a time when the defensive trenches of the region against external pressures were particularly weakened. To begin with, "financialization of the oil markets, enhanced supply security, declining oil prices and the weakening of OPEC implied that the 'oil weapon' had become a less reliable tool to resolve the…[the crises of state-led development] in the region". What is more, these economic uncertainties had been intensified by the long-lasting effects of the militarization of the region since the late-70s (Nakhaei 2020, 175). In the case of Iraq, the juxtaposition of these changes in the political economy of oil with the economic crisis that had emerged as a result of the 8-eight-yeat war with Iran, played a key role in the Iraqi power bloc's decision to invade Kuwait (Alnasrawi 2001, 206). To return to the main issue. What needs to be highlighted here is that economic vulnerabilities of the region in this constellation "allowed the United States to use economic incentives and threats for enhancing its strategic depth in the region" (Nakhaei 2020, 65). For instance, Egypt "was quick to seize the opportunity to obtain much-needed debt relief in return for its military and diplomatic support for the Allied attack on Iraq" (Owen 2004, 116) while the United States cancelled economic aid to Yemen for voting 'no' to Resolution 678 (Bennis and Halliday 2000, 41).

Second, the 'terminal crisis' of the Soviet Union and a crisis management strategy that prioritized détente with the West, excluded an active foreign and security policy towards the Middle East. From the perspective of the Middle East region, the importance of this 'New Thinking' in Soviet foreign policy (and later the pro-western approach in the initial post-Soviet years) cannot be overestimated. After all, the relations of force in the region had been overdetermined by the Soviet-American rivalry since the inauguration of the bi-polar world order, and even more so since the 70s, when the Middle East became "a scene of continuous east–west maneuvering…for strategic positions in the third world" (F. Halliday 2005, 99). Given the narrowing of the region's defensive trenches, the prioritization of détente with the West not only made the Gulf War possible, but also allowed the United States to instrumentalize the United Nations for the enforcement of the 'sanctions warfare regime' (Rubinstein 1994; Hammoudi 2019, 8).

Finally, the Gulf war in particular and the 'sanctions warfare regime' in general laid the foundation of an ever-increasing US military presence through the establishment of military bases, defense agreements, arms transfers and enforcement of No-Fly-Zones. On the one hand, throughout this process, the Middle East became the 'epicenter of Washington's post-cold war military offensive' (Klare 1998, 12). On the other hand, the unparalleled militarization of the region since the 1990s prioritized defense spending, thereby making the unsettled economic situation of Middle East states even more vulnerable to American-led pressures for neoliberlization (Nakhaei 2020, 65).

Having briefly sketched out these colossal changes in the international and regional relations of force, I will now turn to a discussion of the three-layered imperialist strategy through which the 'sanctions warfare regime' materialized;

the 'war on rogue states', 'internationalization qua cantonization' and asymmetrical containment.

6   The War on Rogue States

As much as the breakdown of the Soviet Union facilitated the American-led neoliberal offensive against the dominated formations, it also presented an enormous challenge to the persistence of 'imperialism under American hegemony'. After all, the Soviet Union had consistently presented a strategic threat to all the Atlantic powers and as such compelled them to manage their contradictions under the hegemonic position of the United States. Against this background, the demise of the bi-polar world order could facilitate the intensification of intra-imperialist rivalries at a time when the dominated formations had become exceedingly vulnerable to external pressures (Nakhaei 2020, 63). In this sense, the United States' central role in the inauguration of the 'sanctions warfare regime' was not merely about the projection of American military and political might in a post-Soviet era. Rather, this was the cornerstone of a larger strategy; creation of a *fait accomplis* situation of 'war in permanence', which would 'replace' the threat of communism. This gains an added significance, when one considers the geostrategic importance of Middle East in general and Iraq in particular. It is then not a coincidence that the 'war on rogue states' and later the 'war on terror' came to be "exceptionally concentrated in the Middle East" (Hinnebusch 2003, 235; Klare 1998, 12), and more specifically in Iraq.

7   'Internationalization qua Cantonization'

As I iterated before, the decline of the bi-polar world order permitted, if not forced the United States to break up the resistance to the neoliberal offensive in the South more aggressively through multiplicity of old and new tactics. Among these tactics, what Sabah Alnasseri calls "internationalization qua cantonization" is of particular relevance. That is, the fracturing (de-nationalization, sectarianization, cantonization) of 'formerly politically constituted spaces' through a 'violent opening'; a 'first step' towards the privatization of power and economy in peripheral states which were unwilling to abide by the neoliberal offensive (Alnasseri 2004; 2009). Though not exclusive to the case of Iraq, the 'sanctions warfare regime' is a concrete manifestation of this tactic. This does not only concern the economic, territorial and political 'de-sovereignization' of Iraq which I previously elaborated on, but also the *intended* consequences of this process. On the one hand, the 'sanctions warfare regime' violently forced Iraq back to "pre-industrial social patterns for survival...[as] tribal, religious and ethnic bonds of community reciprocity and exchange re-emerged as central institutions bridging personal and social security" (Ismael and Ismael 2005, 615). On the other hand, the *Ba'ath* regime propagated these social relations to ensure its survival by mediating and/or perpetuating divisions among the old social forces that the 'sanctions warfare regime' had resuscitated. By way of example, one can refer to Saddam's uneasy alliance with the Kurdistan Democratic Party (KDP) against the Patriotic Union of Kurdistan (PUK) during the 'Kurdish civil war', "enhancing the position of the Sunni and Shiite institutions and teaching centers" (Alnasseri 2009) and 're-tribalization' through granting resurrected tribes "specific authority over such matters as limited revenue collection and law enforcement" (Abdullah 2006, 83). Here again, the United States facilitated this process by allowing the brutal suppression of the 1991 uprisings and making "the population directly dependent" on the regime(Alnasseri 2009).

In an a posteriori sense, we can argue that the cantonization of Iraq in and through the 'sanctions warfare regime' was certainly a 'first step' towards the radical neoliberlization of Iraq that occurred after the 2003 invasion (Alnasseri 2004, 2009). Nonetheless, what is necessary here is to situate the American imperialist strategy of cantonization in relation to what I term asymmetrical containment.

8   Asymmetrical Containment

Ever since the outbreak of Iran-Iraq war, the United States had pursued a policy of 'dual containment' towards both countries by ensuring that neither was on a position of victory during the war. After all, undermining the Soviet's position in the Middle East was to a large extend predicated on the mutual weakening of Iran and Iraq, both of which had strong anti-American elements in their foreign orientations (Nakhaei 2020, 195). At the same time, the mutual weakening of Iran and Iraq was central to enhancing Israel's security. That is not the lease because Iran and Iraq were both attempting to increase their strategic depth in the region through replacing the role that Egypt had historically played vis-vis Israel prior to the signing of the Egypt-Israel peace treaty.

With the decline of the bi-polar world order, the 'sanctions warfare regime' developed in conjunction with a similar process in Iran. Put differently, Iran was also subject to intensifying economic sanctions while the country was excluded from the post-Gulf War security arrangements as well the 'peace process' (Amirahmadi 1997, 49; Parsi 2007, 154; Habibi 2013). Hence, in the years following the conclusion of Iran-Iraq war, the policy of dual containment remained firmly in place. This may be explained by pointing to a two-fold process. On the one hand, the 'containment' of Iraq and Iran as 'rogue states' and 'sponsors of terrorism' was central to the *fait accomplis* construction of the New World Order. On the other hand, this policy would maintain the balance of forces in favor of American allies in the region. For instance, the combined effect of the embargo on Iraq and the economic sanctions on Iran allowed American allies, mainly Kuwait and Saudi Arabia, to increase their share in the oil market. This in turn enabled these countries to settle their war debts, purchase American arms and finance American military bases (Alnasseri 2004; 2009).

Nonetheless, the crucial point here is that neither the intensity nor the scope of the sanctions or the political and military pressures on Iran were comparable to the 'sanctions warfare regime' in Iraq. That is, far from experiencing an economic blockade, or political and territorial 'de-sovereignization', post-war Iran was actually integrating into European circuits of capital (Nakhaei 2020). As such, it is crucial to highlight that in the conjuncture following the Gulf crisis, the policy of dual containment was gradually modified to what may be termed 'asymmetrical containment'. The multifaceted reasons behind the asymmetrical nature of dual containment in this period demand their own discussion. However, the main reasons behind such modification in United States' containment policy becomes clear if we consider Washington's push for the 'peace process' against the background of the first intifada. It is true that the first intifada had provided both Iran and Iraq the opportunity to enhance their strategic positioning in the region by expanding their influence on the Palestinian struggle. Nonetheless, the major weight of Iran's influence remained within Lebanon while some forces within Iran's post-war power bloc began to tacitly support the peace process (see Parsi 2007, 142–152). In sharp contrast, Iraq had managed to become the "major financial and political supporter of the Palestinian intifada", "strengthen Arab solidarity with the establishment of regional co-operative economic councils" and host a "summit of twenty-one Arab countries in June 1 1990". In this sense, all indications were pointing towards Iraq's assumption of Egypt's historical in the Palestinian struggle role prior to Camp David Accords. This is perhaps best captured by the way in which Iraq led the efforts on rehabilitating Egypt to the Arab League (Aziz 2000, 130). From this perspective, the unequivocally heavier burden of dual containment on Iraq relates to the American-led efforts in incapacitating the possibility of Iraq gaining a leadership role in the Arab world, at a time when Washington was ensuring Israel's security through pushing for the 'peace process'.

9   Conclusion

My observations above indicate that the three-layered imperialist strategy through which the 'sanctions warfare regime' materialized were relatively successful from the perspective of America's geo-strategic positioning in the Middle East. That is to say, Iraq was fragmented, its social fabric destroyed, and it remained on the sidelines as the 'peace process' was institutionalized. At the same time, by allowing a weakened, yet existing *Ba'ath* regime to remain intact, the United States managed to keep potential Iranian influence in Iraq at bay. What is more, the 'sanctions warfare regime' facilitated an increasing American military presence in the region which in turn had a key role in Washington's later military campaigns.

This is not to say that there were no limitations to this three-layered strategy. 'Illicit trade' between Iraq and its neighbors including Iran, the signing of oil contracts between Iraq, France, Russia and China and removing the cap on Iraq's oil exports after 1999 all show the increasing regional and international opposition to the sanctions (see Katzman and Blanchard 2007). Nonetheless, the essential point here is that the violent condensation of the contradictions of the 'New World Order' in Iraq allowed the 'sanctions warfare regime' to persist, prepare the ground for the 2003 invasion and delay a possible popular history. That is, without the 'sanctions warfare regime', there would neither be a weakened *Ba'ath* regime nor an occupation, but very likely a revolution!

References

Abdullah, Thabit. (2006). *Dictatorship, Imperialism and Chaos: Iraq since 1989.* Nova Scotia; London: Zed Books.

Alnasrawi, Abbas. (2001). "Iraq: Economic Sanctions and Consequences, 1990–2000." *Third World Quarterly* 22 (2): 205–218. https://doi.org/10.1080/01436590120037036.

Alnasseri, Sabah. (2004). "Imperial(istisch)e Kriege und Kantonisierung oder." *Die Internationalisierung peripherer Staaten* 96 (24).

Alnasseri, Sabah. (2009). "Understanding Iraq." *Socialist Register* 44 (44): 77–100.

Amirahmadi, Hooshang. (1997). "The Spiraling Gulf Arms Race." In White, Paul J., and Logan, William Stewart (eds.), *Remaking the Middle East.* Nationalism and Internationalism. Oxford: Berg.

Aruri, Naseer. (2000). "America's War Against Iraq: 1990–1999." In Arnove, Anthony (ed.), *Iraq Under Siege: The Deadly Impact of Sanctions and War*, 23–33. Cambridge, MA: South End Press.

Aziz, Barbara Nimri. (2000). "Targets—Not Victims." In Arnove, Anthony (ed.), *Iraq Under Siege: The Deadly Impact of Sanctions and War*, 127–136. Cambridge, MA: South End Press.

Bennis, Phyllis, and Denis J. Halliday. (2000). "Iraq: The Impact of Sanctions and US Policy." In Arnove, Anthony (ed.), *Iraq Under Siege: The Deadly Impact of Sanctions and War*, 35–46. Cambridge, MA: South End Press.

Gellman, Barton. (1991). "Allied Air War Struck Broadly in Iraq." *The Washington Post*, 23 June.

Gray, Christine. (2002). "From Unity to Polarization: International Law and the Use of Force against Iraq." *European Journal of International Law* 13 (1): 1–19.

Habibi, Nader. (2013). "The Iranian Economy in the Shadow of Sanctions." In Alizadeh, Parvin, and Hakimian, Hassan (eds.), *Iran and the Global Economy: Petro Populism, Islam and Economic Sanctions*, 172–198. Routledge.

Halliday, Denis. (1999). "The Impact of the UN Sanctions on the People of Iraq." *Journal of Palestine Studies* 8 (2): 10.

Halliday, Fred. (2005). *The Middle East in International Relations: Power, Politics and Ideology*. Cambridge/New York, NY: Cambridge University Press.

Hammoudi, Ali. (2019). "Iraq, Imperialism, Political Economy, and International Law." In Ness, Immanuel, and Cope, Zak (eds.), *The Palgrave Encyclopedia of Imperialism and Anti-Imperialism*, 1–18. Cham: Springer International Publishing. https://doi.org/10.1007/978-3-319-91206-6_118-1.

Hinnebusch, Raymond A. (2003). *The International Politics of the Middle East*. Regional International Politics Series. Manchester; New York: Manchester University Press.

Ismael, Tareq Y., and Jacqueline S. Ismael. (2004). *The Iraqi Predicament: People in the Quagmire of Power Politics*. London; Sterling, VA: Pluto Press.

Ismael, Tareq Y., and Jacqueline S. Ismael. (2005). "Whither Iraq? Beyond Saddam, Sanctions and Occupation." *Third World Quarterly* 26 (4–5): 609–629.

Jessop, Bob. (2010). "The Continuing Ecological Dominance of Neoliberalism in the Crisis." In Saad-Filho, Alfredo, and Yalman, Galip L. (eds.), *Economic Transitions to Neoliberalism in Middle-Income Countries: Policy Dilemmas, Economic Crises, Forms of Resistance*, 24–39. Routledge Studies in Development Economics. London; New York: Routledge.

Katzman, Kenneth, and Christopher M. Blanchard. (2007). "Iraq: Oil-For-Food Program, Illicit Trade, and Investigations." Congressional Research Service.

Klare, Michael. (1998). "The Rise and Fall of the 'Rogue Doctrine': The Pentagon's Quest for a Post-Cold War Military Strategy." *Middle East Report*, no. 208: 12.

Nakhaei, Nima. (2020). "State and Development in Post-Revolutionary Iran." Doctoral Dissertation, Toronto: York University.

Owen, Roger. (2004). *State, Power and Politics in the Making of the Modern Middle East*. London; New York: Routledge.

Parsi, Trita. (2007). *Treacherous Alliance: The Secret Dealings of Israel, Iran, and the United States*. New Haven: Yale University Press.

Resolution 661. (1990). "United Nations Security Council Resolution 661—UNSCR."

Resolution 688. (1991). "United Nations Security Council Resolution 688—UNSCR."

Richter, Paul. (1999). "No End Is in Sight to U.S. Air Campaign Over Iraq." *Los Angeles Times*, 3 March.

Rubinstein, Alvin Z. (1994) "Moscow and the Gulf War: Decisions and Consequences." *International Journal* 49 (2): 28.

Simons, Geoff. (1996). *The Scourging of Iraq: Sanctions, Law and Natural Justice*. 2nd ed. London: Mcmillan.

Sponeck, H.C. von. (2006). *A Different Kind of War: The UN Sanctions Regime in Iraq*. New York: Berghahn Books.

World Health Organization, Division of Emergency and Humanitarian Action. (1996). "The Health Conditions of the Population of Iraq since the Gulf Crisis," no. WHO/EHA/96.1.

CHAPTER 14

Writing Out Empire: The Case of the Syria Sanctions

Greg Shupak

Since the end of the Second World War, the United States has been the world's leading political, economic, and military power. America's capitalist economy ensures that it is an internally stratified society wherein the US bourgeoisie, alongside its international allies, makes decisions about US stewardship of the global system with minimal input from the American working class. Analytic clarity, therefore, requires that discussions of US imperialism highlight the centrality of the American ruling class in determining the global policies that the US state pursues. Central to these is the question of how the American ruling class approaches rivals. As the US and its partners attempt to manage economic, political, and ecological instability, the global capitalist empire that the US heads is as concerned as ever with subduing challengers and enveloping territories and populations that are not currently fully within its grasp. As John Bellamy Foster writes,

> the dollar-oil-Pentagon regime, backed by the entire triad of the United States/Canada, Europe, and Japan, is exerting all of its military and financial power to gain geopolitical and geo-economic advantages. The goal is to subordinate still further those countries at the bottom of the world hierarchy, while putting obstacles in the way of emerging economies, and overthrowing all states that violate the rules of the dominant order.
> 2019

Economic sanctions play an indispensable role in that project. They are a mode of control used to attack the populations of countries with governments that sections of the American ruling class regard as a barrier to their interests. Syria provides an example. The Syrian state was periodically willing to work with its American counterpart, siding with the US in the 1991 Gulf War and later participating in America's extraordinary rendition torture program. Nevertheless, the US government has, with brief periods of partial respite, carried out economic and political aggression against Syria for more than forty years. The American state has consistently made clear that it is doing so because the Syrian government helps inhibit US ruling class goals in Palestine, Lebanon, Iraq, Iran, and thus also in Syria itself. In this chapter, I show that US government sanctions have done significant harm to the Syrian economy, and thus also to the Syrian masses' quality of life, for most of the century. Since the start of the 2011 war, the sanctions have inflicted severe harm on Syrians, undermining their access to food and medicine and exacerbating inflation and unemployment. The measures in the United States' Caesar Act (2019) have played a central role in pushing the Syrian population to the edge of starvation.

My argument is not that the economic crisis in Syria is only a result of US sanctions: in the 2000s, Bashar al-Assad's government pursued neoliberal reforms and, by late 2010, the social supports that had previously existed in the country came apart (Kadri and Matar 2019, 1–2). Still less is my position that the policies of the United States and its allies are the sole reason that Syrians are suffering as their country has gone through a decade long war that has been, often simultaneously, a popular uprising against a dictatorship, a civil war, and an international proxy war. Yet I demonstrate that the American ruling class and its international partners have wrought acute material deprivation in Syrians' lives in pursuit of imperial goals in the region and have done so while the consequences have been perfectly clear. Leading US media outlets, I also show, have obfuscated the sanctions' role in the socio-economic destruction of Syria, diminishing the likelihood of American audiences understanding how the government under which they live is culpable in a humanitarian crisis.

1   History of Sanctions against Syria

American sanctions on Syria long predate the 2011 war. Syria has been on the US' "State Sponsors of Terrorism" list since it was first created in 1979 in accord with the Export Administration Act. Syria's inclusion has been based largely on its support for Hizballah, which has fought back against American and Israeli attacks on Lebanon, and for the Palestinian resistance groups Hamas and Palestinian Islamic Jihad (Hersh 2003). Though countries on the list cannot receive foreign assistance funds from the United States, amid a short thaw in relations between Syria and the United States from 1974–1979, American aid helped fund work on Syria's water supply, irrigation, rural roads, and electrification, as well as health and agricultural research. Being on the list also meant that the US Secretary of Commerce and the Secretary of State would have to notify Congress before licensing the export of goods or technology worth more than $7 million to Syria; amendments in 1985 and 1986 lowered this threshold to $1 million and, in 1989, mandated notification irrespective of value. The

Omnibus Diplomatic Security and Antiterrorism Act of 1986 and Omnibus Budget Reconciliation Act of 1986 respectively banned US military equipment sales to Syria and denied foreign tax credits on income or war profits from Syria with both laws citing ostensible Syrian government support for terrorism. A 1994–95 amendment to the Foreign Assistance Act of 1961 mandates that the United States withhold a proportionate share of contributions to international organizations for programs that benefit Syria and seven other countries. Under the Antiterrorism and Effective Death Penalty Act of 1996, the US President is required to withhold aid to third countries that provide assistance or lethal military equipment to countries on the terrorism list though the President can waive this provision if they conclude that doing so is in the "national interest" (Sharp 2010a, 6–8). Such policies were porous. For example, in 2005, the US sold Syria $100 million worth of corn (Sharp 2010b, 19).

The 2003 Syria Accountability and Lebanese Sovereignty Restoration Act marked a significant escalation of US efforts to isolate and subvert Syria. The act reduces American diplomatic contacts with Syria and restricts travel by Syrian diplomats inside the US while banning US businesses from operating or investing in Syria, landing in or overflight of the United States by Syrian aircraft, and all American exports to Syria except food and medicine. The law does so with reference to what the US described as Syria's occupation of Lebanon (*Syria Accountability and Lebanese Sovereignty Restoration Act* 2003, sec. 5). The Lebanese government disputed this characterization, saying Syria was there at Lebanon's request; the US dismissed this position on the grounds that Lebanon's government was allegedly a Syrian puppet (Strindberg 2004). The act also says the sanctions are based on Syria's alleged "development of weapons of mass destruction" (WMDs). Strindberg points out that in both 2003 and 2004 Syria put forth proposals at the UN for making the Middle East a nuclear weapons free zone and the US vetoed the proposal in both cases (pp. 62–63); he also quotes a ranking Western diplomat in the Syrian capital as saying that the Syrians "certainly have no nuclear weapons, nor the capabilities or intentions of developing them. They have no biological capabilities" (Strindberg 2004, p. 63). The Syria Accountability Act likewise accuses Syria of importing oil in violation of sanctions on Iraq and of providing "support for acts of international terrorism" while claiming that it's necessary to "hold Syria accountable for its role in the Middle East, and for other purposes." The deeds referred to in the last sentence include "Hizballah, Hamas, the Popular Front for the Liberation of Palestine, and the Popular Front for the Liberation of Palestine-General Command." The bill goes on to say Syria allows Hizballah and other militant organizations to attack Israeli outposts at Shebaa Farms (*Syria Accountability and Lebanese Sovereignty Restoration Act* 2003, sec. 2), territory that both Syria and Lebanon say is Lebanese but that Israel claims is part of the Syrian Golan Heights that Israel occupied in 1967 ("Fate of Sheeba Farms on Hold Until Israeli Withdrawal" 2008) and illegally annexed in 1981. The Syria Accountability Act also rationalizes sanctions on the grounds that Syrian policy enables Hizballah to control "the Israeli-Lebanese border and much of southern Lebanon" as the group "continues to attack Israeli positions" and "allows Iranian Revolutionary Guards and other militant groups to operate freely in the area" (*Syria Accountability and Lebanese Sovereignty Restoration Act* 2003, sec. 2). In these respects, the sanctions were explicitly enacted because they interfere with US imperial prerogatives in the region such as subduing Iraq, out maneuvering Iran, and attempting to quell Hizballah and Palestinian resistance to US-Israeli efforts to dominate Lebanon and Palestine.

In 2004, the Bush administration issued an executive order building on the Syria Accountability and Lebanese Sovereignty Restoration Act. The order claims that Syria constitutes "an unusual and extraordinary threat to the national security, foreign policy, and economy of the United States" to the point that it was allegedly necessary to "declare a national emergency to deal with that threat." The order declared that "all property and interests in property" be "blocked and may not be transferred, paid, exported, withdrawn, or otherwise dealt in" when the US determines that these "propert[ies] and interests in property" belong to persons who meet one of several conditions. These include "contributing to the Government of Syria's" support for "any person whose property or interests in property are blocked under United States law for terrorism-related reasons, including, but not limited to, Hamas, Hizballah, Palestinian Islamic Jihad, the Popular Front for the Liberation of Palestine, the Popular Front for the Liberation of Palestine-General Command." A further condition for the 2004 sanctions is "significantly contributing to any steps taken by the Government of Syria to undermine United States and international efforts with respect to the stabilization and reconstruction of Iraq" (Exec. Order No. 13338, 2004). Thus, the measures were explicitly applied to people involved in Syrian government actions that were anathema to the US ruling class. These include Syrian support for the Palestinian armed struggle against Israeli colonization as Palestinian liberation forces represent a threat to American capital's extensive economic and political investments in Israel. They also include aid that the American state said Syria provided to the Iraqi resistance to the US military occupation of Iraq following Washington's 2003 invasion of the country, movements that kept American planners from securing total control over Iraq. The US government likewise objects to assistance to Hizballah, which the Americans have long detested because of its defence of Lebanon from US-Israeli attacks during the Lebanese Civil War and Israel's

2006 invasion of the country, because of its fight against Israel's occupation of south Lebanon, and because of its partnership with Iran, the linchpin of state level regional opposition to US hegemony.

A 2008 executive order said that the Syrian government, and "other persons contributing to public corruption related to Syria," were continuing these regional activities through means including "misusing Syrian public assets" or "misusing public authority" in a fashion that "entrenches and enriches the Government of Syria and its supporters." Anyone that the US deems to be part of such endeavours would have their "property or interests in property ... blocked," if it came within reach of the American government, and prevented from being transferred, exported, withdrawn, used as payment, or "otherwise dealt in" (Exec. Order No. 13460, 2008). In the intervening years, the US had also accused Syria of involvement in the assassination of former Lebanese Prime Minister Rafiq Hariri, and the deaths of 22 others, and applied sanctions to anyone that the US claimed was connected to the violence (Exec. Order No. 13399, 2006).

The Syrian uprising began in March of 2011 amid what is often called the "Arab Spring," a series of large protests across many countries in North Africa and West Asia that had toppled governments in Tunisia and Egypt. Syria had undergone a decade of economic liberalization that was "accompanied by major socioeconomic dislocations, including drought and depopulation in rural areas, a dramatic rise in semi-urbanization and informal housing, black market activity, increasing unemployment, and a decaying social safety net.... Th[e] combination of political repression, deteriorating socioeconomic standards, and the spillover effects of the Arab uprisings created the immediate context in which the Syrian uprising began" (Abboud 2015, 337). In April 2011, the Obama administration levied sanctions against the assets of anyone it said committed or supported human rights abuses in Syria (Exec. Order No. 13572, 2011). A month later, the US blocked transactions involving property belonging to senior Syrian government officials as well as anyone Washington deems "an agency or instrumentality of the Government of Syria, or owned or controlled, directly or indirectly, by the Government of Syria" or anyone who materially backs such persons. In August, the United States banned the import of Syrian oil and, under pressure from the Obama administration, the European Union did the same the following month, with the Arab League, Turkey, Canada, and Australia adopting sanctions on Syria or expanding existing ones (Phillips 2016, 86).

In April 2012, the US added further sanctions to Syria and Iran, actions that were described as targeting the countries' abilities to conduct electronic surveillance of the opposition in both countries and to disrupt their communications networks. This policy targets the property of people the US says are connected to Syria and Iran carrying out these activities and bans such persons from entering the United States (Exec. Order No. 13606, 2012). A month later, the Obama administration applied the same punishments to non-Americans who do business with Syria or Iran that contravenes US sanctions or helps another person to do so, a policy that is justified in part on the grounds of "Iran's or Syria's support for international terrorism" (Exec. Order No. 13608, 2012).

The Caesar Act, which was folded into the US' National Defense Authorization Act for 2020, imposes sanctions on a "foreign person" who knowingly "sells or provides significant goods, services, technology, information or other support that significantly facilitates the maintenance or expansion of the Government of Syria's domestic production of natural gas, petroleum or petroleum products." The act also says that the US president will apply sanctions to a "foreign person" if they "knowingly, directly or indirectly, provid[e] significant construction or engineering services to the Government of Syria" (*National Defense Authorization Act for Fiscal Year 2020*, sec. 7412) It goes on to explain that part of its "strategy" is to "deter foreign persons from entering into contracts related to reconstruction in the areas" that are "under the control of— (A) the Government of Syria; (B) the Government of the Russian Federation; (C) the Government of Iran" (*National Defense Authorization Act for Fiscal Year 2020*, sec. 7413). These provisions enable the US ruling class to punish citizens of any country should they invest in rebuilding Syria's shattered economy, by revitalizing key sectors like natural gas or petroleum, or the massive physical destruction that has occurred during the war.

2   Starving Syria: The Impacts of Sanctions on Syria's Population

The sanctions' economic impact was minimal prior to those that George W. Bush's administration applied. Even these were not as devastating as later measures because US-Syria trade was already limited: Syria's sole airline had never operated flights to America, and trade with the EU, Russia, and southeast Asia could fill the void for Syria (Strindberg 2004, 56–57). Nevertheless, the George W. Bush-era sanctions did have significant effects. By 2005, US sanctions were "taking their toll—derailing a major gas project" that had been awarded to a US-Canadian consortium of Petro-Canada, Occidental and Petrofac (Husari 2005). A *New York Times* report published two years later, which looks at power failures and electricity shortages in Syria, notes that while there were legal criteria under which American companies could invest in Syria, "some have hesitated, and energy businesses like Conoco Phillips and

Marathon Oil have pulled out over the past three years." Andrew Tabler, then editor of *Syria Today Magazine* and subsequently director for Syria on the National Security Council's Middle East Affairs Directorate during the Trump administration, says in the *Times* article that "Syria now finds itself in a situation where the number of companies that can build big power facilities are limited, and the ones that can do this have apparently followed the American lead because they fear the repercussions of doing business here" (Naylor 2007).

In 2008, Turkcell withdrew its bid on Syriatel after the American government sanctioned Syriatel's primary stakeholder, Rami Makluf. A 2010 Congressional Research Service report claims that "U.S. sanctions against Syria have clearly dissuaded some U.S. and some foreign businesses from investing in Syria" as trade restrictions "have prevented the country's national air carrier, Syrian Air, both from repairing the few Boeing planes in its fleet and from procuring new planes from Europe, since Airbus uses certain American content in its planes" (Sharp 2010b, 18). In December of the previous year, the US rejected Airbus' request to sell planes to Syria because, on average, 40 percent of an Airbus plane's component parts are of US origin (Sharp 2010b, 18). Similarly, Patriot Act sanctions against the Commercial Bank of Syria "deterred private Western banks from opening branches inside Syria" (Sharp 2010b, 19).

As the sanctions have become harsher in the years following the start of the 2011 war, so have their effects. The boycotts of Syrian oil applied in 2011 pounded the country, particularly the EU's embargo, because almost all of Syria's pre-war 150,000 barrels per day of oil exports went to the EU, principally to Italy and Germany: in 2005–2010, approximately 20 percent of Syria's total budget revue came from oil revenue. The Syrian Center for Policy Research estimates that 28.3 percent ($6.8 billion) of Syria's total GDP loss in 2011–12 was linked to sanctions and that more than half of this reduction ($3.9 billion) was from the oil sector. While some Syrian businesses linked to the government were able to get around the oil sanctions by using *Seychelles-based* shell companies, the effort to block the sale of Syrian oil affected much of the population. 3.1 million Syrians were pushed into poverty in 2011–12, an estimated 877,000 of them because of sanctions (Phillips 2016, 87–88).

Furthermore, a June 2012 Commodity Intelligence Report from the United States Department of Agriculture discusses how sanctions undermine food security in Syria: "The net result of international actions has been to trigger a major depreciation in the Syrian currency (50%), dramatically increase domestic inflation, significantly deplete government financial reserves, and seriously restrict trade. Though current sanctions do not officially target food or agricultural commodities, restrictions imposed on Syrian banks and trading firms have somewhat impeded the country's ability to finance needed imports" (Dahi 6 Mar. 2019). Joshua Landis also points to sanctions as one of four principal reasons that inflation in Syria had exploded by the spring of 2012, alongside hoarding, a 30 percent tariff on any goods coming from Turkey, and the government's reduced ability to pay for subsidies. The US-EU ban on oil imports applied the previous August and September, respectively, were costing $400 million a month while the sanctions' banking restrictions had reduced trade with neighbouring Iraq by 10 percent (Landis 2012, 80).

An October 2012 report from the Danish Institute for International Studies (DIIS), commissioned by the Danish Ministry of Foreign Affairs, finds that sanctions have helped erode international confidence in the Syrian economy thereby contributing to an increase in unemployment. They have also played a part in decreasing salary levels and, therefore, in the fall of Syrians' purchasing power. This reduced purchasing power has undermined access to food across the country. In these ways, "the sanctions add to the socioeconomic costs of the conflict and are likely to exacerbate pre-existing socioeconomic difficulties, particularly affecting the lower social strata of the population" (Lyme 2012, 6–7). DIIS also notes that the ban on transactions in US dollars has reportedly made it almost impossible to carry out financial transactions through Syria using international and regional banks. To avoid breaching the sanctions, international and regional financial institutions have over-complied and been extremely reluctant to serve Syrians. Thus, all Syrian citizens with bank accounts and credit cards, face serious problems when they try to carry out transactions. Since all international transactions have been affected, the sanctions have "indirectly" hampered import of medical items and food, including essential staples like wheat, the import of which Syria relies on for half of its national consumption (Lyme 2012, 49–50).

Though medicine and food are exempt from the economic measures taken against Syria, over-compliance with the sanctions has resulted in problems with importing food and medicine. While the domestic pharmaceutical industry produced 90 percent or more of the medicine consumed in Syria at the time of DIIS' report, this production required importing active agents, machines and equipment. International financial institutions' reluctance to deal with Syrian companies complicates importing, as do increased production costs caused by fuel shortages and higher raw material prices. Consequently, the consumer prices of medicine reportedly rose and there were shortages of pharmaceuticals (Lyme 2012, 61).

As the conflict was about to reach its second anniversary, Doctors Without Borders/ Médecins Sans Frontières (MSF) noted that, before the war, Syria "had a well-functioning health system" with "trained health workers, medical expertise and its own pharmaceutical industry. But today, those resources are almost completely depleted, on all sides of the frontlines. Health networks have broken down because of supply problems and drug shortages resulting from the collapse of the pharmaceutical industry or indirectly from international sanctions imposed on Syria" ("Syria Two Years On: The Failure of International Aid" 2013). In the first three years following the 2011 sanctions, Ella Wind and Omar S. Dahi (2014, 135) point out, "Syrian enterprises and regional partners ... [had] signed virtually no new export contracts." Wind and Dahi note that

> One impact of the sanctions has been an acceleration of the depletion of Syria's foreign exchange reserves. The government has drawn heavily upon these stores of cash as oil revenue dried up. According to a report by the SCPR, the sanctions caused 28 percent (or roughly $6.8 billion) of the losses to GDP in 2011 and 2012. The report also concluded that the sanctions had the worst impact on the lower social classes, given the rise in prices of food staples such as bread and the higher cost of heating oil.
> 2014, 135

A year later the journal *European Security* published an article noting the role of sanctions in more than doubling the price of basics such as milk, eggs and rice, and a threefold increase in the cost of heating oil. Its author, Erica S. Moret, contends that sanctions have led to difficulties importing medicines, which has hindered the treatment of chronic illnesses, including diabetes and respiratory diseases, as well as common contagious illnesses (2015, 130).

In 2017, World Health Organization officials said that doctors in the Damascus Children's Hospital cancer ward face a critical shortage of specialist drugs to treat their patients because western sanctions, as well as the military conflict, have severely restricted pharmaceutical imports. While medical supplies are largely exempt from the sanctions, a 90 percent drop in the value of the Syrian pound has made some pharmaceuticals prohibitively expensive. The sanctions, furthermore, prevent many international pharmaceutical companies from dealing with the Syrian government and hinder foreign banks that are handling payments for imported drugs (Nehme 2017).

With the war in its eighth year, the sanctions had created "severe hardships for the population," preventing damaged utility generators from being repaired, continuing to drive down the value of Syria's currency, and increasing unemployment by helping bring about small businesses' collapse. Together with an escalation in the cost of necessities such as food, heating oil, and medicines, sanctions contributed to severe hardships for the population. Sanctions also share responsibility for the lack of essential medicines, and prosthesis, and medicines for those with long-term chronic conditions for physical and mental health (Sen 2019, 201).

In August 2020, two months after the Caesar Act came into effect, millions of Syrian civilians were having to choose between buying food and taking precautions against COVID-19 as "Poverty and deprivation worsened dramatically since the US introduced all-embracing sanctions on Syria on 17 June under the Caesar Syria Civilian Protection Act" (Cockburn 2020a). The victims of the blockade "are the poor and the powerless who suffer since the price of foodstuffs has risen by 209 per cent in the last year" (Cockburn 2020a). The US government is

> stoking a humanitarian catastrophe in a bid to deny a victory to Russia and Iran, the two main supporters of Assad during the conflict. Confirming this aim, the US special representative for Syria, James Jeffrey, says that US policy is to turn Syria into "a quagmire" for Russia, like the one the US faced in Vietnam, and to give the US a degree of control over Syria similar to what it had in Japan at the end of the Second World War.
>
> COCKBURN 2020a

The US ruling class is driving Syrians deeper into poverty, denying them food and increasing their susceptibility to COVID-19, as a strategy for dominating Syria and thwarting geopolitical rivals from Moscow and Tehran. By October 2020, the Caesar Act had "turned all Syrians, pro and anti-Assad, into economic pariahs subjected to a crippling economic siege. The embargo led to the collapse of the Syrian currency and a steep rise in the price of basic foodstuffs, with wheat, rice and bulgur tripling in price. This happened in a country where the World Food Programme said in June that "famine could very well be knocking at the door" (Cockburn 2020b).

Similarly, a December 2020 *Foreign Policy* article reports that the sanctions are "forcing the country into famine." The article notes that:

> According to the World Food Program, 9.3 million Syrians are unsure where their next meal is coming from, an increase of around 1.4 million in the first six months of the year. Moreover, northeast Syria, the country's breadbasket, is under the control of the United States' Kurdish allies the Syrian Democratic Forces, which are yet to come to an agreement with the regime on grain supply.... U.S. sanctions on oil and gas meant only Iranian crude found its way to Syria. Lack of that basic resource has had a ripple effect on the agriculture and energy sectors, also impacting local

businesses. More than 80 percent of Syrians now live below the poverty line.

The article goes on to say that:

> Senior Western diplomats have told Foreign Policy on many occasions that sanctions are the West's last leverage against Assad to pressure him to release political prisoners, ensure the safe return of refugees, and agree to a political reconciliation that, if carried out sincerely, would eventually mean him leaving power. They insist that paying for Syrian reconstruction, including of infrastructure like power plants and irrigation systems that are necessary for the country's food security and daily life, will end up strengthening the regime's oppression.
>
> VOHRA 2020

These comments indicate that the policy is to starve the Syrian population until the dictatorship they live under dissolves itself. James Jeffrey, a long time US diplomat and Special Representative for Syria Engagement from 2018–2020, also describes the US' approach to the country as being driven by the goal of thwarting its government. He said that the US has secured a "military stalemate" in which US forces and their allies have prevented the Assad government from reclaiming territory it has lost during the war while sanctions have "crushed" Syrian government (Magid 2020).

3   Writing Out Empire: US Media Silences on the Syria Sanctions

The preceding section demonstrates that it was clear by the end of 2012 that sanctions were undermining Syrians' access to food and medicine. To investigate whether US media's coverage of these shortages informed their audiences that the policies of the US and its allies are culpable for these problems, I searched[1] the archives of the three highest circulation newspapers in the United States: *The Wall Street Journal*, *USA Today*, and *The New York Times* (Turvill 2020). I ran queries with Factiva, the media aggregator, to identify

---

[1] My search results contain all types of material that these outlets produce, including multimedia and online publications as well as print; I use the term "works" in a way that should be understood to encompass all of these materials. The search results include letters to the editors but exclude corrections: without this exclusion, the results include documents from *USA Today* that exclusively list corrections and are sometimes tens of thousands of words long.

WRITING OUT EMPIRE: THE CASE OF THE SYRIA SANCTIONS

stories in these outlets that contained any variation of all three of the words, "Syria," "food," and either "short" or "scarce" such as "Syrian," "foodstuffs," "shortage," and "scarcity." I then did the same but added any form of the word "sanction." These search terms are expansive so as to reduce the likelihood of missing pertinent articles.[2] The rationale for taking an approach with these limitations is that, in the interest of comprehensiveness, it is better to have search results with irrelevant material than ones that exclude relevant articles. Despite the imperfections I have identified, this methodology allows the exercise to serve its primary purpose, which is to generate a broad snapshot of major US media coverage of food and medicine scarcity in Syria since the onset of the 2011 war, and to assess how much of it mentions the sanctions.

My queries of the *Journal*, *USA Today*, and *Times'* archives for discussions of the Syrian food shortages and sanctions encompass material from between May 27, 2012 and the end of 2020. I use May 27, 2012 as a start date because that is the day the *Times* published an article by Harvey Morris (2012) that clarifies that there is a relationship between the sanctions and food scarcity in Syria, the first story I can find in any of these outlets that does so. Once this information appears in the *Times*, it is a matter of public record that requires minimal research to uncover and is, therefore, accessible to journalists and editors at all three papers.

In the period under consideration, 972 works in the *Journal* contain any variation of "Syria" combined with "food" and either "short" or "scarce." When versions of "sanction" are added to the search, Factiva finds 155 in the *Journal*, or 15.9 percent of the results. *USA Today* had 70 pieces with the first set of terms and 11 of them, or 15.7 percent, also contain some form of the word "sanction." The *Times* ran 1,803 stories containing any variation of all three of the words "Syria," "food," and "short" or "scarce." Of the 1,803 pieces, 165 of them, or 9.1 percent, also mention some form of the word "sanction."

I ran the same searches of the papers' archives but replaced variants of the word "food" with those of "pharmaceuticals" and "medicine" and then added variants of "sanction." I did so for the archives covering March 6, 2013 to the

---

2   This method's limit is that using these relatively broad search terms produces results that include material that is impertinent to the subject under consideration. For instance, "Climate Change Doomed the Ancients" (Cline 2014) is included in the search results because it discusses Syria and mentions food shortages but in the context of a drought in the Mediterranean in 1200 B.C. Searches that include the word "sanction" require a similar note of caution. For example, a *Journal* article (White 2012) that appears in the results quotes an opposition activist from Homs describing a food shortage in the area and, after a nine-paragraph interval, notes that Turkey has applied sanctions; at no point does the article say that any country's sanctions have contributed to food shortages in any part of Syria.

end of 2020. I chose March 6, 2013 because that is the day that MSF noted the role of sanctions in the collapse of Syria's pharmaceutical industry. In addition, the DIIS report documenting the same relationship had been released the previous October. This search, like the ones I did about food and sanctions, returns results that are not germane. A *Journal* article (Vyas and Dube 2019), for instance, contains the word "sanctions" and the phrase "medicine shortages" but the piece is about Venezuela: Syria comes up because of a quote from Cynthia Arnson of the Woodrow Wilson Center discussing analogies between the two countries.

282 *Journal* articles in that period contain versions of the words "Syria" paired with versions of either "short" or "scarce" and versions of "pharmaceuticals" or "medicine." Adding the word "sanction" to the search generates 61 results, or 21.6 percent. Searching *USA Today* using the former combination of words yields 33 pieces and adding varieties of the word "sanction" returns 5 pieces, which is 15.1 percent. For the *Times*, the results are 509 stories when variations on "sanctions" are left out and 61, or 11.9 percent, when variations on "sanction" are included.

My research indicates that the sanctions' role in making it more difficult for Syrians to access food has been significantly under-reported in leading US media outlets. The searches I ran provide a macro analysis of whether major American media outlets' coverage of food and medicine shortages in Syria brought the economic sanctions that the United States and its allies applied to Syria into the discussion. Though these figures include stories with a focus other than food and medicine shortages in Syria since the start of the 2011 war, it is unlikely that many pertinent works are left out. While the numbers on how many stories are relevant are less precise than would be ideal, this research points to a clear, broad pattern: the vast majority of material that the three most widely read American newspapers ran on food and medicine shortages in Syria fail to mention that sanctions are a crucial cause of these problems. Yet, as I show earlier in this chapter, a substantial body of evidence demonstrating that the sanctions are an important factor in these scarcities has been available throughout the period of coverage being examined. This gap in media coverage wrongly communicates to audiences that the United States and its partners are not responsible for the scarcities of food and pharmaceuticals in Syria. Writing the empire out of the story erects a barrier to public understanding of this aspect of Syria's devastation and thus also to building a mass movement against such policies.

4   Conclusion

Imperialism strives to be a totalizing world system. The capitalist ruling class that manages the US-led empire encircles recalcitrant peoples, choking them off militarily, politically, and economically. Sanctions are one such mode of attack More than four decades of sanctions on Syria, which the US has explicitly and repeatedly said that it is applying on the grounds of Syrian non-compliance with the US regional agenda, have culminated in the US and its partners starving the Syrian civilian population. The American-led alliance is doing so largely because the Syrian government has supported the Palestinian and Lebanese struggles against American and Israeli aggression and been seen by the US as supporting the Iraqis' as well. That the Syrian state is situated alongside Iran in a regional counterpoint to US ruling class objectives, and with Russia in an international one, further explains America's economic warfare on Syria. However, the three highest circulation American newspapers have obscured how the sanctions undercut Syrians' ability to get food and medicine. These economic measures should be understood not as a form of collective punishment inflicted on the Syrian population in addition to the war but as a dimension of that war, and *The Wall Street Journal, USA Today*, and *The New York Times* as purveyors of war propaganda by omission.

References

Abboud, Samer. (2015). "How Syria Fell to Pieces." *Current History* 114 (776): 337–342.

Bellamy Foster, John. (2019). "Late Imperialism." *Monthly Review* 71 (3).

Cline, Eric H. (2014). "Climate Change Doomed the Ancients." *The New York Times*, 28 May.

Cockburn, Patrick. (2020a). " 'A Choice Between Bread and Masks': Syrians Face Calamity as Trump's New Sanctions Combine with Surging Coronavirus." *The Independent*, 21 August.

Cockburn, Patrick. (2020b). "The Next Gaza Strip? Daily Battle of Survival for Those Left in Idlib." *The Independent*, 6 October.

Dahi, Omar. (2019). "Syria: Donor Conditionality, Sanctions, and the Question of Justice." *Conflict Research Programme Blog*, 6 March.

"Executive Order 13338 of May 11, 2004, Blocking Property of Certain Persons and Prohibiting the Export of Certain Goods to Syria." Federal Register, 69.93 (2004): 26749–26754. https://home.treasury.gov/system/files/126/13338.pdf.

"Executive Order 13399 of April 25, 2006, Blocking Property of Additional Persons in Connection With the National Emergency With Respect to Syria." Federal Register, 71.82 (2006): 25059–25061. https://home.treasury.gov/system/files/126/13399.pdf.

"Executive Order 13460 of February 15, 2008, Blocking Property of Additional Persons in Connection With the National Emergency With Respect to Syria." Federal Register, 73.32 (2008): 8991–8993. https://home.treasury.gov/system/files/126/13460.pdf.

"Executive Order 13572 of April 29, 2011, Blocking Property of Certain Persons With Respect to Human Rights Abuses in Syria." Federal Register, 76.85 (2011): 24787–24789. https://www.govinfo.gov/content/pkg/FR-2011-05-03/pdf/2011-10910.pdf.

"Executive Order 13606 of April 22, 2012, Blocking the Property and Suspending Entry Into the United States of Certain Persons With Respect to Grave Human Rights Abuses by the Governments of Iran and Syria via Information Technology." Federal Register, 77.79 (2012): 24571–24574. https://www.govinfo.gov/content/pkg/FR-2012-04-24/pdf/2012-10034.pdf.

"Executive Order 13608 of May 1, 2012, "Prohibiting Certain Transactions With and Suspending Entry Into the United States of Foreign Sanctions Evaders With Respect to Iran and Syria." Federal Register, 77.86 (2012): 26409–26411. https://home.treasury.gov/system/files/126/fse_eo.pdf.

Fantz, Ashley. (2012). "Will Asma al-Assad Take a Stand or Stand By Her Man?" *cnn*, 22 August.

France 24. (2008). "Fate of Sheeba Farms on Hold Until Israeli Withdrawalm," 14 August.

Hersh, Seymour. (2003). "The Syrian Bet." *New Yorker*, 28 July.

Husari, Ruba. (2005). "Syria Courts Russians to Counter Sanctions." *Oil Daily*, 28 January.

Kadri, Ali, and Linda Matar. (2019). "Introduction: Syria in the Imperialist Cyclone." In Linda Matar and Ali Kadri (eds.), *Syria: From National Independence to Proxy War*, 1–25. London: Palgrave Macmillan.

Landis, Joshua. (2012). "The Syrian Uprising of 2011: Why the Asad Regime is Likely to Survive to 2013." *Middle East Policy* 18 (1): 72–84.

Lyme, Rune Friberg. (2012). *Sanctioning Assad's Syria*. Copenhagen: Danish Institute for International Studies.

Magid, Jacob. (2020). "Ex-Syria Envoy Felt Trump Was Unqualified. Now He's Sad to See Administration Go." *Times of Israel*, 5 December.

Moret, Erica S. (2015). "Humanitarian Impacts of Economic Sanctions on Iran and Syria." *European Security* 24 (1): 120–140.

Morris, Harvey. (2012). "From Massacres to Shortages, Syria Is Under Pressure." *The New York Times Blogs*, 27 May.

National Defense Authorization Act for Fiscal Year 2020. Public Law 116-92, *U.S Statues at Large* 133 (2019): 1198–2316. https://www.congress.gov/116/plaws/publ92/PLAW-116publ92.pdf.

Naylor, Hugh. (2007). "Tired of Energy Ills, Syrians Doubt the West Is to Blame." *The New York Times*, 15 August.

Nehme, Dahlia. (2017). "Syria Sanctions Indirectly Hit Children's Cancer Treatment." *Reuters*, 15 March.

Phillips, Christopher. (2016). "International Institutions and the Slide to War." In *The Battle for Syria: International Rivalry in the New Middle East*, 83–104. New Haven, CT: Yale University Press.

Sen, Kasturi. (2019). "The Political Economy of Public Health in Syria: Some Global and Regional Considerations." In Linda Matar and Ali Kadri (eds.), *Syria: From National Independence to Proxy War*, 188–208. London: Palgrave Macmillan.

Sharp, Jeremy M. (2010a). *Syria: Background and U.S. Relations*. CRS Report No. RL33487. Washington, DC: Congressional Research Service. https://digital.library. unt.edu/ark:/67531/metadc503617/m1/1/high_res_d/RL33487_2010Mar03.pdf.

Sharp, Jeremy. (2010b). *Syria: Issues for the 112th Congress and Background on U.S. Sanctions*. CRS Report No. RL33487. Washington, DC: Congressional Research Service. https://www.refworld.org/pdfid/4d2d98572.pdf.

Strindberg, Anders. (2004). "Syria Under Pressure." *Journal of Palestine Studies* 33 (4): 53–69.

Syria Accountability and Lebanese Sovereignty Restoration Act. Public Law 108-175, *U.S Statues at Large* 117 (2003): 2482–2489. https://www.congress.gov/108/plaws/publ 175/PLAW-108publ175.pdf.

"Syria Two Years On: The Failure of International Aid" *Doctors Without Borders*, 6 March. https://www.doctorswithoutborders.org/what-we-do/news-stories/news/ syria-two-years-failure-international-aid.

Turvill, William. (2020). "Top Ten US Newspaper Circulations: Biggest Print Titles Have Lost 30% of Sales Since 2016 Election." *Press Gazette*, 22 October.

Vohra, Anchal. (2020). "Assad's Syria Is Starting to Starve Like Saddam's Iraq." *Foreign Policy*, 2 December.

Vyas, Kejal, and Ryan Dube. (2019). "U.S. Tightens Curbs on Venezuela." *The Wall Street Journal*, 26 February.

White, Gregory. (2019). "Russian Envoy Begins Mission in Syria." *The Wall Street Journal*, 8 February.

Wind, Ella, and Omar S. Dahi. (2014). "The Economic Consequences of the Conflict in Syria." *Turkish Review* 4 (2): 132–140.

CHAPTER 15

The Blockade on Yemen

Shireen Al-Adeimi

1   Introduction

Modern warfare often conjures the image of one army fighting another in physical battles until one surrenders or is otherwise defeated by the stronger army. Less visible forms of warfare are economic impositions by stronger countries on weaker ones such as embargoes and sanctions, which involve either the full or partial prohibition of trade with a country. Though sanctions have long been used against individuals or states such as Cuba, North Korea, and Russia, their use was escalated by former President Obama, who used them more than any other president (Fishman 2017). Thus, without sending troops or dropping bombs, sanctions can pressure, deter, or punish states and actors whose actions do not align with US foreign policy goals by banning or restricting trade (e.g. Cuba and Iran) or imposing financial and visa restrictions against specific individuals. In Yemen, a country reeling from over six years of war, warring parties backed by three different US administrations are practicing an ancient, more primitive form of warfare akin to siege warfare.

A siege is "a military blockade of a city or fortified place to compel it to surrender" (Dictionary 2002). Thus, in siege warfare, a group is surrounded from the outside and is prevented from accessing vital supplies such as food until they surrender to the invading army. Modern times have facilitated an upgrade to such siege warfare, as the siege on Yemen—henceforth referred to as a blockade—does not only restrict entry of food and other essential supplies through land, but also by air and sea.

The US Navy defines blockades as, "belligerent operation[s] to prevent vessels and/or aircraft of all States, enemy as well as neutral, from entering or exiting specified ports, airfields, or coastal areas belonging to, occupied by, or under the control of an enemy State" (US Navy 2017).

After years of unrest following the Yemeni Revolution, the US-backed Saudi-led coalition began bombing Yemen. Weeks later, the UN Security Council passed Resolution 2216, which recognized the Saudi-led invasion and called on Member States to prevent the transfer of "arms...technical assistance, training, financial or other assistance" to Yemen's Houthis by inspecting, "all cargo to Yemen, in their territory, including seaports and airports" (UN General

Assembly 2015). Thus, under the guise of an arms embargo, the coalition began preventing commercial trade and the entry of food, fuel, and medicines into the country, and preventing most Yemenis from seeking refuge in other countries (al-Salmi 2015). In late 2017, the coalition went as far as imposing a total blockade that even prevented humanitarian organizations from operating within Yemen. Though this total blockade has since been "lifted", the coalition continues to impose a ban on trade and commercial imports (Yaqub 2018), despite the country's reliance on imports for 90% of its needs, and severely restricts aid, medicine, and fuel shipments (France 24 2020). The Saudi-led coalition's fuel blockade has caused famine in parts of Yemen by turning Hodeidah port into a "ghost town" with hundreds of aid trucks at a standstill, unable to deliver lifesaving aid to Yemenis (CNN 2021), despite receiving clearance through the UN Verification and Inspection Mechanism (UNVIM). The compounding effects of bombardment and blockade have caused a humanitarian crisis unlike any other in the world today.

2   War in Numbers

Yemen, a country of 30 million people, is located in the southern tip of the Arabian Peninsula, south of Saudi Arabia and West of Oman. The fighting that began in 2015 has led to what the UN calls, "the world's worst humanitarian crisis" (United Nations News 2017). While accurate figures are difficult to obtain, more than 112,000 people are reported to have been killed in the violence (ACLED 2020). Unlike other regional conflicts that saw millions of people seeking refuge to Europe and other countries, only 275,000 Yemenis were able to seek refuge and asylum in neighboring Somalia and Ethiopia, while more than 3.6 million Yemenis are displaced internally (UNHCR 2021). Additionally, 24 million people in Yemen—80 per cent of the population—is in need of humanitarian assistance, while 2 in 3 people cannot afford food, leaving half the country on the "brink of starvation" (*ibid.* 2021). At least 70 percent of Yemenis do not have access to safe drinking water and adequate healthcare (2021), thereby leaving them vulnerable to preventable illnesses.

The crisis is often described as "man-made"—that is, it is not due to natural environmental factors such as drought or floods. Rather, the devastation is the result of the systematic targeting of civilians through aerial bombardment as well as a blockade that has trapped most civilians in the country and has prevented vital supplies from entering Yemen. Deaths due to the blockade are even more difficult to confirm than those accounted for by the bombing. Since December 2016, UNICEF has estimated that a child under the age of five dies every 10 minutes due to malnutrition and preventable illness (UNICEF 2016). Though the total figure is not reported, a tally of this statistic would indicate that over 210,000 children between the ages of birth and five have already died during four of the six years of the ongoing war. This figure does not include all children who have died of malnutrition and preventable illnesses, nor does it encompass all people in Yemen who have died from such causes. Additionally, it may never be known how many people died while awaiting dialysis, organ transplant, cancer treatment, or even over-the-counter medication.

These deaths are not the consequence of living in a poor country; they are the consequence of a deliberate campaign that has targeted fighters and civilians alike. Those imposing the blockade on Yemen are among the world's wealthiest countries: neighboring Saudi Arabia and the United Arab Emirates with full military support from the United States, United Kingdom, and France. This chapter will provide an overview of the background of the conflict and highlight the ways in which the blockade has destroyed Yemen's healthcare and economy, leading to what can be reasonably described as an ongoing genocide (Bachman 2019).

3　　Conflict Background

Yemen's geopolitical significance lies in its strategic location: the country controls Bab al-Mandeb strait (Sedghi 2017), where 6.2 million barrels of oil and oil products travel daily to Europe and Asia (U.S. Department of Energy 2019). Its location and status as the Middle East's poorest country left it vulnerable to intervention from its richer, oil-producing neighbors such as Saudi Arabia and the UAE, as well as oil-reliant countries like the US and the UK. Notably, China built its first and only foreign base on the other side of this strait in 2017 in Djibouti (Jacobs and Perlez 2017). The following sections detail the events that destabilized Yemen and signaled a shift in leadership that is openly hostile to Saudi Arabia and the United States, thereby prompting these countries to intervene militarily and subsequently plunge Yemen into its current humanitarian crisis.

3.1　*Colonial and Post-Colonial Divisions*

Prior to 1990, Yemen was divided into two countries that were ruled by separate colonial rulers: Northern Yemen was part of the Ottoman Empire until it collapsed in 1918, while southern Yemen was under British control (in various forms) from 1839 until 1967 (Al-Adeimi 2019). In 1962, a coup backed by Egypt's Gamal Abdel Nasser overthrew the Mutawakkilite Kingdom in northern

Yemen and led to the establishment of the Yemen Arab Republic (YAR or North Yemen) (Reidel 2018). The Mutawakkilites were supported by other monarchies: Saudi Arabia, Jordan (2018), and the United Kingdom; however, they failed to regain control after years of fighting. Southern Yemen, on the other hand, eventually became the People's Democratic Republic of Yemen (PDRY or South Yemen)—the Arab world's first, and to date, only Marxist-Leninist state (Al- Adeimi 2019).

Over two decades later, as the Soviet Union was in its final throes and therefore unable to economically support the nascent PDRY, leaders in both parts of the country began talks that led to Yemen's unification in May 1990 (Hurd and Noakes 1994). By then, Saleh had already ruled YAR since 1978, and became the leader of the united Republic of Yemen thereafter. The unity, however, was challenged in 1994 when tensions led to an aggressive war launched by Saleh after southern leaders declared secession from the North. This took place following years of marginalization and exploitation of southern resources by Saleh and other northern elites (Kambeck 2016). Saleh's violent response to this discontent, however, only led to further discord between southern and northern Yemenis, the former of whom now felt they were under a forced unity (Al-Adeimi 2019).

3.2   New and Renewed Insurgencies

In 2007, al-Hirak al-Janoubi (the Southern Movement) was formed, challenging Saleh's rule and renewing calls for secession from the North. Though their goals were to secede from the rest of Yemen, they too joined the 2011 protesters calling for Saleh's ouster. In the years after the 1994 civil war and before the 2011 protests, a different group in another part of the country posed yet another challenge to Saleh. The Ansarullah—or the Houthis as they are commonly known—began building a movement in the northern Yemeni province of Sa'dah, challenging Saleh's corruption and his alliance with Saudi Arabia and the United States. Though often described as proxies of Iran, the Houthis are an independent group that gained prominence after Saleh violently responded to their challenge. While they practice a sect of Shi'a Islam known as Zaydism, so too did Saleh and approximately 40% of Yemenis. As such, Houthis are neither a religious minority nor is their cause sectarian driven. However, they did oppose the growing influence of Wahhabi Islam in Yemen, especially in their Saudi-bordering province of Sa'dah (S. Weir 1997).

Between 2004 and 2010, Saleh responded by waging six wars against the Houthis, some of which were fought directly with the Saudi army. Though he succeeded in killing their leader—Hussein al Houthi—Saleh's wars did nothing to stop the growing Houthi movement. Thus, by 2010, Yemen had only been united for 20 years, was ruled by a dictator and a corrupt class of elites, and Saleh's rule was challenged by the Hirak in the South and Houthis in the North. This, along with growing discontent among Yemenis following decades of economic and political challenges, set the stage for the protests in 2011. Like those in the southern Hirak, the Houthis also joined the Yemeni masses who were demonstrating against Saleh's rule.

3.3 Revolution

In January 2011, a popular Yemeni uprising sought to oust President Ali Abdullah Saleh's 33-year undemocratic regime. Unlike its neighbors in the Persian Gulf region, overthrowing a dictator seemed possible; after all, unlike Saudi Arabia, Oman, the United Arab Emirates, or any other country in the Arabian Peninsula, Yemen was a republic with a history of deposing British colonists in the South and Yemeni monarchs in the North of the country. Thus, encouraged by the fall of strongmen in Tunisia and Egypt, Yemenis also peacefully protested in hopes of overthrowing their own dictator.

3.4 Power Shifts

Though the protests began peacefully, they took a violent turn in May when longtime Saleh allies—the Islamist Islah party—joined calls for Saleh's ouster and mounted an armed challenge when he refused to step down. After a failed assassination attempt and the recovery that followed, Saleh finally resigned in November of that year following mediation by the Gulf Cooperation Council (GCC), leaving his Vice President of 17 years, Abd Rabbu Mansour Hadi, temporarily in charge (Popp 2015). While the GCC agreement outlined the transition process, it ignored vital political forces within Yemen: the Houthis and the Hirak (2015). As Hadi faltered during the following two years, Saleh remained powerful and retained control over much of the Yemeni armed forces (Kasinof 2012), highlighting yet another failure of the GCC agreement. This position allowed him to forge new and unexpected alliances when the Saudi-led coalition attacked Yemen in 2015.

In late 2014, following mass protests after the Yemeni government lifted fuel subsidies, the Houthis took over the capital Sana'a (Craig 2014). In the weeks that followed, they signed onto a UN-mediated unity government, but later derailed this transition process by placing Hadi under house arrest. Hadi, in turn, resigned and left the capital to Aden, which prompted the Houthis to follow him, sparking an armed confrontation (Popp 2015). Despite these upheavals, Jamal Benomar, the former UN special envoy for Yemen, notes that Yemeni parties were able to reach a compromise and he was "in discussions with Saudi officials regarding the venue for a signing ceremony" (Beonomar 2021). Two days later, the Saudi-led coalition began bombing Yemen "with no warning" (Benomar 2021). Amidst the chaos, it became clear that an unlikely alliance had formed: Saleh and the Houthis joined forces to resist the Saudi and UAE coalition that began bombing Yemen ostensibly on behalf of Hadi. This alliance led to the nearly three years of cooperation between these former foes until it finally broke down in December 2017 and ended with Saleh's killing by the Houthis. Since then, the Houthis have assumed the role of de facto government in Yemen, and currently pose the only organized resistance against the Saudi and UAE coalition that is still bombing, blockading, and occupying parts of Yemen. Meanwhile, Hadi remains in Saudi-Arabia, the Hirak formed a UAE-backed political party (the Southern Transitional Council), and the two formed a unity government despite their divergent goals and years of armed clashes (Staff 2020).

4   Bombs, Blockades, and Their Consequences

4.1   *Warring Parties*

The coalition led by Saudi Arabia and the United Arab Emirates also included Qatar (until 2017) and Morocco (until early 2019). Bahrain, Jordan, Egypt, Sudan, and Kuwait remain part of the coalition. Countries fueling the war through arms sales to Saudi Arabia and the UAE include the United States, United Kingdom, Canada, Spain, France (which also provides logistical sup- port), Italy, and others. While it was not officially part of the coalition, the support of the United States and the United Kingdom is indispensable to the coalition; a 2019 UN report noted these countries may be complicit in potential war crimes (Raghavan 2019). Both countries have personnel in the command room who provide targeting assistance to the coalition (Graham-Harrison 2016), while the US also trains soldiers and pilots, maintains and repairs vehicles and aircraft, and provides other military contracts that total at least $120 million per month (Vergun 2018). Until late 2018, the US also performed the vital task of refueling coalition jets midair (Stewart 2018), thereby allowing fighter jets to remain in Yemen's airspace for longer periods of time. Without such extensive targeting, logistical, intelligence, and arms support from the US and other Western allies, Saudi Arabia and the UAE are arguably unable to wage a war at this magnitude. The Houthis, on the other hand, are limited to missiles and drones, and receive nominal support from Iran, which is likely limited to financial and political support (Transfeld 2017) given the extensive blockade placed by the aforementioned countries that would make the transfer of weapons virtually impossible (despite claims to the contrary).

4.2   Systematic Targeting of Civilians

In March 2016, Human Rights Watch cited an unpublished UN document that noted findings from a Panel of Experts that, "the coalition's targeting of civilians through air strikes, either by bombing residential neighborhoods or by treating the entire cities of Sa'dah and Maran in northern Yemen as military targets, is a grave violation of the principles of distinction, proportionality and precaution." The report continued, "[i]n certain cases, the Panel found such violations to have been conducted in a widespread and systematic manner" (Human Rights Watch 2016). Such targeting of civilians, however, was not limited to airstrikes that destroyed much of Yemen's infrastructure, hospitals, schools, bridges, roads, water plants, food production sites, and other civilian and structures; it also manifests in the blockade on Yemen.

Soon after the blockade was imposed in 2015, Yemen's hospitals began to shut down due to a lack of diesel (Borger 2015). The resulting collapse of the economy, healthcare, and sanitation systems led to the outbreak of diseases as well as 80% of the population left reliant on foreign aid for survival. The compounding effects of the relentless bombardment and occupation campaign by Saudi, the US, and other allies, as well as the blockade imposed by these countries' armies, navies and air forces, led to many "worsts" over the next few years.

4.3   The Blockade's Impact on Health

As of 2021, Yemen is undergoing four active outbreaks: cholera, diphtheria, dengue, and COVID-19 (World Health Organization 2021), and there are fears of a potential polio outbreak (Mohareb and Ivers 2019). In June of 2017, a joint statement by UNICEF and the WHO called the cholera outbreak in Yemen "the worst cholera outbreak in the world" (World Health Organization 2017). Prior to this, Haiti had suffered the worst outbreak in modern times, which killed 9,000 people and infected nearly 800,000 people in the 2010s. By comparison, the ongoing cholera outbreaks in Yemen have so far killed over 4,000 Yemenis and infected nearly 2 million Yemenis between 2016 and August 2020. Cholera, a waterborne disease that transmits in unsanitary conditions (Qadri, Islam, and Clemens 2017), is much less deadly when fluid replacement is administered (Phelps et al. 2018). In a country where well over half the population lacks access to healthcare and clean water, however, re-hydration is not an option. A country does not experience simultaneous outbreaks such as this simply due to war. In Yemen, the blockade has directly led to these, and other, severe health conditions.

When fuel was either partially or fully blocked from entering a country, facilities such as water pump stations and hospitals could no longer function. Additionally, lack of funds to pay for sanitation workers' salaries and fuel scarcity limited the function and repair of sanitation vehicles (Weir 2019), conditions became rife for diseases transmitted through fecal-oral system such as cholera. Furthermore, when vaccinations could no longer be delivered to the vast majority of the population (Mohareb and Ivers 2019), those vulnerable to such diseases could not be inoculated against them. Amidst these conditions, another outbreak, diphtheria, re-emerged. This bacterial disease that transmits through respiratory contact (Organization 2018) had all but disappeared from Yemen until 2017: The last recorded case of diphtheria was in 1992, and the last outbreak was in 1982 (Medecins sans Frontières 2017). One generation later, Medecins sans Frontières's emergency coordinator Marc Poncin noted, "the ongoing war and blockade are sending Yemen's health system decades back in time" and has allowed this "neglected and forgotten disease" to reemerge due to the "a blockade on supplies including medicines and vaccines." He added, "[t]he blockade on fuel has meant that patients cannot afford to travel to the very few health centers still operating across the country. This is crucial, because if people infected are unable to access treatment regularly, diphtheria can spread in the body and be fatal in up to 40 percent of the cases" (2017).

Yet another outbreak, the global COVID-19 pandemic, has also severely impacted Yemen's already battered healthcare system. With more than half of all healthcare facilities in Yemen either closed or partially functioning (Sidani and Al-Wesabi 2020), accurate testing and tracking of COVID-19 cases is not feasible. Also, in a country where water is scarce and most of the population is weakened by malnutrition, the effects of COVID-19 in Yemen have the potential of inflicting maximum harm on civilians (Al-Adeimi 2020). Though confirmed cases remain relatively low and Houthi authorities failed to "admit the full scale of the outbreak," (Devi 2020), the case mortality rates of 27 percent are the highest in the world (Cao, Hiyoshi, and Montgomery 2020). Thus, the collapse of Yemen's healthcare came as a result of years of bombardment that targeted health facilities (including several airstrikes of MSF-run hospitals) (Almosawa and Nordland 2016; Gladstone 2019), coupled with the blockade that severely limits medicine, vaccines, and medical equipment (Mohareb and Ivers 2019), as well as fuel and other life-saving essentials.

4.4   *The Blockade's Impact on the Economy*
Prior to the blockade, 54 percent of Yemenis lived under $2 per day, and Yemen was the poorest country in the Middle East (Childress 2015). Today, Yemen could become the world's poorest country (UN Development Programme 2019). Yemen's gross domestic product (GDP) went from an all-time high of $43.2 billion in 2014 to $22.6 billion in 2019. Similarly, the gross national income (GNI) per capita dropped from $1,460 in 2014 to $940 in 2018 (World Bank 2020a). The blockading of

oil exports, which had been the largest source of foreign currency prior to the war (World Bank 2020c), have contributed to the collapse of the Yemeni economy. Further, the decision to move the Central Bank of Yemen to Aden in 2016, led to the inability of authorities in the North to pay millions of salaried government workers, creating widespread poverty (World Bank 2020b). The bifurcated Yemeni Riyal (YER) has also plummeted from 215 to one US dollar (USD) in 2015 to 760 YER in 2018 (Editorial 2018). The same report attributes this depreciation partly to "import restrictions due to closure of ports"—i.e., as a result of the blockade (Assessment Capabilities Project 2020). Thus, households' purchasing power suffered in a country that is almost entirely dependent on imports (2020).

In the last days of the Trump presidency, his administration moved to designate the Houthis as a foreign terrorist organization (FTO), a move that was condemned by aid groups working in Yemen, the United Nations, and others (OCHA 2021), for its potential to escalate famine in Yemen (Council 2021). Though reversed by Biden, this move represents one in a series of calculated attempts at siege warfare: When bombing civilian infrastructure failed to achieve the US/Saudi coalition's goals, a blockade was imposed. When the combined effects of the blockade and the systematic targeting of food production sites also failed to wrestle Yemen from the Houthis, aid was used as a weapon of war. This was seen through the Trump government's aid cuts to Northern Yemen, and their attempted influence over the UN to suspend aid to the majority of Yemenis (Lynch and Gramer 2020). Though famine has not been declared in Yemen (likely due to pressures on the UN by Saudi Arabia and the US, its biggest donors), a genocide against the Yemeni people is still unfolding.

5   Winners and Losers

According to Article 2 of the United Nations Convention on the Prevention and Punishment of the Crime of Genocide, adopted in 1948, defines genocide as follows: Any of the following acts committed with intent to destroy, in whole or in part, a national, ethnical, racial or religious group, as such: (a) Killing members of the group; (b) Causing serious bodily or mental harm to members of the group; (c) Deliberately inflicting on the group conditions of life calculated to bring about its physical destruction in whole or in part; (d) Imposing measures intended to prevent births within the group; (e) Forcibly transferring children of the group to another group.

In the case of Yemen, as has been highlighted in this chapter and noted by others (Bachman 2019), it can be argued that all these conditions have been met. Six years into the war on Yemen, the "Decisive Storm" intervention launched by Saudi Arabia and its allies was neither decisive (their stated goal to restore Hadi to power has failed), nor characteristic of a storm that ends seemingly as quickly as it begins. The situation remains unwinnable for the foreign parties involved, who have struggled to maintain control through aerial bombardment and the use of foreign and local mercenaries (Brennan 2020). The Houthis, on the other hand, are now the de facto rulers in much of the former North Yemen, where approximately 70% of the population lives. Much of the former South Yemen is controlled by the coalition, though it is ruled by a fraught alliance between the UAE-backed southern secessionists (the STC) and the Saudi-backed Hadi government (despite their divergent goals that have caused numerous armed confrontations). Additionally, groups such as al-Qaeda in the Arabian Peninsula (AQAP), who the coalition has at times used in their fight against the Houthis (BBC 2016), remain active in southern areas. Exceptions to the North/South control are two former northern governorates that remain battlefronts, Ma'rib and Taiz. Though the war is likely unwinnable for this coalition, there have been clear and unmistakable losers: Yemeni civilians.

Years of bombardment and blockade have inflicted maximum harm of the Yemeni civilian population. And while the scars left behind by bombs are visible, the trauma left experiencing war and being deprived of one's basic needs will be long-lasting. The United Nations estimates that half of all Yemeni children suffer stunted growth (Falk 2019), with Guterres warning that Yemen is "now in imminent danger of the worst famine the world has seen for decades" (UN Security Council 2020). Long after the bombs stop dropping and the blockade is fully lifted, Yemenis who have survived the war will continue to suffer the consequences of being starved and denied their basic human rights. To prevent more Yemenis from starvation and certain death, however, the conflict in Yemen must be recognized for what it is—a genocidal campaign waged by the world's richest countries on one of the world's poorest. And while the bombing and lifting of the blockade will alleviate the short-term suffering, the long-term political, social, and economic implications will resonate for decades to come.

References

ACLED. (2020). "Research Hub: War in Yemen." ACLED Data 2020.

Al-Adeimi, Shireen. (2020). "5 Years of U.S.-Saudi War Have Left Yemen Highly Vulnerable to a Coronavirus Outbreak." *In These Times*, 24 March.

Al-Adeimi, Shireen. (2019). "The U.S.-Backed Coalition Can't Agree on Why It's Bombing Yemen." *In These Times*, 12 September.

Almosawa, Shuaib, and Rod Nordland. (2016). "Bombing of Doctors Without Borders Hospital in Yemen Kills at Least 15." *The New York Times*, 8 August.

Assessment Capacities Project. (2020). "Volatility of the Yemeni Riyal: Drivers and impact of Yemeni Riyal's volatility, Thematic report."

Bachman, Jeffrey. (2019). "A 'synchronised attack' on life: the Saudi-led coalition's 'hidden and holistic' genocide in Yemen and the shared responsibility of the US and UK." *Third World Quarterly* 40 (2): 298–316.

British Broadcasting Corporation. (2016). "Yemen conflict: Al-Qaeda seen at coalition battle for Taiz." BBC *News*, 22 February.

Benomar, Jamal. (2021). "In Yemen 'Diplomacy is Back.' What Next?" *Newsweek*, 19 February.

Borger, Julian. (2015). "Saudi-led naval blockade leaves 20m Yemenis facing humanitarian disaster." *The Guardian*, 5 June.

Brennan, David. (2020). "Yemenis Demand U.S. Arrest American Mercenaries Accused of 'Blatant' War Crimes." *Newsweek*, 12 February.

Cao, Yang, Ayako Hiyoshi, and Scott Montgomery. (2020). "COVID-19 case-fatality rate and demographic and socioeconomic influencers: worldwide spatial regression analysis based on country-level data." BMJ *Open* 10 (11).

Childress, Sarah. (2015). "In Yemen, Everyday Life Goes from Bad to Worse." *Public Broadcasting Services*, 15 April.

CNN. (2021). "Famine has arrived in pockets of Yemen. Saudi ships blocking fuel aren't helping." CNN *News* Online, 10 March.

Craig, Iona. (2014). "What the Houthi takeover of Sanaa reveals about Yemen's politics." *Al Jazeera America*, 25 September.

Devi, Sharmila. (2020). "Fears of "highly catastrophic" COVID-19 spread in Yemen." *The Lancet* 385: 10238.

Falk, Pamela. (2019). "Half of kids in Yemen under five have stunted growth, UN says." CBS *News*, 3 July.

Fishman, Edward. (2017). "Even Smarter Sanctions: How to Fight in the Era of Economic Warfare." *Foreign Affairs* 96, 6:102–110.

France 24. (2020). "Yemen fuel supplies 'weaponised', putting millions at risk." *France 24*, 10 July.

Gladstone, Rick. (2019). "Saudi Airstrike Said to Hit Yemeni Hospital as War Enters Year 5." https://www.nytimes.com/2019/03/26/world/middleeast/yemen-saudi-hospital-airstrike.html.

Graham-Harrison, Emma. (2016). "British and US military 'in command room' for Saudi strikes on Yemen." *The Guardian*, 15 January.

Human Rights Watch. (2016). "Yemen: Embargo Arms to Saudi Arabia."

Hurd, Robert, and Greg Noakes. (1994). "North and South Yemen: Lead-up to the Break-up." WRMEA, 1 August.

Jacobs, Andrew, and Jane Perlez. (2017). "U.S. Wary of Its New Neighbor in Djibouti: A Chinese Naval Base." *The New York Times*, 25 February.

Kambeck, Jens. (2016). "Returning to Transitional Justice in Yemen: A Backgrounder on the Commission on the Forcibly Retired in the Southern Governorates." Center for Applied Research in Partnership with the Orient Reports, July 2016.

Kasinof, Laura. (2012). "Protesters Set New Goal: Fixing Yemen's Military." *The New York Times*, 28 February.

Lynch, Colum, and Robbie Gramer. (2020). "Pompeo to Pressure U.N. Over Aid to Yemen." *Foreign Policy*, 2 March.

Médecins Sans Frontières. (2017). "From cholera to diphtheria—shattered health system battles a new threat." Press Release.

Mohareb, Amir M., and Louise C. Ivers. (2019). "Disease and Famine as Weapons of War in Yemen." *The New England Journal of Medicine* 380 (2): 109–111.

OCHA. (2021). "Briefing to the Security Council on the humanitarian situation in Yemen."

Phelps, Matthew, Mads Linnet Perner, Virginia E. Pitzer, Viggo Andreasen, Peter K.M. Jensen, and Lone Simonse. (2018). "Cholera Epidemics of the Past Offer New Insights Into an Old Enemy." *Journal of Infectious Diseases* 217 (4): 641–649.

Popp, Ronald. (2015). "War in Yemen: Revolution and Saudi Intervention." *CSS Analyses in Security Policy* 175.

Qadri, Firdausi, Taufiqul Islam, and John D. Clemens. (2017). "Cholera in Yemen — An Old Foe Rearing Its Ugly Head." *The New England Journal of Medicine* 377.

Raghavan, Sudarsan. (2019). "U.N. report says U.S., Britain, France may be complicit in potential war crimes in Yemen." *The Washington Post*, 3 September.

Reidel, Bruce. (2018). "A Brief History of America's Troubled Relationship with Yemen." *The Brookings Institute Reports*, 22 October.

al-Salmi, Wajdi. (2015). "Yemen Authorises Arab Naval Blockade." *Al Araby*, 12 April.

Sedghi, Hamideh. (2017). "Trumpism: The Geopolitics of the United States, the Middle East and Iran." *Socialism and Democracy* 31 (3): 82–93.

Sidani, Rana, and Sadeq Al-Wesabi. (2020). "Survey reveals extent of damage to Yemen's health system." *The World Health Organization*, 6 November.

Stewart, Phil. (2018). "U.S. halting refueling of Saudi-led coalition aircraft in Yemen's war." *Reuters*, 9 November.

Transfeld, Mareike. (2017). "Iran's Small Hand in Yemen." *The Carnegie Endowment*, 14 February.

U.S. Department of Energy, Energy Information Administration. (2019). "The Bab el-Mandeb Strait is a Strategic Route for Oil and Natural Gas Shipments."

United Nations (UN) Children's Fund. (2016). "Malnutrition amongst children in Yemen at an all-time high, warns UNICEF."

UN Development Programme. (2019). "Prolonged conflict would make Yemen the poorest country in the world, UNDP study says." https://www.undp.org/content/brussels/en/home/presscenter/pressreleases/prolonged-conflict-would-make-yemen-the-poorest-country-in-the-w.html.

UN General Assembly. (2015). *Resolution Adopted by the Security Council at its 7426th meeting, on 14 April 2015*. S/RES/2216.

UN High Commission on Refugees. (2021). "Yemen Humanitarian Crisis."

UN Security Council. (2020). "Secretary-General's statement on Yemen."

United Nation News. (2017). " 'Catastrophic' Humanitarian Blockade in Yemen Putting Millions at Risk, UN Warns." *UN News*, November.

Vergun, David. (2018). "Army builds sustaining military partnership with Saudi Arabia." *US Army Reports*.

Weir, Doug. (2019). "How Yemen's conflict destroyed its waste management system." *The Conflict and Enviornment Observatory*, 1 August.

Weir, Shelagh. (1997). "A Clash of Fundamentalisms: Wahhabism in Yemen." *Middle East Report* 204: 22–26.

The World Bank. (2020a). "Data: Republic of Yemen." *2020 Annual Report*.

The World Bank. (2020b). "World Bank Yemen Macro-Poverty Outlook." October 2020.

The World Bank. (2020c). "Yemen's Economic Update." April 2020.

World Health Organization. (2021). "Epidemic and pandemic-prone diseases."

World Health Organization. (2018). "Immunization, Vaccines and Biologicals: Diphtheria."

Yaqub, Farhat. (2018). "2017: A Year in Review." *The Lancet* 390 (10114): 2753–2754.

CHAPTER 16

The US War on Venezuela

Gregory Wilpert

It is long past time that the people of the United States and the so-called "international community" recognize that sanctions against the people of entire countries constitute an act of war. The chapters in this book about US sanctions against different countries are a testament to why sanctions must be considered an act of war. The case of Venezuela probably represents one of the more devastating and extreme applications of sanctions since the sanctions that were imposed on Iraq before the 2003 Iraq war.

Even though non-UN approved sanctions are illegal according to international law (Happold and Eden 2016) the US government reserves the right to impose sanctions on any country of its choice. But why is the US so willing to defy international, regional, and even national law when it imposes economic sanctions on countries? Based on the Venezuelan experience, one can identify at least two main reasons for why the US does this. First, there is the publicly declared goal of bringing about regime change in the country. After all, in order to put an end to the Latin American "Pink Tide" of leftist governments, the US has been able to engineer or support regime change in five out of eleven countries that were previously governed by the left or center-left.[1] In cases where military coups did not prove to be doable—mainly in countries where the left was solidly in control of their military (Cuba, Venezuela, and Nicaragua)—the US has resorted to sanctions as a way of "convincing" the governments to leave office. The US did this, despite the fact that it has been well established in numerous academic studies that economic sanctions do not

---

1   The 11 Latin American countries that had left or center-left governments in the 2000's included Cuba, Venezuela, Nicaragua, Haiti, Bolivia, Honduras, Ecuador, Argentina, Uruguay, Chile, and Paraguay. Of these, five were defeated through either military or legislative coups: Haiti (2004), Honduras (2009), Paraguay (2012), Brazil (2016), and Bolivia (2019). Only in Argentina, Uruguay, and Chile were center-left governments defeated at the ballot box— and in each of these cases the governments were not particularly leftist. Ecuador was an exceptional situation in that Lenin Moreno was elected on a center-left platform in 2017, as the successor to the leftist government of Rafael Correa, but he rapidly switched to a neoliberal-right platform once in office. Meanwhile, Cuba, Venezuela, and Nicaragua, continue to suffer from US-sponsored regime-change operations.

bring about regime change.[2] The official reasons for the regime change effort are to protect human rights, to end allegedly massive government corruption, and to end drug trafficking. However, given official US government support for human rights violators such as Saudi Arabia and drug producing countries such as Colombia, these justifications are hardly credible. US Secretary of State Mike Pompeo even admitted, in March 2019, that the Trump administration hopes to worsen Venezuela's humanitarian crisis: "The circle is tightening, the humanitarian crisis is increasing by the hour. (...) You can see the increasing pain and suffering that the Venezuelan people are suffering from" (Pompeo 2019).

Rather, far more likely is that the United States seeks regime change for any government, anywhere in the world, that does not accede to the opening of its economy to international capital. This has been the end-result in every country where the US succeeded in engineering regime change in the past. And this has been especially true for countries with enormous oil reserves, such as Iran, Iraq, and Venezuela.[3] One could argue that since many other countries with large oil reserves also have state-owned oil companies, which the US does not seek to change, such as Saudi Arabia, that this is not a significant motivation for regime change. However, this first motivation combines with the second likely motivation.

The second reason the US government launches economic sanctions is that they serve as an excellent warning to the rest of the world not to oppose the United States or to implement redistributive or anti-capitalist economic policies. Countries that do pursue such policies are driven to ruin by sanctions and serve as excellent examples of why "socialism does not work." It is thus no wonder that in the 2020 US presidential campaign Republicans repeatedly pointed to Venezuela as an economic basket case with the argument that this is what the US would look like if someone like Bernie Sanders (or even Joe Biden) became president.

A third reason for why the US seeks regime change, which is closely related to the previous one, is that it consistently seeks to defeat governments that

---

2 For example, former CIA Deputy Director David Cohen under Obama makes a strong case for why sanctions would never work when they aim for regime change: "The logic of coercive sanctions does not hold, however, when the objective of sanctions is regime change. Put simply, because the cost of relinquishing power will always exceed the benefit of sanctions relief, a targeted state cannot conceivably accede to a demand for regime change" (Cohen and Weinberg 2019). See also Shagabutdinova and Berejikian (2007).

3 According to the most recent certifications of oil reserves, in 2011 Venezuela officially surpassed Saudi Arabia as the country with the largest oil reserves in the world, at just over 300 billion barrels, or 17.5% of all reserves (OPEC 2020).

pursue a foreign policy that undermines or counters US foreign policy. That is, governments that aim to develop a "multi-polar" world, foster South-South cooperation, or in any other way develop independence from US hegemony, they become a target for regime change.

In the following pages I will first outline a brief history of recent US policy towards Venezuela. Then, I summarize the devastating economic, social, and political consequences of sanctions. Finally, in the third section, I revisit the issue of the motivations behind US policy towards Venezuela. I conclude with some thoughts about what social movements could do to put an end to US sanctions policies.

1   A Brief History of US Foreign Policy towards Venezuela

When Hugo Chávez first assumed the presidency of Venezuela in January 1999, relations with the US government, then under President Bill Clinton, both sides seemed to think that it was possible to have good relations between the two countries. All of this changed, however, when George W. Bush became president, especially in late 2001 when Chávez condemned the US bombing of Afghanistan in the harshest terms. As Chávez moved further to the left, requiring foreign oil companies to pay significantly higher royalties for oil extraction, US foreign policy towards Venezuela was increasingly geared towards regime change, at first via open and covert support for the opposition and for military coups. Then, beginning in 2015, under President Obama, with the additional help of economic sanctions, the US further intensified the noose around Venezuela's neck.

Since coup attempts to put an end to the Bolivarian Revolution[4] failed, the US government gradually began undermining the government of Venezuela via sanctions to further destabilize the government and help the opposition. The first sanctions were already introduced in July 2003, when the US cut off all Export-Import Bank credits to Venezuela (Weisbrot 2003). Such credits are essential for the smooth functioning of bilateral trade because they help bridge delays in international payments. Next, in 2004 and 2005, the Bush

---

4   Chávez and his supporters referred to his presidency as the start of the "Bolivarian Revolution," in reference to Simon Bolívar, who liberated Venezuela and much of South America from Spanish colonial rule. Chávez's revolution aimed to complement representative democracy with participatory democracy, to reverse decades of neoliberal economic policy, to redistribute the country's oil wealth, and to pursue a foreign policy that prioritizes South-South relations instead of US-Venezuela relations, among other things.

administration cut off US arms sales to Venezuela, forcing Venezuela to demo-
bilize its aging F-16 fighter jets and to spend billions on the purchase of new
Russian-made Sukhoi jets. Then, in late 2008, the Bush administration began
its first official sanctions on Venezuelan government officials, beginning with
the Venezuelan minister of the interior, the head of the military intelligence
service, and the head of the civilian intelligence service (Wilpert 2008).

Relations between the US and Venezuela did not evolve much during the
Obama presidency, except towards the end of Obama's second term in office,
he signed the "Venezuela Defense of Human Rights and Civil Society Act of
2014," which imposed sanctions on Venezuelan officials who had been accused
of human rights violations. Then, in March of 2015, Obama signed Executive
Order 13692, which claimed that human rights violations in Venezuela represent an "unusual and extraordinary threat to the national security" of the
United States. Both of these measures led to the imposition of sanctions against
high-level Venezuelan government officials. The designation of Venezuela as
a serious national security threat to the United States is laughable, but it is
required by US law for the imposition of most types of sanctions.

The patently false claim that Venezuela represents a threat makes a mockery
of the International Emergency Economic Powers Act of 1977, which is the law
that requires a finding of a threat to national security before imposing sanctions. The timing of these new sanctions, though, was probably well calculated
because they came a few months after Obama re-opened diplomatic relations
with Cuba. In other words, the tougher stance towards Venezuela was most
likely intended to counterbalance the improved relations with Cuba. Once the
Obama administration had laid the spurious legal groundwork for economic
sanctions, it was a relatively small step for Trump to dramatically intensify, first
by adding more and more government representatives to the list of sanctioned
individuals. Then, in August 2017, Trump cut Venezuela off from practically all
financial transactions. According to a White House statement, it would ban
all "dealings in new debt and equity issued by the government of Venezuela
and its state oil company..." (Lilley 2017) Even though these sanctions were
supposed to only affect credit-related transactions in the US, they ended up
affecting practically all of Venezuela's financial transactions around the world
as banks engaged in "over-compliance" so as to avoid even the remotest possibility of being punished by the US government.

The Trump administration further emphasized this point when the government's Financial Crimes Enforcement Network (FinCen) issued a letter in
September 2017 warning that "all Venezuelan government agencies and bodies,
including SOEs [state-owned enterprises] appear vulnerable to public corruption and money laundering" (Rodriguez 2018). American banks' reaction to

this was swift and major banks proceeded to close bank accounts associated with the Venezuelan government. The immediate consequence was that trade between the US and Venezuela, Venezuela's largest trading partner at the time, slowed down tremendously because export-import credits and financial transactions for trade could no longer be processed. Another reason trade became so difficult was because the international Clearing House Interbank Payments System (CHIPS) is reliant on less than 50 correspondent banks, each of which must have a branch office in the United States. This leaves CHIPS highly subject to US law.

The Trump administration dealt the most devastating blow to the Venezuelan economy when it basically issued a full-scale embargo on Venezuela in January 2019 to coincide with the administration's recognition of Juan Guaidó as the self-declared "interim" president of Venezuela. The US government prohibited all trade with Venezuela's state-owned oil company Petróleos de Venezuela, S.A. (PDVSA), which until 2018 was still sending 35.6% of Venezuelan oil exports to the US (Weisbrot and Sachs 2019a). Later that year the Trump administration turned over control of the PDVSA-owned but US-based oil company Citgo to Guaidó appointees, thereby effectively removing an estimated $5.2 billion in assets and approximately $1 billion in annual dividends from Venezuelan government control. Also, the US froze approximately $9 billion in Venezuelan gold reserves and $3.4 billion in trade credits (*ibid.*).

Another indication that the US economic sanctions on Venezuela are practically total—a blockade, in effect—was the seizure in August 2020 of four Iranian tankers loaded with gasoline and headed for Venezuela. US officials halted the tankers in the Strait of Hormuz by threatening ship owners, insurers, and captains with sanctions (Neumann 2020). As the tanker incident illustrates, the sanctions were basically tightened at every opportunity that the Trump administration found. All direct economic transactions between the US and Venezuela have now been blocked as the Trump administration kept looking for extra-territorial application of the sanctions so that the blockade against Venezuela becomes as total as possible (Reuters 2020).

Just to make sure that the US was deploying absolutely every possible avenue of pressure against Venezuela, the Department of Justice announced in October 2020 that President Maduro, as well as 14 other top government officials are being indicted for "narco-terrorism" and drug trafficking. The US would offer bounties for their arrest to the tune of $15 million (for Maduro) to $5 million (Department of Justice 2020). However, even the US Drug Enforcement Administration (DEA) admits, in its 2019 report, that, "The majority of the cocaine and heroin produced and exported by Colombian TCOs [Transnational

Criminal Organizations] to the United States is transported through Central America and Mexico" (Drug Enforcement Admionistration 2019).

During the first half of February 2021, the United Nations sent Alena Douhan, a Special Rapporteur "on the negative impact of unilateral coercive measures on the enjoyment of human rights" to Venezuela. Her analysis of the sanctions echoes practically all of the points made in this chapter. But her preliminary report also points out the complete illegality, according to international law, of the sanctions regime. The report states,

> ...unilateral sanctions against the oil, gold, mining and other economic sectors, the state-owned airline and the TV industry constitute a violation of international law, and their wrongfulness is not excluded with reference to countermeasures. The announced purpose of the 'maximum pressure' campaign—to change the Government of Venezuela—violates the principle of sovereign equality of states and constitutes an intervention in the domestic affairs of Venezuela that also affects its regional relations.
>
> Office of the High Commissioner on Human Rights 2021

Upon taking office in January 2021, the Biden administration decided to continue the Trump administration's draconian Venezuela sanctions, as well as committing itself to continuing the recognition of Juan Guaidó as so-called "interim" president of Venezuela. The Biden administration's determination to hold on to sanctions on Venezuela even led to the first blockage of the WTO's dispute resolution mechanism since its founding in 1999, when the US representative to the WTO rejected Venezuela's request to have the sanctions examined for their compliance with WTO rules (Baschuk 2021).

2   Economic Consequences of US Sanctions

It ought to be obvious that the harsh sanctions on Venezuela would be devastating to its economy. After all, what country in the world would not be devastated when its export earnings are reduced from $3,200 per person per year in 2012 to less than $200 per person per year in 2020?[5] This represents a

---

5   Figures from the Venezuelan economist Francisco Rodriguez 2020. This chapter refers to these figures as oil revenues that are available for Venezuela to spend on imports per capita. Considering that oil export revenues pay for almost 100% of Venezuela's imports, it is fair to say that per capita oil export revenue and per capita import spending is roughly the same.

94% decline in hard currency income available for imports. Considering that Venezuela has historically depended on importing about 75% of the food it consumes and 90% of its medical supplies, this means a dramatic decline in the availability of currency for imported food and medicine (Oliveros 2020, 8). Venezuela thus suffered the worst economic decline in the history of the country (and in the history of all of Latin America) between 2017 and 2020, with GDP declining by 15.7% in 2017, 19.6% in 2018, and another 25.5% in 2019. The Economic Commission for Latin America and the Caribbean (CEPAL) predicts another contraction of 26% for 2020 (CEPAL 2020).

Venezuela's far-right opposition under self-declared president Guaidó and the Trump administration nonetheless claim that the economic collapse is the fault of the Maduro government and not of the sanctions. A common argument for this has been that Venezuela's economic decline already began in 2015, when the economy contracted by 3.9%. That same year, inflation almost tripled, from 68.5% in 2014, to 180% in 2015 (*ibid.*). Inflation kept climbing every year, until it reached hyperinflation levels in 2018. No doubt, some of Venezuela's economic problems can be traced to inflation, which has to do with the government's monetary policies (Wilpert 2019). However, the collapse of the country's oil industry, and along with that of its imports, are far more directly tied to the sanctions (Weisbrot and Sachs 2019b).

Oil prices hit a new low of $26 per barrel in early 2016, which combined with the already existing difficulties of importing badly needed supplies for maintaining Venezuela's oil production. The combination of reduced revenues for imports and the increasing complications of the sanctions meant a dramatic decline in oil production in Venezuela. Oil production was still at 2.4 million bpd (barrels per day) in late 2015, but by 2020 it dropped to 339,000 bpd, a decline of 86% in five years (Rodriguez 2020) Similarly, Venezuela's 1.3 million bpd refining capacity ground to an almost complete standstill during the same time. Both refineries and oil production facilities need constant maintenance, for which replacement parts must be imported, and which has been made practically impossible under the circumstances of the US economic sanctions. This has also meant severe gasoline shortages within Venezuela, leading to food supply problems, not only for transporting food, but also for planting and harvesting. This, in turn, led to an estimated one fifth loss in domestic food production (Yapur 2020). By late 2020, Venezuela was forced to import as much as 300,000 bpd of gasoline (Parraga 2020). The only way gasoline purchases can be carried out, though, is via swaps for asphalt, naphtha, natural gas, fuel oil, or crude oil, since international financial transactions are prohibited under the sanctions regime.

3   Social Consequences of US Sanctions

Officially the US government claims that its economic sanctions have exemptions for the import of food and medicines. However, this is blatantly false. While it is true that food and medicine are not included in the official sanctions policies, in practice it has become extremely difficult for Venezuela to import anything because of the sanctions against all financial transactions. In addition to halting financial transactions, since oil is Venezuela's primary source of foreign income (92%), the sanctions on the oil industry have meant a massive reduction in revenues to pay for imports.

Even in cases where imports are specifically designed to take advantage of the food and medicine allowance, the US government has intervened to stop such transactions, such as when it sanctioned shipping companies in June 2020, which were involved in an oil-for-food swap agreement with Mexico (Vaz 2020a). Even Iran and Iraq, which until recently faced some of the world's harshest and most comprehensive sanctions in recent memory, had oil-for-food programs, which Venezuela does not have.[6] According to some estimates, food and medicine imports declined by 78% between 2013 and 2018 (Weisbrot and Sachs 2019a, 16). It is very likely that they continued to decline in the following two years between 2018 and 2020.

As a result of this massive reduction in life-saving essentials, Venezuela is facing the possibility of famine for the first time in its history, according to the UN (Deen 2020). Already, the health impact has led to the loss of approximately 40,000 deaths in 2017 and 2018, according to a study conducted by the economists Mark Weisbrot and Jeffrey Sachs, who looked at excess mortality data for these two years (Weisbrot and Sachs 2019a). The Global Network Against Food Crises and the Food Security Information Network ranked Venezuela's food crisis as being the fourth worst in the world in 2019, ranked by the number of people affected.[7] The extremely difficult access to medicines puts everyone with a deadly health condition at risk, including 80,000 people with HIV, 16,000 in need of dialysis, 16,000 with cancer, 4 million who suffer from diabetes and hypertension.

Even when international institutions offer relief funds, the US has gone out of its way to block them. For example, in March 2020 the IMF offered $1 trillion

---

6   The Venezuelan opposition-affiliated economist Francisco Rodriguez has thus argued in favor of an oil-for-food program for Venezuela (Rodriguez 2019).

7   Yemen, Dem. Rep. of Congo, and Afghanistan occupied the top three places for that year. According to this report, 9.3 million Venezuelans, or 32% of the total population, faced a food crisis requiring urgent action. Please see Food Security Information Network 2020.

to countries to cope with the COVID-19 pandemic, with no strings attached. When Venezuela requested $5 billion of these funds, they were denied with the argument that Maduro is not the president of Venezuela, even though the UN recognizes the Maduro government. This in addition to the denial in 2019 of $400 million in IMF Special Drawing Rights (SDRS) that Venezuela technically has a right to access (Laya and Vasquez 2020).

It is little surprise that there has been a massive wave of migration out of Venezuela in the past few years because of the sanctions and linked economic crisis. This migration has probably attracted more attention than any other social consequence of the sanctions, but media rarely connect it to the sanctions and generally overstate the extent of the migration. That is, according to most estimates mentioned in the media, over 5 million Venezuelans have emigrated between 2013 and 2019 (e.g. Nebehay 2019). However, a more accurate estimate would probably be that of the Venezuelan opposition-affiliated economics institute ENCOVI, which conducted a survey of Venezuelan households and places the figure at around half that, at about 2.5 million (Emersberger 2020). Even the lower number is significant, though, and has affected all areas of daily life in Venezuela, but especially regarding "brain drain," where the country's younger university-educated generation has left in large numbers.

4   Political Consequences of Sanctions

Sanctions' effect on a country's politics is often not considered, even though the US government usually hopes—against all evidence (e.g. Cohen and Weinberg 2019)—that they will result in regime change. But there are several important impacts that ought to be considered in the case of Venezuela, including how the sanctions have contributed to greater political polarization, to increased political violence, to the solidification of the government's power, and to increased grassroots solidarity and mutual aid.

No doubt, Venezuela's political sphere has been polarized ever since Chávez was first elected. From the start of his presidency this has been a serious problem because it created obstacles for governing and for a normal give and take between political parties (Wilpert 2007). However, just as the opposition gradually began to learn to live with the Bolivarian Revolution, to accept the 1999 constitution, and to engage in real political dialogue with the Maduro government in 2017 and 2018, the Trump administration's sanctions, and political interference were instrumental in torpedoing the agreement (Boothroyd 2018; Wilpert 2018). These government-opposition negotiations had been on the verge of signing an agreement for early presidential elections in which the opposition would have participated, but in the last minute they withdrew at the urging of the US State Department. Given the intensifying economic crisis, some opposition leaders and the US government no doubt believed it would be better to hold out for a coup instead of a presidential election that would only have changed control over the national executive, but none of the other branches of the state.

Indeed, political violence and mobilizing for a coup was the route that the more radical faction of the opposition undertook once again after the May 20th, 2018, presidential election, which the radical opposition faction boycotted. Actions that this segment of the opposition undertook were an assassination attempt on August 4th, 2018, the attempted coups of February 23rd and April 30th, 2019, and the paramilitary incursion of May 3rd, 2020 (Vaz 2020b). None of these would probably have happened, had the US government not intensified the sanctions throughout the same period and convinced the opposition to boycott the 2018 presidential election.

At the time that the US-backed opposition is engaging in political violence, it should be no surprise that the Maduro government would solidify its hold on power. The sanctions and the political violence constitute the context in which President Maduro organized elections in May 2017 for an all-powerful constituent assembly to revamp the constitution. Also, sanctions are an important reason for why Maduro and the United Socialist Party of Venezuela (PSUV) has tried to marginalize internal "chavista" dissidents from the political process (Fuentes 2020).

Chavista dissidents, who are at times very critical of President Maduro but who have generally not turned against him completely or joined the opposition, are a growing movement in Venezuela. Partly this is the result of the Bolivarian movement having roots long before Chávez's election, in the grassroots neighborhood assemblies and other organizations, which eventually turned into communal councils and communes, which Chávez actively encouraged during his presidency. The sanctions have also influenced grassroots organizations, in that neighborhoods have had to mobilize in solidarity with the poorest, to help each other survive and overcome the economic crisis that the harsh sanctions regime has caused. Sometimes these grassroots efforts have been promoted directly be the Maduro government, such as in the case of the distribution of so-called "CLAPs" (Spanish acronym for Local Provision and Production Committees), where the government provides basic food staples and household items for a minimal fee and distributes them through locally organized volunteers, who are often connected to the local communal councils, which are direct-democratic neighborhood citizen assemblies. In other cases, citizens gather, at times through the communal councils, at times on an ad-hoc basis, to make sure all members of their community have access to basic needs, such as food, water, and electricity (Ciccariello-Maher 2013; Martinez and Gabbert 2018; and Ciccariello-Maher 2020).

5   Geopolitics of the Sanctions against Venezuela

As mentioned in the introduction, given the suffering that the US sanctions have caused the people of Venezuela, it is impossible to believe the US government's claim that they are being imposed in the name of protecting human rights. Rather the far more likely explanation is that the sanctions are designed to prevent any effort to create an alternative project, both within Venezuela as well as internationally.

Domestically, Venezuela has represented an alternative to the dominant neoliberal project ever since Chávez first became president in 1999. Economically, shortly after his election, Chávez reestablished state control over the state-owned oil company PDVSA, required transnational oil companies to pay significantly higher royalties for oil extraction, initiated urban and rural land reforms, and redistributed much of the oil boom's increasing revenues to the general population via countless new social programs in health, education, and housing. Politically, the Chávez government supported increased political participation, both via the representative electoral system by registering previously disenfranchised poor Venezuelans to vote, as well as via the creation of grassroots neighborhood organizations known as the communes and communal councils (Wilpert 2007; Tinker-Salas 2015; Azzellini 2018). There is some debate within the international left as to the extent to which the Maduro government still represents an economic and political alternative. However, despite this debate, the fact remains that it was the political and economic trajectory that Chávez first set in motion that is so objectionable to the world's ruling elites. This trajectory, known as the Bolivarian Revolution, remains to this day a compelling project for most Venezuelans, and one that the world's capitalist class continues to oppose, even if Maduro has deviated from this project's trajectory to some extent.

Internationally, Chávez also constructed an alternative to the dominant paradigm of neoliberal globalization. In an effort to strengthen South-South cooperation he spear-headed the creation of numerous new regional organizations, such as the Union of South American Nations (UNASUR), the Community of Latin American and Caribbean States (CELAC), PetroCaribe, and the Bolivarian Alliance (ALBA). Together with other center-left governments in the region at the time, he also helped prevent the Free Trade Agreement of the Americas

(FTAA). Every step of the way Chávez, and then Maduro, worked to oppose US efforts to impose neoliberal globalization on Venezuela and its allies.

Another crucial question for understanding the geopolitics of the US sanctions against Venezuela has to do with whether the US government is pursuing its opposition to the Bolivarian Revolution in the hope of opening Venezuela for US-based capital, for transnational capital in general, or for some other purpose?[8] The predominant assumption among critics of US foreign policy and US imperialism tends to be that the US government is opposing Venezuela in order to extend the US empire for the benefit of US capital. However, as the sociologist William I. Robinson points out in numerous critiques of this assumption, there are serious reasons to believe that there is hardly any such thing as "US capital" anymore (Robinson 2014). The US state ended up implementing neoliberal globalization in a way that did not specifically favor US capital, but capital in general.[9]

This does not mean that transnational capital is the only motivating factor in US foreign policy choices. After all, US politicians also need to maintain their legitimacy by getting reelected, so they do need to pay at least some attention to public opinion. However, since the US public pays relatively little attention to foreign policy, especially if it does not involve outright military conflict and dying soldiers, the public's concerns carry far less weight in foreign policy than in domestic policy making. One consideration regarding the public that does play an important role, at least with regard to Venezuela, is the presence of expatriate Venezuelans and Cubans in the important "swing state" of Florida. Appeasing this constituency, despite their relatively small number, has always been an important consideration for presidents of both parties, with regards to these two countries.

---

8   For now, I will lump all administrations that confronted Venezuela's Bolivarian Revolution, of presidents Bush, Obama, Trump, and most recently Biden, in one conceptual framework. Whether this is justified or whether they need to be differentiated is something I will examine more closely later.

9   Despite their disagreements with Robinson about the salience of a Transnational Capitalist Class, Panitch and Gindin (2012) make a similar argument, where they present the history of how the US ruling class implemented neoliberal globalization in the interests of capital in general, not just for US-based capital. According to them, "The American state, in the very process of supporting the export of capital and the expansion of multinational corporations, increasingly took responsibility for creating the political and juridical conditions for the general extension and reproduction of capitalism internationally" (ibid., 6). Also: "U.S. military interventions abroad were primarily aimed at preventing the closure of particular places or whole regions of the globe to capital accumulation. This was part of a larger remit of creating openings for or removing barriers to capital in general, not just U.S. capital" (ibid., 11).

In other words, different approaches towards Venezuela among different US presidents are not so much the result of different interests that they intend to pursue, but the result of different strategic considerations. In the case of the Republicans and of President Trump in particular, this strategy has meant the pursuit of regime change in Venezuela by using as much as force as possible, just short of engaging in an actual military confrontation, while disguising the regime change effort in humanitarian and US-nationalist discourses. In the case of the Democrats and of President Obama (and probably President Biden), it has also meant the pursuit of regime change, justified by humanitarian rhetoric, but taking into account the additional consideration of how to involve US allies in pursuit of this goal.

It is tempting to believe that the Trump administration, because of its nationalist rhetoric, was pursuing the interests of US capital and not of transnational capital in general. According to this assumption, the US is not only pursuing regime change in Venezuela but is also attempting to prevent Russian and Chinese involvement in Venezuela, so that after a regime change Venezuela would pursue more favorable relations with US-based oil companies. However, despite Trump's rhetoric, Trump's actual trade policy track record shows no indication that he favored US-based transnational corporations to the detriment of foreign-based ones.[10]

Luckily for Venezuela, there are several countries around the world that are very interested in supporting Maduro, both for their own economic reasons as well as out of a sense of solidarity among sanctioned countries. Countries that fall into this category are above all Cuba, Russia, Iran, and China. Each of these has significantly increased their trade and cooperation with Venezuela since Chávez first became president. Every tightening of sanctions against Venezuela, though, has led to efforts to increase Venezuela's trade and cooperation with each of these countries. In other words, if the sanctions were designed to reduce or prevent the deepening of Cuba's, Iran's, China's, or Russia's relations with Venezuela, they have actually had the exact opposite effect.

---

10   For example, despite Trump's rhetoric that the US-China trade war would benefit US workers and US businesses, all evidence suggests that it actually hurt US workers and businesses. See, for example, Hass and Denmark 2020. Arguably, one of the main objectives of the US-China trade war was to get China to stop favoring its own companies through subsidies, which, if it had been achieved, would have placed all companies that compete with China on a more even footing, not just US companies.

6   Conclusion

How can concerned citizens, activists, and politicians confront and the deadly sanctions regime that it is imposing on Venezuela? The first step, given that most people do not pay much attention to the sanctions and their effects, is to make sure that more people are aware of exactly how devastating the sanctions are. They are, in effect, an act of war, against which the affected population has practically no recourse. The United States is taking advantage of its privileged position in the world, as the holder of the global reserve currency, to deploy sanctions as an inexpensive means for overthrowing governments, even though they also are a very ineffective means.

Coupled with a greater understanding of the sanctions' devastating and war-like effects, it is necessary to develop a greater realization that they are also in violation of international law. While appeals to international law might not mean much nowadays, given that so many countries and especially the US constantly violate it, only an international outcry can reverse this trend. Next, the sanctions also violate US law, which, in theory, is more actionable. However, given that US courts regularly refuse to rule on anything that impinges on foreign policy, the US Congress needs to step up and create stricter legislation governing sanctions. One such proposal has been introduced by Rep. Ilhan Omar of Minnesota, with the "Congressional Oversight of Sanctions Act" (HR 5879), whereby sanctions could only be imposed with congressional approval.

Finally, and perhaps most effectively, countries around the world need to recognize that by allowing the US to have a stranglehold on the global financial system, via the US dollar, they have given the US far too much undeserved and illegitimate power. Luckily, more and more countries are beginning to recognize this now, especially as a result of the sanctions regimes that the US has been imposing and proposals for an alternative financial system are increasing. Hopefully, such an alternative system, which would be fairer for everyone, will come about sooner rather than later.

References

Azzellini, Dario. (2018). *Communes and Workers' Control in Venezuela: Building 21st Century Socialism from Below*. New York: Haymarket Books.

Baschuk, Bryce. (2021). "U.S. Disrupts WTO Dispute Meeting Over Venezuela Sanctions Fight." *Bloomberg News*, 26 March. https://www.bloomberg.com/news/articles/2021-03-26/u-s-disrupts-wto-dispute-meeting-over-venezuela-sanctions-fight.

Boothroyd, Rachael. (2018). "Venezuelan Opposition Abandons Talks in Dominican Republic, Dismisses Deal with Gov't." Venezuelanalysis.com, 8 February. https://venezuelanalysis.com/news/13647.

CEPAL. (2020). "Economic Survey of Latin America and the Caribbean 2020: Main conditioning factors of fiscal and monetary policies in the post-COVID-19 era." http://repositorio.cepal.org/bitstream/handle/11362/46071/89/ES2020_Venezuela_en.pdf.

Ciccariello-Maher, George. (2013). We Created Chávez. Durham: Duke University Press.

Ciccariello-Maher, George. (2020). "Venezuela: Communes Against Sanctions." Viviremos: Venezuela vs Hybrid War, edited by Claudia de la Cruz, Vijay Prashad, and Manolo de los Santos. New York: International Publishers.

Cohen, David, and Zoe A.Y. Weinberg. (2019). "Sanctions Can't Spark Regime Change." Foreign Affairs, 29 April. https://www.foreignaffairs.com/articles/united-states/2019-04-29/sanctions-cant-spark-regime-change.

Deen, Thalif. (2020). "UN Warns of an Impending Famine With Millions in Danger of Starvation." IPS, 27 November. http://www.ipsnews.net/2020/11/un-warns-impending-famine-millions-danger-starvation/.

Department of Justice. (2020). "Nicolás Maduro Moros and 14 Current and Former Venezuelan Officials Charged with Narco-Terrorism, Corruption, Drug Trafficking and Other Criminal Charges." Department of Justice Press Release, 5 October. https://www.justice.gov/opa/pr/nicol-s-maduro-moros-and-14-current-and-former-venezuelan-officials-charged-narco-terrorism.

Drug Enforcement Administration. (2019). "2019 National Drug Threat Assessment," 30 January.

Emersberger, Joe. (2020). "UN agencies not above playing politics with statistics." ZNet Blog, 24 December. https://zcomm.org/zblogs/the-un-is-not-above-playing-politics-with-its-mortality-statistics/.

Fuentes, Federico. (2020). "Venezuela: Could rebellion in the ranks spell trouble for Maduro?" Green Left Weekly, 18 October. https://www.greenleft.org.au/content/venezuela-could-rebellion-ranks-signal-end-maduro.

Happold, Matthew, and Paul Eden. (2016). Economic Sanctions and International Law. Oxford: Hart Publishing.

Hass, Ryan, and Abraham Denmark. (2020). "More pain than gain: How the US-China trade war hurt America." The Brookings Institute. https://www.brookings.edu/blog/order-from-chaos/2020/08/07/more-pain-than-gain-how-the-us-china-trade-war-hurt-america/.

Laya, Patricia, and Alex Vasquez. (2020). "IMF Won't Lend to Venezuela Because Maduro Lacks Recognition." Bloomberg, 18 March. https://www.bloombergquint.com/markets/venezuela-requests-5-billion-from-imf-to-fight-coronavirus.

Lilley, Sandra. (2017). "Trump Administration Announces Strong Financial Sanctions On Venezuela." *NBC News*, 25 August. https://www.nbcnews.com/news/latino/trump-administration-announces-strong-financial-sanctions-venezuela-n796101.

Martinez, Alexandra, and Karin Gabbert. (2018). *Venezuela desde adentro*. Fundación Rosa Luxemburg, Oficina Andina.

Nebehay, Stephanie. (2019). "Venezuela exodus set to top 5 million as long-term needs grow, officials say." *Reuters*, 23 October. https://www.reuters.com/article/us-venezuela-security-un-idUSKBN1X21MM.

Neumann, Scott. (2020). "U.S. Seizes Iranian Fuel From 4 Tankers Bound For Venezuela." *National Public Radio*, 14 August.

Oliveros, Luis. (2020). "The Impact of Financial and Oil Sanctions on the Venezuelan Economy." *Washington Office on Latin America*, October 2020. https://www.wola.org/2020/10/new-report-us-sanctions-aggravated-venezuelas-economic-crisis/.

Office of the High Commissioner on Human Rights. (2021). "Preliminary Findings of the Visit to the Bolivarian Republic of Venezuela by the Special Rapporteur on the Negative Impact of Unilateral Coercive Measures on the Enjoyment of Human Rights." https://www.ohchr.org/EN/NewsEvents/Pages/DisplayNews.aspx?NewsID=26747&LangID=E.

OPEC. (2020). "Annual Statistical Bulletin 2020." https://asb.opec.org/ASB_Charts.html?chapter=10.

Panitch, Leo, and Sam Gindin. (2012). *The Making of Global Capitalism*. New York: Verso Books.

Parraga, Marianna. (2020). "Venezuela's refinery woes send fuel imports soaring." *Reuters*, 5 December.

Pompeo, Mike. (2019). "Remarks to the Press." US Department of State, 11 March. https://www.state.gov/secretary/remarks/2019/03/290269.htm.

Reuters. (2020). "U.S. Fines Copa Airlines $450K for Transporting Passengers Between U.S., Venezuela," 17 June. https://www.reuters.com/article/usa-copa-holdings-venezuela/update-1-u-s-fines-copa-airlines-450k-for-transporting-passengers-between-u-s-venezuela-idUSL1N2DU2RN.

Robinson, William I. (2014). *Global Capitalism and the Crisis of Humanity*. New York: Cambridge University Press.

Rodriguez, Francisco. (2020). "The United States Helps Venezuela's Regime Survive." *Foreign Policy*, 20 October. https://www.foreignaffairs.com/articles/venezuela/2020-10-09/united-states-helps-venezuelas-regime-survive.

Rodriguez, Francisco. (2019). "Why Venezuela needs an oil-for-food programme." *The Financial Times*, 27 February. https://www.ft.com/content/804b2040-39d2-11e9-b856-5404d3811663.

Rodriguez, Francisco. (2018). "Crude Realities: Understanding Venezuela's Economic Collapse." *Washington Office on the Americas*, 20 September. https://www.venezuelablog.org/crude-realities-understanding-venezuelas-economic-collapse/.

Shagabutdinova, Ella, and Jeffey Berejikian. (2007). "Deploying Sanctions While Protecting Human Rights: Are Humanitarian 'Smart' Sanctions Effective?" *Journal of Human Rights* 6 (1): 59–74.

Tinker-Salas, Miguel. (2015). *Venezuela: What Everyone Needs to Know*. Oxford: Oxford University Press.

Vaz, Ricardo. (2020a). "US Sanctions Shipping Companies, Torpedoes Venezuela Oil-for-Food Deal." Venezuelanalysis.com, 2 June. https://venezuelanalysis.com/news/14894.

Vaz, Ricardo. (2020b). "Venezuelan Armed Forces: Paramilitary Incursion Neutralized." Venezuelanalysis.com, 3 May. https://venezuelanalysis.com/news/14861.

Weisbrot, Mark. (2003). "Washington Pursues Dangerous Policy in Venezuela." *Center for Economic and Policy Research*, 25 September. https://www.cepr.net/washington-pursues-dangerous-policy-in-venezuela/.

Weisbrot, Mark, and Jeffrey Sachs. (2019a). "Economic Sanctions as Collective Punishment." *Center for Economic and Policy Research*, 25 April. https://cepr.net/report/economic-sanctions-as-collective-punishment-the-case-of-venezuela/.

Weisbrot, Mark, and Jeffrey Sachs. (2019b). "Economists Use "Fuzzy Graphs" to Challenge Data on the Human Cost of Trump Sanctions on Venezuela," *Center for Economic and Policy Research*, 30 April. https://cepr.shorthandstories.com/venezuela-sanctions-response/index.html.

Wilpert, Gregory. (2007). *Changing Venezuela by Taking power: The History and Policies of the Chávez Government*. New York: Verso Books.

Wilpert, Gregory. (2008). "U.S. Retaliates against its Ambassador's Expulsion from Venezuela." Venezuelanalysis.com, 12 September. https://venezuelanalysis.com/news/3793.

Wilpert, Gregory. (2018). "Venezuela's Highly Unusual Presidential Election." *New Internationalist*, 17 May.

Wilpert, Gregory. (2019). "The Origins of Venezuela's Economic Crisis." *The Real News Network*, 2 April.

Yapur, Nicolle. (2020). "A Fifth of Food Output is Wasted in Famine-Threatened Venezuela." *Bloomberg News*, 26 June.

CHAPTER 17

Trying to Unbalance Russia: The Fraudulent Origins and Impact of US Sanctions on Russia

Jeremy Kuzmarov

In late August 2020, the Trump administration extended its Russia sanctions policy into the small East German town of Sassnitz. The town was supporting an $11 billion Russian pipeline, Nord Stream 2, which would double the capacity for natural gas to flow directly from Russia to Germany. Sassnitz's port supplied a Russian pipe-laying ship involved in Nord Stream 2. Residents feared that the sanctions, which the Biden administration waived, would cut their town off from the US commercially and exclude it from the global financial system, causing a new recession. The Trump administration, with backing from Poland and the Baltic nations, had long opposed the pipeline, seeing it as an instrument for Russian leverage over Germany, Ukraine and Central Europe. Defenders of the project said that Washington was really angling to sell Europe its more expensive liquified natural gas. Heiko Maas, the German foreign minister stated that "the U.S. administration was disrespecting Europe's right and sovereignty to decide itself where and how we source our energy" (Eddy and Erlanger 2020).

Maas' remarks underscore how economic sanctions are part of a global "great game" for control over energy resources, which results in the trampling of nations' sovereignty. In the midst of the COVID-19 pandemic, the Trump administration announced new punitive measures on a nearly daily basis, with one-fourth of people on Earth now living in countries suffering from US sanctions (Norton 2020; Tétrault-Farber 2020). The sanctions targeting Russia have extended to the Russian Defense Ministry's 48th Central Research Institute, which worked with other non-military medical centers to develop and test the world's first COVID-19 vaccine, called Sputnik 5. The research institute was targeted because of its alleged role in Russia's chemical and biological warfare program, though the institute successfully developed and tested vaccines against Ebola, Middle East Respiratory Syndrome (MERS), and a universal flu vaccine.

In April 2020, a Russian company sent ventilators to the United States as a form of humanitarian aid to help overwhelmed hospitals treat coronavirus patients. It was later revealed that this Russian firm had been under US sanctions since 2014 (Norton 2020) The above facts highlight the absurdity of the

American sanctions, which were ostensibly imposed for human rights purposes, but were detrimental to human rights and health, and have not worked.
The purpose behind the US sanctions was outlined in a 2019 report issued by the
RAND Corporation, the leading Pentagon think-tank, entitled "Overextending
and Unbalancing Russia." This report assesses how an array of foreign policy
measures—from encouraging domestic protests to providing lethal aid to
Ukraine to undermining Russia's image abroad—might weaken and destabilize Russia. The project's researchers found that "economic cost-imposing measures" held particularly high likelihood of success. These included an expansion of US energy production, which would expand world supply and depress
global prices hence hurting Russia, and the imposition of deeper trade and
financial sanctions if these sanctions were "comprehensive and multilateral"
(Dobbins 2019).

Russia's President Vladimir Putin has been targeted under the sanctions
because he has restored Russia's independence and economic strength from
the Boris Yeltsin era (1991–2000). After the fall of the Soviet Union, Yeltsin
rapidly privatized the post-Soviet economy in a way which fueled corruption
and benefited a new class of oligarchs while impoverishing ordinary Russians.
State industries were sold off for a fraction of what they were worth, and the
social safety net was destroyed (Mettan 2017). Yeltsin furthermore acquiesced
to the expansion of the North Atlantic Treaty Organization (NATO) towards
Russia's border, which Communist Party leader Gennady Zyuganov likened to
a "Versailles" for Russia—a reference to the 1919 conference in which Germany
was humiliated by the Western allies (Lippmann 1997; Tóme 2000). An advisor
to the Foreign Ministry said that Russia was being treated "like a colony" [of the
United States], which Putin has set out to reverse (Stent 2015, 25).

While keeping the capitalist structure as Yeltsin's handpicked successor
intact, by the mid 2000s Putin had begun to restore Russia's economic sovereignty. He did so by prosecuting corrupt oligarchs, blocking capital flight, and
reasserting Russian control over the Central Bank and Russian industries that
had been taken over by foreigners (Miller 2018). One of the investors who fell
afoul of Putin's new order was William F. Browder, the grandson of the former
communist party leader Earl Browder and hedge fund billionaire, who was
omnipresent in the media and in government halls pushing for the institution
of economic sanctions against Russia.

In 2013, Browder was found guilty in Russian court of failing to pay 552 million rubles in taxes ($16 million) and illegally buying up shares in Gazprom,
for which he was sentenced in absentia to nine years in prison (Giraldi 2018).
Browder accused the Russian government of perpetrating a $230 million tax
scam against his company, Hermitage Capital, though there is strong evidence

to indicate that he and his associates were behind the massive fraud. His tire-less promotion of sanctions has been in turn designed to divert attention away from this fact. Private lobbyists have often played an important role in driving US foreign policies. What is unique though in this case is that a white-collar criminal has singlehandedly helped to increase the risk of global nuclear war.

1   A New Battlefield for the United States

Economic sanctions can be defined as a "political act that utilizes economic instruments to either affect a change in the domestic or foreign policy of a tar-get state or undermine and weaken the authority and effectiveness of its govern-ment" (Connolly 2018, 11) According to Robert Blackwill and Jennifer Harris of the Council on Foreign Relations, the United States has been the principal coun-try imposing sanctions, with more than 120 instances over the past one hundred years (Blackwill and Harris 2016). After the September 11 attacks on the World Trade Center, the Bush administration tried to use sanctions to cripple what it considered to be rogue banks that financed terrorism or rogue regimes. The Obama administration followed suit by carrying out record sanctioning, target-ing left-wing governments and others which were defiant of US global designs (Blackwill and Harris 2016). Jack Lew, Obama's Treasury Secretary, said that eco-nomic sanctions are "a new battlefield for the United States, one that enables us to go after those who wish us harm without putting our troops in harm's way" (quoted in Wright 2017, 132). The sanctions directed against Russia are unique because it is the first time they have been applied against a member of the UN Security Council and former member of the G-8. The usual norm is to target weak and vulnerable Third World nations. The other distinctive facet is that the sanc-tions were first initiated through lobbying directed by a businessman who had been evicted from the targeted country and prosecuted for white collar crime.

2   The Browder-Magnitsky Hoax

The United States inaugurated the sanctions against Russia in December 2012 in an action that marked the beginning of the new Cold War. Russian President Vladimir Putin called the US-Russia sanctions a "provocation" designed to undermine the future of American-Russian relations" and said that they were "shortsighted and dangerous" and an "overt interference into our internal affairs" (Palmer 2012).

Prior to that time, the Obama administration had been advancing a "reset" policy that was designed to improve US Russian relations and had resulted in the New Strategic Arms reduction Treaty (START). START limited, albeit marginally, the number of nuclear and ballistic missile launchers and nuclear warheads deployed by each side. During the 2012 presidential debates, Obama depicted his opponent Mitt Romney as a relic of the 1980s when he suggested Russia had come to supersede al Qaeda as the greatest national security threat, telling Romney that the Cold War had ended twenty years ago (Kuzmarov 2019). By December 2012, however, Obama had signed into law the Magnitsky Act, a bill first promoted by Senator Ben Cardin (D-MD), which was designed to punish those responsible for the death of supposed Russian whistleblower Sergei Magnitsky. Curiously, only seven of the sixty targeted individuals had anything to do with Magnitsky, suggesting Magnitsky was but a pretext (*ibid.*).

Magnitsky was said to have been the lawyer of Bill Browder who was murdered in an Alcatraz like prison in Russia (Butyrka) after he had exposed a Russian government scam to rob taxpayers of $230 million by filing fictitious returns after seizing Browder's company. Browder told this story in his bestselling 2015 book, *Red Notice: A True Story of High Finance, Murder, and One Man's Fight for Justice.* The book would make for a good Hollywood thriller spotlighting government corruption and abuses in the Russian criminal justice system and the noble fight by a reformed "red" who gives up his lucrative business career to achieve redemption for his crusading friend caught up in a Kafkaesque nightmare (Browder 2015).

If only the story were true.

A film that has been blacklisted in the US directed by Andrei Nekrasov and written by Torstein Grude, *The Magnitsky Act: Behind the Scenes* (Piraya Films) and book by Hedge Fund Manager Alex Krainer, *The Killing of William Browder: Deconstructing Bill Browder's Dangerous Deception* (2017) revealed serious inconsistencies in Browder's story. Notable among these is the fact that Magnitsky was not actually a lawyer, as Browder claimed, but a tax accountant. There is no evidence also that Magnitsky was a whistleblower; rather he was questioned by Russian authorities as a suspect in Browder's tax scam.

In the early 2000s, Magnitsky had been hired by Browder to set up an offshore structure that Russian investigators would later say was used for tax evasion and illegal share purchases by Hermitage. In August 2019, the European Court of Human Rights ruled that the Russian [government] had "good reason to arrest Sergei Magnitsky for Hermitage tax evasion" (Nekrasov

2016; Krainer 2017; Komisar 2020). According to Andrei Nekrasov, Magnitsky was an expert in "circumventing the laws and regulations" which required foreigners like Browder to pay more for business and stock shares. In 2016, Browder was charged by Russian authorities with murder in Magnitsky's death. The evidence to back up the murder charge is an intercepted communication from Western intelligence agencies, which allegedly exposes an operation called Quake designed to "start a scandal or significant news trigger to discredit the Russian Federation in the eyes of the international community." Operating under the code name "Agent Solomon," Mr. Browder, with Britain's MI-6 and Russian opposition leader Alexei Navalny (AKA "Agent Freedom"), is said to have arranged for "proxies in the Russian federal penitentiary service to arrange the termination of any medical services for Magnitsky" (Kramer 2017). Similar accusations were previously aired on Russian state television but dismissed by independent analysts because the communication was found to have had spelling errors that derived from flawed Russian translation.

Browder himself repeatedly changed his story and posted a deceptive power point of Magnitsky's death certificate. Information from the website he provided a link to indicated that there were no signs of a violent death (Komisar 2020). Dr. Robert C. Bux, a forensics expert who wrote a report on Magnitsky's death, stated that there was no evidence that Magnitsky had been beaten to death, as Browder claimed. Magnitsky's mother Natalia believes that her son's death stemmed from negligence on the part of prison staff rather than murder. Confirming this assessment, a Russian commission that led to the dismissal of twenty-one prison employees, concluded that Magnitsky was never tortured in prison but died likely of a heart condition and the negligence of prison staff, not murder (Walker 2013; Krainer 2017).

Mr. Nekrasov told this chapter's author in an interview that he spoke off-the-record with a Doctor Kratov from the Butyrka prison, who was indicted and tried in Russia for negligence in his treatment of Magnitsky (he was acquitted but traumatized by the experience). According to Nekrasov, "Kratov said that in his personal opinion there was a chance that Magnitsky had indeed been killed (he died of a heart attack officially) but that in that case only Browder and company could have been behind it. Theoretically it is possible to organize such a killing from outside a jail in Moscow, even if there is no evidence of it in our case in my view. What is clear, however, is that only Browder stood to benefit from Magnitsky's death, while the authorities needed Magnitsky alive, as a witness against Browder" (Personal Interview with Author, October 2017).

The US embassy significantly had never raised any outcry in the period that Magnitsky was in prison, and Browder never discussed his case or assisted in his defense after his arrest. Hermitage also never had any mention of it on its website, turning Magnitsky into a martyr only later. When I asked why the US embassy never displayed any concern for Magnitsky's case when he was still in jail, ambassadors John Beyrle (2008–2012) and Michael McFaul (2012–2014) refused to answer.

3   A Foreign Version of a Russian Oligarch

Browder's book *Red Notice* provides fascinating detail about how Browder rebelled against his left-wing family by "putting on a suit and tie and becoming a capitalist" (Browder 2015). After receiving his M.B.A. at Stanford University, Browder worked for the investment banking firm Salmon Brothers, where he turned a $25 million investment in privatization vouchers in Russia into a $125 million stock portfolio. He then started up his own investment firm, Hermitage Capital, with help from Syrian Israeli banker, Edmund Safra, an owner of the Republican National Bank of New York which had sold tens of billions of dollars in US dollar notes to corrupt Russian banks who profited from the privatization voucher scheme.

In 2008, *New York Times* reporter Clifford J. Levy described Browder as a "foreign version of the Russian oligarchs who earned their fortunes in the mass privatization after the fall of the Soviet Union" (Levy 2008). A lot of his wealth was obtained through illicit means. He was implicated in a scam, for example, where Hermitage relocated its entities to the Republic of Kalmykia in southern Russia, which offered low tax rates and incentives for hiring disabled employees. Hermitage did the latter but only on paper (Krainer 2017).

Hermitage's parent company was HSBC Bank, a financial partner of billionaire George Soros, who lost even greater than Browder sums when Putin took control over Russia's Central Bank and economy and appears to be using Browder as their front man. Told by his mentor Safra "not to shy away from kicking up a scandal to protect his interests," Browder provided financial support to Maryland's Democratic Party Senator Ben Cardin's campaigns through Ziff Brothers, a firm associated with Hermitage, which gave over $1 million to Democratic Party candidates in the 2016 election (Browder had made stock trades for Ziff in Moscow and was using it to try to purchase shares of Gazprom, the large Russian natural gas company). From 2013–2018, Mr. Cardin also received $33,7000 from Lockheed Martin, $20,005 from Northrop Grumman and $22,500 in 2012 from the Carlyle Group. The source of his funding would plausibly explain his support for the Magnitsky bill, and a Russophobic Senate study promoting an escalation of the new Cold War.

John Hobson famously emphasized in his 1902 classic *Imperialism* how the British empire was driven by financial elites seeking outlets for new investments and who unduly influenced government policy. With regards to the United States, Hobson wrote that "it is Messrs. Rockefeller, Pierpont Morgan, Hannah, Schwab, and their associates who need imperialism ... because they desire to use the public resources of their country to find profitable employment for the capital which otherwise would be superfluous" (Hobson 2010 [1902], 83).

Mr. Browder follows in the same tradition in this neoliberal era. He and his backers have been extremely successful in using their wealth and political connections to sway public opinion against Putin and in driving forward the new Cold War, of which the sanctions policy is an important cornerstone. At one point, Browder called Secretary of State John Kerry—a lukewarm supporter of the Magnitsky Act—"Putin's lapdog" and purveyor of an "appeasement policy" (Krainer 2017). This kind of poisonous language suggests that Browder is part of a planned political campaign, driven by powerful financial and "deep state" interests who profited from the plunder of Russia in the 1990s.

4   New Cold War and American Double Standards

During Obama's second-term, American-Russian relations deteriorated further when the US backed a coup d'état in Ukraine in February 2014 against the pro-Russian leader Viktor Yanukovych, which led to a secessionist drive by the eastern provinces and outbreak of civil war. Russia responded by annexing Crimea after a referendum on the future of the province, and by supporting guerrilla rebels in Eastern Ukraine fighting the American backed Ukrainian regime, which had the support of the pro-fascist Azov battalion (de Ploeg 2017). Russian intervention in Eastern Ukraine and annexation of Crimea became a basis for expanding the Russia sanctions, which targeted Eastern Ukrainian and Crimean leaders. Russian-speaking Ukrainians it should be noted had felt threatened by the post-coup Ukrainian government, which pushed for the use of the Ukrainian language in schools and purged Yanukovych's supporters and former communists from government (Weir 2014; Arel 2018).

In March 2014, President Obama signed an executive order condemning Russia's seizure of Crimea and imposed sanctions on individuals and entities deemed to have undermined Ukraine's "democratic processes or institutions" (Landler *et al.* 2014; Connolly 2018). Further rounds of sanctions targeted two Ukrainian separatists—Aleksey Naydenko and Vladimir Vysotsky—involved in organizing elections in the breakaway East, which the US State Department called a "sham" (*Al Jazeera* 2019). Eastern Ukrainians however felt differently about the elections. Crimeans had meanwhile voted overwhelmingly to rejoin Russia, while the head of the private US intelligence firm Stratfor told a Russian paper that the Obama administration was behind "the most blatant coup in history [in February 2014]" (Chernenko and Gubuev 2015; Sakwa 2016; Kovalik 2018). The lack of democracy in Ukraine was apparent in the banning of the communist party and jailing of Ukrainian-Russian journalist Kirill Vyshinski for conducting a supposed "information war" (Vyshinsky and Bartlett 2019), though sanctions were never contemplated against Ukraine.

Between 2012 and 2019, the Obama and Trump administrations imposed more than 60 rounds of sanctions on Russian individuals, companies, and government agencies. In August 2018, the Treasury Department's Office of Foreign Assets Control listed 491 Russian people and entities who were affected, compared to 146 from China and 335 from Iran (Trojanovski 2018). A key factor underlying these numbers was the fracking revolution and adoption of new methods in horizontal drilling which transformed the United States into a leading energy producer and lessened dependence on Russia and other oil producing countries like Venezuela and Iran, which could now be crushed through sanctions (Bellamy Foster, Holleman, and Clark 2019, Clemente 2019).

In February 2019, Senators Lindsey Graham (R-SC) and Robert Menendez (D-NJ) introduced the Defending American Security from Kremlin Aggression Act (DASKAA), or the "sanctions bill from hell," amidst an escalating climate of Russophobia. The bill called for designating Russia as a "state sponsor of terrorism" for its actions in Syria, and the blacklisting of large Russian state banks and energy firms, restrictions on new Russian sovereign debt transactions and Russian uranium imports, and new sanctions on Russian political figures and oligarchs. Menendez told *Reuters* that the bill was "the next step in tightening the screws on the Kremlin and will bring to bear the full condemnation of the U.S. Congress so that Putin finally understands that the U.S. will not tolerate his behaviour any longer" (Zengerle 2018).

On September 24th, 2020, another harsh sanctions bill titled "Holding Russia Accountable for Malign Activities" was introduced by five prominent Senators—Chris Coons (D-Del), Marco Rubio (R-Fl), Ben Cardin (D-Md), Mitt Romney (R-Utah) and Chris Van Hollen (D-Md) in response to the alleged poisoning of Russian opposition figure Alexei Navalny, though proof of the latter was never firmly established (Harris 2020; Peters 2020).[1] President Joe Biden followed up by imposing new sanctions on March 2nd, 2021, claiming that a US intelligence finding—which was never made available to the public—had determined Russia's guilt (Kuzmarov 2021). The "Holding Russia Accountable for Malign Activities" bill generally fits a disturbing pattern in which sanctions are advanced in response to unsubstantiated allegations.[2] In August 2019, the Trump administration passed a round of sanctions in response to Putin's alleged use of nerve gas to poison Sergei Skirpal, a former Russian military intelligence officer, and his daughter Yulia, which independent investigators believe was part of a set-up orchestrated by British intelligence (O'Neill 2018; Porter 2018). The Skirpals were found on a park bench mere miles from a secret military lab capable of manufacturing Novichok (Kuzmarov 2021). The Obama administration before that had imposed more sanctions after Russian troops supposedly shot down of a Malaysian airliner. A fire near the crash site destroyed key evidence that might have implicated the Ukrainian military, however, and the US withheld evidence from investigators (Parry 2014, 2015).

5   Economic Impact of the Sanctions

The consequences of the economic sanctions have been quite severe on Russia. Thirty-nine percent of Russian business leaders said the sanctions hurt their business and told regional governors they were creating serious problems for the oil and gas sector (Pismennaya 2018; Stubbs and Nikolskaya 2018). Food prices soared, with the price of cabbage doubling, and pork increasing by nearly a third (Birnbaum 2015). The IMF estimated that sanctions linked to the 2014 invasion of Ukraine cost Russia one to 1.5% of GDP by mid-2015 (Harrell

---

1   Doctors in Omsk, Siberia where Navalny was transported after his flight carried out an emergency landing thought he was suffering from a metabolic disorder caused by a drop in sugar levels. Aleksandr Murakovsky, the head doctor of the hospital's emergency department, told the press they did not find poison.

2   Another example is North Korea where sanctions were extended after North Korean leader Kim Jung-Un was accused of killing his half-brother Kim Jong Nam at Kuala Lampur International airport, though a Malaysian investigation did not find any proof that Kim Jung-Un was involved. Yet another round of sanctions was imposed when the North Korean security services were accused of killing an American tourist, Otto Wambier, though again proof that Wambier was tortured was never firmly established, and he may have died from his own health problems. See A.B. Abrams, *Immovable Object: North Korea's 70 Years at War with American Power* (Atlanta: Clarity Press, 2020).

2019). At a meeting in St. Petersburg, Putin said that Russia lost over $160 billion due to the sanctions' impact on foreign investment (Bow Group 2015).

Political analyst Thomas J. Wright points out that the sanctions combined with the fall in oil prices contributed to the collapse of the Russian ruble, whose value fell from 34 rubles to the dollar on July 1, 2014 to 69 to one on January 30, 2015. This resulted in significant inflation, which made imports more expensive and depressed incomes and wages. Spending cuts were initiated in health care and education, fitting a pattern in which governments transfer the economic burden of sanctions to the poorest and most marginalized groups. Russian Gross Domestic Product (GDP) contracted by 4.6 percent from July of 2014 to July of 2015—its greatest drop since 2009. Inflation rose to 11.4 percent in 2014 and was at a 15.8 percent annual rate by August 2015. Living standards plummeted for the first time since the 1990s. Stock market returns were reduced by 6.5%. International air travel fell by 20 percent, car sales fell by 36 percent, and shops stopped stocking many Western food products (Bow Group 2015; Wright 2017).

6   Putin Responds

Sanctions expert Richard Connolly points out how Putin's administration "used a range of tools and resources to cushion targeted sectors from the worst effects [of the sanctions]." This included a shift towards "greater reliance on domestic resources—or Russification—and forging closer relations with non-Western countries." According to Connolly, the Russian state response to sanctions was "coordinated, substantial and sophisticated" (Connolly 2018, 4). It was enabled by the rapid economic growth that was previously achieved, which resulted in a swelling of government tax revenues and rebuilding of state capacity from the Soviet era.

In August 2015, Putin formed a Russian government commission for import-substitution chaired by former president Dmitri Medvedev. Denis Mamturov, the Minister for Industry and Trade, presented a detailed plan that included more than 2,000 projects across 19 branches of the economy with the goal of reducing the share of imported goods. 235 billion rubles ($4.5 billion) were allocated to be spent directly from the federal budget over the coming five years as a system of tax credits and favorable loans for certain businesses was set up. According to Mamturov, by the summer of 2017, 22 sectors of the economy were receiving state support to stimulate import-substitution.

Putin at the same time began challenging foreign direct ownership over key sectors of Russia's economy targeted under the sanctions. He initiated a process of nationalizing privately owned oil companies, which produced oil production technologies, redefined production sharing agreements that privileged foreign companies, which Putin described as "colonial," and brought back under tight state control major Russia energy giants, Yukos, Sibneft and Gazprom. Through these measures, oil and gas production in Russia remained at or above pre-sanctions levels (Connolly 2018).

Crucial also was Putin's support for the development of energy extraction equipment in Russia through direct state funding and subsidized loans, which were used to offset dependence on imports. Russian companies began producing their own intelligent geo-navigational equipment used in drilling, and Putin in October 2014 approved the creation of a state-owned oil services company, RBC, whose aim was to duplicate services provided by Haliburton and Baker Hughes (Kramer 2014). According to Connolly, the strategy of direct state subsidization of the industry "represented a deviation from the previous trajectory of economic policy which had largely left the industry to the vagaries of the market" (Connolly 2018). Annual output in oil and gas equipment grew by four percent in 2015 following the repudiation of neoliberal doctrine and 14 percent in 2016. In 2018, Russia's oil exports totaled $130 billion, up nearly 40 percent from the year before (Clemente 2019).

A growth pattern was seen in other industries including the pharmaceutical and automotive industries, which produced 79 percent of cars sold in Russia in 2016 (Hellevig 2017). In 2017, 85 percent of Russian household appliances were produced domestically and Russian companies were developing their own cutting edge technological products such as a hydraulic excavator used in mining endeavors, a Thulium fiber laser for surgical application and bulldozers of high technical quality which were affordable in ruble terms. Putin's government also supported development of a new banking card payment system called the Mir to ensure the sovereignty of domestic payments after Visa and Master card ceased to serve some Russian banks, and set up an alternative transaction system called Swift. Russian farmers were a big winner of Putin's import substitution policy as the share of imported food in Russia declined from 25 to 10 percent following the institution of sanctions and the country became the world's top wheat exporter. Russia also became nearly self-sufficient in sugar and meat products; a domestic cheese manufacturer tripled its output and domestic production displaced imports of pork and chicken (Hellevig 2017).

The New York Times reported in March 2020 that Russia's newfound self-sufficiency in agriculture combined with lowering of debt and bulging financial reserves made the country better positioned than most others to withstand the economic shocks bred by the Coronavirus. $600 billion in gold and hard currency reserves had been built in part through a policy of writing into the budget an artificially low estimate for the global price of oil, with all tax on profits above that level going into the national piggy bank. Because of the country's self-sufficiency in agriculture, the government could now spend its reserves on economic recovery rather than needing to prop up the ruble to keep imported food affordable (Kramer 2020).

As far as geopolitics, Putin successfully used the backdrop of sanctions to advance his idea of a Eurasian Union tying Central Asian economies with Russia. Gazprom paid a mere $1 to take control of Kyrgyzstan's gas company, now called Gazprom Kyrgyzstan, in a deal matched by similar Russian state investments in nuclear, hydroelectric and oil sectors across Russia's "near abroad" (Blackwill and Harris 2016). Putin also expanded trading ties with China. In 2018, trade between the two countries grew to $108 billion (Kramer 2019). When Chinese Premier Xi Jinping visited Russia in June 2019, Putin took him on a boat tour around the historic city of St. Petersburg to solidify the mutual alliance. A jealous United States responded by staging an incident in which the US cruiser Chancellorsville brushed a Russian vessel in the Philippines sea while making it look like Russia had engaged in provocative maneuvers (a photo showed two Russian sailors sunbathing, which undermined this claim). The goal of the United States was to skew world opinion against Russia to justify its bellicose policies, however, these policies were not working.

Kirill Dmitriev, CEO of Russia's Direct Investment Fund told CNBC that the "sanctions hurt the United States more than Russia" largely because "a lot of people were moving away from (the) dollar, because lots of dollar transactions were getting restricted" (Ellyatt 2019). These comments epitomize how the sanctions policy has not only failed to achieve its stated goals of weakening Russia and deterring its intervention in Ukraine but backfired and harmed the US economy. Putin's largely effective response to the sanctions prevented his political competitors from gaining ground on him (Leander and Sakhrin 2017). In February 2015, while he was being vilified in Western media, Putin was incredibly ranked the world's most popular politician (Boren 2015). This honor exposes the farcical nature of the sanctions policy whose main accomplishment has been to enflame tensions between the US and Russia and contribute to the dangerous climate of the new Cold War, where the risk of nuclear conflagration grows ever greater by the day.

References

Al Jazeera. (2019). "U.S., Canada, EU Hit Russia With Fresh Sanctions Over Ukraine." *Al Jazeera*, 15 March.

Arel, Dominique. (2018). "Language, Status, and Loyalty in Ukraine," *Harvard Ukrainian Studies* 35: 233–264, https://www.husj.harvard.edu/articles/language-status-and -state-loyalty-in-ukraine.

Bellamy Foster, John, Hannah Holleman, and Brett Clark. (2019). "Imperialism in the Anthropocene." *Monthly Review*, July–August 2019.

Birnbaum, Michael. (2015). "A Year into the Conflict with Russia are Sanctions Working?" *The Washington Post*, 27 March.

Blackwill, Robert, and Jennifer Harris. (2016). *War by Other Means: Geoeconomics and Statecraft*. Cambridge, MA: Harvard University Press.

Boren, Zachary Davies. (2015). "The World's Most Popular Politicians: Putin's Approval Rating Hits 86%." *The Independent*, 27 February.

Bow Group Research Paper. (2015). "The Sanctions on Russia," 9 August.

Browder, Bill. (2015). *Red Notice: A True Story of High Finance, Murder, and One Man's Fight for Justice*. New York: Simon & Schuster.

Chernenko, Elena, and Alexander Gubuev. (2015). "Stratfor's Chief's 'Most Blatant Coup in History." *Kommersant* , 20 January. https://russia-insider.com/en/politics/ stratfor-chiefs-most-blatant-coup-history-interview-translated-full/ri2561.

Clemente, Jude. (2019). "Does the U.S. Import Oil from Russia?" *Forbes Magazine*, 18 April.

Connolly, Richard. (2018). *Russia's Response to Sanctions: How Western Economic Statecraft is Reshaping Political Economy in Russia*. New York: Cambridge University Press.

Dobbins, James. (2019). *Overextending and Unbalancing Russia: Assessing the Impact of Cost-Imposing Options*. Santa Monica, CA: RAND Corporation.

Eddy, Melissa, and Steven Erlanger. (2020). "German Port Faces Ruin Under U.S. Sanctions." *The New York Times*, 26 August.

Ellyatt, Holly. (2019). "Sanctions on Moscow Hurt the U.S. Long-Term, Russia's Wealth Fund Head Says." *CNBC*, 23 January.

Giraldi, Philip. (2018). "Bill Browder Escapes Again." *Global Research*, 2 June. https:// www.globalresearch.ca/bill-browder-escapes-again/5642767.

Harrell, Peter. (2019). "How to Hit Russia Where it Hurts: A Long-Term Strategy to Ramp Up Economic Pressure." *Foreign Affairs*, January 2019.

Harris, Roger. (2020). "NYT Releases Sequel of Putin the Poisoner: The Incredulous Case of Mr. N." *Counterpunch*, 29 September. https://www.counterpunch.org/2020/ 09/29/nyt-releases-sequel-of-putin-the-poisoner-the-incredulous-case-of-mr-n/.

Hellevig, Jon. (2017). "Russia's Import-Substitution—Impressive results by Carrots and Sticks." *Arawa,* 26 July. https://www.awaragroup.com/blog/russias-import-subs tituton/.

Hobson, John A. (2010 [1902]). *Imperialism: A Study.* London: Cambridge University Press.

Komisar, Lucy. (2017). "The Man Behind the Magnitsky Act: Did Bill Browder's Tax Troubles in Russia Color Push for Sanctions." *100 Reporters,* 20 October.

Komisar, Lucy. (2020). "U.S. & UK Intensify Campaign Against Russia; UK Harks Back to First Pillar of New Cold War, the Magnitsky Hoax." *Committee for East-West Accord,* 6 July. https://www.thekomisarscoop.com/2020/07/u-s-uk-harks-back-to-first-pil lar-of-new-cold-war-the-magnitsky-hoax/.

Kovalik, Dan. (2018). *The Plot to Control the World: How the US Spent Billions to Change the Outcome of Elections Around the World.* New York: Simon & Schuster.

Krainer, Alex. (2017). *The Killing of William Browder: Deconstructing Bill Browder's Dangerous Deception.* Monaco: Equilibrium.

Kramer, Andrew E. (2014). "The 'Russification' of Oil Exploration." *The New York Times,* 29 October.

Kramer, Andrew E. (2017). "Conspiracy Claims Devour Magnitsky Murder Inquiry." *The New York Times,* 23 October.

Kramer, Andrew E. (2019). "China and Russia Leaders Criticize US for Tariffs and Sanctions." *The New York Times,* 8 June.

Kramer, Andrew E. (2020). "Thanks to Sanctions, Russia is Cushioned from Virus' Economic Shocks." *The New York Times,* 10 April.

Kuzmarov, Jeremy. (2019). *Obama's Unending Wars.* Atlanta: Clarity Press.

Kuzmarov, Jeremy. (2021). "Is Russian Opposition Leader Alexei Navalny a Key Prop in a Psychological Warfare Operation Designed to Bring Down Vladimir Putin?" *CovertAction Magazine,* 13 March. https://covertactionmagazine.com/2021/03/13/ is-russian-opposition-leader-alexey-navalny-a-key-prop-in-a-psychological-warf are-operation-designed-to-bring-down-vladimir-putin/.

Landler, Mark, Annie Lowrey, and Steven Lee Myers. (2014). "Obama Steps Up Russia Sanctions in Ukraine Crisis." *The New York Times,* 20 March.

Leander, Per, and Alexey Sakhrin. (2017). "Russia's Trump." *Jacobin,* 11 July.

Levy, Clifford J. (2008). "An Investment Gets Trapped in Kremlin's Vise." *The New York Times,* 24 July.

Lippman, Thomas. (1997). "Clinton, Yeltsin Agree on Arms Cuts and NATO." *The Washington Post,* 22 March.

Mettan, Guy. (2017). *Creating Russophobia: From the Great Religious Schism to Anti-Putin Hysteria.* Atlanta: Clarity Press.

Miller, Chris. (2018). *Putinomics: Power and Money in Resurgent Russia.* Chapel Hill, NC: University of North Carolina Press.

Nekrasov, Andrei, with Thorstein Grude. (2016). *The Magnitsky Act: Behind the Scenes* (Piraya Films).

Norton, Ben. (2020). "U.S. Sanctions Russian Research Institute That Developed Covid-19 Vaccine." *The Gray Zone Project*, 28 August. https://thegrayzone.com/2020/08/28/us-sanctions-russian-research-institute-covid-19-vaccine/.

O'Neill, John. (2018). "The Strange Case of the Russian Spy Poisoning." *Consortium News*, 13 March.

Palmer, Doug. (2012). "Obama Signs Trade, Human Rights Bill That Angers Moscow." *Reuters*, 14 December.

Parry, Robert. (2014). "Flight 17 Shoot-Down Scenario Shifts." *Consortium News*, 3 August.

Parry, Robert. (2015). "Fake Evidence Blaming Russia for MH-17." *Consortium News*, 18 May.

Peters, Andrea. (2020). "Russian Oppositionist Alexei Navalny Flown to German Hospital After Doctors Dispute Poisoning Claim." *World Socialist Web Site*, 22 August. https://www.wsws.org/en/articles/2020/08/22/nava-a22.html.

Pismennaya, Evgenia. (2018). "Russian Business Says Sanctions Hurt Despite Kremlin Optimism." *Bloomberg News,* 27 November.

de Ploeg, Chris Kaspar. (2017). *Ukraine in the Crossfire*. Atlanta: Clarity Press, 2017.

Porter, Gareth. (2018). "Another Dodgy British Dossier: The Skirpal Case." *Consortium News*, 21 April.

Sakwa, Richard. (2016). *Frontline Ukraine: Crisis in the Borderlands*. London: I.B. Tauris.

Stubbs, Jack, and Polina Nikolskaya. (2018). "'Russia in the Doldrums?' New U.S. Sanctions to Weigh on Recovery," *Reuters*, 9 April.

Stent, Angel. (2015). *The Limits of Partnership: U.S.-Russian Relations in the 21st Century*. New Jersey: Princeton University Press.

Tétrault-Farber, Gabrielle. (2020). "Russian Ventilators Sent to U.S. Made Firm under U.S. Sanctions: Russia Newspaper." *Reuters,* 3 April.

Tomé, Luis José Rodrigues Leitao. (2000). "Russia and NATO's Enlargement." NATO Research Fellowship Program, 1998–2000. Final Report, June.

Trojanovski, Jon. (2018). "Russia Keeps Getting Hit with Sanctions. Do They Make a Difference." *The Washington Post*, 22 August.

Vyshinsky, Kirill, and Eva Bartlett. (2019). "'They Just Want Me in Prison': Eva Bartlett Interviews Jailed Ukrainian Journalist Kirill Vyshynsky." *Mintpress News*, 25 February.

Walker, Shaun. (2013). "Russia Drops Inquiry Into Death of Sergei Magnitsky." *The Independent*, 19 March. https://www.independent.co.uk/news/world/europe/russia-drops-inquiry-into-death-of-sergei-magnitsky-8541205.html.

Weir, Fred. (2014). "Ukraine Purge: Communists, Cronies and Crooks Face the Axe." *The Christian Science Monitor*, 16 October.

Wright, Thomas J. (2017). *All Measures Short of War: The Contest for the 21st Century and the Future of American Power.* New Haven: Yale University Press.

Zengerle, Patricia. (2018). "U.S. Senators Introduce Russia Sanctions 'Bill from Hell.'" *Reuters*, 2 August.

CHAPTER 18

The Political Economy of US Sanctions against China

Zhun Xu and Fangfei Lin

One important sign of an increasingly unstable global capitalism has been the visible tension between the US and China in the last decade. The tension, so far, has been mostly driven by the aggressions from the US side. This was evident from the American "pivot to Asia" under the Obama administration, as Lieberthal (2011) claims: "Obama moved boldly to shift the center of gravity among the key multilateral organizations in Asia…and leading them to take approaches favored by Washington but are neuralgic for Beijing." However, it was under the Trump administration that the negative opinions on China became much more explicit in the US mainstream media and politics. Even though there are many things that the Trump administration, establishment Republicans and the Democrats would strongly disagree with each other, they have reached a holy alliance regarding containing China.

The resentment and perhaps some regret over the "soft" approach towards China is now visible among some US elites. In July 2020, Mike Pompeo, the US Secretary of State, made a speech titled "Communist China and the Free World's Future" in a symbolic venue, the Richard Nixon Presidential Library and Museum. Pompeo lamented the failure of the US' China strategy, arguing that US engagement with China since Nixon benefited China at the expense of the US economy and "way of life"; and it did not induce China to evolve "towards freedom and democracy" (Pompeo 2020). In another blunt racist revelation in 2019, Kiron Skinner, a former Director of Policy Planning at the United States Department of State, highlighted the threat of China since "it's the first time that we will have a great-power competitor that is not Caucasian." All these opinions have been preparing new ground for sanctions against China. In many such narratives, China previously was someone that needs to be and can be saved by peaceful engagement/education of the West. Now China has somehow become uneducable and needs to be taught its place in the world.

Since the founding of the People's Republic in 1949, China was for a long time a target of the strictest US-led sanctions. A trade embargo was not lifted until the normalization of the US-China relationship in the early 1970s. Since then, China has deeply integrated into the global capitalist economy and become a major producer and trader. Despite certain long-term trade restrictions and occasional exceptions, the US has largely refrained from imposing significant new sanctions on China. Thus, it is concerning to see the emerging new hostility from the US and the resulting new sanctions on a large number of Chinese companies, universities, and research institutions.

The return of US sanctions against China poses two important questions for understanding both the working and the crisis of global capitalism. First, we need to understand the causes behind this new wave of sanctions: is it a short-term measure from the US capitalists which could change with a new administration, or a long-term policy change that will bring back part of the experiences during the Cold War? Second, we can explore whether these sanctions will make an impact on both the Chinese economy and politics, particularly the industrial upgrading of and labor conditions in the Chinese industries, as well as China's relationship with the West and the global south.

This chapter explores these questions from a political economy perspective, which debunks some of the allegations behind the US sanctions and examines the consequences of such sanctions in the context of global capitalist crisis We argue that the baseless sanctions are imperialist responses to the crises of global capitalism of which China has been an integral part. However, such actions only hurt the working people in both US and China, and will tend to destabilize global capitalism even more. The next section briefly reviews the history of the US-China relationship after 1949. The third section examines the current US sanctions against China and their consequences. The last section concludes the chapter.

1   The Evolving US-China Relationship

When the Chinese Communist Party (CCP) defeated the Guomindang (Nationalist) Party in 1949, the US did not seem to immediately make a firm decision on its strategy towards the new socialist country. The US government, although still supporting the Guomindang regime in Taiwan economically, was at least preparing to cut its military aid to the Guomindang (Cohen 2019, 183–184). As Cohen (2019) suggests, the US government was ready to live with the new China and would not intervene further in the Chinese civil war (the reunification with Taiwan). Meanwhile, the US already started to impose trade restrictions on China as part of its broader Cold War policies. In 1948, the value of US exports to China was 273.4 million USD, but it dropped to 82.6 million USD in 1949, and 33 million in 1950 (January to August) (Tao 1997). Industrial goods such as fossil-based products declined by more than 90 percent and the remaining was mostly cotton since it was not strategically significant (Tao 1997).

The Korean civil war in 1950 prompted the US to take a more aggressive stance against China. After the war broke out, the US government immediately sent its Seventh Fleet to the Taiwan Strait to prevent the Chinese revolution from moving into Taiwan and essentially started establishing Taiwan as an anti-communist outpost. The US later upgraded its sanctions to a total embargo and seized all Chinese government assets and some private Chinese assets in the US after China intervened in the Korean War (Tao 1997). US controls on strategic trade with China were even stricter than those imposed against the Soviet Union, which was known as the "China Differential" (Meijer 2015).

All these US-led aggressions made China choose to side closely with the USSR. Thanks to the massive economic and technical support from the USSR and the Soviet bloc, China was able to start its rapid industrialization despite the sanctions in the 1950s. However, the political and economic tensions between China and the USSR starting from the late-1950s gradually deteriorated the Sino-Soviet relationship. This was further aggravated by the sudden withdrawal of Soviet technicians in 1960. This forced China to explore trade relationships outside the Soviet bloc in the 1960s, which was also in the interest of the US as it hoped from the beginning to separate China away from the Soviet Bloc.

The effort to diversify trade partners worked well for China. As early as 1966, more than half of Chinese imports came from major capitalist economies such as Japan, Western Europe, Canada, and Australia, though the US trade embargo was still in place (Chen 2006). Hong Kong also played a special role in the anti-sanction struggle (Tao 1997). It was virtually impossible to cut the connections and legal/illegal trading routes between Hong Kong and the mainland. The CCP decided to not liberate Hong Kong immediately as the British-occupied city essentially served as a door through which China could break through the embargo. Thus, China was able to use the commercial interest of US allies to effectively reduce the damage from the US sanctions.

At the same time, the US was facing great challenges by the revolutionary struggles in Vietnam and beyond. It had some strong incentive to have a working relationship with China, partly to isolate Vietnam and partly to take advantage of the Sino-Soviet split (Meijer 2015). The Chinese leadership under Mao was also interested in the normalization of its relationship with the US-led capitalist world and gaining access to advanced technology and capital equipment. The trade embargo was partially lifted after Nixon's visit to Beijing in 1972 and China increased its foreign trade by 74 percent in a year (Chen 2006). A real change in the US-China relationship had to wait until the rise of the post-Mao leadership in China and the increasing tension between the US and the USSR following the war in Afghanistan. The new Chinese leadership, led by Deng Xiaoping, was determined to break away from Maoism and thus much more enthusiastic in developing a close collaboration with the US-led capitalist world. Meanwhile, the Carter administration was also looking for more explicit strategic cooperation with China. This quickly led to the US further loosening trade restrictions on China (allowing military equipment sales) and forging military collaboration between the two countries (Meijer 2015). The close collaboration was based on a common strategic interest against the USSR throughout the 1980s, and then a common business interest for the elites from both countries to work together after the demise of the USSR. The political turmoil in China at the end of the 1980s led to a brief period of US sanctions, but many of those were quickly lifted (Mann 1991). The US established Permanent Normalized Trade Relations with China in 2000 and, with support from the US and others, China joined the World Trade Organization in 2001.

Despite some major differences in their politics and ideologies, since the rise of neoliberalism China and the US have been playing largely complementary roles in the global economy. This was made possible first by industrial relocation/outsourcing in the US starting from the 1980s. Moreover, China dismantled its rural collectives in the 1980s and privatized much of urban state-owned enterprises in the 1990s, creating a large reserve army of labor. US firms outsourced less sophisticated industries to China, while the post-structural reform working class in China proved to be sufficiently flexible, productive, and cheap to make China the leading workshop of the world. The US business community in general has greatly benefited from such a relationship (sometimes called the Chimerica) as it provides cheaper consumer goods and lowers interest rates (Ferguson and Xu 2018). China has also enjoyed a very rapid rate of capital accumulation and growth and accumulated a large sum of foreign reserves.[1] At the same time, the US-China relationship is far from equal. The US monopolizes science and technology whle China mostly produces or assembles cheap commodities for the US and others. Despite its rapid economic growth, China remains in the semi-periphery category in terms of its position in the world division of labor; a large part of China's massive foreign reserves was also held in US dollar assets, which in essence constitute China's informal tribute to US imperialism (Li 2020).

---

1 From a critical perspective, the working classes in both countries have not fared well in the process. For example, the labor shares of national income in both US and China have had some significant decline during the neoliberal era.

The stability of such a fundamentally collaborative but hierarchical relationship is the very basis of the post-cold-war global economy that we live in. Thus, it is of clear importance to understand the origins of the recent new sanctions and whether this means the beginning of the end of the current global order.

2   Examining Recent Sanctions

For years, the US has been blaming China for many of its own problems. However, under Trump anti-Chinese sentiments have reached a historic high. For example, one of his high-level advisors, Peter Navarro, made his name by writing fearmongering books such as *The Coming China Wars* and *Death by China*. Trump himself is a master demagogue and for years, he has blamed China for "stealing" US jobs and technology. After all, the Trump administration started the prolonged trade war with China by imposing new tariffs first on solar panels and washing machines (Schlesinger and Ailworth 2018), and later on a large number of Chinese products.

Many accusations directed at China by the US government are misleading at best. China does enjoy a huge trade surplus with the US, but actual gains from trade are exaggerated. According to Ma *et al.* (2015), foreign-invested enterprises operating in China created nearly 45% of the domestic content in Chinese exports, whereas processing Chinese-owned enterprises only contributed by less than 5%. Moreover, in terms of income distribution, foreign factory owners captured more than half of the value of Chinese exports. China has seen some dramatic industrial expansion in the last few decades, but this was mainly based on domestic capital. For example, the United Nations Conference on Trade and Development (2020) documents that the foreign direct investment (FDI) only constitutes 2.3 percent of China's gross capital formation in 2019, which was lower than the number in the US (5.6 percent) or the world (7 percent).

Moreover, US firms outsourced to China and other countries not due to some secret scheme of the Chinese government but primarily because of cheaper productive labor and the massive market. Since these foreign companies make their own investment decisions on a profit basis, it would be indeed absurd to assume the Chinese government can somehow force global capital to give away technology and sacrifice profits. As for the number of jobs, although total urban employment increased dramatically, the neoliberal reform starting from the late 1990s that prepared China for the export boom cost the Chinese workers more than 50 million jobs in the urban formal sector, and those formal jobs were never restored (Chen and Xu 2017). As a comparison, according to Scott and Mokhiber (2020), the alleged number of US job losses due to the trade deficit with China was 3.7 million between 2001 and 2018.

Although related to broad claims such as job/technology theft, the most recent US sanctions are based on more concrete allegations. We divide these newly implemented sanctions into three categories: first, sanctions against enterprises because of their relationship with the Chinese military; second, sanctions against enterprises based on the Chinese trade with US "enemies" such as Iran; and finally, sanctions against local governments and enterprises because of alleged human rights violations, such as the case in Xinjiang.

The first category involves the question of military connections. A large number of firms and universities in China have been under export control with the Entity List and Unverified List (often a precursor to the Entity List). Students in some leading universities in China suddenly lost access to standard software such as Matlab, as the US firm MathWorks has suspended its service for these universities (Chen 2020). The list also includes institutions that do not have a clear connection with the military. For example, it includes Anhui Institute of Metrology, which is an institution providing service of measurement in Anhui Province; and it also includes Renmin University, which is a leading university famous for social sciences and humanities.

It is quite hypocritical to accuse Chinese universities of having military connections when all the leading US universities and many large companies have deep connections with the US imperialist military force which has invaded countries around the world and keeps an active military force around China. In one grant for research equipment alone, the US Department of Defense gave 49 million USD to 91 institutions in 2020 (US Department of Defense 2019). In the same year, the US Department of Defense also gave out about 434 million under "University Research Initiatives" (Association of American Universities 2020.Moreover, the US enthusiastically sold military equipment to China not long ago (Meijer 2015).

The second category is closely related to the US sanctions on Iran. Since 1979, the US has imposed various sanctions on Iran. This was partly loosened by the Joint Comprehensive Plan of Action (JCPOA) between the five permanent members of the UN Security Council (China, US, France, Russia, Britain) plus Germany and Iran. The JCPOA basically allowed Iran to reduce/redesign its nuclear facilities in exchange for significant sanction relief. However, in 2018 the Trump administration quickly withdrew from the JCPOA and re-imposed sanctions. This has had some major impacts on Iran as companies around the world have abandoned their investment/trade plan with Iran. For example, the Swedish corporation Ericsson once collaborated with Iran's second-largest mobile operator MTN-Irancell to develop 5G network, but later was forced to leave Iran due to the US pressures (Khaasteh 2020). Some Chinese firms have been doing business with Iran despite the sanctions, including ZTE and Huawei. Both ZTE and Huawei are telecommunications equipment companies. Huawei is a leading producer in the global market and has been promoting its 5G network around the world. It made steady progress in Iran after competitors like Ericsson left (Khaasteh 2020). While the US government has long been accusing Huawei of spying the foreign countries for the Chinese government with no evidence, they started with ZTE first. In 2017, ZTE pleaded guilty to exporting US technology to Iran and North Korea and was fined 1.2 billion USD (US Department of Justice 2017). In 2018, the US government announced that ZTE did not do enough to discipline its employees who were involved in the violation of the sanctions and banned US companies from providing exports to ZTE for seven years (US Department of Commerce 2018a). This paralyzed ZTE's business as it relied on the core technology from the US. Later the ban was lifted after ZTE paid another 1.4 billion USD and replaced the entire board of directors and senior leadership (US Department of Commerce 2018b).

The US started to deal with Huawei a few months after reaching an agreement with ZTE in 2018. In December 2018, by the request of the US, the Canadian government arrested Huawei's top executive Meng Wanzhou, daughter of its founder and CEO Ren Zhengfei. Meng and Huawei were accused to have violated the US sanctions on Iran. The arrest based on the alleged company's violation of sanctions was a bold move. As Jeffrey Sachs, a leading American economist commented, the United States rarely arrests senior businesspeople for alleged crimes committed by their companies, and "to start this practice with a leading Chinese businessperson—rather than the dozens of culpable US CEOs and CFOs—is a stunning provocation to the Chinese government, business community and public" (Sachs 2018). The US government later put Huawei among others on the so-called Entity List, which prevents Huawei from accessing items produced domestically and abroad from US technology and software (US Department of Commerce 2020). This has caused major disruptions in Huawei's production, as like ZTE, Huawei is reliant on US chips and technology (Pham 2020).

With the leading role of US technology in the global economy and the long arm of the US jurisdiction, the case of Huawei perfectly showcased the imperialist power of the US. The US's sanctions and arrests directed against these Chinese firms is reinforcing the brutal sanctions on Iran. More importantly, it is a blunt threat to all the countries that the US is quite resourceful and determined in implementing severe punishment to those who dare to challenge US interests and its sanctions.

The last category of sanctions is linked to the alleged violation of human rights, particularly in the Xinjiang Uyghur Autonomous Region (XUAR). Since 2019, the Trump administration has imposed a series of harsh sanctions on Chinese organizations and enterprises in the name of concerning human rights violations and abuses targeting Uyghur and other ethnic minorities in Xinjiang. In October 2019, the US Department of Commerce took the lead to add 28 Chinese organizations to its Entity List, including twenty government organizations in XUAR and eight high-technology companies throughout China. These entities were accused to be "implicated in the implementation of China's campaign of repression, mass arbitrary detention, and high-technology surveillance" (US Department of Commerce 2019). In May 2020, the US announced its intention to penalize 33 Chinese entities for helping the Chinese government spy on the Uyghur population (Shepardson and Freifeld 2020). In early July 2020, the US issued the Xinjiang Supply Chain Business Advisory in warning companies of legal, economic, and reputational risks of doing business with Chinese firms involved in human rights abuses (US Department of State, Department of the Treasury, Department of Commerce and Department of Homeland Security 2020), and then announced to sanction one Chinese government entity and four government officials, including Chen Quanguo, the Communist Party Secretary of XUAR in connection with human rights abuses against ethnic minorities in Xinjiang (US Department of the Treasury 2020). On December 2, 2020, the US officially ban cotton and cotton products imports from the Xinjiang Production and Construction Corps (XPCC) (Lawder and Patton 2020).

The US attacks on the violations of human rights in Xinjiang can be specifically identified as two major issues: Uyghurs 'genocide' and coercive or forced labor in Xinjiang. In June 2020, a report written by Adrian Zenz and published by Jamestown Foundation claimed that, according to China's official statistics, Xinjiang's natural population growth rate has sharply declined from 2015 to 2018, since the Chinese government has implemented a large-scale campaign of compulsory sterilization towards Uyghur women and other Muslim minorities and promoted the policy of 'Han colonialism' in Xinjiang (Zenz 2020a). The rumors of forced Uyghur labor in Xinjiang mainly originated in a report from Cave *et al.* (2020) entitled "Uyghurs for Sale" published by the Australian Strategic Policy Institute (ASPI) in March 2020. In the report the Chinese government was accused of facilitating a mass coercive labor transfer of Uyghurs to factories. In mid-2020, new rumors have begun to spread that the Xinjiang government has forced Uyghurs, especially the graduates of vocational education and training centers, to engage in onerous cotton-picking work in XPCC's cotton fields. Most US sanctions towards the XPCC and its officials and the ban on cotton/cotton products from Xinjiang, particularly after July 2020, have been imposed under the banner of opposing and prohibiting the acts of forced labor.

The reports backing up these sanctions afford no factual support for the claim that Xinjiang has carried out the policies of 'genocide' or 'Han Colonialism'. Since 1978, the population growth rate of ethnic minorities, especially Uyghurs, has been higher than that of Xinjiang's Han population. From 2010 to 2018, the Uyghur population rose from 10.17 million to 12.71 million, while the Han population in Xinjiang merely increased to 9.01 million from 8.82 million (Li 2021). Also, Xinjiang revised its population and family planning regulations in 2017, granting the same and equal policy to all ethnic groups: urban couples can have two children, rural couples can have three (Xinjiang Uygur Autonomous Region Health Commission 2019). Rumors of 'forced Uyghur labor' are also inconsistent with the history and current situation of the cotton industry in Xinjiang. Around 2000, Xinjiang has become China's largest cotton-producing region. Yet, Xinjiang's cotton cultivation at that time was incompatible with the operational requirement of cotton harvest machines, and a large amount of manpower was urgently demanding during the cotton harvest period. Hundreds of thousands of migrants, thereupon, have seasonally moved from central and eastern provinces to Xinjiang's cotton fields. It should also be noted that the occurrence of Uyghur cotton pickers, as labor migrants in Xinjiang's cotton fields, is not a newly emerging phenomenon. Some news reports suggest that, around 2003, or even earlier, many Uyghur farmers from Hotan or Kashgar have embarked on their migrant journey of working as seasonal cotton pickers in Aksu (Xu *et al.* 2005). Their motives for seasonal migration varied little from that of Han seasonal cotton pickers from inner provinces, unrelated to forced labor but largely derived from the desire for increasing cash income to maintain or improve livelihood that has been greatly affected by commodification of subsistence during the process of China's capitalist agrarian changes after 1978. Since the number and scale of Uyghur cotton pickers was much smaller than those who migrated from inner provinces, they did not receive widespread media coverage and attention. However, it is undeniable that the group of Uyghur cotton pickers has been a key and long-standing labor force for manual cotton harvesting.

Since 2010, the labor demand for manual cotton pickers, who have been rapidly replaced by machines, has dramatically decreased in northern Xinjiang. However, mainly restricted by the dilemmas of land fragmentation and existing cotton varieties' inadaptation in machinery harvesting (Deng and Ning 2020), southern Xinjiang, though accounting for nearly 70 percent of the total cotton-producing area in Xinjiang, has yet to fully implement machinery cotton harvesting—the percentage in south Xinjiang was merely 34.7 percent in 2019 (Department of Finance of Xinjiang Uygur Autonomous Region 2020). Thus, the labor demand still exists in southern Xinjiang. As we previously mentioned, enrolling Uyghur cotton pickers has been commonly seen in cotton fields of south Xinjiang. Based on one of the authors' (Fangfei Lin) field observations in 2013, both XPCC's companies and private cotton planters in Aksu had widely recruited Uyghur migrants through private relations or Uyghur labor agents. Cotton planters there prefer hiring Uyghur migrants, merely because they can reduce the cost of travel expenses that are paid for Uyghur migrants, though the salary of Uyghur migrants is basically the same as that of Han migrants. In this sense, hiring Uyghur migrants in Xinjiang's cotton fields definitely is a market-driven employment, unrelated to "forced labor".

These facts debunk the accusation appearing in Zenz (2020b) that the Chinese government has deliberately impeded the development of machine-based cotton harvesting in order to compel the Uyghurs to conduct heavy cotton-picking work. The varying degree of mechanization among Xinjiang's cotton production probably is closely related to the unbalanced developmental status of agrarian capitalization in Xinjiang—this exact problem is worth discussing further yet will not be thoroughly analyzed in this article. In short, the labor demand of Uyghur seasonal cotton pickers in south Xinjiang is largely decided by its relatively low degree of agricultural capitalization, not due to the 'special treatment' towards labor migrants of a certain ethnic minority.

The US has not provided an adequate factual basis for its allegations of forced labor or compulsory birth control towards the Uyghurs in Xinjiang. So, what is the motivation for the United States launch a range of sanctions against China over Xinjiang? An analysis from the perspective of political economy requires us to examine which group's interests will be harmed and which group will ultimately benefit through those issued sanctions. Sautman argues that the case of Tibet, in which the narratives of China practicing 'genocide' and 'Han colonialism' in Tibet have been circulated and uncritically accepted by the media and politicians in the West, reflects political mobilization dominated by the West, "where charges go unchallenged due to confusion over what is genocide, the sacralized popularity of the Dalai Lama, a constructed image of Tibetan victimhood, anti-Communism, and anti-Chinese racism" (Sautman 2006, 257). This logic also can apply to examinations of the US accusations against Xinjiang's human rights, that through constructing the Uyghur victimhood to "obtain a bottomless line of moral credit" (Todorov 2003), the US and some Uyghur political speculators might fulfill the unreasonable demands or achieve their political goal of discrediting China. US accusations about human rights violations in Xinjiang, as Prashad (2020) remarks, "are being made for political and commercial ends not on strictly human rights grounds".

3 Conclusion

Like other sanctions, the recent US sanctions on China are unlikely to help the people in either country. For example, the US ban on cotton in Xinjiang will have severely negative impacts on the livelihoods of Xinjiang cotton farmers, whose human rights seems to be totally neglected by the Trump administration while imposing the sanctions. Textile enterprises in Xinjiang, including those providing the Uyghurs with guaranteed and reasonably paid employment, also have confronted the threat of bankruptcy because of the US cotton ban. Based on one of the authors' short conservation with an official of the Xinjiang Cotton Textile Association in December 2020, he admitted that the US cotton ban will have a significant impact on Xinjiang's cotton textile industry, but for now, the losses have yet to be precisely estimated. Will the US government be responsible for these Uyghurs who may lose their jobs? The answer is most likely no. These sanctions do not help the US economy and create jobs for the US people either. Even if it does suppress certain industries or firms in China, US capital can easily outsource jobs elsewhere. And the Chinese and US economy are closely interconnected in the global economy. The US theoretically cannot delink from China without a fundamental change in the global political economy that probably means a major capitalist crisis. As Rennemo (2020) writes, given China's importance, the United States "risks harm to its sanctions tool, longstanding alliances, and ultimately its geopolitical position if its posture remains one dimensional and overly coercive."

How the US-China relations evolve in the next 10–20 years might be vital for the survival of world capitalism. In terms of its position in the world economy, China has not and is not competing with the US. But China has been able to maintain its rapid growth, relative political autonomy with a ruling communist party over the last few decades, which posed some uncertainty (rather than challenge) to the US-led imperialist order. The US could well tolerate such minor uncertainty when capitalism is going strong throughout much of the neoliberal era. But this all changes when the capitalist world started struggling with secular stagnation and deepening political crisis, particularly after the global financial crisis.

The US ruling class needs an "Other", an enemy, and this paranoia makes them desperate in identifying the potential threats to its rule. China serves as such a perfect scapegoat. The US thus wrongly interpret the deep problems of capitalism as some power struggles and competition with China, even though China has been a major supporting pillar of the existing capitalist world economy. The sanctions against China are destroying the neoliberal global economy, which will only make capitalism even more unstable everywhere.

References

Cave, Danielle, James Leibold, Kelsey Munro, and Nathan Ruser. (2020). "Uyghurs for Sale." *Australian Strategic Policy Institute*, 1 March. https://www.aspi.org.au/report/uyghurs-sale.

Chen, Xin-zhu J. (2006). "China and the US trade embargo, 1950–1972." *American Journal of Chinese Studies*: 169–186.

Chen, Yilin. (2020). "Trending in China: Chinese Students Barred From Using Common Computer Code As US Sanctions Bite." *Caixin*, 11 June. https://www.caixinglobal.com/2020-06-11/trending-in-china-chinese-students-barred-from-using-common-computer-code-as-us-sanctions-bite-101566010.html.

Chen, Ying, and Zhun Xu. (2017). "Informal employment and China's economic development." *The Chinese Economy* 50 (6): 425–433.

Cohen, Warren I. (2019). *America's response to China: a history of Sino-American relations*. Columbia University Press.

Deng, Yahui, and Shuo Ning. (2020). "Xinjiang jicaimian fazhan xianzhuang ji yixiewenti jiejue yu zhanwang" 新疆机采棉发展现状与一些问题解决与展望 [The Status Quo of the Development of Mechanical Cotton Picking in Xinjiang and the Solutions and Prospects of Some Problems]. *Mianhua kexue* 棉花科学 5: 26–29.

Department of Finance of Xinjiang Uygur Autonomous Region 新疆维吾尔族自治区财政厅. (2020). "Xinjiang weiwuer zizhiqu mianhua shengchan xianzhuang touru fenxi" 新疆维吾尔自治区棉花生产现状投入分析 [Analysis on the Input of Cotton Production in Xinjiang Uygur Autonomous Region], 19 October. http://czt.xinjiang.gov.cn/czt/xwlb/202010/8deb5ef5eb1f4a26b237d57c59605300.shtml.

Ferguson, Niall, and Xiang Xu. (2018). "Making Chimerica great again." *International Finance* 21 (3): 239–252.

Khaasteh, Reza. (2020). "How US Sanctions Drove Iran Into Huawei's Arms." *The Diplomat*, 22 October. https://thediplomat.com/2020/10/how-us-sanctions-drove-iran-into-huaweis-arms.

Lawder, David, and Dominique Patton. (2020). "U.S. Bans Cotton Imports from China Producer XPCC Citing Xinjiang 'Slave Labor.'" *Reuters*, 3 December. https://www.reuters.com/article/usa-trade-china-xinjiang-idUSKBN25Z2BK.

Li, Minqi. (2020). "China: Imperialism or Semi-Periphery?" Working paper, Department of Economics, University of Utah.

Li, Xiaoxia. (2021). "Xinjiang diqu renkou biandong qingkuang fenxi baogao" 新疆地区人口变动情况分析报告 [Analytic Report on Population Changes in Xinjiang]. *China Daily*, 7 January. https://cn.chinadaily.com.cn/a/202101/07/WS5ff6a127a3101e7ce973991e.html.

Lieberthal, Kenneth G. (2011). "The American Pivot to Asia." *Brookings Institute*, 21 December. https://www.brookings.edu/articles/the-american-pivot-to-asia.

Ma, Hong, Zhi Wang, and Kunfu Zhu. (2015). "Domestic content in China's exports and its distribution by firm ownership." *Journal of Comparative Economics* 43 (1): 3–18.

Mann, Jim. (1991). "Many 1989 U.S. Sanctions on China Eased or Ended." *The Los Angeles Times*, 30 June.

Meijer, Hugo. (2015). "Balancing conflicting security interests: US defense exports to China in the last decade of the cold war." *Journal of Cold War Studies* 17 (1): 4–40.

Pham, Sherisse. (2020). "New Sanctions Deal 'Lethal Blow' to Huawei: China Decries US Bullying." *CNN*, 18 August. https://edition.cnn.com/2020/08/17/tech/huawei-us-sanctions-hnk-intl/index.html.

Pompeo, Michael. (2020). "Communist China and the Free World's Future." *US Department of State*, 23 July. https://www.state.gov/communist-china-and-the-free-worlds-future.

Prashad, Vijay. (2021). "Trade and Tensions Between the U.S. and China." *Monthly Review Online*, 3 August.

Rennemo, Andrew. (2020). "With China Sanctions, America Pushes the Limits of Its Financial Power." *The Diplomat*, 19 June. https://thediplomat.com/2020/06/with-china-sanctions-america-pushes-the-limits-of-its-financial-power.

Sachs, Jeffrey. (2018). "The U.S., not China, is the real threat to international rule of law." *The Globe and Mail*, 12 December. https://www.theglobeandmail.com/opinion/article-the-us-not-china-is-the-real-threat-to-international-rule-of-law.

Sautman, Barry. (2006). "Colonialism, Genocide, and Tibet." *Asian Ethnicity* 3: 243–265.

Schlesinger, Jacob M., and Erin Ailworth. (2018). "U.S. Imposes New Tariffs, Ramping Up 'America First' Trade Policy." *The Wall Street Journal*, 22 January. https://www.wsj.com/articles/u-s-imposes-trade-tariffs-signaling-tougher-line-on-china-1516658821.

Scott, Robert E., and Zane Mokhiber. (2020). "Growing China trade deficit cost 3.7 million American jobs between 2001 and 2018." *Economic Policy Institute*. https://www.epi.org/publication/growing-china-trade-deficits-costs-us-jobs.

Shepardson, David, and Karen Freifeld. (2020). "Dozens of Chinese Companies Added to U.S. Blacklist in Latest Beijing Rebuke." *Reuters*, 23 May. https://www.reuters.com/article/us-usa-china-blacklist/dozens-of-chinese-companies-added-to-u-s-blacklist-in-latest-beijing-rebuke-idUSKBN22Y2QR.

Tao, Wenzhao. (1997). Jinyu yu fan jinyu: wushi niandai zhongmei guanxi zhong de yichang yanzhong douzheng [sanctions and anti-sanctions: a serious struggle in Sino-US relations in the 1950s]. *Zhongguo shehui kexue* 3: 179–195.

Todorov, Tzvetan. (2003). "The Lunchbox and the Bomb." *Project Syndicate*, 2 August.

United Nations Conference onTrade and Development. (2020). "World Investment Report 2020." United Nations.

US Department of Commerce. (2018a). "Secretary Ross Announces Activation of ZTE Denial Order in Response to Repeated False Statements to the U.S. Government," 16 April. https://www.commerce.gov/news/press-releases/2018/04/secretary-ross -announces-activation-zte-denial-order-response-repeated.

US Department of Commerce. (2018b). "Commerce Department Lifts Ban After ZTE Deposits Final Tranche of $1.4 Billion Penalty," 13 July. https://www.commerce.gov/ news/press-releases/2018/07/commerce-department-lifts-ban-after-zte-deposits -final-tranche-14.

US Department of Commerce. (2019). "U.S. Department of Commerce Adds 28 Chinese Organizations to its Entity List," 7 October. https://www.commerce.gov/news/ press-releases/2019/10/us-department-commerce-adds-28-chinese-organizations -its-entity-list.

US Department of Commerce. (2020). "Commerce Department Further Restricts Huawei Access to U.S. Technology and Adds Another 38 Affiliates to the Entity List," 17 August. https://www.commerce.gov/news/press-releases/2020/08/commerce -department-further-restricts-huawei-access-us-technology-and.

US Department of Defense. (2019). "DOD Awards $48.9 Million to Universities for Major Research Equipment," 20 November. https://www.defense.gov/Newsroom/ Releases/Release/Article/2021937/dod-awards-489-million-to-universities-for -major-research-equipment/.

US Department of Justice. (2017). "ZTE Corporation Agrees to Plead Guilty and Pay Over $430.4 Million for Violating U.S. Sanctions by Sending U.S.-Origin Items to Iran," 7 March. https://www.justice.gov/opa/pr/zte-corporation-agrees-plead-guilty-and -pay-over-4304-million-violating-us-sanctions-sending#:~:text=ZTE%20Corporat ion%20has%20agreed%20to,making%20a%20material%20false%20statement.

US Department of State, Department of the Treasury, Department of Commerce and Department of Homeland Security. (2020). "Risks and Considerations for Businesses with Supply Chain Exposure to Entities Engaged in Forced Labor and other Human Rights Abuses in Xinjiang," 1 July. https://www.bis.doc.gov/index.php/documents/ pdfs/2569-xinjiang-supply-chain-business-advisory-final-for-508/file.

US Department of the Treasury. (2020). "Treasury Sanctions Chinese Entity and Officials Pursuant to Global Magnitsky Human Rights Accountability Act," 9 July. https://home.treasury.gov/news/press-releases/sm1055.

Xinjiang Uygur Autonomous Region Health Commission 新疆维吾尔自治区卫生 健康委员会. (2019). "Xinjiang Uygur Autonomous Region Population and Family Planning Regulations" 新疆维吾尔自治区人口与计划生育条例, 9 May. http://wjw .xinjiang.gov.cn/hfpc/zcwj1/201905/ab39b45654db43879a1ce8782d117624.shtml.

Xu, Junfeng, Zhanjun He, and Chunhui Zhao. (2005). "Baiwan Shihuagong 'jian'zou Xinjiang shiliuyi yuan" 百万拾花工'拣'走新疆16亿元 [Millions of cotton pickers take away 1.6 billion *yuan* from Xinjiang]. *Xinhua News*, 26 November.

Zenz, Adrian. (2020a). "Sterilizations, IUDs, and Mandatory Birth Control: The CCP's Campaign to Suppress Uyghur Birthrates in Xinjiang." *Jamestown Foundation*, 21 July. https://jamestown.org/wp-content/uploads/2020/06/Zenz-Internment-Sterilizations-and-IUDs-UPDATED-July-21-Rev2.pdf?x67063.

Zenz, Adrian. (2020b). "Coercive Labor in Xinjiang: Labor Transfer and the Mobilization of Ethnic Minorities to Pick Cotton." *Center for Global Policy*, 14 December. https://cgpolicy.org/wp-content/uploads/2020/12/20201214-PB-China-Zenz-1-3.pdf.

PART 3

Resistance to Economic Sanctions and Economic Sanctions as Resistance

∵

CHAPTER 19

Blowback to US Sanctions Policy

Renate Bridenthal

The hardships imposed by the US and UN, which continue and even increase, have been well documented. President George W. Bush approved over 1,800 sanctions, President Barack Obama over 2,000 and President Trump over 3,700 sanctions. All these were imposed on foreign governments, central banks, and individuals. As is well-known, sanctions rarely achieve their goals of changing the regimes or even the practices of their targets. However, less well-known is the widening circle of unintended consequences. These include encouragement of illicit trade and smuggling, the alienation of US allies whose commercial and financial relationships are interrupted, and challenges to the dollar, the hegemonic currency of trade and thus of sanctions enforcement. Some countries are trading with each other in their local currencies, others are hoarding gold as a hedge, and alternative digital currencies are being created. Just as the pound sterling was slowly replaced as the dominant currency of reserves and trade by a rising dollar in the 1920s when the British Empire began its demise, so also the dollar, as the face of United States global dominance, may be facing a similar fate. While the impact of sanctions is not the only reason for this, it does contribute and so can be seen as *blowback* to US policy of trying to impose its will on other countries. Sanctions turn out to be both a symptom and a cause of the US failed pursuit to retain global dominance.

In his evocatively titled *Busted Sanctions: Explaining Why Economic Sanctions Fail*, Bryan R. Early shows how third parties, including US allies, have continuously undercut US sanctions (Early 2015). Among other unintended consequences, allies may profit from sanctions against a target country by stepping into the US place of trade thereby reducing sanctions' efficacy. Thus, the European Union developed a trading mechanism INSTEX (Instrument in Support of Trade Exchanges), to bypass US sanctions and to continue trade with Iran. Early in 2020, INSTEX enabled the export of medical goods from Europe to the pandemic-hit country (Euractiv 2020). Even American firms can benefit by dealing with a sanctioned state through a third party, especially if that third party is protected from retaliation by a military alliance with the US This may seem counter-intuitive except that such firms realize that they are less likely to be punished for working through an ally which their government needs politically. This has been the case of American trade with Iran through the middleman port of Dubai (Early 2015).

Until the recent crackdown by its capital, Abu Dhabi, the United Arab Emirates (UAE), used the port city of Dubai, across the Persian Gulf from Iran, as an *entrepot* for trade with Iran. Mysteriously, US imports markedly rose to Dubai as did Dubai's re-exports to Iran, along with smuggling. The goods even included spare parts for Iran's American-made military hardware and computers, as well as ordinary items. Oil was a major export from Iran, and France, Germany, Italy, and China traded for oil with Iran via Dubai as the city grew in global importance. Dubai also set up free trade zones in which goods could be repackaged, reprocessed, or modified, providing cover for firms evading sanctions. Some items could be repackaged as supposedly illicit Chinese copies and then returned to their licit versions in Iran in a process of reverse-counterfeiting. In these zones, major high-tech multinationals set up shop, including Microsoft, Oracle, Hewlett-Packard, Cisco Systems, IBM, Compaq, Sun Microsystems, and Intel as well as those in India, Iran, and China. All this went on under the nose of the US Navy, which made 300 port calls in Dubai in 1995 and over 500 port calls ten years later. The reason for this contradiction lies in the strategic importance of the UAE to the US, thanks to a defense accord of 1994, which inadvertently gave it political cover for sanctions-busting. Thus, even Halliburton in 2005 won contracts to develop oil and gas fields in Iran (*ibid.*).

In the last decade and a half, international concern that Iran may have violated the Nuclear Non-proliferation Treaty forced the UAE government to crack down on sanctions-busting. The US, backed by UN sanctions, pressured foreign banks to stop dealing with sanctioned Iranian entities. Some of these measures have been effective, especially with respect to proliferations-sensitive strategic transactions. However, Dubai continues to act as a way station for trade with Iran, China being a major customer for its oil (Foundation for the Defense of Democracies 2020).

A new round of sanctions imposed by President Trump in October 2016 on Iranian banks revealed ongoing US frustration with the failure of previous ones to bring Iran to heel. However, this has not been without political cost. These moves have distanced American allies some of whom have fiercely objected on the grounds of protecting their investments as well as allowing payment for humanitarian and medical aid for Iran's population, badly hit by the corona virus pandemic (Verma 2020). Sanctioned states are also drawing together. In 2020, Iran sent Venezuela five tankers of oil to blend with Venezuela's tar-like crude and to help it prop up its production after US sanctions cut off access to equipment and buyers for its oil (Kassia and Zerpa 2020). Iran and China are also coming closer together. They have negotiated closer economic relations in telecommunications, banking, infrastructure, and oil. In 2020 they agreed on a $400 billion trade and military partnership. An adversarial united front against US sanctions is a boomerang in the making.

The failure of sanctions to affect Russian policies is even more dramatic in that Russia may actually have benefited in some way from them. Russia's political economy has a strong state sector that overcame sanctions through import substitution, development of alternative financial structures, and a closer relationship with China. As US imports of food declined, the Russian agricultural sector grew, such that "Russian farmers are in the best shape they've ever been" and Russia, by 2016, had become top wheat exporter in the world (Twigg 2019). Despite sanctions imposed by the European Union, European states like Germany have not diminished their trade with Russia much. Despite US political objections, Germany continues also to import Russian oil in significant quantities (Trading Economics 2021). And although Germany temporarily halted completion of the Nordstrom Pipeline which will carry oil from Russia to Germany and into other European countries via the Baltic Sea, citing sanctions on Russia for allegedly poisoning its opposition leader Alexei Navalny, pipe laying has resumed (*Financial Times* 2021).

Sanctions on Russia and China have also brought the two together in various ways. China has increased its oil imports by more than half and 25% of Russia's trade with China is now in their national currencies (RT Business 2021). They are cooperating in developing the Arctic Ocean which, due to global warming, has opened a northern sea route for East-West trade. Russia has the longest shoreline on it, giving it access to offshore reserves of oil and to onshore port construction by China's Silk Road Fund and the China Development Bank. The launch of the Polar Silk Road signals significant cooperative infrastructure development. In sum, it has been said that Russia would have more to lose by the removal of sanctions than by new ones (Jian 2020).

Using new financial structures that allow Russia to trade in local currencies rather than the dollar, it also has resumed relations with other sanctioned countries such as Cuba and Venezuela. It is building power plants and restoring railroads in Cuba, as well as cooperating on joint projects in the areas of energy, metallurgy, information technology, telecommunications, space research, combating climate change, biotechnology, public health, and the pharmaceutical industry (Simes 2020). Russia sent a first batch of its COVID-19 vaccine to Venezuela; it also helped China purchase oil indirectly from Venezuela by using a Switzerland-based unit of Rosneft, Russia's state-owned oil company, which made it appear as if the oil's origin was Malaysia (Cohen and Parraga 2020).

But besides the failure of many of the US sanctions, there has been grow-ing backlash, of which perhaps the most significant political effect has been Russia's growing diplomatic closeness to China. This is not just a failure of sanctioning both, but a major setback to the US geopolitically in its growing rivalry with China. Russia's military combined with China's economic might would make a powerful challenge to US global hegemony. Besides their strong commercial ties, the two countries have shared military technologies. Should tensions worsen with the US, a military alliance is not out of the question (Isachenkov 2020). China has similarly affirmed its strategic commitment to Russia (Zhang 2020).

The new great power rivalry, seen by some as a new cold war, puts US allies in a difficult middle position, entwined, as most are, with both. Thus, European business and political communities resent US sanctions for shutting them out of the Chinese market. The European financial establishment has effectively ignored the sanctions by agreeing to a landmark mutual investment deal with China. Europe may no longer see the US as its indispensable patron, but rather view itself as a swing vote in the rivalry (Lau 2020). Meanwhile, in Asia, a Quadrilateral Security Dialogue (QUAD) connects Japan, India, and Australia with the US as a potential NATO to "contain" China. And yet the China-domi-nated Regional Economic Partnership Agreement (RCEP), is a trade bloc that includes these countries as well as fifteen others, including South Korea, the Philippines, Singapore, and Vietnam (Petri and Plummer 2020).

Finally, China has begun to use sanctions policy on its own behalf. Thus, after the Dalai Lama's visit to Mongolia in 2017, China raised tariffs on its min-ing products. When Norway's Nobel Peace Prize was awarded to a Chinese dis-sident, its exports to China were curtailed. And when South Korea agreed to host the US THAAD missile defense system, China urged its travel industry to discourage tourism to South Korea. Most recently, China has even taken on the US directly by issuing new rules against global companies that comply with US sanctions against its industries. This positions such companies between the competing countries and may result in them putting pressure on the US gov-ernment to relax some sanctions. This is not exactly tit-for-tat, as US sanctions are greater in number and heft, but does indicate a kind of diplomatic blow-back in the further chilling of relations (Aggarwal and Reddie 2020).

The most egregious use of sanctions policy has been that against the International Criminal Court. Aggrieved by the court's opening investiga-tions into alleged US assisted war crimes in twelve countries, including Sudan, Myanmar, and Afghanistan, President Trump issued an executive order on June 11, 2020, that authorized asset freezes and family entry bans against ICC officials and makes it more difficult to enforce international criminal law prohibiting genocide, war crimes, and crimes against humanity. This move has additionally alienated major US allies and founding members of the ICC, like France, Germany, and other important members of the European Union, as well as the United Nations (Lorber 2020).

Financially, the most looming blowback to US sanctions policy is the growing set of challenges to dollar hegemony. Since the major currency of international trade is the US dollar, official sanctions are carried out in the denial of dollar-denoted trade with targeted countries. Besides evading use of the dollar by resorting to trade in local currencies, there has been an attempt to strengthen other currencies, notably Russia's ruble and China's renminbi, by increasing their gold backing. Until the global pandemic of 2020, there was a kind of gold rush by major central banks, not only of Russia and China, but also of Germany and Turkey, to hoard the precious metal (Siegner 2019; Siefong 2019). The purpose was to prepare for a possible future of a multi-currency monetary system. Even the governor of the Bank of England, Mark Carney, opined that the dollar-centric system wouldn't hold (*The Economist* 2020). And Europe has entered the fray, reacting to US sanctions on its trade with Iran. A European Commission paper proposes a greater role for the Euro to avoid excessive reliance on the dollar for financial stability (Brundsen 2021).

But perhaps the most novel challenge to the dollar is the emergence of digital currency. For a time, Bitcoin was seen in that role, but it soon became an object of speculation, which made it useless as a medium of exchange. Other similar attempts like Etherium and Libra faced similar obstacles. However, block chain technology has been used by states like North Korea, which has evaded US sanctions using cryptocurrencies (Sanger 2020). In January 2019, 70 percent of central banks planned work on sovereign digital currencies. As potential reserve assets, central bank digital currencies can threaten the globally hegemonic position of the US dollar, undermining its capacity to enforce sanctions, among other things. Digital currencies can avoid cross-border payments through the Society for Worldwide Interbank Financial Telecommunication (SWIFT) network, which has been a powerful tool for US sanctions (Aggarwal and Marple 2020). Surprisingly, even Christine LaGarde, former head of the International Monetary Fund and currently President of the European Central Bank has espoused digital currencies of central banks. Her view: "We are at a historic turning point. A new wind is blowing, that of digitalization. ... Should central banks issue a new digital form of money? I believe we should consider the possibility to issue digital currency. There may be a role for the state to supply money to the digital economy" (Lagarde 2018). While JP Morgan expressed concern to this apparent threat to US dollar dominance, eight other major banks including

HSBC and Citi collaboratively launched a blockchain in trade finance in Singapore and similar initiatives have been launched in Oman and Europe. In tune with the times, the Biden administration's head of the Security and Exchange Commission, Gary Gensler, has taught blockchain and cryptocurrency at MIT, which means he is prepared to regulate upcoming financial technologies.

China has gone the furthest in this direction, creating a digital gold-backed Renminbi which it plans to launch as a real rival to the US dollar in international trade. One emerging market at a time, China is building a global payments infrastructure that could become linked through an international currency (Ferguson 2019; Tooze 2021). This response to US weaponization of its dollar dominance could lead to the world dividing into a US dollar zone, a Eurozone, and a digitalized Renminbi-zone that likely embraces a large part of the total global emerging markets. At the very least, the Renminbi could network the countries in China's Belt and Road Initiative (Coisdealbha 2021). In addition, China has developed a challenge to the dollar-based SWIFT system of payments, through its Cross-Border Interbank Payment System (CIPS) which, as of April 2020, has participants in 95 countries (Hillman 2020).

China's digital challenge to the dollar actually originated in the 2008 financial crisis. The overprinting of dollars led to high inflation outside the US and so China, as the country with the world's largest foreign-exchange reserves, lost relative purchasing power. This led the People's Bank of China to consider that the Renminbi should go international. China-US relations have worsened considerably since then, leading China gradually to reduce its holdings of US treasury bonds by $22 billion down to $1.06 trillion in 2020. It regards the printing of dollars as a form of soft default and the possible confiscation of China's foreign-exchange reserves as a hard default, both exacerbating the call for "dedollarization" in China. However, there is internal debate in China about the pros and cons of an internationalized Renminbi. A fully international currency has drawbacks as well as privileges, including vulnerability to market volatility. Therefore, China continues to assert state power over private financial power (Dongsheng 2020).

To preempt possible US financial sanctions should relations worsen, China has approved BlackRock, Citigroup, and JPMorgan Chase to expand their businesses in its financial markets. However, the US has blacklisted some corporations from investing in Chinese companies that could possibly contribute to China's military. These include the oil company CNOOC and smartphone manufacturer Xiaomi which has surpassed Apple by units sold (*Financial Times* 2020). Some tension emerged within the US government about further blacklisting Alibaba, Tencent and Baidu, some of China's largest technology companies. The Pentagon and State Department wished to do so on grounds of national security, but the Treasury Department prevented it over concern for potential US investor losses. As an expert has observed: "Economic imperatives are certainly overriding political concerns" (quoted in *Financial Times* 2020).

A major form of US-China rivalry is technology, in which supremacy is likely to have major political effects. Therefore, as for finance, the US has imposed sanctions on Chinese technology company Huawei on the grounds that it can deliver sensitive information to the Chinese government and its military. In fact, Huawei is a private company owned by about half of its employees who are entitled to stock options (Towson 2020). Nevertheless, Meng Wanzhou, the daughter of its founder and its chief financial officer, was arrested in December 2018 in Vancouver, Canada, on allegations that she had violated US sanctions against Iran, another sanctioned country, by selling it telecom equipment through its subsidiary Skycom. Having fought extradition to the US and imprisonment, she has since been released home to China. Huawei's success in offering 5G, the fifth generation of cellular networks that can connect many devices in real time, has brought it a higher rating than Apple's latest iPhone 12. However, Huawei's reliance on chips made by the Taiwan Semiconductor Manufacturing Company have made it vulnerable to US sanctions on chipmakers supplying it and so its stocks are dwindling. As a result of this political compulsion replacing market forces, Apple gained nearly ⅓ in sales. But other American firms that produce chips are negatively affected in a specific kind of blowback. Chip sales to China "drive semiconductor research and innovation here in the [United States], which is critical to America's economic strength and national security," according to John Neuffer, president and CEO of Semiconductor Industry Association, a trade group representing American chipmakers. Qualcomm, Micron and others that had supplied Huawei have experienced collateral damage (Pham 2020). And Huawei is planning a chip plant of its own in Shanghai so as ultimately to rely exclusively on Chinese made machinery rather than on a global supply chain. But the technology is complex and will take several years. Meanwhile, the damage to Huawei is real as many countries have succumbed to US pressure to sanction it. Of course, Australia, Canada, New Zealand, United Kingdom, the four countries that join the US in the Five-Eyes intelligence network, have accepted the sanctions. And while the German government allows Huawei technology in 5G mobile networks, the European Union recommends that its members resist it. Huawei is challenging the measures in courts across Europe (Boston and Woo 2020).

Conclusion

The ultimate effect of US sanctions policy trends toward isolating the United States or, at least toward dividing the world into two competing power blocs with middling powers negotiating their positions between them. US alliances are fraying at the edges, the dollar is more seriously challenged than ever, and American technology is fighting to stay in the lead. Should the global technology networks really divide into competing power blocks, the effect on research and development for pandemics and climate change would be immensely damaging to all parties. Thus, the ultimate blowback is not only the probable failure of the US to retain world dominance, but a cascading set of events that could lead to global disaster.

References

Aggarwal, Vinod, and Tim Marple. (2020). "Digital Currency Wars? US-China Competition and Economic Statecraft." *Global Asia* 15 (4).

Aggarwal, Vinod, and Andrew W. Reddie. (2020). "New Economic Statecraft: Industrial Policy in an Era of Strategic Competition." *Issues & Studies: A Social Science Quarterly on China, Taiwan, and East Asian Affairs* 56 (2).

Boston, William, and Stuart Woo. (2020). "Huawei Gets Conditional Green Light in Germany as Government Approves Security Bill." *The Wall Street Journal*, 16 December.

Brundsen, Jim. (2021). "EU Sets Out Plan to Curb Dollar Reliance in Post-Trump Era." *Financial Times*, 16 January.

Cohen, Luc, and Marianna Parraga. (2020). "Special Report: How China got Shipments of Venezuelan Oil Despite U.S. sanctions." *Reuters*, 12 June.

Coisdealbha, Dónal. (2021). "China's Digital Currency." *Socialist Voice*, 6 January.

Dongsheng, Di. (2020). "The Economics and Politics of China's Currency Internationalization." *Global Asia*, June.

Early, Bryan. (2015). *Busted Sanctions: Explaining Why Economic Sanctions Fail*. Stanford University Press.

The Economist. (2020). "America's aggressive use of sanctions endangers the dollar's reign." *The Economist*, 18 January.

Euractiv.com. (2020). "EU's INSTEX mechanism facilitates first transaction with pandemic-hit Iran." https://www.euractiv.com/section/global-europe/news/eus-instex-mechanism-facilitates-first-transaction-with-pandemic-hit-iran/.

Ferguson, Niall. (2019). "America's Power is on a Financial Knife Edge." www.niallferguson.com, 15 September.

The Financial Times. (2021). "Gazprom to Restart Nord Stream 2 Construction." *The Financial Times*, 10 January.

Foundation for the Defense of Demcoracies. (2020). "UAE continues to serve as hub for Iranian sanctions evasion."

Hillman, Jonathan. (2020). "China and Russia: Economic Unequals." *Center for Strategic and International Studies*, 15 July.

Isachenkov, Vladimir. (2020). "Putin: Russia-China Military Alliance Can't Be Ruled Out." *Associated Press News*, 22 October.

Jian, Yang. (2020). "China's Economic Initiatives in the Arctic." *Global Asia*, December.

Kassia, Lucia, and Fabiola Zerpa. (2020). "Venezuela and Iran defy U.S. sanctions with new tanker delivery." *World Oil*, 14 September.

Lagarde, Christine. (2018). "Winds of Change: The Case for New Digital Currency." *The International Monetary Fund Reports*, 13 November.

Lau, Stuart. (2020). "All EU Member States Back China Investment Deal, Sources Say." *South China Morning Post*, 28 December.

Lorber, Eric. (2020). "Trump's Sanctions on International Court May Do Little Beyond Alienating Allies." *The New York Times*, 26 February.

Petri, Peter, and Michael Plummer. (2020). "RCEP: A new trade agreement that will shape global economics and politics." *The Brookings Institute*, 16 November.

Pham, Sherisse. (2020). "New Sanctions Deal 'Lethal Blow' to Huawei. China Decries U.S. Bully." *CNN Business*, 18 August.

RT Business. (2021). "De-dollarization in overdrive: Russia & China boost settlements in national currencies to 25%." *Russia Today*, 3 January.

Sanger, David. (2020). "North Korea's Internet Use Surges, Thwarting Sanctions and Fueling Theft." *The New York Times*, 11 June.

Siefong, Myra. (2019). "Why Russian and Chinese central banks will keep buying gold." *Market Watch*, 13 September.

Signer, Eric. (2019). "New U.S. Sanctions Spark Blowback Against Federal Reserve Note Dollar System." *FX Street: The Foreign Exchange Market*, 3 June.

Simes, Dimitri. (2020). "Putin is resurrecting Russia's Cold War Pact with Cuba." *The Spectator*, 6 February.

Tooze, Adam. (2021). "The Rise and Fall and Rise (and Fall) of the U.S. Financial Empire." *Foreign Policy*, 15 January.

Towson, Jeffrey. (2020). "Huawei's Employee Stock Ownership Plan (ESOP) is "Meritocracy Plus Partnership" at Scale in China Tech." www.jefftowson.com, 20 October.

Trading Economics. (2021). "Germany Imports from Russia." 2021 Data. Twigg, Judy. (2019). "Russia Is Winning the Sanctions Game." *The National Interest*, 14 March.Verma, Premash. (2020). "U.S. Issues Additional Sanctions Against Iranian Banks." *The New York Times*, 9 October.

Zhang, Judy. (2020). "China-Russia ties won't be broken, declare Xi and Putin in signal to Biden." *South China Morning Post*, 29 December.

CHAPTER 20

International Solidarity against US Counterinsurgency

Sarah Raymundo

This chapter documents lessons learned from building international solidarity from a Global South perspective; advancing a vision of former colonized peoples who continue to "share a common struggle for national sovereignty, self-determination, dignity, and equality for future generations (Philippines-Bolivarian Venezuela Friendship Association nd)." These lessons of solidarity point to (1) some of the limitations of the current framing of US counterinsurgency in relation to anti-imperialist struggles and; (2) the processes from which this reframing obtains; (3) and the actual conduct of insurgent states like the Bolivarian Republic in building socialism through establishing, maintaining, and sustaining communes. These experiences are advanced through budling international solidarity through historical struggles as well as the current conduct of national liberation movements that hold fast to an anti-imperialist politics.

1   Shared History

The Philippine-Bolivarian Friendship Association (PBVFA) was established in 2008 to cultivate friendship between the Filipino anti-imperialists and people's movement and the Bolivarian Republic of Venezuela. The solidarity association is facilitated by a common colonial history shared among the peoples of the Philippines and Venezuela. Both countries were subjects of Spanish colonialism and each also share a history of anti-colonial movements that were forged and secured in the Battle of Carabobo of 1821 in Venezuela and the Katipunan Revolution of 1896 in the Philippines.

The Battle of Carabobo was the crucial victory which brought independence to Venezuela and became the basis for Simon Bolivar to establish the foundation of Gran Colombia in South America and Central America, encompassing present-day Venezuela, Colombia, Panama, Ecuador, Peru, and Bolivia. The Katipunan Revolution of the Philippines was the first national revolution in Asia to defeat a Western colonizing power, thus inspiring the development of revolutionary anti-colonial consciousness throughout Asia. The Katipunan Revolution played a crucial role in rousing Chinese revolutionary anti-imperialists in the late-nineteenth and early-twentieth centuries, under the leadership of Sun Yan Sen (Simbulan 2009).

The historical and geographic bearing of these seminal anti-colonial struggles set the crucial stage for the consolidation anti-imperialist movements in both countries and the proliferation of global anti-imperialist movements in the nineteenth and twentieth centuries .

The anti-imperialist struggles in both Venezuela and the Philippines directed against American domination largely shape each nation's conduct in the unfolding anti-imperialist movements in each country and have significant reverberations worldwide, both in the past and in the present.

The Bolivarian process that initiated the process of seizing power from the US and its local comprador leaders is punctuated with the movements in the 1980s and 1990s, culminating in the election of Hugo Chávez as president of Venezuela in 1998. In the following decades, Chávez and the Bolivarian revolutionary movement has undertaken a significant role in forging a global anti-imperialist movement dedicated to defending political independence, establishing economic sovereignty, and protecting cultural norms of Global South nations made subservient to the neoliberal capitalist policies of the US and its western allies. Meanwhile, the anti-imperialist movements in the Philippines continue to battle the Philippine State, a bureaucratic machine mired by imperialist and comprador interests, with an alternative national agenda committed to empowering the people, thus cementing class and national oppression.

The friendship association between the peoples of the Philippines and Venezuela is a peaceful engagement with the unfinished revolutions of Bolivar and Bonifacio. Both insurgencies and popular struggles had and continue to oppose restrictive measures, containment strategies and direct atrocities committed by US-supported counterinsurgencies. However, keen observers and participants in international solidarity work may regard the framing of insurgency and counter-insurgency purely as military actions in a war as quite limiting in comprehending the emergent dynamics of these polar opposites. In the so-called post-colonial world, the battle cry of anti-colonial and socialist revolutions are no longer just the demands of underground armed movements but also of the urban and rural working classes.

The anti-colonial vision of the armed revolutionaries of the Katipunan is celebrated by its inheritors as the source of Philippine independence. Yet full decolonization has yet to take place in a country whose independence was commandeered by the US shortly after it was won by the armed uprising. Virulent colonial legacies of the Spanish and US variants remain, dividing nationalist dispositions into reactionary and revolutionary modes of envisioning and striving for a truly independent nation. But in times of chauvinistic and fascist appropriation of power, various sectors rise up and assert their concrete vision of independence linked to establishing genuine nationhood and being/becoming Filipino.

The US-Marcos dictatorship spawned a peasant-worker alliance that concretized independence through the people's demand for an end to land grabs with a call for land to the tillers and for jobs with a concrete proposal for national industrialization. The 1986 People Power Revolution was none other than the continuation of the anti-colonial revolution waged by Bonifacio's Katipunan. However, it can only continue the unfinished revolution by taking into account the inter class hierarchies created by colonialism and subsequently cemented by a comprador bourgeoisie subordinate to the modern imperialist system. The peasant-worker alliance constitutes the masses of people battling a comprador state that links the Philippines to an imperialist system led and facilitated by the US.

In 1808, Simon Bolivar led the South American campaign for independence from Spanish rule. The struggle for sovereignty was not a revolutionary sweep but a series of political interventions unifying military and parliamentary forms of consolidation. From the successful Battle of Boyaca (1819), Bolivar established a National Congress within three years, and defeated the huge Spanish military expeditionary force culminating in the Battle of Carabobo in 1821, which paved the way for complete independence. The legacy and actual machinery of colonialism and imperialism created local oligarchs that eventually divided and installed puppet regimes.

The Bolivarian Revolution led by Hugo Chávez transformed the political and economic character of the Venezuelan society from an oil proxy of the US to a nation defined by the Bolivarian process (Global Research 2019). The emphasis on this revolution being a Bolivarian process follows the vision of Chávez. It is a transition of a suffering and oppressed nation towards a country that generates insurrection and rebellion for the rights of the majority (Chávez Frías 2015). The process continues, enjoying the support of the majority of Venezuelans through an electoral process. This US sanctions on Venezuela are the fatal attacks of an imperialist state against a former neo-colony. Sanctions in this context function as a tool to punish a whole nation that dares to enjoy the right to self-determination.

2   Counterinsurgency as Liberal Democratic Tool

The fatal sanctions imposed by the US on Venezuela exceed counterinsurgency campaigns conducted by the US, the earliest of which was for the Philippine-American War. Distinguishing between combatants and civilians is a basic principle that warrants the use of force in an armed conflict situation. But US sanctions on Venezuela target the whole population. The same can be said of the "war on terror" or the counterinsurgency program of the Philippine State against the national liberation struggle that carries out a program for land redistribution and national industrialization.

Counterinsurgency—a comprehensive campaign of violent suppression against forces regarded as threats to US hegemony—was brutally imposed by the US upon its hijack of the 1896 Revolution and the ruthless destruction of all forms of anti-imperialist defiance. It must be stressed that in the Philippines, this led to the genocide of whole populations. While Filipinos and Venezuelans share a common struggle against US imperialism for which the US unleashes its counterinsurgent program, the mechanisms of this punitive imperialist scheme differ. US counterinsurgency has inflicted severe violence and attacks on the Bolivarian Republic of Venezuela for the purpose of government destabilization and regime change. Meanwhile, the White House assigns to the Philippine state the responsibility of implementing counterinsurgency as the core of the latter's internal security policy. In actual practice, counterinsurgency is not just a military undertaking but legitimized state actions that blast all forms of resistance.

For the PBVFA, recognizing the impacts of US counterinsurgency on struggling peoples means opposing its flagrant violation of national sovereignty and the people's economic and political rights. It is crucial to recognize US imperialism in all its forms: wars of aggression, sanctions as economic war and massive disinformation. The anti-imperialist stance of the Bolivarian Republic of Venezuela and the movement for national liberation toward socialism in the Philippines are Global South movements. But their actions are not contained by geography.

The US nuclear war planning inside the Pentagon has been exposed and opposed not only by Global South anti-war activists and anti-imperialists but by people from within the elite departments of US intelligence and US government. Figures like Philip Agee founder of Covert Action, formerly of the CIA, Attorney General and US Senator Ramsey Clark, Paul Johnstone a former senior Pentagon analyst are only a few of those who initially worked for US world hegemony and subsequently saw through its destruction and dedicated their efforts at exposing and opposing Washington's reckless aggression toward its opponents.

This may sound contrary to the dictum of liberal democracy, which the US seeks to uphold and "export" around the world. However, US democracy was and remains to be the staunchest enemy of anti-colonial revolutions of colonized peoples in the Third World. The history of colonial wars in the name of democracy, manifest destiny and civilization stretches back to the colonial wars waged against peoples in the 19th and 20th centuries. The US war on Spain that eventually led to the neo-colonization of Cuba, Puerto Rico and the Philippines by US imperialism. France, Germany and Great Britain were all imperialist nations that claimed democracy as the guiding principle of governance. Such a claim did not stop the first World War to explode in Europe.

This US-style bourgeois liberal democracy is a democracy for the economic and political elite, thus democracy for capitalism and imperialism. The history of anti-colonial socialist struggles shows that the US export of liberal democracy and its implementation at home are an imperialist state's mechanisms for counterinsurgency. They come in different forms from covert and overt military actions to free market and free elections.

In the history of modern states, any alliance between an imperialist power like the US and a client state like the Philippines can only be a partnership that uses terrorism as pretext to carry out endless wars of aggression against the people. The hostilities experienced by the critics of the tyrannical Duterte regime—incarceration of dissenters, killings of activists and the fake drug war—are instances of state terrorism perpetuated to maintain US global hegemony. It is with this experience that the national liberation movement in the Philippines understands that the US imperialist war on Venezuela will not stop with the new faces in the White House.

The Biden Administration has taken steps to tighten the blockade against Venezuela through the Bolivar Act (US Congress 2021). The US war aggressors even dare to mislead by actually using the acronym BOLIVAR as a title for a US bipartisan law. United against Venezuela, democrat and republicans intend to intensify prohibitions on contracting with persons that have business operations with the Maduro regime.

At the height of the global pandemic last year, US President Trump chose to violate international law and bombard the world with another wave of massive disinformation by charging President Nicolás Maduro and other senior officials with narco-terrorism (US Department of Justice 2020). Meanwhile, President Maduro's prompt and decisive leadership announced a series of measures to protect Venezuelans from the dire effects of the coronavirus crisis. Among them are a six-month suspension of commercial and residential rent, including capital and loan interest payments. A special government bonus and wages for small and midsize companies is reserved for workers to be paid for by the Venezuelan government until September 2020; and a comprehensive agricultural plan that will subsidize food boxes for 7 million families, among others (Dobson 2020).

3   Solidarity vs. Sanctions

US economic sanctions on Venezuela, which for years have undermined full social and economic development in the country, will not stop the Bolivarian Republic from serving its people in these most difficult economic times. This is in stark contrast to Trump's failure to contain the exponential spread of the virus and provide an immediate healthcare response. This capacity on the part of the Bolivarian Republic is also expressed by journalist and university professor, Jessica Dos Santos: "There isn't one single nation that has come out better after a US or NATO intervention. In addition to that, intervention presupposes that we don't have the capacity to solve our own problems, and I firmly believe that we can (Marquina and Gilbert 2020)."

The Bolivarian state's capacity to serve the people is also articulated by Venezuelan student organizer Nick Nieto in an interview with the author:

> Where in the world can you find a country gripped by neoliberal policies—and it is worse here in Venezuela as it is besieged by sanctions and all forms of war against a nation fighting for its own sovereignty—in which its government struggles hard to provide free education, food stamps, assist the poorest of the poor to have a roof under their heads? Where in this neoliberal world is that kind of service to the people by a government attacked by U.S. Imperialism, day in and day out, can you find a country like that?
>
> Author Interview, January 12, 2019

In the same visit to Venezuela as an international guest representing the PBVFA on the occasion of Maduro's inauguration as President of the Bolivarian Republic, this writer would also meet with women commune organizers and fishermen. In this meeting, the organizers stress the leading role of women in the communes, which is not part of tradition but a fairly new practice that they need to cultivate. A community leader herself, Molly explains that

...women have always been responsible for holding their families together, especially in times of severe crisis. Our new role as commune leaders takes in this practice but now with reinforced by political power bestowed upon us by the Bolivarian process. It has not been easy but actual and formal power can make a difference in combating patriarchy.

Author Interview, January 2019

Molly brought with her one of her comrades who is a fisherman. He claims to have grown up in a household in which his own mother had to do so much with so little power.

So women as commune leaders is not a familiar experience for me. We did not have communes, we only had poor living conditions and we were never sure where to get food or how to survive the next day. I will not say that I have fully understood our present situation but at least I can say that we are united on a plan and respecting women and their capacities is not against that plan.

Author Interview, January 13, 2019

A meeting between the representatives from the Ministry of Popular Power for Communes Social Protection and international guests took place earlier that day. In her presentation, Minister Blanca Eekhout provides an interesting take on people's communes (Eekhout 2019).

They are to be approached as a process that is part of the larger historic Bolivarian process. One of the first proposals of Comandante Chávez in February 1998 is to "once again found the Republic and call for a constitutional process. For the first time ever, famers workers, Indigenous Peoples, Afro-descendants, social movements and other sectors were called upon to found the new Republic. From that moment, the transformation of Venezuelan society began."

EEKHOUT 2019

The 1999 Constitutional Convention commenced the process of constructing popular laws. Eekhout recounts that one of the key laws pertained to the building of a communal economy. These are laws for planning that gave people the necessary tools for deciding what is to be done. And one of the important tasks is for "socialism to have a concrete basis within the communes." She adds that as early as the war for independence, "Bolivar understood that in order to form a republic, you have break inequality and you have to bring about the real unity of the people." The basic Bolivarian principle emerged once Bolivar broke the laws of slavery.

> From here forward, he said, there is only one class of people, we are all citizens. Bolivar ordered that we unite and build a republic. But it is impossible to build a republic if 80% of the population are not recognized as citizens. This is the idea that gave life to the communes, although it is yet to become a reality.
>
> EEKHOUT 2019

This re-founding, which involved the participation of popular classes is what, in the words of the Minister,

> gave rise to the attempted overthrow of the Chávez government in 2002. Once the people started making laws that destroy the monopoly of land, recognize the rights of Indigenous Peoples, establish territories that belong to the people who work here, and recuperate income from the petroleum industry, the bases for imperialism and elite rule is also destroyed. But this overthrow was thwarted by alternative means of communication installed in local communities as well as by the union between the civilian population and the military.
>
> EEKHOUT 2019

Those elements were already present barely four years into the Bolivarian process. The same process also involved the implantation of social missions. Eekhout shares that the education mission effectively battled illiteracy and turned Venezuela as the second most important country in Latin America with people involved in university-level education. She adds that the social missions also included health programs called "within the barrio program" with full support of the Cuban government. The housing mission, she adds,

> has constructed 2.5 million houses (as of January 2019). This is all happening in the middle of U.S. imperialist economic sabotage, boycott, terrorism. We are still in the process of building the communes in spite of all US imperialist attacks and despite the death of President Chávez, which is the biggest challenge that the communes ever faced.
>
> EEKHOUT 2019

Currently, the Bolivarian Republic has organized "3,060 communes based on community councils of various communities."

The economic task of helping people commits the Bolivarian government to build the communes based on the communes of farmers, workers, and other sectors like the youth and women-led committees for gender equality. The militia is also part of the communes that people form themselves to defend this country (Eekhout 2019).

The communes are also sites of production involving businesses serving social concerns, which Chávez and Maduro enabled. There are banks in the commune facilitating various needs and local business. This continued development of this incipient process has been affected by US sanctions. But the idea of producing things within the commune persists, even on a small scale.

> For example, the Bolivarian government pays for the uniforms of students and has, for the opening of the school year in September, sourced four million of those school uniforms from textile plants located in several communes. This is especially important because in December last year [1998], we systematically studied and planned for an economy that will effectively respond to problems relating to inflation. In addition to what the communes are producing, the government has also purchased textile products abroad and distributed these to communes. This initial step is crucial in building a platform for communes to produce things independently in order to protect the people from economic terrorism inherent in the capitalist market. It is important to sustain our economy that is not solely based on petroleum industry, as one of the great attacks on our country was through the manipulation of the price of petroleum, which eventually led to the sabotage of the industry
>
> EEKHOUT 2019

Following the great victory of October 2, 2012, Comandante Chávez called for a radical change in " the direction of the ship." Eeckout refers to the new direction that Chávez had begun to navigate when he made a public appeal for the communes. Chávez warned that "if we do not construct a great union of the communes then we are going to lose the battle. Communes or nothing!" But when Chávez died, Eeckout intimates, the "empire got the chance to ruin the whole thing." For this reason, Maduro emphasized that for the "Bolivarian process to continue, the formation of the communes is imperative" (Eekhout 2019).

In other words, state consolidation in the Bolivarian Republic of Venezuela rests on the consolidation of the communes. It is for this reason that communes must be founded on a social base made up of a consolidated organizations of farmers and workers. Asked how local business figures in the communes, Eeckout explains that social business belongs to a collective as they have been inserted in the communes.

> The process of building and uniting workers collectives are crucial so that even capitalist businesses can be controlled by communes in any given area. There are still collectivities of workers forming traditional unions. But our idea is to build workers organizations that are socialist in orientation.
>
> EEKHOUT 2019

As for the impact of the US economic war against Venezuela on workers communes, Eeckout cites an interesting realization on the part of the workers and even private industries.

> They have realized that much of what they produce ends up going out of the country, which makes the very process of production vulnerable to economic sabotage. Therefore, it is crucial to fight not only for the control over production but also to be able to determine where these products go.
>
> EEKHOUT 2019

This realization compels them to unite with the efforts of the commune where they are located. In this instance, even owners of local factories and workers are united against global commodity chains imposed by an imperialist system. But only from the perspective of building the communes. And doing so, as Chávez had envisioned, means uniting all the communes. Eeckout summons one of the greatest insights of Chávez: "A commune isolated does not have any value at all. We have to bring them all together so we can organize and accomplish what is to be done."

What is striking about meeting fishermen, farmers, workers, women leaders from the communes, representatives of Indigenous Peoples, professors, and students is their confidence. It is not the confidence that one may observe in the ways of the rich. It is a confidence that exudes pride derived from daily struggles, which they share with such joyful enthusiasm. They patiently explain their experiences in their own language. They invite you to their communes. They want you to see things they have built with their own hands but always in the context of a collective undertaking.

They teach you the most important lesson about the US sanctions regime: imperialism and sovereign nation-states in the Global South cannot co-exist without a persistent anti-imperialist struggle and socialist planning.

The PBVFA was also part of the Foro de Sao Paulo held in Caracas, Venezuela (July 25–28, 2019). More than a thousand anti-imperialist activists from Left parties and social movements from all continents affirmed that three-fourths of all sovereign nations in the world also recognize Nicolas Maduro as the democratically elected and re-elected president, and hence, is the legitimate head of state. Thousands of Venezuelans assembled in Caracas to witness the Foro's presentation of the event's delegates. One of them is former National Democratic Front of the Philippines Chief Consultant Luis Jalandoni who addressed the Venezuelans in Spanish as most Filipinos of his generation were required to acquire Spanish proficiency in school. The huge crowd cheered Luis upon his mention of the dual state power in the Philippines that allows for the communist New People's Army to wage an armed revolution and build organs of political power similar to the communes in Venezuela.

Shortly after this event, the US inflicted a total economic blockade issued through an Executive Order dated August 9, 2019. It is nothing new but it is a breach of the rules of international law and order. That Trump-inflicted blockade shows how US imperialism seriously seeks to not only illegally freeze the assets of the Bolivarian Republic. The same blockade warranted the seizure of a ship in Panama Canal containing 25 thousand tons of soy-made products meant for delivery to Venezuela. Clearly, the blockade arbitrarily justifies the US action to block the Venezuelan people's right to food.

In the eyes of US imperialism, a nation like Venezuela that refuses US imperialist privatization of its key economic sectors, control over its oil and finance should be isolated, and its people punished severely. The US also uses brazen tactics such as commanding other nations to be complicit to its criminality by imposing the same sanctions on Venezuela. This is a breach of international peace, sovereignty and equity among nations, and justice.

This illegal and fatal blockade is another attempt at imposing US imperialist version of "national security" on the world. US imperialism has used "national security" as an excuse for its endless wars. This US-controlled fascist tyranny insults the people of Venezuela by painting their duly elected president as a "usurper of power" while drumming up support for treasonous puppets like Juan Guaido who already was rejected by the Venezuelan people.

The Filipino people's transnational struggle against US imperialist-state sponsored tyranny and for national sovereignty can only be fruitful and victorious when waged with anti-imperialist citizens and freedom fighters worldwide.

To capture the concrete reality of our time, we need to proceed with concrete analysis of concrete conditions. US imperialism is the principal enemy. Our current situation is different from the conditions that partly shaped two imperialist wars. The First and Second World Wars involved opposing military coalitions. In our time, NATO had and continues to unleash horrific wars as the sole military coalition controlled by US Imperialism.

Meanwhile, The Bolivarian Republic of Venezuela is clearly at the forefront of the global anti-imperialist movement. The Bolivarian process is not only a successful struggle for national freedom waged by Venezuelans but also a continuing struggle for socialism in the 21st century. Amidst the drain of value from the Global South to the Global North and the policy of permanent war by the US Counterinsurgency State, the Bolivarian process is a struggle of every nation colonized anew by US imperialism. For the oppressed yet fighting workers and farmers of the Philippines, Venezuela is a moment in a long series of victories and challenges endured by the proletariat—our Russia in 1917, our China in 1949 our Cuba in 1959, our Vietnam in 1975 our Iran in 1979, our Venezuela from Hugo Chávez to the current Bolivarian Revolution.

References

Chávez Frías, Hugo. (2015). *The Blue Book*. 18. Caracas: Obsequio Gobierno Bolivariano.

Dobson, Paul. (2020). "Venezuela announces 6-month rent suspension, guarantees workers' wages, bans lay-offs." *People's World*, 24 March.

Eekhout, Blanca. (2019). "Minister's Statements," 13 January.

Global Research. (2019). "Venezuela: From Oil Proxy to the Bolivarian Movement and Sabotage. Abysmal Poverty under US Proxy Rule: An Interview with Michel Chussodovsky." *Global Research Center*, Venezuela, 10 February.

Preamble. (n.d.). The Philippines-Bolivarian Venezuela Friendship Association.

Marquina, Cira Pascual, and Chris Gilbert. (2020). *Venezuela The Present As Struggle Voices from the Bolivarian Revolution*, 200. New York: Monthly Review Press.

Simbulan, Roland G. (2009). *Forging a Nationalist Foreign Policy: Essays on U.S. Military Presence and the Challenges to Philippine Foreign Policy*, 162–163. Quezon City: Ibon Center.

US Congress. (n.d.). Bolivar Act. n.d.

US Department of Justice. (2020). "Nicolás Maduro Moros and 14 Current and Former Venezuelan Officials Charged with Narco-Terrorism, Corruption, Drug Trafficking and Other Criminal Charges," 26 March.

CHAPTER 21

Boycott and Sanctions as Tactics in the South African Anti-Apartheid Movement

Jesse Bucher and Stuart Davis

While previous case studies in this collection have focused on the process through which the United States and allies leverage sanctions against states perceived as competitors, threats, or both, the case study of the anti-apartheid boycott and sanctions movement in South Africa offers an alternative vision of how sanctions might be employed within the context of grassroots social movement mobilization. Beginning as a grassroots movement against the South African government's system for institutionalizing a pattern of racial hierarchy along what former prime minister and chief designer of apartheid Hendrik Vorwoerd labeled "differences that are permanent and not man-made" (cited in Nesbitt 2004, 18), the anti-apartheid movement offers a oft-cited case study on the role of sanctions in bringing about successful regime change. However, a closer analysis illustrates that while the anti-apartheid sanctions campaign presents a case of a sanctions regime that works on behalf of marginalized groups, its success is linked to the movement's shift from a liberationist framework fighting against an oppressive ethno-state and the ideological and economic order that supported it to a diplomatic framework focused on gaining political legitimacy through encouraging corporate social responsibility (csr) as a way of translating struggle into terms legible to global corporations and capitalist states.

This chapter will not revisit debates over the degree to which the boycott and sanctions campaigns initiated by the anc did or did not cause the end of the apartheid government in South Africa in 1994. Contemporaneous and retrospective analyses from Martin (1992), Horne (1996), Mangaliso (1997), Thomson (2012), and many others have addressed this question at length. Instead, we will analyze how the movement's trajectory can help us map the political and economic conditions under which a grassroots sanctions movement can succeed in gaining transnational support. Our central through-line is a comparative analysis of two historical moments within the anti-apartheid movement that weaponized economic activity as a tool for fighting the apartheid state: *the moment of boycott* and *the moment of sanctions*. We acknowledge that each of these moments represents a complex period with contradictory impulses. In the comparison between these two moments, we track the shift from the liberationist tactical employment of boycott as part of a guerrilla struggle against the apartheid system to a discourse on political representation yoked to a model of consumer citizenship where corporations are empowered as partners of states in the fight against racial injustice.

In the 1950s, the African National Congress increasingly recognized that three modalities existed for tackling the problem of apartheid: boycott, sanction, and war. For each of these modalities, relative time scale was important. Boycott, for example, was supposed to be a short-term response to apartheid since these actions originally lasted for short periods of time to call attention to the conditions brought on by apartheid policies. Sanctions, which needed the support of external states, was a longer-term prospect. However, war was, in the ANC's formulation, supposed to be the modality/act that would eventually defeat the problem of apartheid. These three modalities were supposed to carry out the resistance to apartheid. In practice, and especially within the political realm, however, boycott gained immense political currency. While boycott started as an *economic* response, it grew over time in political importance. Many people joined the boycott movement, and used it, and over time, the ANC struggled to contain its use as it began to fold in larger corporations and other nation-states, including several that were previously supportive of the apartheid government (namely, the US). What began as a domestic boycott drive eventually grew in importance beyond the initial expectation that ANC leader Nelson Mandela and others had in the 1950s to incorporate larger international calls for desisting in trade with companies linked to the apartheid regime that would ultimately result in the Comprehensive Anti-Apartheid Act of 1986 in the United States.

Initially, the ANC saw boycott and sanctions as part of the same constellation. However, a central assertion of this chapter is that the boycott movement lost its revolutionary potential when incorporated with CSR initiatives (most apparent in the 1977 Sullivan Principles) and state-to-state sanctions. In other words, boycott articulated as CSR and sanctions corrupted a political movement that leveraged boycott to challenge apartheid. The Sullivan Principles and other Reagan-era policies support this corruption thesis as they attempt to create a type of compromise between the impulse to boycott/sanction and the impulse to maintain CSR. Ultimately, we are pointing out that there are incongruent relationships between these modalities. The prevailing academic literature makes it seem like there is a seamless relationship between boycott, sanctions, and the end of apartheid. We argue that this was not the case in practice.

1   Introduction to Boycott as Strategy

In his 1958 article, "Our Struggle Needs Many Tactics," Nelson Mandela wrote about the strategic use of boycotts in the evolving struggle against apartheid:

> Perhaps it is precisely because of its effectiveness and the wide extent to which various organizations employ it in their struggles to win their demands that some people regard the boycott as a matter of principle which must be invariably applied at all times and in all circumstances irrespective of the prevailing objective conditions. This is a serious mistake for the boycott is in no way a matter of principle but a tactical weapon whose application should, like all other political weapons of struggle, be related to the concrete conditions prevailing at the given time.
>
> MANDELA 1958, 14–15

Mandela's writings on boycott captured a transitional phase in the ANC's struggle against apartheid. For much of the 1950s, Mandela had helped lead non-violent forms of resistance to apartheid including the 1952 Defiance Campaign that expanded coordinated acts and intentional defiance of apartheid laws and policies. The broad goal of the Defiance Campaign was to broaden opposition to apartheid by creating a united front of a range of racially distinct political formations. As Mandela would later write: "[t]he government saw the campaign as a threat to its security and its policy of apartheid. They regarded civil disobedience not as a form of protest but as a crime and were perturbed by the growing partnership between Africans and Indian. Apartheid was designed to divide racial groups, and we showed that different groups could work together" (Mandela 2013, 133). While the campaign failed to halt the passage of apartheid legislation and, by Mandela's own assessment, went on for too long (Mandela 2013, 139), the membership of the ANC nevertheless soared in 1952, resulting in the ANC as the most prominent anti-apartheid organization in South Africa.

The relative successes (prompting mass opposition to apartheid) and limitations (eventual decline in support and effectiveness) of the Defiance Campaign likely informed Mandela's writings on the utility of boycott. The strategies embodied in these liberation movements—especially the deliberate use of boycotts—reveal some of the ways in which Mandela started to craft alternative political philosophies capable of challenging the dominance of apartheid. These philosophies of boycott are important for three reasons. First, they unpack a broader relationship between economic and political subjects in South Africa and elaborate how colonial and apartheid power prefigured an

emergent neo-liberal order. Second, the writings on boycott treat the act of boycott as a tactical action, a weapon, used to achieve specific goals in the larger
framework of a struggle for liberation and emancipation. Third, they create
a precedent for the sustained implementation of an international anti-apartheid sanctions campaign which grew exponentially following the banning of
major political organizations in 1960, and the African National Congress and
the Pan African Congress—an Africanist organization that split from the ANC
in 1959—went into exile and formed military wings (uMkhonto we Sizwe and
Poqo respectively).

In the late-1950s, boycott formed a provisional step in the broader move
towards the military struggle against apartheid. In this way, we can see how
Mandela's approach to boycott formed a link between previous anti-colonial
struggles around the world (in which boycotts were widely deployed), and a
wider insurgency against apartheid (which consolidated forms of neo-liber-
alism drawn out of an earlier colonial order). It is these renderings of boycott
and, later, sanction that merit further attention and explanation. Both boycott
and sanction campaigns respectively set out patterns of response that—while
not always capable of sustaining a shift in state control—pointed to ways
in which economic and political subjectivity have merged since WWII. As
awareness campaigns, they illuminate the merger of political and economic
responses while advancing potential strategies for change. It is even more troubling, therefore, that imperialist powers like the US and multinational corporations would later employ and commandeer these strategies in the name of
anti-apartheid struggle.

While economic inequity and class dynamics long framed South African
politics, the growth of the apartheid state formally secured a politics of political subjectivity sustained by permanent links between race, economic status,
and political access. Thus, one of the main political challenges that Mandela
and others faced in the 1950s was to find a way of avoid being folded into the
categories of belonging promulgated by the apartheid state. The most prominent response to this problem appeared in the Freedom Charter, adopted by
the Congress of the People in 1955, which endorsed the ideals of a "free and
democratic South Africa" (Mandela 2013, 174).

The effort to implement economic, political, and cultural boycotts and sanctions in response to the formation and expansion of the apartheid state generated
an unprecedented effort from the 1950s until the end of apartheid in the 1990s.
The long duration of this movement and the multiple state and non-state actors
who sustained it further capture the complex and often overlooked mixture
of factors that shaped Cold War-era transnational politics. While much scholarly attention has focused on the role of Western powers in the anti-apartheid

boycott and sanctions movement, it is worth recalling that other African political parties and states, as well as postcolonial Asian countries, were the first to
develop boycotts and sanctions against apartheid. The goal of this chapter is to
expand analysis of the boycott and sanction movement against apartheid to
address how the campaign originated from within anti-colonial movements that
anticipated a post-war neo-liberal order. These initial considerations of boycott
and, after the late-1950s, sanctions, recognize the increasingly merged roles of
consumer and citizen. It was because of conditions internal to the experience of
apartheid that these overlaps became so heightened.

To unpack these claims, we will closely examine some of Mandela's political writings from the late-1950s that detail the potential uses and impacts of
boycotts through a series of dedicated political statements. In its cold calcu-
lating logic, apartheid had removed the final vestiges of the types of liberal
colonial political institutions of trusteeship that Mandela and others had once
responded to as the hallmark of racism in the 1940s. Indeed, at the start of his
political career, Mandela vociferously reacted to the forms of colonial trusteeship that massively reduced political possibility for the vast majority of people
in South Africa. Yet, apartheid went even further by removing the vague promises of colonial trusteeship and replacing them with a plan for 'separate development' that intensified forms of racial and ethnic control of populations.
Prior to the formal state project of apartheid, and especially during the period
of economic growth fueled by WWII, there remained the slim possibility that
upward economic mobility among sections of the Black middle class would
slowly lead to political access. Indeed, much of the renewed energy that gave
rise of the ANC-YL in the 1940s extended from the belief that the pace of political access needed to be quickened. With the implementation of apartheid policies, these avenues of political change were rapidly eroded.

2   Background to ANC's Employment of Boycott

There is a contentious history of the meaning, tactic, strategy and efficacy of
boycotts and sanctions in the academic study of South Africa. Boycotts, in particular, have been around longer, in part because boycotts have been easier to
organize and generate by groups that lacked direct forms of political power.
Most of the early boycotts were an extension of anti-colonial movements
inside of South Africa. Amongst the first were those led by Afrikaners who
boycotted British businesses and Indian owned businesses at select moments
in the early twentieth century. Afrikaners, especially in the late 19th and early
20th centuries, engaged in anti-British (anti-colonial) projects. They did not

want to be folded into the broader British empire and placed great emphasis on establishing independent republics beyond the reach of the British imperial power. At the end of the 19th century, and in the aftermath of the 'mineral revolutions', it was increasingly impossible for the Afrikaner states to remain outside of British control. In this context, Afrikaner boycotts of British goods could be conceived of as a form of anti-colonial politics, but one that cast itself simultaneously as particular form nationalism with a deeply entrenched anti-liberal attitude. In this regard, they resisted the hegemony of British empire which included British goods and the Indian merchants who sold British goods. The other widespread use of boycott came in the 1940s through 1950s before and immediately after the implementation of apartheid rule. The ANC and later the PAC both used boycotts to launch campaigns of peaceful protest against apartheid laws that curtailed freedom of movement between town and country.

The 1940s in South Africa, especially the early 1940s brought with it new economic opportunities for Africans, especially in South Africa's bourgeoning urban centers. The economic opportunities occurred in a moment of political possibility when it seemed likely that colonial forms of liberalism would expand to draw in broader participation. Prior to the onset of apartheid, the rule governing race relations and political access in South Africa was a form of 'trusteeship': a reigning attitude that held that black South Africans needed a paternal state to control the country for them. Apartheid included both the expansion of the psychology of trusteeship ('you are not an adult') but also to cut off the kinds of opportunities made available under British liberal colonialism.

Against this backdrop, it is worth asking about the specific role of boycott that was called into play by a nascent political movement of opposition to apartheid. The boycott was not merely about showing an outpouring of popular power. Rather, they were more fundamentally about forging a political blockade that exceeded apartheid's instrumentalization of race and ethnicity in a program of population control. Apartheid's logic held that people belonged to distinct races and ethnic group (separate development), so a politics that could appeal to efficient economic activity (boycott) had immense importance.

Against this oppressive system and the ideological systems that justified it, Nelson Mandela developed his specific theorization of boycott by learning from his experiences with and knowledge of anti-colonial movements. In these settings, especially under the conditions of colonial trusteeship, it was possible to be an "economic adult" but a "political minor." In other words, there was a place for black subjects in the sphere of economic production as workers but not in politics as citizens. As a strategically deployed activity, boycott allowed for a targeted response to the economic and political institutions and practices that substantiated the state itself. For Mandela, the distinction between boycott and sanction was important because it captured some of the differences between the anti-colonial struggles, and the place of formerly colonized countries in the emerging international order of the Cold War.

Mandela is often thought of as a participant in boycotts and other non-violent struggles, and as an object of sanctions (the Free Mandela campaign). But he is less understood as a theorist of boycott. However, along with Walter Sisulu, Mandela wrote in the 1950s about boycott as a tactical weapon of political struggle. Mandela's consideration of the boycott as a tactical weapon places it within a broader history of anti-colonial political movements. However, as Mandela developed a political philosophy of boycott in the context of apartheid, he anticipated the further merging between political and economic subjectivity that would grow in the post-WWII world order.

3   Theorizing Boycott as a Tactic in the Struggle against Apartheid

In the 1950s Mandela reviewed the differences between boycott as an unbending principle and boycott as a purposeful tactic. He notes:

> In point of fact total and uncompromising opposition to racial discrimination in all its ramifications and refusal to co-operate with the Government in the implementation of its reactionary policies are matters of principle in regard to which there can be no compromise. In its struggle for the attainment of its demands the liberation movement avails itself of various political weapons one of which might (but not necessarily) be the boycott. It is, therefore, a serious error to regard the boycott as a weapon that must be employed at all times and in all conditions.
>
> MANDELA 1958, 16

In this way, Mandela perceived the conditions that made the struggle against apartheid different from other anti-colonial struggles. There was a real risk—when boycott became categorical rather than strategic—of giving in to the conditions of race war and losing the capacity to respond to the folding together of politics and economy.

As a strategic action, Mandela also illuminated the fact that, amidst neo-liberal conditions, the most economically and politically vulnerable people are the most exposed and vulnerable. Thus, when used strategically rather than constantly, boycott insulates them from their broader vulnerabilities. Mandela's definition is useful because in his evaluation, boycott becomes a unique and selective strategy rather than an inviolable principle. He opens up the possibility of considering the weapons that were available to a political movement that had to consider its own current political moment as well as the moment that came next—the creation/manifestations of a new state.

Both Mandela and Walter Sisulu emphasized the role of boycott as a strategy rather than a constant political policy or principle. They claimed, in the late-1950s, that boycott should be used at particular moments and under specific conditions as a step that preceded war. Boycott provided an economic and political strategy (it targeted products and industries as well as elections). Mandela and Sisulu wrote at a time when the Congress Movement, led by the ANC, attempted to broaden is political base and begin to imagine a new set of political, economic, and social relations that would follow apartheid. The Congress Movement's vision took form in the 1955 Freedom Charter.

To expand mass awareness about the objectives of the Freedom Charter, both Mandela and Sisulu realized that boycott could inculcate a robust response. As Sisulu put it: Boycotts "have raised the political consciousness of the people, brought about a greater solidarity and unity among the masses. In this way they have raised the peoples' organizations to a higher level, demonstrating the correctness of the action" (Sisulu 1957, 13). Sisulu described participation in existent institutions, advisory broads, governments, and all forms of collaboration as tactically important: "Once we differentiate between the principle and the tactic, in other words, in this case to know that the boycott is a tactic and the rejection of reactionary political institutions can include participation in them with a view to rendering important the system that gives rise to them" (ibid., 15). This shift further reflects the steady entrenchment of apartheid—in the 1950s Mandela still talked about parliamentary changes: "People who accept racial discrimination and who wish to co-operate [sic.] with the Government in in the oppression and exploitation of their own people on the one hand and participation in such elections not because of any desire to co-operate [sic.] with the Government but in order to exploit them in the interest of the liberation struggle on the other hand" (Mandela 1958, 16). Yet, this approach failed during the 1958 and 1961 elections in which the ethno-nationalist Afrikaner National Party expanded its seats, elections that bookended the 1960 referendum to form the South African Republic.

By 1960, the peaceful struggle against apartheid had run out of options. After peaceful protest at Sharpeville, and in tandem with the banning of ANC and PAC, and the later split from Great Britain to form a republic, the struggle against apartheid became an armed struggle. War itself was a weapon of political struggle. At the same time, boycott, sanction, and divestment emerged as a part of the international campaign against apartheid. Trade and other forms of exchange faced sanctions and divestment, academics, sports federations, and other cultural actors began to implement boycotts against South African participation, or of participating in events in South Africa at all. And later, in the 1970s and especially the 1980s, the schools boycott expanded inside of South Africa.

There was additional crossover between boycott and other modalities of protest, specifically strikes. As Mandela described in his statement, 'General Strike' in May 1961: "We are the people of this country. We produce the wealth of the gold mines, of the farms, and of industry. Non-collaboration is the weapon we must use to bring own the government. We have decided to use it fully and without reservation" (Mandela 1961). But and here is the important feature of boycott, the boycott or strike must be a targeted tactic rather than a universal policy because the goal is not to end politics but to create a new politics altogether. As a tactic, a weapon, boycott must produce something new even as it destroys something that already exists. In this regard, the specific connection between boycott and anti-colonial politics is particularly interesting because they both keep focus on future political formations.

Since boycott has important origins in anti-colonial struggles, especially in India and Ireland, it also connects to debates about the role of armed insurrection. In some parts of the African continent—especially in the settler colonies of Algeria and Kenya—military insurgencies arose against colonial states in the 1950s. When Mandela wrote about the tactical use of boycott, he realizes that war against the apartheid state was impending: "It is accepted and recognized that the people of South Africa will win their freedom as a result of the amount of pressure they will put up against the reactionary policies of the Government. Under a United Party Government, it will still be necessary to wage a full-scale war on racial discrimination" (Mandela 1958, 16). This expanded sense of the relationship between boycott and "full-scale war" is interesting because, on the one hand, it anticipates the formation of MK and the initiation of a sabotage campaign. It allowed, strategically, a politics of holding the moral high ground, and tried to limit political expectations amidst a longer buildup to inevitable warfare.

Mandela had studied anti-colonial war, especially during his visits to Algeria in 1961 (Hyslop 2014). As Mandela wrote in *Long Walk to Freedom*, his recognition of the need to utilize armed struggle stemmed from a long-running commitment to pragmatic tactics. While living underground in 1961, he read Karl von Clausewitz's *On War*, later writing that "Clausewitz's central thesis, that war was a continuation of diplomacy by other means, dovetailed with my own instincts" (Mandela 2013, 276). When preparing to initiate the military struggle, Mandela weighed four approaches, including sabotage, guerilla warfare, terrorism, and open revolution (Mandela 2013, 282). As he described, "[g]uerilla warfare was a possibility, but since the ANC had been reluctant to embrace violence at all, it made sense to start with the form of violence that inflicted the least harm against individuals: sabotage" (*ibid.*, 282). Importantly for Mandela, sabotage—with its deliberate and targeted use of tactical violence—smoothed the path to future reconciliation. As such, Mandela's application of sabotage overlapped with his earlier description of boycott. Like other leaders who emerged from anti-colonial struggles, Mandela was always mindful of the people of a future state that did not yet exist. Mandela had a desire to produce a reconciled, democratic state *after* apartheid and, as such, he saw the importance of less damaging actions (like boycott and sabotage) that could create political change without doing permanent damage to the country's population. Permanent, unending boycott would have unintended consequences for those who were carrying out the boycott. As a strategic action, Mandela's version of the boycott could preserve the life and existence of those who were part of the collective cause and that made the movement possible in the first place.

For Mandela, boycott is a kind of practical weapon. It is a weapon that destroys, in targeted ways, specific political institutions or political bodies. It does this because political systems, like economic ones, need to generate flow. Just like you can withhold money from an economic system (bus boycotts), you can also remove people from a political system to disrupt the very flow of politics. An aspect of boycott policies has been an appreciation that the anti-colonial struggle must attend to the creation of a politics that is yet to come. Writing in the 1950s, both Mandela and Sisulu addressed this question, and anticipated some of the claims that Frantz Fanon would later make when describing anti-colonial struggles later in the 1950s. Thought of as a tactical weapon, the boycott anticipates anti-colonial war. It is the step before armed struggle which both the ANC and PAC would adopt in 1960. Mandela and Sisulu were thinking about two layers of strategy—the domestic interior of South Africa, but also the large anti-colonial struggle. This is, for Mandela, also a subversive war. Boycott used strategically can preserve life or at least expose less life to suffering or bodily harm. Like guerilla attacks and the sabotage campaigns of the early 1960s, boycotts demonstrated that it was apartheid that resulted in a damaged life and a vulnerable psyche. A boycott that touched the surface lightly concentrated focus on apartheid itself.

4   The Shift from Boycott to Sanctions in the 'South African State
     in Exile': Solidarity within African States, the Global South, and
     Settler Colonial States

Unsurprisingly, the first countries to support sanctions against the apartheid government ruling South Africa were ones that had similar experiences with anti-colonial struggles. 'Sanction' as a term literally meaning to 'impose a penalty on' only came into use after 1956. The word stems from a verb related to the enactment of law—a verb that came into use at the end of the 1700s. Thus, the sense of imposing a penalty is connected to a world order that came into existence after the Second World War, and was framed around a neo-liberal biopolitics which allows people outside of one's own country to die or face death. This was also part of the logic of apartheid—the expanded political and economic order of colonialism to implement an apartheid system.

When the USA finally sanctioned apartheid South Africa, anti-colonial politics were tellingly often overlooked. This owes to the difference that has increasingly emerged between boycott/sanction as tactic in struggle and boycott/sanction as a form of corporate social responsibility. In this regard, the American sanctions movement, while well intentioned by some, was the sign of a shift towards a boycott/sanctions movement dominated by a neo-liberal economic order in which 'corporate social responsibility' became more important than genuine support for political freedom. In other words, a corporation could capture a sense of 'freedom' not just through free and unrestricted markets, but also through freedom from the sense that the corporation itself was complicit (or to use Sisulu's phrase, 'collaborating') with the apartheid state. This became linked to a notion of CSR defined as being able to demonstrate freedom from collaboration to free up the strength of one's marketable public image.

The shift from a perspective foregrounding the interrelatedness between apartheid and racial capitalism embedded in the initial boycott movement towards a CSR was accompanied by shifts in self-definition in anti-apartheid activists: as support for the apartheid government faded within the international community and its multilateral institutions (like the UN), the ANC's diplomatic profile was enhanced. Transnational anti-apartheid economic activism took the form of both formal sanctions either passed by multilateral organizations or adopted by individual states as well as consumer-led divestment campaigns (Marsh and Szanya 2000). Beginning with India's severance of trade with the apartheid regime at the first meeting of the United Nations in January 1946 (Hamilton 1946), formal sanctions developed gradually throughout the 1960s–1970s and included a UN arms trade ban in the early 1960s, an OPEC ban on petroleum trading in 1973 and (perhaps most famously) the

US Comprehensive Anti-Apartheid Act of 1986 (Klotz 1995; Levy 1999). These
sanctions complimented divestment tactics: the targeting of individual corporations or stakeholders by divestment activists was viewed as a tactical
counterpoint to the diplomatic work of lobbying legislators or states to support sanctions (Posnikoff 1997; Knight 2001). The most visible element of the
divestment and boycott initiative was the Sullivan Principles whose synthesis
of corporate and legislative outreach was perhaps most totally synthesized in
Mandela's 1993 tour of the United States (Nesbitt 2004, p. 169).

   The cumulative effect of the sanctions and divestment movement is hard to
gauge; it is difficult to distinguish the effects of its pressure from South Africa's
increasingly diminishing appeal as a borrower (Levy 1999) and the impact of
the thawing of the Cold War on strategic support for the Apartheid regime
(Martin 2013). Relatedly, the Sullivan Principles proved difficult to enforce
and even more difficult to measure in terms of impact. Still, Martin (2013) has
argued that the economic situation of the apartheid government was damaged
by the ability of ANC as state-in-exile to push a contraction in trading partners
for both imports and exports. Though its impact proves difficult to gauge, the
divestment and sanctions element of the movement has been celebrated as a
unique contribution: a group of anti-racist grassroots activists facing extreme
violence from a recalcitrant, backwards-looking and oppressive state were
able to create a post-ideological coalition that eventually toppled the racist
aggressor.

5   Lessons from the Anti-Apartheid Boycott and Sanctions Movement

In its highly visible tactical role in the overthrow of apartheid rule, the ANC's
boycott/sanctions campaign offers a powerful example of how a grassroots
sanctions initiative working on behalf of marginalized populations can lead
to tangible political change. However, the ANC's success in courting international support was accompanied by a perspectival shift away from an earlier
radical critique of the foundation of apartheid in racial capitalism. This was
a victory of a power bloc in the ANC which viewed the party as a multi-class
political formation. This shift served a tactical function as it gave the movement a symbolic malleability that allowed it to depict its aims and politics
as compatible with a wider array of organizations, politicians, and movements. As Clifford Bob (2002, 2005) has argued at length, the effectiveness
of an anti-state or dissenting movement in winning support within transnational support networks is inextricably linked to how the movement defines

itself for external stakeholders. The loss in translation of the anti-colonial liberationist aspect of anti-apartheid sanctions advocacy accompanying the movement's transnationalization made the movement more legible to both liberal social movements abroad and the international community of states. However, this shift towards the diplomatic register expressed through the ANC's self-representation as a state-in-exile within the international community represents an adoption of political liberalism and the language of citizenship and rights for non-white South Africans over a more expansive engagement with the economic and political predicament in South Africa. This kept ANC policy within the political goals of the Freedom Charter, which was ultimately a program of minimum political demands of rights. In a critique that directly engages this shortening, Peter Hudson sums up this shift in the deeper political alignment as "a critique of the underlying notions of immutable races without an understanding of the political-economic relations that shaped it" (Hudson 2018).

6   Conclusion: Forgetting the Human Costs of Boycott

For Mandela, the act of boycott as guerilla tactic contained the negotiation of human costs, particularly in relationship to vulnerable populations. This is where he is imagining the state that is yet to come; a state that cares about its citizens. However, the shift to sanctions as form of statecraft indexes a routine non-acknowledgment of human costs. Returning to the tactical model of boycott as guerilla tactic provides a tool for weaponizing consumption that is grounded in political economy and subaltern politics. There is a common mistake which holds that Western powers like the United States are the only ones who are able to imagine boycotts and sanctions as a global process that targets specific places when necessary. This overlooks the fact that boycott was also integral to anti-colonial struggles. It is troubling that corporations have taken up the process of boycott and sanction when it is strategically convenient.

References

Bob, Clifford. (2002). "Political Process Theory and Transnational movements: Dialectics of protest among Nigeria's Ogoni minority." *Social Problems* 49 (3): 395–415. DOI: https://doi.org/10.1525/sp.2002.49.3.395.

Bob, Clifford. (2005). *The Marketing of Rebellion: Insurgents, Media, and Transnational Activism.* London: Cambridge University Press.

Hamilton, Thomas. (1946). "India Calls on U.N. to Discuss Friction with South Africa." *The New York Times*, 24 June.

Horne, Gerald. (1996). "Who Lost the Cold War? Africans and African Americans." *Diplomatic History* 20 (4): 613–626.

Hudson, Peter J. (2018). "To Remake the World: Slavery, Racial Capitalism, and Justice." *The Boston Review.* https://bostonreview.net/forum/remake-world-slavery-racial-capitalism-and-justice/peter-james-hudson-racial-capitalism-and.

Hyslop, Jonathan. (2014). "Mandela on War." In Rita Barnard (ed.), *The Cambridge Companion to Nelson Mandela.* New York: Cambridge University Press.

Klotz, Andrew. (1995). "Norms Reconstituting Interests: Global Racial Equality and US Sanctions Against South Africa." *International Organization* 49 (3): 451–478.

Knight, Richard. (2001). "Sanctions, Divestment, and US Corporations in South Africa. In Robert Edgar (ed.), *Sanctioning Apartheid.* Trenton, NJ: Africa World Press.

Levy, Philip I. (1999). "Sanctions on South Africa: What Did They Do?" *The American Economic Review* May 1999: 415–420.

Mandela, Nelson. (1958). "Boycott is not an Inflexible Principle: Our Struggle Needs Many Tactics." *Liberation* 29 (February): 14–17.

Mandela, Nelson. (1961). "General Strike." https://omalley.nelsonmandela.org/omalley/index.php/site/q/03lv01538/04lv02009/05lv02032/06lv02037.htm.

Mandela, Nelson. (2013). *The Long Walk to Freedom.* New York: Little, Brown and Company.

Mangaliso, Mazamo. (1997). "South Africa: Corporate Social Responsibility and the Sullivan Principle." *The Journal of Black Studies* 28 (2): 219–238.

Marsh, Paul, and Thomas Szanya. (2000). "The South African Retrospective Case." *Identifying Potential Ethnic Conflict: Application of the Process Model*, 133–187. New York: Rand.

Martin, William. (1992). "Southern Africa and the World-economy: Regionality and Trade Regimes." In Immanuel Wallerstein, Sergio Viera, and William Martin (eds.), *How Fast the Wind? Southern Africa, 1975–2000.* Trenton, NJ: Africa World Press.

Martin, William. (2013). "South Africa and the 'New Scramble for Africa': Imperialist, Sub-imperialist, or Victim?" *Agrarian South: Journal of Political Economy* 2 (2): 161–188.

Nesbitt, Francis Njubi. (2004). *Race for Sanctions: African Americans Against Apartheid: 1956–1994.* Bloomington, IN: University of Indiana Press.

Posnikoff, Jonathan. (1997). "Divestment with South Africa: 'They Did Well by Doing Good.'" *Contemporary Economic Policy* 15 (1): 76–86.

Sisulu, Walter. (1957). "Boycott as a Political Weapon." *Liberation* 23 (February): 12–15.

Thomson, Alex. (2012). "A More Effective Constructive Engagement: US Policy Towards South Africa after the Comprehensive Anti-Apartheid Act of 1986." *Politikon: South African Journal of Political Studies* 39 (3).

Wheatcroft, Geoffrey. (1998). "Toppling Apartheid." *The New York Times*, 11 November.

CHAPTER 22

Settler Colonialism, Imperialism and Sanctions from Below: Palestine and the BDS Movement

Corinna Mullin

Lenin famously remarked, "There are decades where nothing happens; and there are weeks where decades happen." I began writing this chapter in the months before the May 2021 escalation of Israeli settler colonial violence against the Palestinian people that resulted in hundreds of Palestinian deaths, injuries, and arrests, as well as widespread infrastructure and property theft and destruction—just the latest chapter in close to a century long process of Palestinian dispossession and oppression. Although one could hardly describe the preceding years of persistent global Palestine solidarity organizing as "nothing happen[ing]", the intensity of these past few weeks brought home the meaning of Lenin's refrain.

As in the past, the recent upsurge in pro-Palestine organizing has been sparked by yet another massacre in Gaza, part of what Israeli strategists refer to in racist language as "mowing the grass", signifying its genocidal intent. Yet, it is not only Palestinian victimization that has moved people globally to act. It is the "sumoud" (steadfastness) of the Palestinian people in the face of such violence, and their fierce commitment to resistance and liberation that inspires people around the world to reaffirm their solidarity. The last Israeli massacre in the open-air prison that is Gaza in the summer of 2014 led to a familiar cycle- the resurgence of Palestine solidarity organizing in imperialist centers, quickly followed by Zionist backlash. The standard tactics include harassment and defamation as well as lawfare, resulting in the repression and even criminalization of Palestine solidarity organizing, especially in the United States, France and the United Kingdom. The campaign to push governments, institutions and organizations to adopt the International Holocaust Remembrance Alliance (IHRA) definition of anti-Semitism, effectively equating anti-Zionism with anti-Semitism, is one of the most recent examples of attempts to stifle pro-Palestinian organizing through legal and administrative means (Fadel and Salti 2020).

But the upsurge of action provoked by the latest round of Israeli violence and resistance feels different. To begin with, it comes on the heels of massive waves of protests in the US against the racist institutions of organized violence, ongoing Indigenous organizing for material decolonization across Turtle Island (also known as the United States), as well as the combined economic-health-climate crises of the past year, which have contributed to heightening the awareness and political (re)engagement, especially of young people. In addition, the display of unified resistance across the colonially fragmented parts of Palestine (Gaza, 1948 Palestine and the occupied West Bank and East Jerusalem) to the brutal repression and accelerated colonial violence, extensively captured and circulated through social media, has injected a new burst of energy into the global solidarity movement.

Although there are numerous ways in which solidarity is expressed, the Boycott, Divest and Sanctions (BDS) movement has become a bellwether of pro-Palestine sentiment across the globe. BDS is a "Palestinian-led movement for freedom, justice and equality founded in 2005 that upholds the simple principle that Palestinians are entitled to the same rights as the rest of humanity" (Palestinian Campaign for the Academic and Cultural Boycott of Israel 2021). Inspired by the South African anti-apartheid movement, BDS as a form of non-violent advocacy of Palestinian liberation has clearly gained strength over the past few weeks with the number of labor actions, academic and student statements as well as diverse protest tactics calling for BDS increasing exponentially.

That the imperialist core has become a site of some of the most vocal pro-Palestine organizing as well as robust repression should not come as a surprise. Since its inception, Israel has been intimately connected to imperialist interests in the region. As Abdul Wahab Kayyali (1977, p. 98) explained, the creation of a Jewish state in the region was seen as a strategic opportunity in the context of European imperialist expansion, "which necessitated the search for new sources of raw materials and markets for the finished products, in addition to securing the lines of commercial and military communication." Britain in particular had a "desire to keep any rival European power away from the Suez Canal—crucial for security the sea passage to India" (Allday 2021). It was this imperialist aim that led the UK to push for the particular post- World War I settlement, institutionalized in the League of Nations mandate, that saw the British assume control over historic Palestine, "wast[ing]' little time in fostering the conditions needed for Zionist colonization to flourish" (Salaita 2021; Sayegh 1965). In the context of the Cold War, Israel was deemed central to the imperialist agenda of stifling Arab nationalism and self-determination in the region (Kayyali 1977).

Although it was the British who played a crucial role in the foundation of Israeli settler colonial rule, the US soon inherited the mantle, becoming the cornerstone of what the Palestinian nationalist and anti-imperialist writer and activist Ghassan Kanafani referred to as the "Zionist-Imperialist alliance". Ex-NATO commander Alexander Haig bluntly explained the importance of Israel to the US ruling class, arguing Israel is "the largest American aircraft carrier in the world that cannot be sunk, does not carry even one American soldier, and is located in a critical region for American national security" (Carol 2019).

Most analyses focus on the amount of official US aid to Israel as the main axis of this relationship. Indeed, the figures are stark. Since its founding in 1948, the US has provided over $134 billion (adjusting for inflation, roughly $252.7 billion as of March 2018) in military and economic aid. In the past few decades it has been around $3.1 billion per year, and most recently, $3.8 billion a year. These figures are presented to substantiate the argument that Israel is a burden on US taxpayers: in the absence of support for Israel, imagine how much money would be available to invest in life sustaining goods and institutions, including quality public education, free health care and affordable housing. But the reality that often gets obscured in this approach is how much wealth is actually accumulated as a result of US support for Israel.

A political economy of US support for Israel reveals the material basis of the US-Israel relationship. This includes Israel's central role in the US dominated military/security/industrial complex—a central mode of accumulation under racial capitalism—as well as for expanding and protecting US empire, facilitating value drain from the periphery to the center of the global economic system. As William Robinson (2020, p. 106) has argued, the Israeli economy, similar and connected to imperialist core economies, "feeds off local, regional and global violence, conflict, and inequalities." For those committed to liberation in the US and Europe, the fight for Palestine is both a duty (because it is our economic, military and political support that enables and maintains Israel's colonial violence and oppression) and a necessity (as Robyn D.G. Kelley put it: "Fighting for decolonization of Palestine is Fighting for decolonization of the planet").

As demonstrated by the most recent drive to expand the number of peripheral (particularly Arab) states that have normalized relations with Israel, another aim of the Imperialist-Zionist matrix of power is to undermine the possibilities for alternative political, social and economic projects based on solidarity and self-determination within the Arab world as well as the broader global South. Due to the increasing incorporation of post-colonial states within this matrix, the BDS movement has a growing appeal to activists located in the global South.

In this chapter, I will explore the background context of the BDS movement as well as its development across time and space since the call was first made by Palestinian civil society organizations in 2005. It will begin with an exploration of the history of boycotts and sanctions as tactics of resistance to slavery, racial capitalism and colonialism. Considering the role of western imperialism in enabling and sustaining settler colonial rule in Palestine, the chapter will go on to examine the achievements and hurdles of the BDS movement in the imperialist core, with a focus on the United Kingdom and the United States. In the period following independence, most global South states expressed support for the Palestinian liberation struggle. However, the imperialist driven counter-revolution which followed, including the overthrow of revolutionary governments, as well as more subtle forms of political, economic and military intervention designed to undermine and discipline global South sovereignty, often entailing some level of interaction with Israel, has meant that the BDS movement has by necessity spread to parts of the global South—even to those states that have not officially normalized relations with Israel, in particular on the African continent and West Asia. The chapter will also consider these global South Palestine solidarity movements, focusing on two in particular: Tunisia and South Africa. It will conclude by arguing that although BDS is an important tactic in materially and discursively dismantling Israeli settler-colonialism, it should not, as many organizers have pointed out, be considered the only form of legitimate resistance. As with past anti-colonial struggles, it is for the people who are colonized to determine the means through which they will achieve their liberation. Radical solidarity means that we follow the Palestinian lead. That includes recognizing their right, under international law, to resort to armed resistance (National Lawyers Guild 2021).

1   A Brief History of the Use of Sanctions and Boycotts from Below

Throughout the modern history of interstate relations, sanctions have most often been used as a tool of power, designed to reinforce the status quo or to achieve political and economic outcomes that are not possible through other forms of 'soft' or 'hard' power alone. As the world's leading imperialist power, it is not surprising that the United States currently deploys the largest number of sanctions against other countries as a means to reinforce its dominance. Currently, one third of the globe is subjected to US sanctions. Not only do sanctions by design "cause untold death and devastation," a reality laid bare in the current health crisis, but also, as Lauren Smith (2020) demonstrates, "economic sanctions serve to justify and conceal theft, through asset freezes and seizures, at a rate only previously accomplished through invasion and occupation." US sanctions trigger currency devaluation, inflation, and increased unemployment, as well as reduced access to food, power, industrial equipment, and medicine. In other words, in the hands of US empire, sanctions are a neocolonial tool designed to prevent global South development.

However, sanctions are not only a tool of power but can and have also been effectively wielded by resistance movements, most notably by the anti-apartheid movement which called on allies across the globe to boycott, sanction and divest from apartheid South Africa. The movement encompassed everything from grassroots organizing to lobbying at the United Nations. It was officially launched in June 1959 at a meeting of South African exiles and their supporters. Socialist anti-colonial leader and founding Tanzanian president, Julius Nyerere explained its purpose: "We are not asking you, the British people, for anything special. We are just asking you to withdraw your support from apartheid by not buying South African goods" (Hjelmgaard 2013). The boycott attracted widespread support from students, trade unions and leftist activists in the UK initially, and eventually across the globe.

The anti-apartheid movement intensified following the Sharpeville massacre on 21 March 1960, when 69 unarmed protesters were shot dead by the South African police, escalating its campaign to include demands for the complete political and economic isolation of apartheid South Africa (Graham and Fevre 2020). The movement achieved an early victory with the adoption by the UN General Assembly in November 1962 of Resolution 1761, a non-binding resolution establishing the UN Special Committee against Apartheid and calling for the imposition of economic and other sanctions against South Africa. Following passage of this resolution, the anti-apartheid movement organized an international conference on sanctions in London in April 1964 targeting the imperialist centers and greatest enablers of apartheid South Africa, the US and UK (Gurney 1960). Although it took decades, the BDS movement, together with armed struggle and other forms of collective action eventually succeed in pressuring the South African government to negotiate with the African National Congress (ANC).

The tactic of the boycott has much longer roots as part of the repertoire of anti-colonial resistance, often combined with other forms of collective action such as strikes and sit-ins. Although it was employed by abolitionists in the US and UK in the 1790s, it wasn't until 1880 that the English term was first used to describe the action taken by Irish peasants who rose up against the English landowner, Charles Cunningham Boycott (Wills 2018). He was responsible for collecting rents from tenants and evicting those who couldn't pay. In the context of Ireland's "Land War" of 1879–1882, bought about by four years of crop failures, the perpetual precariousness of the rural poor, and rising nationalism of the Home Rule movement, in 1879 the Irish National Land League formed, campaigning for fair rents and better living conditions. The League encouraged

Boycott's employees to withdraw their labor, and launched a campaign of iso-lation against Boycott in the local community (Hickey and Doherty 2003).

Boycotts also featured prominently in the anti-colonial struggles of the 20th century. One of the earlier examples was the boycott of Italian products in the mid 1930s, organized by the International African Friends of Ethiopia (IAFE) against the fascist Italian invasion of Ethiopia. The group was founded by C.L.R. James, and other renown members included Jomo Kenyatta of Kenya and Amy Ashwood Garvey of Jamaica. Though these efforts failed to prevent the invasion of Ethiopia, they helped build strong transnational networks and "popularized the notion that economic action could be a weapon of the weak—an idea further pushed by Communist organizers who supported many of these movements." A resolution issued by the 1945 Pan-African Congress in Manchester, UK, reminded workers: "Your weapons—the Strike and the Boycott—are invincible" (Coates 2020).

In the struggle for independence in Ghana, the anti-colonial leader Kwame Nkrumah described the centrality of "all legitimate and constitutional means" to resist British imperialism, including "strikes, boycotts and non-cooperation" (Nkrumah 1971, p. 112). Before armed resistance began in earnest, the Algerian anti-colonial struggle also deployed non-violent forms of collective action. For example, on April 25, 1952, a general strike and boycott was declared as part of a day of mourning in solidarity with the thousands of Tunisian independence activists who had been arrested and the hundreds killed in recent months by French colonial forces (Rahal 2013). And in Kenya, the anti-colonial Mau Mau movement utilized boycotts as part of its arsenal of resistance (Hyde 2000).

Boycotts also played an important role in anti-racist and Black freedom struggles in the US. Perhaps most famously, the Montgomery Bus Boycott, a yearlong boycott beginning in 1955 in which Black people avoided using city transportation in Montgomery, Alabama, to protest the arrest of civil rights organizer Rosa Parks for refusing to give up her seat on the bus to a white man. There was also the 1960 Greensboro boycott protesting segregation and unequal treatment primarily at the Woolworth store in Greensboro, North Carolina. This was followed by the Patronage Movement led by Rev. Leon Howard Sullivan and his group of 400 ministers targeting local businesses in Philadelphia, which was "inspired by the national attention garnered by the Greensboro" boycott and "was widely heralded as a victory for the civil rights movement and was replicated by other organizations across the country including Martin Luther King Jr.'s Southern Christian Leadership Conference (SCLC)" (Ann Levy 2018).

The latest iteration of the struggles for Indigenous Black and Brown lib-eration includes renewed calls for boycotts of companies and institutions responsible for the ongoing oppression, exploitation and dispossession of racialized communities in the US. This includes the protest movement against the Dakota Access Pipeline (DAPL) and other partner entities that caused a number of delays due to protests, sit-ins and boycotts from 2014 to 2017, primarily organized by the Standing Rock Sioux Tribe and other Indigenous tribes with ancestral lands along the path of the proposed pipeline. DAPL and associated companies lost at least $7.5 billion from the actions, and DAPL's parent company, Energy Transfer Partners (ETP), saw a 20 percent decline in its stock price over that period (Kelly 2018). The abolition movement received increased attention following the George Floyd and Breonna Taylor uprisings in the summer of 2020, including various calls to divest from and abolish the racist institutions of organized violence, including the police, prisons, ICE, homeland security, and the military (Kelley 2020).

2   The Palestinian-Led Boycott, Divestment and Sanctions Movement

In 2005, the BDS movement was launched by 170 Palestinian unions, refugee networks, NGOs, and organizations representing Palestinians living under settler-colonial and apartheid rule as well as in exile.

> The movement urges nonviolent pressure on Israel until it complies with international law by meeting three demands:
> 1. End its occupation and colonization of all Arab lands and dismantle the Wall;
> 2. Recognize the fundamental rights of the Arab-Palestinian citizens of Israel to full equality; and
> 3. Respect, protect, and promote the rights of Palestinian refugees to return to their homes and properties, as stipulated in UN resolution 194
>
> PACBI 2021

The Palestinian Campaign for the Academic and Cultural Boycott of Israel (PACBI) was founded in April 2004 in Ramallah. It has since been integrated into the larger BDS movement, and is a founding member of the Palestinian BDS National Committee (BNC), tasked with overseeing the academic and cultural boycott aspects of BDS. The US arm of PACBI, the United States Association for the Academic and Cultural Boycott of Israel (USACBI), was founded in 2009.

The BDS movement builds on the history of Palestinian multi-pronged resistance, dating back to the earliest forms of nationalist struggle in 1918 and including the strikes, protests and armed resistance of the 1936–1939 anti-colonial revolution (Kanafani 1972), as well as the first and second Intifadas where the strategy of "non-cooperation, which emphasized the boycott of everything relating to the occupation (which parallels the strategy of ungovernability in the South African liberation struggle) was employed (Jamjoum 2021).

From the beginning, Zionist funded campaigns in the imperialist core have sought to sabotage the BDS movement, through programs that surveil, harass and repress individuals, organizations and institutions speaking out and organizing on behalf of Palestinian liberation. Lawfare has been a central tactic of the Zionist attacks on Palestine solidarity, including anti-BDS legislation and lawsuits aimed at sabotaging BDS efforts as well as the campaign to push governments and institutions to adopt the IHRA definition of anti-Semitism, which conflates anti-Zionism and the boycott of Israel with anti-Semitism and has been sharply criticized by rights groups, lawyers, and academics (MEMO 2021). In the weeks following the May 2021 escalation of settler colonial and apartheid violence against the Palestinian population, the BDS campaign received a boost, with scores of university students, faculty and staff, social movements and trade unions issuing statements and resolutions affirming or reaffirming support for BDS as well as taking more direct action.

3   BDS in the Imperialist Core

Considering the UK's foundational role in enabling settler-colonial rule in Palestine, it is unsurprising that the UK has been the site of one of the most robust BDS movements. The movement really took off in 2010 when the 120,000 member University and College Union (UCU), Britain's largest trade union for academics and academic-related staff in higher education, voted to support the BDS campaign and sever ties with the Israeli organization of trade unions, the Histadrut. Tom Hickey, from the University of Brighton, explained the rationale, including Histadrut's support for "the Israeli assault on civilians in Gaza" in January 2009, arguing that the organization "did not deserve the name of a trade union organization" (Paul 2010). The UCU's boycott motion demanded the "isolation of Israel while it continues to act in breach of international law" and called to "campaign actively" against Israel's trade agreement with the European Union. In that same year, the Scottish Trade Unions Congress (STUC) "endorsed a report recommending the STUC support a boycott and divest from Israeli companies, call for sanctions against Israel, and encourage positive investments in the Occupied Palestinian Territories" (STUC 2009). The movement gained steam in 2014, when The National Union of Teachers (NUT), the largest teachers' union in Europe, passed a resolution backing a boycott of companies profiting from Israel's illegal settlements and occupation of the West Bank and Gaza Strip. That was followed by the 2014 Unite the Union vote to develop a "campaigning and leverage strategy around BDS," recognizing that the "oppression faced by ordinary Palestinians at the hands of their colonial oppressors and the way in which their plight is used as a political bargaining chip cannot be allowed to continue" (PSC 2014). In 2019, The *British Society for Middle Eastern Studies* voted overwhelmingly to support the Palestinian call for BDS.

There has been significant pushback in the UK from the start, with a relentless campaign to demonize and delegitimize organizers, scholars and politicians (including former head of the Labour Party, Jeremy Corbyn). This racist, anti-Palestinian campaign most recently culminated in a legal battle between the British government and the Palestine Solidarity Campaign (PSC) that began in 2016 when the Department for Communities and Local Government issued guidance prohibiting the Local Government Pension Schemes (LGPS) from engaging in divestment from foreign states and the UK defence industry, including on the basis that they trade in products produced in the illegally occupied Palestinian territories (MEMO 2021). In April 2020, the PSC won its Supreme Court appeal, reinforcing the right of LGPS to divest from Israel. In response, the Prime Minister's office announced in May 2021 that it would enact "reforms" designed to "to ensure a coherent approach to foreign relations," and would "stop public bodies from imposing their own approach or views via boycott, divestment, or sanctions campaigns" (MEMO 2021). The battle continues.

Despite high levels of support, especially among the latest iteration of the Black, Indigenous and other People of Color liberation movements, BDS in the US has also faced significant legal and political challenges from the Zionist lobby. Students and faculty, in particular Palestinian, Muslim, Arab, have been especially vulnerable to racist attacks on Palestine solidarity organizing on university campuses. Where they are not the ones to initiate restrictions, university administrators have often caved into pressure from Zionist organizations such as Canary Mission, CAMERA and Hillel out of fear of the "public relations fallout that Title VI complaints—and their invocations of 'hostile' or "unsafe" environments—are designed to manufacture" and have therefore subjected critics of Israel to extra scrutiny or restricted or condemned their speech (Palestine Legal 2016). This happens in many ways: 1) collaboration with the local police departments, FBI and other institutions of organized violence to surveil Palestinian, Muslim, Arab and pro-Palestinian organizing on campus; 2) directly or indirectly accusing individuals and groups organizing in solidarity with Palestine of being anti-Semitic; 3) failing to protect students and faculty from the weaponization of Title VI/IX; 4) failing to protect students and faculty from racist, anti-Palestinian attacks; and, 5) using bureaucratic barriers and administrative obstacles designed to hamper student organizing for Palestinian rights. The latter measures "include creating impediments to reserving rooms and forcing students to obtain advance approval for events, pay security fees, and attend mandated meetings with administrators" (Palestine Legal 2016).

There is also the lawfare side of BDS repression. As of 2021, 35 states have passed bills and executive orders designed to discourage boycotts of Israel. The majority of them have been passed with broad bipartisan support. Most anti-BDS laws have taken one of two forms: contract-focused laws requiring government contractors to promise that they are not boycotting Israel; and investment-focused laws, mandating public investment funds to avoid entities boycotting Israel. Civil rights organizations, including the National Lawyers Guild (NLG), the American Civil Liberties Union (ACLU), Center for Constitutional Rights (CCR) and the Council on American–Islamic Relations (CAIR) have challenged many of these laws in court for violating the right to free speech. Most recently, a federal court in the US state of Georgia ruled that a law created to discourage the Palestinian-led BDS movement was in violation of the First Amendment, making Georgia the fifth state to have such legislation struck down after Kansas, Arizona, Texas and Arkansas (Middle East Eye 2021).

Yet despite these very real hurdles, BDS organizing continues apace in the US. The anti-racist and anti-imperialist lawyer's association, National Lawyers Guild, was one of the first national organizations to adopt BDS in 2007. The Association for Asian American Studies was the first scholarly organization to adopt BDS in April 2013, explaining that it aligned with the organization's overall orientation which "seeks to advance a critique of U.S. empire, opposing U.S. military occupation in the Arab world and U.S. support for occupation and racist practices by the Israeli state." The American Studies Association followed suit with its own BDS resolution in April 2013, followed by the Native American and Indigenous Studies Association (December 2013), Critical Ethnic Studies (2014), the National Association of Chicana and Chicano Studies (April 2015), and the National Women's Studies Association (November 2015).

There have also been more targeted victories, with the divestment of pensions and other funds from corporations that benefit from Palestinian oppression, including the 2012 announcement that pension giant TIAA-CREF would divest its Social Choice fund from Caterpillar, and later from Veolia and

SodaStream (USCPR 2019). A host of faith-based organizations have chosen to divest from Israeli Apartheid, including the 18 United Methodist Church Annual Conferences- representing thousands of churches and hundreds and thousands of members, which adopted 30 resolutions and statements calling for divestment between 2005–2015. In 2007, the National Coalition of American Nuns publicly urged the boycott of Caterpillar, while in 2008, the American Friends Service Committee approved a "Israel-Palestine Investment Screen" (USCPR 2019). The Majilis Ash-Shura/Islamic Leadership Council of New York, endorsed BDS in 2017, and in 2018, The Episcopal Church voted to "divest from Israel's human rights abuses" (USCPR 2019).

Historically, the mainstream US labor movement has aligned itself with "labor Zionism," supporting Israeli wars and opposing Israeli settler colonial and apartheid rule (Adely and Letwin 2021). The AFL-CIO has been one of Israel's "staunchest defenders and a generous financial supporter," and many US labor leaders- including AFL-CIO president Richard Trumka, Retail, Wholesale and Department Store Union president Stuart Appelbaum, and American Federation of Teachers (AFT) president Randi Weingarten openly oppose BDS (Schuhrke 2021). Attitudes began to shift in the aftermath of the 2014 Israeli massacre in Gaza. Since then, there have been some limited labor victories in the fight to adopt BDS. In 2014, the United Auto Workers [UAW] Local 2865, representing over 14,000 workers at the University of California, became the first major US labor union to endorse BDS. A year later, the UAW International Executive Board (IEB) informed UAW Local 2865 that it had nullified the vote, claiming endorsement of the boycott would interfere with the "flow of commerce to and from earmarked companies" (Vasquez 2016). The United Electrical Workers, Radio, and Machine union (UE) adopted a resolution endorsing BDS at its national convention in August 2015.

The most recent escalation of settler colonial and apartheid violence has caused a resurgence of labor activity around BDS including numerous solidarity statements, many issued by the AFL-CIO's closest international allies such as the Canadian Labour Congress, the UK's Trades Union Congress, the Irish Congress of Trade Unions and the International Trade Union Confederation. In addition to statements, unions in Italy and South Africa have organized direction actions, with a dockworker's union in the Italian port city of Livorno refusing to load weapons bound for Israel, while a South African dockworkers union similarly boycotted an Israeli cargo ship in the port of Durban (Forrest 2021).

There has also been a flurry of unions in the US passing BDS resolutions, signifying a renewed interest in taking on the Zionist lobbies in various sectors. One of the most significant displays of US labor solidarity with Palestine recently occurred when the United Educators of San Francisco, Local 61 of the AFT, which represents 6,200 school teachers and staff, adopted a "Resolution in Solidarity with the Palestinian People" on May 19, making it the first K-12 teachers union in the US to do so (Greschler 2021). The resolution states that "as public school educators in the United States of America, we have a special responsibility to stand in solidarity with the Palestinian people because of the 3.8 billion dollars annually that the US government gives to Israel, thus directly using our tax dollars to fund apartheid and war crimes." Similar BDS resolutions have advanced with United Teachers Los Angeles (UTLA), the second largest AFT local in the nation, and a resolution was passed by the AFT affiliated City University of New York's Professional Staff Congress in June 2021.

4   BDS in the Periphery

Although Arab populations "have ceaselessly shown solidarity with the Palestinians since Britain issued the Balfour Declaration in 1917," including through the provision of fighters, weapons, funds and legal support for the Palestinian resistance, reactionary, "Arab regimes...have always put their own national interests first," establishing ties with the settler colonial state when it has suited their interests, with the Hashemite Amir Faisal's deal with the British in 1919 presenting the first example of such "collaboration" (Massad 2020). After the backlash experienced following official normalization by Egypt (1979) and Jordan (1994), other Arab heads of states were reluctant to do so openly. However, the increased imbrication of regional states within US empire over the past several decades has reinforced mutual though unequal relations of dependency. In the absence of popular legitimacy, many governments have increased their arms purchases and military alignments with the US in order to maintain power, making them particularly vulnerable to calls for normalization.

In the last year of the Trump presidency, normalization agreements were negotiated with United Arab Emirates (August 2020) and Bahrain (September 2020). Both agreements were part of the "Abraham Accords: Declaration of Peace, Cooperation, and Constructive Diplomatic and Friendly Relations", one of the signature achievements of the Trump administration as part of its aggression towards Iran and buffering of support for settler colonial rule in Palestine. The Palestinian BDS National Committee (2020) expressed the feeling of many people in the region, exclaiming: "The UAE and Bahrain's dictators are selling out the Palestinian people, ignoring their own citizens, for their belligerent and capitalist interests." Morocco became the 5th Arab country to normalize relations with Israel in December 2020, in exchange for the United States officially recognizing Morocco's sovereignty over Western Sahara, which it has occupied since 1976 when Spain relinquished its colonial claim over the territory (Visram 2017). Joseph Massad (2020) was scathing in his analysis of the deal, pointing out that in exchange for receiving "US legitimisation of its takeover and annexation of the Western Sahara," the government "sacrificed Palestinian rights enshrined in international law to obtain benefits for themselves." This was in line with the reactionary leadership of the entire region, Massad explained, with the Arab League, itself "an enemy of Palestinian interests since its establishment...refus[ing] to condemn these peace deals even though they contradict its standing policy."

Most African states broke relations with Israel in the post-colonial era and have consistently supported Palestinian rights in international fora. The preamble of the African Charter of Human Rights, ratified by all African states except South Sudan, affirms their "duty to achieve the total liberation of Africa... and undertaking to eliminate colonialism, neo-colonialism, apartheid, Zionism and to dismantle aggressive foreign military bases and all forms of discrimination."

The Palestinian struggle has been deemed central to the pan-African liberation project. The Organization of African Unity—the precursor to the African Union—in its 12th ordinary session held in 1975, became the first international body to recognize the inherent racism in Israel's Zionist ideology by adopting Resolution 77 (XII) (Baroud 2020). It also drew connections between Palestinian oppression and settler colonial rule on the African continent, pointing out "that the racist regime in occupied Palestine and the racist regimes in Zimbabwe and South Africa have a common imperialist origin, forming a whole and having the same racist structure and being organically linked in their policy aimed at repression of the dignity and integrity of the human being" (*ibid.*). This Resolution was cited in UNGA Resolution 3379, adopted in November of that same year, which determined that "Zionism is a form of racism and racial discrimination". Resolution 3379 remained in effect until it was revoked by the General Assembly in 1991, under intense US pressure (Baroud 2019).

In his address at the International Day of Solidarity with the Palestinian People in 1997, Nelson Mandela proclaimed that "our freedom is incomplete without the freedom of the Palestinians." Similarly, as the Palestinian BDS National Committee has noted (2021), "Palestinian self-determination is closely connected with Africa's pursuit of genuine independence." As freedom fighters in the region are well aware "African and Palestinian liberation movements have long stood in active mutual solidarity for self-determination, while Israel has consistently supported colonial and neocolonial powers on the continent" (*ibid.*).

Tunisia is home to one of the most active BDS movements on the African continent. The history of Tunisian solidarity with Palestine dates back to the 1948 Nakba when many young Tunisian men risked their lives to fight alongside Palestinians in the anti-colonial resistance (Al Jazeera 2020). Post-independence Tunisian governments have always claimed support for Palestine, with the PLO invited to relocate to Tunis in 1982, after being forced to leave Lebanon. However, many activists have expressed skepticism about the sincerity of this solidarity and have used the political opening provided by the 2010–2011 uprising to call for an investigation into the role of the Tunisian Security establishment's role in the assassination of Palestinian leader and high-ranking Fatah official Khalil Al Wazir (popularly known as Abu Jihad) in 1988, as well as other Mossad operations on Tunisian soil. The BDS movement grew in the aftermath of the 2010–2011 uprising, where demands of protesters for "dignity" and "social justice" included an analysis of former President Ben Ali's subordinate relationship with the West, leading to Tunisia's failure to adopt a stronger stance in solidarity with Palestine. Many Tunisians now feel more work must be done to resist Tunisia's unofficial relations with the Zionist state (Kawas 2016).

On the 7th anniversary of the uprising, 100 Tunisian academics, artists, intellectuals and journalists called for the academic and cultural boycott of Israel. The appeal states in its preamble that "the recent recognition by US President Trump of Jerusalem as the capital of Israel, with the proven complicity and support of some Arab regimes, offers Arab citizens a cruel but salutary reminder of the progress of the rampant normalization of relations of the Arab world with the Zionist colonial state." Leaders of major civil society organizations have joined this call, including the largest trade union (UGTT), women's, student's and human right organizations. The signatories pledge to "fight all forms of normalization of relations of the Arab world with the Zionist colonial state" (Tunisian Campaign for the Academic and Cultural Boycott of Israel 2018). In light of the recent escalation of settler colonial and apartheid violence, Tunisian activists have called once again on the Tunisian parliament to pass legislation criminalizing normalization with Israel (Saidani 2021).

The Palestinian liberation movement was among the closest and most reliable allies of the African National Congress in leading the fight against apartheid in South Africa at a time when Israel was the apartheid regime's closest trading and arms partner. Unsurprisingly, BDS has received widespread support from South Africans. Archbishop Desmond Tutu, known for his anti-apartheid and human rights activism, is one of the most prominent South Africans to endorse BDS. He came to this position after visiting occupied Palestine and comparing the conditions there to conditions in apartheid-era South Africa (Tutu 2012). In 2012, the South African National Congress (ANC) party gave BDS its blessing, stating, "the Palestinians are the victims and the oppressed in the conflict with Israel." The Congress of South African Trade Unions (COSATU) fully endorsed BDS in July 2011. During the 2014 Israel–Gaza conflict, COSATU vowed to "intensify" its support for BDS, picketing Woolworths for stocking Israeli goods.

In 2020, the South African BDS (SA BDS) movement accelerated its organizing efforts, supporting the Palestinian civil society call for global solidarity to resist the Trump-Kushner "Deal of the Century." Referring to the agreement by its popular moniker, they explained the "steal of the century...would violate fundamental principles of international law, including the right to self- determination and the prohibition of the annexation of territory by force." The SA BDS Statement attracted the endorsement of more than 250 prominent South Africans, including, religious leaders, former cabinet ministers, veterans of the liberation struggle, trade unionists, human rights defenders, journalists, and ex-political prisoners, as well as leaders from elsewhere on the continent. The Statement called on the South African government to spearhead a sanctions campaign against Israel in the UN.

5   BDS: The "Floor Not the Ceiling" of Global Palestine Solidarity

Although the resurgence of the BDS movement in the imperialist core and globally give us cause to celebrate, it should not come at the expense of delegitimizing other forms of Palestinian resistance, including the internationally recognized right to armed resistance, or of criminalizing different types of solidarity, including direct action. One of the most powerful demonstrations of Palestine solidarity in the wake of the recent escalation of settle colonial violence was the forced closure in the UK of two factories run by the largest Israeli arms manufacturer, Elbit Systems. Activists with the group Palestine Action explained the protest: "For the sake of the protection of life and human rights, direct-action against Elbit Systems is a moral duty" (Ayoubi 2021). Several Palestine Action members were arrested, demonstrating some of the material risks involved in direct forms of solidarity. As many organizers have reminded us, BDS should be "the floor not the ceiling" of the global Palestine solidarity movement (Decolonize this Place 2016).

References

Adely, Suzanne and Letwin, Michael. (2021). "Bottom-Up Labor Solidarity for Palestine Is Growing." *Labor Notes*, 26 August. https://www.labornotes.org/blogs/2021/08/bottom-labor-solidarity-palestine-growing.

Abdullah Sayegh, Fayez. (1965). *Zionist colonialism in Palestine*. Research Center, Palestine Liberation Organization.

Al Jazeera. (2020). "In the Footsteps of a Tunisian Hero." *Al Jazeera*.

Allday, Louis. (2021). "The Cause of Anti-Colonialism and Liberation is One: Fayez Sayegh's Zionist Colonialism in Palestine." *Liberated Texts*, 23 March. https://liberatedtexts.com/reviews/the-cause-of-anti-colonialism-and-liberation-is-one-fayez-sayeghs-zionist-colonialism-in-palestine/.

Ann Levy, Jessica. (2018). "On the Limits of Boycotts as a Political Tool." *Black Perspectives*. https://www.aaihs.org/on-the-limits-of-boycotts-as-a-political-tool/.

Ayoubi, Nur. (2021). "Israel-Palestine: Activists in UK shut down second Israeli arms factory in a week." *Middle East Eye*, 25 May. https://www.middleeasteye.net/news/israel-palestine-uk-arms-factory-activists-shut-down-second.

Baroud, Ramzy. (2020). "Palestine in the Global South: Israel's 'Scramble for Africa'." *Afro-Middle East Centre*, 9 December. https://www.amec.org.za/palestine-israel/item/1707-palestine-in-the-global-south-israel-s-scramble-for-africa.html.

Baroud, Ramzy. (2019). "Israel's scramble for Africa: Selling water, weapons and lies." *Al Jazeera*, 23 July. https://www.aljazeera.com/opinions/2019/7/23/israels-scramble-for-africa-selling-water-weapons-and-lies.

Carol, Steven. (2019). *Understanding the Volatile and Dangerous Middle East: A Comprehensive Analysis*. Bloomington, IN: iUniverse.

Coates, Benjamin. (2020). "A Century of Sanctions." *Origins: Current Events in Historical Perspectives* 13 (4).

Fadel, Mohammad and Salti, Shireen. (2020). "In Canada, the IHRA definition has begun to stifle pro-Palestinian voices." *+972 Magazine*, 28 December. https://www.972mag.com/canada-ihra-antisemitism-palestinians/.

Forrest, Adam. (2021). "Italian port workers refuse to load shipment of arms headed for Israel." *The Independent*.

Graham, Matthew, and Fevre, Christopher. (2020). "Boycotts, rallies and Free Mandela: UK anti-apartheid movement created a blueprint for activists today." *The Conversation*, 4 April. https://theconversation.com/boycotts-rallies-and-free-mandela-uk-anti-apartheid-movement-created-a-blueprint-for-activists-today-134857.

Greschler, Gabriel. (2021). "San Francisco's teachers union becomes first K-12 union to endorse BDS movement." *Sun Sentinel*, 27 May. https://www.sun-sentinel.com/florida-jewish-journal/fl-jj-san-francisco-teachers-union-endorse-bds-movement-20210527-z43voimn5bdz7kpv75txkd2crm-story.html.

Gurney, Christabel. (2000). " 'A Great Cause': The Origins of the Anti-Apartheid Movement, June 1959-March 1960." *Journal of Southern African Studies* 26 (1):123–144.

Hickey, D.J., and Doherty, J.E. (2005). *A New Dictionary of Irish History from 1800.* Dublin, Ireland: Gill & Macmillan.

Hjelmgaard, Kim. (2013). "Britain played vital anti-apartheid role." *USA Today,* 5 December. https://www.usatoday.com/story/news/world/2013/12/05/mandela-brit ain-anti-apartheid-movement/2418803/.

Hyde, David Nicholas. (2000). *Plantation Struggles in Kenya: Trade Unionism on the Land 1947–63.* School of Oriental and African Studies PhD.

Jamjoum, Hazem. (2021). "Liberation, Wonder, and the 'Magic of the World': Basel al-Araj's *I Have Found My Answers." Liberated Texts.* https://liberatedtexts.com/revi ews/liberation-wonder-and-the-magic-of-the-world-basel-al-arajs-i-have-found -my-answers/.

Kanafani, Ghassan. (1972). "The 1936–39 Revolt in Palestine." New York: Committee for a Democratic Palestine.

Kawas, Hanna. (2016). "Is Tunisian Security Complicit in the Murder of Palestinian Leaders?" *Palestine Chronicle,* 31 December. https://www.palestinechronicle.com/ is-tunisian-security-complicit-in-the-murder-of-palestinian-leaders/.

Kayyali, Abdul-Wahab. (1977). "Zionism and Imperialism: The Historical Origins." *Journal of Palestine Studies* 6 (3): 98–112.

Kelley, Robin D.G. (2020). "What Abolition Looks Like, From the Panthers to the People Calls to defund prisons and policing is neither new nor hopelessly utopian." *Level,* 26 October. https://level.medium.com/what-abolition-looks-like-from-the-panth ers-to-the-people-6c2e537eac71.

Kelly, Sharon. (2018). "Energy Transfer and Banks Lost Billions by Ignoring Early Dakota Access Pipeline Concerns." *Truthout,* 8 December https://truthout.org/articles/ene rgy-transfer-and-big-banks-lost-billions-in-dakota-access-pipeline/.

Massad, Joseph. (2020). "How the Arab League helped dissolve the Palestinian question." *Middle East Eye,* 15 September. https://www.middleeasteye.net/opinion/how -arab-league-helped-dissolve-palestinian-question.

Middle East Eye. (2021). "US: Georgia court rules anti-BDS legislation unconstitutional," 24 May. https://www.middleeasteye.net/news/us-georgia-court-rules-anti-bds-law -unconstitutional.

Middle East Monitor. (2021). "UK tries to curb BDS as Israel's apartheid status become impossible to dispute." *MEMO,* 12 May. https://www.middleeastmonitor.com/ 20210512-uk-tries-to-curb-bds-as-israels-apartheid-status-become-impossible-to -dispute/.

National Lawyers Guild. (2021). "Statement in Solidarity with the People of Palestine in their Struggle Against the Settler Colonial State of Israel." *NLG.* https://www.nlg .org/statement-in-solidarity-with-the-people-of-palestine-in-their-struggle-agai nst-the-settler-colonial-state-of-israel/.

Nkrumah, Kwame. (1971). *Ghana: The Autobiography of Kwame Nkrumah*. New York: International Publishers.

Palestinian Campaign for the Academic and Cultural Boycott of Israel (PACBI). (2021). "What is BDS." https://bdsmovement.net/what-is-bds.

Palestine Solidarity Campaign. (2014). "Unite votes to support Palestinian rights." *Palestine Solidarity Campaign*. https://www.palestinecampaign.org/britains-larg est-union-unite-votes-strengthen-work-boycott-divestment-sanctions/.

Palestine Legal. (2016). "The Palestine Exception to Free Speech: A Movement Under Attack in the US." *Palestine Legal*. https://palestinelegal.org/the-palestine -exception.

Paul, Jonny. (2010). "Britain's largest academic union cuts ties with Histadrut." *Jerusalem Post*, 2 June. https://www.jpost.com/international/britains-largest-acade mic-union-cuts-ties-with-histadrut.

Rahal, Malika. (2013). "Algeria: Nonviolent resistance against French colonialism, 1830s-1950s." In Bartkowski, Maciej J. (ed.), *Recovering nonviolent history. Civil resistance in liberation struggles*. Boulder, CO: Rienner.

Robinson, William. (2020). *The Global Police State*. London: Pluto Press.

Saidani, Mongi. (2021). "Tunisian Opposition Calls for Criminalizing Normalization." *Asharq Al-Awsat*, 19 May. https://english.aawsat.com/home/article/2980876/tunis ian-opposition-calls-criminalizing-normalization.

Schurke, Jeff. (2021). "US. Unions Are Voicing Unprecedented Support for Palestine." *In These Times*, 26 May. https://inthesetimes.com/article/palestine-israel-labor-uni ons-afl-cio-aft-bds-gaza.

Smith, Lauren. (2020). "United States Imposed Economic Sanctions: The Big Heist." *Monthly Review Online*, 3 March. https://mronline.org/2020/03/10/united-states -imposed-economic-sanctions-the-big-heist/.

STUC. (2009). "Scottish Trade Unions Call for Boycott of Israel." *STUC Media Centre*. https://www.stuc.org.uk/media-centre/news/636/scottish-trade-unions-call-for -boycott-of-israel.

Tunisian Campaign for the Academic and Cultural Boycott of Israel. (2018). "Tunisian Civil Society Calls for the Academic and Cultural Boycott of Israel on the 7th Anniversary of the Revolution of Freedom and Dignity in Tunisia." *BDS Movement*. https://bdsmovement.net/news/tunisian-civil-society-calls-academic-and-cultu ral-boycott-israel-7th-anniversary-revolution.

Tutu, Desmond. (2012). "Justice requires action to stop subjugation of Palestinians." *Tampa Bay Times*, 30 April. https://www.tampabay.com/opinion/columns/justice -requires-action-to-stop-subjugation-of-palestinians/1227722/.

US campaign for Palestinian Rights (USCPR). (2019). "US BDS Victories." *USCPR*. https:// uscpr.org/campaign/bds/bdswins/#1499798328669-154c6be3-635c.

Vasquez, Mario. (2016). "UAW Overrules Academic Workers BDS Vote Against Israel Despite Finding Strong Turnout, No Misconduct." *In These Times*, 6 January.

https://inthesetimes.com/article/uaw-university-california-local-2865-boycott-divestment-sanctions-israel.

Visram, Nizar. (2017). "The World's Last Colony: Morocco continues occupation of Western Sahara, in defiance of UN." *Open Democracy*, 13 April. https://www.opende mocracy.net/en/north-africa-west-asia/world-s-last-colony-morocco-continues -occupation-of-western-sahara-in-de/.

Wills, Matthew. (2018). "There were boycotts before the word was coined in the 1880s, but ever since then they've always been called after the experience of Captain Charles Boycott." *Daily JSTOR*. https://daily.jstor.org/boycotting-captain-boycott/.

CHAPTER 23

Epilogue

Stuart Davis and Immanuel Ness

Across the 22 chapters in this collection, we note a broad variation in how economic sanctions are defined and enacted in terms of historical moment, national context, relationship to other kinds of military pressure, hegemonic rivalries within the configuration of global imperialism, and other factors. This epilogue attempts to draw connections between different chapters as well as foreground some of the unique differences regarding motivations, triggers, and consequences. In this endeavor, we have structured this epilogues around a few questions paramount to the cohesive framework to which the authors provide their individual contributions.

1   How are sanctions war?

One of the central continuities across each chapter is the notion that sanctions constitute a form of warfare. They are not an 'alternative to war', as they are often framed by policymakers and academics (i.e. Cortright and Lopez 1995); they are, in the words of anti-war activist and political economist Trita Parsi, "an alternative *form of* war" (cited in Petti 2020, emphasis in original). Concomitantly, sanctions are part of a continuous cycle of tactical and strategic policies that preclude and continue afer military engagement, where if war fails, sanctions continue. This position is borne out across the collection. As Karuka's chapter forcibly shows in its historiography of sanctions as military tactic, contemporary economic sanctions regimes are the historical inheritors of medieval siege warfare. They are designed to maximize suffering through a form of starvation politics that cuts off access to life-sustaining supplies for not just leaders of opponent states but for an entire population. This attempt to deny resource access to a population comes up throughout the text. As Elich poignantly details in his discussion of Yugoslavia, the imposition of sanctions and the hyperinflation they engendered created a dire and desperate situation where many had to resort to hunting or foraging for food as a means of survival. In Venezuela, sanctions have facilitated shortages in vital foodstuffs and pharmaceuticals by crippling its ability to import needed supplies—as Wilpert discusses in his chapter.

The starvation politics sanctions thrive on extend well beyond nutrition or access to foodstuffs. As Davis contends, the way that sanctions regimes seek to destabilize and undermine countries like Cuba and Iran create insurmountable barriers for service providers to maintain internet infrastructure; these barriers make it impossible for civilians in these countries to access information or use video conferencing services like Zoom along with other internet platforms. In Iraq, Syria, Yemen, and the other case studies of this book, sanctions regimes served to cut off vital medical supplies for civilian populations.

2   How do sanctions serve imperialism? How do sanctions relate to American ambitions?

One of the central contentions of this collection is that since the dawn of the Cold War economic sanctions have largely served as a tool for the US to achieve its geopolitical ambitions as it expanded into the leading geostrategic world power in the late twentieth century. Economic penalties applied by the US and its allies have varied based on context within a given moment in time. While other studies have discussed the longer history of sanctions within international diplomatic history (Mulder Forthcoming), our authors have centered their analyses on either the post-World War II period where America strove to maintain and expand its global hegemony or the period from about 2010 to the present, as the United States is meeting new geopolitical rivals for its position of military, economic, political, and cultural primacy. Given this historical specificity, *Sanctions as War* highlights the role of sanctions as tools for exercising US geopolitical will on a global stage.

Within this framework we identify two types of imperialist economic sanctions:

The first type is linked to *regime change attempts*; these are either *unilateral* and directed against states whose existence is perceived as direct threat to the goals of the US/its client states or *multilateral* and linked to larger humanitarian movements. Beginning with the embargo on Cuba in the early 1960s, this type of sanction has focused on enforcing punitive measures on institutions, politicians and other elite actors, and especially civilians in countries like Venezuela, Yugoslavia, Yemen, and Syria. *Multilateral* against those who are declared 'rogue states' by an international community dominated by the UN, particularly Security Council permanent members like the US, France, and UK. This includes Iraq, Zimbabwe, North Korea, and Yugoslavia. What unites both unilateral and multilateral sanctions is that they operate according to the perspective where the maximization of human suffering through the application of financial levers will push stakeholders within a given sanc-tioned state to overthrow the government and install a new one—one that is hopefully more amenable to the US.

The second type of imperialist sanction consists of those designed to police the behavior of perceived rivals. These sanctions are directed against states that are politically and economically capable of surviving through autarchy, as they maintain and provide most of the necessities of the working classes, if not the middle classes, and therefore offer competing foreign policy visions. Sanctions of this type include those launched against perceived American opponents including China, Russia, and to a lesser degree Iran. Sanctions launched against these states seem to be less intended to overthrow regimes than to keep potential rivals in check through political discreditation in the West. In this way, sanctions are used more as a sign of spectacular or symbolic strength on the part of the US by demonstrating its ability to shame these potential competitors at any time and in whatever form it desires. Mirrlees' discussion in this collection of the recent application of sanctions against the Chinese technology industry illustrates this point. In addition, American and European sanctions serve also as a cautionary form of intimidation against lesser pow-ers considering to draw closer to potential global and regional adversaries. As advances in technological research and development by Chinese firms began to outpace America counterparts, the Trump administration turned to sanc-tions as a way to 'put China in its place'. The timeline for the Biden adminis-tration's recent sanctions in April-May 2021 against Russia also provide a case of this second type of imperialist sanction: as increasing accusations of poten-tial hacking began to spread, the US immediately turned to ratcheting up eco-nomic sanctions as a form of retroactive payback, even without solid evidence (Tucker 2021).

An analysis of these types of sanctions—those aimed at regime change and those aimed at policing rivals—demonstrates their past and present subordi-nation to the US struggle for geopolitical hegemony.

3   Are economic sanctions effective? When do specific sanctions regimes against a targeted state end?

Another main argument is that sanctions do not generally seem to end when benchmarks are met, as supporters of targeted or 'smart' sanctions maintain (Ahn and Ludema 2019). They end when either a targeted state is destroyed and a new regime sympathetic to US interests is embedded, like successor states of Yugoslavia or Iraq after the overthrow of Sadam Hussein; or there is an internal shift within the culture of the American political elite that accommodates lifting or shifting specific sanctions. Examples of this internal shift include the lifting of some elements of the trade embargo on during the 'Cuban thaw' at the end of the Obama administration (Feinberg 2018) and Biden's pulling back on the most draconian terms of the Trump administration's amplified sanctions against Iran in an effort to return to JCPOA (Psaledakis and Arshad 2021). Conversely, internal shifts in the US government could also fuel the implementation of other sanctions. To draw on a case from this collection: as Kuzmarov details at length, the increase in sanctions launched against Russia in the 2010s cannot be disentangled from rising currents of Russophobia within US elite political culture and the media—particularly after the 2016 US election (see also Tsygankov 2019).

Regardless of these relatively shallow fluctuations in the form and degree of sanctions, our collective analysis maintains the perspective that regardless of political oscillations the historical pattern of employing economic sanctions against states perceived as enemies is consistent. To quote Vijay Prashad's summation of the Trump administration's role in the employment of unilateral sanctions against Venezuela: "Obama forged the spear; Trump hurled it into the heart of Venezuela" (cited in Ciccariello-Maher 2021, 178). Sanctions precede and succeed individual presidents, growing in popularity as the desire for kinetic war fades.

4   If sanctions can be characterized as both brutally humane
       and provenly ineffective, why are they tolerated? How are
       sanctions 'marketed' to the public? Why do people not care more
       about them?

The answer is linked to legitimation through manufacturing consent. Nakahara and Shahin's chapter demonstrates how media coverage buttresses the US ruling class and imperial power. Shupak's discussion of media coverage demonizing any criticism of Western support for the Syrian opposition, Ness's critique of putative "independent" monitoring organizations like human rights NGOs, and Davis's examination of freedom of press activists who provide academic and media ammunition by attributing alleged conflict within targeted states to claims of authoritarian actions of a given government, illustrate the ways that media, NGOs, and many activists do not consider the impact of sanctions. If the US and its Western allies seek out evidence of human rights abuses or violations of press freedoms, since almost every state is culpable, it is unproblematic to adopt them at any time through the support of neutral observers; even if they have no interest in the power gambit leading to economic sanctions. However, almost all human rights organizations have been either established by advocates of regime change of states veering from US policies, or, if genuinely committed to human rights, infiltrated and coopted by the vast tentacles of the US foreign policy establishment.

5   What do anti-imperialist sanctions look like? How can the strategy
        of imposing sanctions as a prescriptive mandate be mobilized
        to support causes that work against the oppressive nature of the
        existing geopolitical order?

By and large, economic sanctions are the exclusive preserve of hegemonic states and are used as a means to maintain and expand military, economic, political, and cultural domination. They are engendered through the political establishment, promoted through government domination over the academy, and disseminated to the public through a compliant and acquiescent media, which lays the foundation for the application of punitive economic sanctions by the US and its hegemonic allies against subordinate states considered to diverge with its sacrosanct neoliberal policies of free trade and who do not adhere to property rights established through centuries of imperialism, engage in misbehavior and do not adhere to political norms. If the stakes are high, and a noncompliant state consolidates power, the US will turn to military intervention, a reason why sanctions are an integral component of war.

The final two chapters of this book, on popular political movements for equality directed at South Africa from the late 1970s-to-late 1980s and Israel from 2000 to the present, offer a diverging perspective on how the imposition of punitive economic policies emerge. As an alternative to hegemonic state sanctions, social movements for popular sanctions against states develop at the level of civil society and are directed to the state, typically absent the legitimating forces of media, academia, and NGOs. In the absence of foundation and state funding, popular movements gain momentum independent of established political parties, the mainstream media, and most monitoring agencies, as major hegemonic states oppose the imposition of sanctions on their allies who regularly break basic norms of international law. This was the case in apartheid South Africa and Israel. Both states maintained geopolitical significance in imposing the strictures of the imperium and have been rarely reproached by the United States and its allies, but boycotts, divestment, and sanctions had been called on both by those aware of their apartheid policies.

South Africa maintained geostrategic significance as a key supplier of precious metals until the end of apartheid in 1994. Indeed, the presence of precious metals in Southern Africa has contributed to global contestation for influence over the governments in the region. Israel serves as a key geostrategic military ally of the US. Israel, a staunch US ally, is not a subject of sanctions but recipient of $3.8 billion a year in US public funding for its military. Furthermore, Israel engages in cooperative and expanding bilateral economic trade. Israeli forces are deployed to support US allies facing military insurgencies, for example Colombia and Honduras in Latin America. In addition, Israel has engaged in covert operations against states that the US has applied economic sanctions; notably Iraq, Iran, Syria, Yemen, and beyond.

The movements for sanctions against apartheid South Africa and Israel represent bottom-up movements that react to open and blatant violation of human rights, privileges conferred on a segment of the population; white South Africans from 1946 to 1994, and Jewish Israelis from 1948 who have appropriated and expropriated the majority of land and left large majorities of non-whites and non-Jews in conditions of utter economic despair. In the case of Israel, the International Criminal Court has charged the state with war crimes committed against noncombatants, including women and children.

Popular pressure first pushed states in the Global South to impose sanctions on South Africa, followed by movements in Europe and the United States, leading to the political and economic isolation of the country. It was not until 1988 that the US applied sanctions against South Africa, after the US Congress overrode a veto by Republican president Ronald Reagan. In view of the absolute disparity in conditions between white and black South Africans, the economic sanctions imposed on the country in the late-1980s diminished the economic prosperity of the dominant minority white population.

In the case of Israel, the same pattern applies. If sanctions were applied, they would only hurt the dominant populations who benefit from settler-colonialism, occupation, and illegal settlements. But popular movements akin to South Africa in the 1970s and 1980s have developed against fierce opposition of the US and its allies and have gained momentum as Israel's policies of subordinating and massacring Palestinians are increasingly met with popular opposition within the 1948 boundaries of Israel and in the territories. Popular opposition is expanding beyond the borders throughout Southwest Asia, Africa, Latin America, and into Europe and North America. Nonetheless, the Israeli state and its allies maintain extraordinary influence in Britain, France, Germany, and within the US government. They have weaponized anti-Semitism to impede the application of economic sanctions. In this way, Israel and numerous sympathetic NGOs in the West seek to equate opposition to Israeli policies

with anti-Semitism, which has mitigated the strength of the growing opposition to its oppressive rule, occupation of Palestinian territories in the West
Bank, and establishment of settlements on lands designated as part of a future
Palestinian state. Consequently, while the movement for sanctions against
Israel is bound to expand, the Israeli state has far more supporters in the West
in addition to a large but declining number of Jews and millenarian Christians
who view support for Israel as a sign of the *End Times*. However, the sanctions
movement is growing in support among the masses and even segments of the
capitalist class, who view the Israeli apartheid as anathema to their interests.

Sanctions that rise from among the socially conscious in the West do eventually percolate to the top echelons of politics, but the process can be slow,
typically occurring over decades. Even if they do not succeed immediately,
they have a record of isolating targeted states. While apartheid South Africa
and Israel today are unequal societies, internal opposition and external economic sanctions have been successful in building movements for change without harming the vast swaths of the population who do not rely on or benefit
from trade. By contrast, sanctions imposed by imperialist hegemons tend to
harm the vast majority of citizens without having tangible consequences on
economic and political elites.

6   Conclusion

Coming full circle, this book seeks to provide evidence that economic sanctions represent a dialectical problematic fully integrated into the study of war
and can also be a weapon for social justice if the powerless seeking equality
have equivalent resources. If offered an accurate account of the circumstances,
sanctions can be applied effectively to create equality among peoples and
even contribute to the alleviation of poverty and lack of adequate resources
for urban and rural dwellers. Applied ethically and universally high disparities
in Gino-coefficients and poverty rates could be narrowed through sanctions
policies aimed at promoting economic redistribution of land and economic
resources. But the beneficiaries of the enormous global wealth gap seek to
expand accumulation through sanctioning states that to a greater or lesser
extent have sought to mitigate poverty and inequality: Cuba, Venezuela,
Yugoslavia and Iran, to name a few. While these divergent projects have had
a range of outcomes, from short term gains—revolutionary Iran—to long
term tangible improvement in the quality of life—Cuba—they all have been
under siege by sanctions. On the grand geo-strategic chessboard, sanctions

threaten the future of humanity through increasing hostilities and bringing
the world closer to nuclear war.

In this book, the editors and contributors have not offered prescriptive solutions to resolve the crisis of sanctions, but sought to document and demonstrate the motivations, causes, and potentially catastrophic consequences of
sanctions.

References

Ahn, Daniel, and Ludema, Rodney. (2019). "Measuring Smartness: The Economic Impact
of Targeted Sanctions against Russia," in *Disrupted Economic Relationships: Disasters,
Sanctions, and Dissolutions*, edited by Tibor Besedes and Volker Nitsch, 131–154.
Cambridge, MA: MIT Press.

Ciccariello-Maher, George. (2021). "Venezuela: Communes Against Sanctions," in
Vivermos: Venezuela vs. Hybrid War, edited by Claudia de la Cruz, Manolo de los
Santos, and Vijay Prashad, 174–190. New York: International Publishers/LeftWord
Books.

Cortright, David, and Lopez, George. (1995). "The Sanctions Era: An Alternative to
Military Intervention." *The Fletcher Forum of World Affairs* 19 (2): 65–85.

Feinberg, Richard. (2018). "A Backstage Pass to the Historic US-Cuba Thaw." *Americas
Quarterly* June 3, 2018.

Mulder, Nicholas. (Forthcoming). *The Economic Weapon: The Rise of Sanctions as a Tool
of Modern War*. New Haven, CT: Yale University Press.

Petti, Matthew. (2020). "Economic Sanctions: An Alternative to War or War by
Alternative Means?" *The National Interest*, 28 April.

Psaledakis, Dimitri, and Arshad, Mohammed. (2021). "Biden Tiptoes through Sanctions
Minefield Towards Iran Nuclear Deal." *Reuters*, 17 May.

Tsygankov, Andrei. (2019). *The Dark Double: US Media, Russia, and the Politics of Values*.
London: Cambridge University Press.

Tucker, Aaron. (2021). "US Imposes Stiff Sanctions on Russia, Blaming it for Major
Hacking Operation." *The New York Times*, 14 April.

Index

Note: 'f' after a page number denotes figure and 't' after a page number stands for table.

www.ingramcontent.com/pod-product-compliance
Lightning Source LLC
Chambersburg PA
CBHW070900030426
42336CB00014BA/2267